Modern British and Irish Criticism and Theory

Also available:

Modern European Criticism and Theory
Modern North American Criticism and Theory

Modern
British and Irish Criticism
and Theory

A Critical Guide

Edited by Julian Wolfreys

Edinburgh University Press

© The Contributors, 2006

First published as part of *The Edinburgh Encyclopaedia
of Modern Criticism and Theory* in 2002

Edinburgh University Press Ltd
22 George Square, Edinburgh

Typeset in Ehrhardt by
Hewer Text UK Ltd, Edinburgh, and
printed and bound in Great Britain by
Antony Rowe Ltd, Chippenham, Wilts

A CIP record for this book is available from the British Library

ISBN-10 0 7486 2450 3 (paperback)
ISBN-13 978 0 7486 2450 8

The right of the contributors
to be identified as authors of this work
has been asserted in accordance with
the Copyright, Designs and Patents Act 1988.

Contents

Preface

Modern British and Irish Criticism and Theory offers the reader a comprehensive, critically informed overview of the development of literary and cultural studies from the nineteenth century to the present day. Beginning with Coleridge and Arnold, examining the contributions of cultural commentators, aestheticians and novelists, and considering the institutionalisation of literary criticism in the universities of England, Ireland, Scotland and Wales, the book addresses in detailed, accessible and rigorous essays the significance of poetics, literary and cultural studies. Over twenty essays contribute to an understanding of the practice of literary studies, providing a perceptive and often provocative series of critical interventions, which, themselves, engage in the very locations from which criticism and theory have emerged. Roughly, though fairly evenly, divided between studies of the work of particular critics, whose texts have produced sea changes in critical attitude and practice, and analysis of the development and institutionalization of literary and cultural studies throughout the twentieth century and at the beginning of the twenty-first, the critics included here focus on, even as they challenge the assumptions behind, the growth and expansion of critical trends and methodologies. The present volume follows therefore a narrative of cultural change and transformation, even as it determines and foregrounds particular contours in that narrative.

   Modern British and Irish Criticism and Theory also opens up the continuous quest for, and affirmation of, multiple cultural voices and identities, often incommensurate with one another, within the study of literature and culture at institutions of higher education. It is a narrative that on the one hand traces the movements, schools of thought and institutional allegiances that have unfolded, often though not exclusively along ideological lines. On the other hand, it considers the ways in which close reading and formal analysis of works of literature have given way historically to more politicized and theorized accounts, only to see certain signs of a return to depoliticized formalism. Involved in this is an implicit investigation, from essay to essay and across the collection of the contest for critical position and articulation of that position through successive generations of literary scholars.

   While emphasizing the practice and theory of literary and cultural criticism in many of its historically specific guises, the present volume also provides extensive critical coverage of related cultural issues in the articles, and the contextual discourses that inform those issues. Clearly the focus is on the institutional practice of criticism, and, with that, an implicit narrative develops concerning acts of institutionalization. Another way to understand this is that there takes place repeatedly instances of accommodation, domestication and, in some cases, normalization of currents of thought imported or translated from other disciplines, other fields of thought and, in the case of so-called high theory from the late 1960s to the 1980s, other cultures of critical thinking.

This is inevitable in any process of institutionalization. It is a matter of what Jacques Derrida has referred to as auto-immunization. Any institution – but it has to be said the university is particularly good at this, and thus exemplifies the means by which institutionalization maintains itself – takes in and makes over just enough of some *other* in order to keep it going. In that act of self-interested maintenance there is also an act of hospitality. Such reciprocity is an inescapable feature of any accommodation. One welcomes the other into one's home, across the threshold, boundary or border as a gesture of hospitality and welcome. But intrinsic to this welcome, inextricably tied up with any such act, is a desire to render the foreign, the other, that which is different, less other, less strange or threatening perhaps. Hospitality assumes both tolerance and neutralization, in order to allow it to carry on with business as usual. The university is wonderfully effective in these processes.

One such place where accommodation might be signalled as also the sign of neutralization is addressed in the present volume, in an essay by Martin McQuillan. McQuillan's essay, 'British Poststructuralism since 1968', rightly points up the ironies in not only its own title but also in the very idea of 'British' as an illusory signifier of ideological and historical neutralization, homogenization and the erasure, discursively and materially, of the other – and of many others. One of the many ironies is in the fact that while so-called poststructuralism – in truth not a movement but merely a convenient term for accommodating and so domesticating the multiple and heterogeneous discourses of critical thinking from continental Europe as these have been translated both into English and into English and North American critical practice – has found a few homes in universities, the radicalism assumed in the name 'poststructuralism' has not extended to a self-reflective caution over the terms 'Britain' or 'British'. Those critics who otherwise would see themselves as champions of otherness, difference, alterity, heterogeneity and so on, can be seen as having fallen into some unthinking cultural hole by assuming a notion of undifferentiated Britishness.

That very risk is run in the title of a volume such as the one you are holding, and the history of the kinds of academic accommodation and questioning in which the present volume is involved, as a collection and through the singular voices of each of the critics who constitute that collection, is given no more acute focus than in the title: *Modern British and Irish Criticism and Theory*. Although a distinction between 'British' and 'Irish' is made in the title, whereby a difference, if not a dissimilarity, is advertised between two cultural practices of criticism and the institutions in which such practices are carried on, the title might be read as presupposing, as Martin McQuillan puts it, ideas of 'continuity, stability and exclusion'. The title does not acknowledge difference, dissimilarity or singularity in culture or practice as these might be or are hypothetically voiced in the universities of Scotland or Wales. In this case, it might be argued, such exclusion, such silencing, is a form of colonialism or imperialism because – and again I cite McQuillan – 'Britain' is a concept involving 'ideological union of heterogeneous identities, around an idea of sovereignty derived from a colonial identity'. As he goes on to add, the only identity that critics working in the universities of Wales, Scotland, Ireland and England *might* share 'might be the nomadic internationalism of the professional academic'. (Seen from another aspect, that internationalism could also be read as a privilege of globalization.)

Of course, to a small extent – and this has not been taken far enough – constitutional reform in 'Britain', so-called, and of 'Britain', has sought to redefine the various cultural identities and their relationships. For many reasons, though, unfortunately too numerous and complex to be investigated here, there is an inescapable ambivalence concerning the terms 'Britain' and 'Britishness', due in no small part to the ideological overdetermination at work in those words. Here, then, is the final irony for now: the title has arrived as an accommodation, however uncomfortable, however problematic, between an English editor and a Scottish academic press. And this has been done in order to accommodate and incorporate in the place of the title those very problematic engagements that, in most if not all of the essays presented herein, are taken up by each of the critics who have contributed, not only in their contributions, but every day, in their teaching and in their research. It remains the responsibility of the reader to perceive in the use of the term 'British' not a coercive or homogenizing imposition but a signal intended to draw attention to the interrogation of the limits of such a cultural and historical denomination, as that analysis takes place directly or otherwise in the practice of criticism in recent decades.

Clearly, then, incorporations are not without consequences. The contributors to the present volume understand this. In such accommodations there also occur the rise of contest and conflict, dialectic and engagement as is implied through my brief reflection on the politics of the title. Not inconsequent to the encounters between a more or less idealized notion of 'community' such as the 'university' are the misreadings and mis-perceptions, the avoidances, the non-reception, and even occasionally the hostilities that provide some of the more visible punctuations within the history of criticism and theory. So, to reiterate: the articles in *Modern British and Irish Criticism and Theory* chart and reflect on the accommodations and resistances, the tolerances and intolerances. In this, each article concerns itself not only with the formalist contours and epistemological parameters of a particular discourse or movement, it also acknowledges the cultural, historical and ideological specificities of the emergence and transformation of criticism. Together and individually, the essays offer to the reader a view of the extent to which philosophy, poetics, politics, aesthetics, linguistics and psychoanalysis are part of the densely imbricated textures of critical practice. Furthermore, while remaining aware of the importance of the various contexts within and out of which criticism has grown, the essays herein also concern themselves with the equally important issue of cross-fertilization between the various academic and intellectual cultures under consideration. *Modern British and Irish Criticism and Theory* thus provides the reader with a comprehension of the key issues with the intention of demonstrating that those issues and the fields into which they are woven are marked by, even as they themselves re-mark, an unending and vital process of hybridization – of methodologies, disciplines, discourses and interests. In this, taken together the essays comprising the present volume question implicitly the very condition of the practice and theory of criticism itself.

In presenting the various facets of critical activity, there have been, necessarily, omissions. This is true of the shaping of any narrative. Even so, it is hoped that the overall contours of critical practice as staged here are not misrepresented and that, concomitantly, the dominant hegemonies of thought in their particular historical and cultural moments are neither distorted nor in some other manner misrepresented. It has to be said that if there is no such thing as a pure discourse, self-sufficient and enclosed from influences, confluences and even contaminations, there is also no such thing as a finite context or group of contexts. One obviously cannot speak of either purely national or universal determinations; equally one cannot ascribe to critical thinking a finite or unchanging condition. The very definition of literary criticism and its institutional manifestations here supposes an identity always in crisis, and always accommodated as such in its mutability. Intellectual cultures, like literary genres, have moments of historical ascendance, ideological transformation and hegemonic dominance. Appearing to lose that dominance, going 'out of fashion' as is sometimes perceived in the more journalistic of interpretations, traces, influences, remain, continuing to be transformed, and so to effect the cultures of criticism in which the reader is presently situated. It is with such issues, such processes and cultures of transformation and translation that *Modern British and Irish Criticism and Theory* is purposely involved.

Julian Wolfreys

1. Samuel Taylor Coleridge (1772–1834) and Matthew Arnold (1822–1888)

In 'The Perfect Critic' (1920), T. S. Eliot performs an early critical variation on the commonplace recognition of Samuel Taylor Coleridge and Matthew Arnold as foundational figures in the history of modern criticism in English: 'Coleridge was perhaps the greatest of English critics, and in a sense the last. After Coleridge we have Matthew Arnold; but Arnold – I think it will be conceded – was rather a propagandist for criticism than a critic, a popularizer rather than a creator of ideas' (Eliot 1957, 1). If this characterization of Arnold does not quite inspire confidence, the tell-tale 'perhaps' in the praise for his predecessor suggests that Coleridge, too, somehow fails to satisfy Eliot's requirements. A remark later on in the same essay confirms this suspicion:

> Coleridge is apt to take leave of the data of criticism, and arouse the suspicion that he has been diverted into a metaphysical hare-and-hounds. His end does not always appear to be the return to the work of art with improved perception and intensified, because more conscious, enjoyment; his centre of interest changes, his feelings are impure. (Eliot 1957, 13)

In the 'Introduction' to *The Sacred Wood*, Arnold's failure to live up to Eliot's definition of a true critic is diagnosed in remarkably similar terms as a swerving from 'the centre of interest and activity of the critical intelligence' (1957, xii) in pursuit of 'game outside of the literary preserve altogether, much of it political game untouched and inviolable by ideas' (1957, xiii). In hindsight, Eliot's observation that both Coleridge and Arnold had trouble keeping the 'centre of interest' of criticism proper firmly in focus would seem to strengthen rather than diminish their claim to foundational status for twentieth-century criticism. For diversions into philosophical hare-and-hounds and the pursuit of political game are hardly exceptional features of contemporary criticism – if anything, they figure prominently among criticism's multiple centres of interest today.

It is tempting to celebrate this apparent decentring of critical practice deplored by Eliot as a welcome turn to impurity, away from what appears as a rigid obsession with the canonical literary artefact as an object of disinterested aesthetic contemplation. Yet such celebration is in danger of repeating the purist obsession it decries. It risks foreclosing the double challenge of literature's constitutive impurity: its resistance not only to the confinement of 'Literature' (or, worse, 'Poetry') to itself as its own self-sufficient 'centre of interest', but also to the programmatic release of literature into the healthy outdoors of philosophico-political relevance. The task of criticism is to monitor this double resistance by allowing for a radical displacement of its centres of interest, including its currently central interest in the displacement of literature itself. The well-founded suspicion that neither Coleridge nor Arnold would recognize themselves in this plea for radical displacement does not in the least disqualify them from ranking among its prime precursors.

Coleridge's early activities were decisively shaped by the reformist energy associated with the French Revolution. In 1794, he developed a scheme, in tandem with Robert Southey, to found a commune in New England on the principles of what Coleridge called 'Pantisocracy': the rule of all as equals. The scheme never materialized but Coleridge continued to divulge his democratic views on religion, politics and education in numerous lectures and in articles in the periodical press, including his own weekly *The Watchman*. He meanwhile published religious and philosophical poetry and began to develop a life-long interest in German metaphysical thought. His greatest poetical works were written around the turn of the century, at a time when his association with William Wordsworth laid the foundations of what was to become British romanticism. Intent on a solid philosophical frame for the proper pursuit of poetry, Coleridge increasingly turned to the construction of ambitious but abortive blueprints for a future comprehensive metaphysics, which were meant to culminate in his projected but never completed magnum opus, the 'Logosophia'. Arguably the most lasting groundwork for this 'total and undivided philosophy' (Coleridge 1983, I, 282) is the *Biographia Literaria* (1817), a sprawling account of his 'literary life and opinions' which, together with his numerous public lectures on literature and criticism, was to become the basis for Coleridge's massive reputation as a literary critic and theorist. His more directly socio-political and moral preoccupations were developed in his *Lay Sermons* (1816–17), the first of which was significantly entitled *The Statesman's Manual* (meaning the Bible but also, in some measure, itself), and in the two most substantial products of his last decade, *Aids to Reflection* (1824) and *On the Constitution of Church and State* (1830). In these last works, Coleridge emerges as a formidable conservative authority calling for the proper establishment of a corporate intelligentsia, a 'permanent, nationalized, learned order, a national clerisy or church' (Coleridge 1976, 69) whose task it is 'to form and train up the people of the country to obedient, free, useful, organizable subjects, citizens and patriots, living to the benefit of the state, and prepared to die for its defence' (54).

On the Constitution of the Church and State was probably Coleridge's most influential contribution to nineteenth-century public thought. Among those 'profoundly influenced by the idea it presented of a Christian society' (Colmer 1959, 165) was Thomas Arnold, Headmaster of Rugby, a powerful figure in the field of public school education and father of Matthew Arnold. Matthew Arnold's early records, however, appear at odds with this missionary ethos of high public purpose. In his first decade as a writer, he produces his most significant poetical works, an arresting body of writing uncomfortably strung between celebrations of nature and melancholy introspection. At the start of that same decade, in 1851, Arnold became an Inspector of Schools, a taxing position he would hold for some thirty-five years and which demanded frequent travelling in England and Europe as well as considerable administrative labour, including the production of educational policy reports. In 1857 he was elected Professor of Poetry at Oxford, the first non-clergyman ever to hold this position, and the first to lecture not in Latin but in English. The lectures he delivered were often published and some found their way into his first series of *Essays in Criticism* (1865), a volume which established his reputation as a critic. This reputation was further consolidated for posterity with his influential collection of essays in political and social criticism, *Culture and Anarchy* (1869), in which he champions the cultivation of culture as an indispensable cohesive agent properly positioning the individual in a state intent on harmonious perfection: true culture, the ongoing encounter with the 'sweetness and light' of 'the best that has been said and thought in the world', is the only defensible centre of authority in a society otherwise doomed to dissolution as a result of the incommensurable interests of its class components – the Barbarians (the aristocracy), the Philistines (the middle class) and the Populace. In the 1870s Arnold addresses the condition of religion and its institutions in modern society in a number of books of which the controversial *Literature and Dogma* (1873) was and remains the most widely read. Subtitled 'An Essay towards a Better Apprehension of the Bible', *Literature and Dogma* calls for a reading of the Bible which would release it from the straitjackets of dogmatic orthodoxy and sectarian dissent and thereby re-establish it as an effective instrument of culture. Such a reading would have to be informed by the critical 'tact' trained in the study of literature. Arnold's last years as an author were devoted to further exercises of this critical tact, collected in a second series of *Essays in Criticism*, published soon after his death.

A first curious similarity between these two critical trajectories is that they both take shape in the aftermath of a relatively short-lived poetic career: Coleridge wrote his major poetry before he turned 35, Arnold before he turned 40, and both suffered from an acute sense of disappointment at what they regarded as an unfulfilled promise. Yet the all too readily available inference that their later critical work is to some extent a second-best exercise in compensation for personal poetic failure – a sad shift away from a centre of interest they could not hold – threatens to obscure the seriousness of their critical commitment. Caught up as they were in the massive reorganization of the universe of discourse accompanying the relatively rapid transition from a largely rural-agrarian to an urban-industrial culture, involving unprecedented demographic expansion and redistribution and the emergence of new social and political entities, Coleridge and Arnold addressed questions whose urgency is not to be trivialized as a function of their own self-assessed shortcomings in the province of poetry. Nor was their continued critical concern with literature merely a form of corporate escapism on the part of a putative literary establishment. The fact that both authors did reserve a crucial role for literature in the attempt to address the pressing issues of the modern condition is all too frequently glibly demystified as an overdetermined escape from these issues in the serene spheres of aesthetic unworldliness. If the hopes they invested in literature seem extravagant, that is because they are: powered by the conviction that literature at its best has a potential for alteration that must be allowed to wander outside the narrow discursive formation to which it is confined. The critical question, however, is whether this alternative extravagance itself can be contained.

Coleridge and Arnold share the twin assumption that theirs is a culture profoundly marked by a disabling imbalance. Their further diagnostic assessments of the nature and history of this imbalance, however, are quite distinct, as are the remedies they advance in order to redress it. Coleridge's is ultimately a profoundly theological cultural ideology, while Arnold resolutely (although not therefore whole-heartedly) advances a secular perspective on culture and its discontents. Reading them in sequence is to follow an important strand in the history of secularization.

In 1800 Coleridge announced his intention to write 'an Essay on the Elements of Poetry' which 'would in reality be a *disguised* system of Morals & Politics' (cit. Coleridge 1983, I, xxxii). When he eventually composed the *Biographia Literaria* some fifteen years later, he proposed a definition of the central faculty without which this disguise could only ever be a wilful travesty. The question whether Coleridge's proposal ultimately succeeds in warding off charges of wilful – and potentially sinister – imposition can be responsibly addressed only in the larger context of what has been called the 'aesthetic ideology' (de Man 1996), of which it is a forceful representative. Here, we are primarily concerned with the internal logic of Coleridge's argument.

The faculty which allows for a transfer from the realm of poetry to that of morals and politics is the Imagination, and an expansive reading of Coleridge's definition of it reveals the principal features of his theological ideology. The imagination in general is 'the living Power and prime Agent of all human Perception' (Coleridge 1983, I, 304). The critical context of this thesis is Coleridge's opposition to the then (at least in Britain) dominant empiricist doctrine, hailing back to John Locke and David Hume, which conferred absolute primacy to sensory experience and thereby, according to Coleridge, reduced the universe to a dead wasteland of determinist materialism, and human society in particular to a mere laboratory for mechanistic utilitarian experiments. Coleridge's resistance to this system found a foothold in the critical philosophy of Immanuel Kant, who took on board Hume's empiricism but developed an alternative perspective leaving room for a dimension transcending the empirical. Most crucial to Coleridge – who, liberally borrowing from contemporary post-Kantian German philosophers, modified Kant's extremely sophisticated system to his own ends – Kant distinguished between two faculties of the mind: the Understanding, the cognitive faculty strictly speaking, concerned with determined certainty derived from sensory experience; and Reason, the faculty of volition and desire concerned with supra-sensory Ideas, chief among them the final purpose of freedom. In order to ensure a proper connection between these two faculties, Kant introduced the mediating faculty of judgement – in Coleridge, this 'intermediate faculty' (Coleridge 1983, I, 125) is the Imagination, which alone can furnish a synthetic view of the universe as a living organic purposive whole in which the human subject participates to the full, as opposed to a mere material aggregate of objects which '(*as* objects) are essentially fixed and dead'. (Coleridge 1983, I, 304). To perceive the world imaginatively is to see it as a living, organic whole with a distinct final purpose. Coleridge leaves little doubt as to the nature of that purpose: the imagination is 'a repetition in the finite mind of the eternal act of creation in the infinite I AM' (Coleridge 1983, I, 304).

The bottom line of Coleridge's ideology, then, is his conviction that to construe the world properly, i.e. imaginatively, is to recognize its ultimate foundation in God. At the close of the *Biographia Literaria*, Coleridge drives the point home by asserting that his true goal has always been 'to kindle young minds, and to guard them against the temptation of Scorners, by shewing that the Scheme of Christianity, as taught in the Liturgy and Homilies of our Church, though not discoverable by human Reason, is yet in accordance with it', ending on an image of 'the Soul steady and collected in its pure *Act* of inward Adoration to the Great I AM, and to the filial WORD that re-affirmeth it from Eternity to Eternity, whose choral Echo is the Universe. Glory to God alone' (Coleridge 1983, II, 248). The implication of this didactic intent is clearly that, although the imagination is taken to be 'the living Power and prime Agent of *all* human Perception', it is under constant threat and in need of cultivation.

Indeed, this was already suggested in the initial definition, where Coleridge distinguishes between the 'primary' imagination (the imagination in general) and the 'secondary' imagination. This latter Coleridge considers as an echo of the former, co-existing with the conscious will, yet still as identical with the primary in the *kind* of its agency, and differing only in *degree*, and in the *mode* of its operation. It dissolves, diffuses, dissipates, in order to re-create; or where this process is rendered impossible, yet still at all events it struggles to idealize and to unify. (Coleridge 1983, I, 304)

Although Coleridge does not develop the point at this juncture, the distinction between the primary and the secondary imagination amounts to a fundamentally hierarchical conception of human society which can either be seen as an uncomfortable supplement to his initially 'broadly "Jacobin" or Democratic' outlook, or indeed as a confirmation of what was in fact from the very outset 'a conservative political philosophy, not greatly different from that of *Church and State*' (Gravil 1990, 6). It is clear, at any rate, that Coleridge considers those endowed with the truly creative secondary imagination as exemplary human beings, and to the extent that poets are indeed endowed with the imagination to this degree, a critical investigation of the elements of poetry could legitimately lay claim to the status of 'a *disguised* system of Morals & Politics'.

The bulk of Volume II of the *Biographia Literaria* constitutes Coleridge's concerted attempt to properly pursue this investigation, primarily through the critical assessment of the poetry of Wordsworth, intent on measuring his achievement against the theoretical definition of '[t]he poet, described in *ideal* perfection', as one who 'brings the whole soul of man into activity, with the subordination of its faculties to each other, according to their relative worth and dignity' and who 'diffuses a tone, and spirit of unity, that blends, and (as it were) *fuses*, each into each, by that synthetic and magical power, to which we have exclusively appropriated the name of imagination' (Coleridge 1983, II, 15–16). In its actual execution, Coleridge's 'practical criticism' here and elsewhere remains a model of acute attention to the technical detail of poetics, as witness, for instance, the constant critical reconstruction and deconstruction in the course of the last century of his definition of the symbol as the pre-eminent product of the creative imagination, vastly superior to the mechanical artifices of allegory (see Day 1996, 105–25). Moreover, Coleridge's emphatic commitment to an articulate reflection on the very premises of criticism has made his work an extremely valuable point of reference in the development of literary theory as such. Yet whether his criticism indeed lives up to his stated intention to develop 'a *disguised* system of Morals & Politics' is questionable. For the 'disguise' is never quite dropped. More precisely: inasmuch as the *Biographia Literaria* contributes to Coleridge's ideological institution of the imagination, it functions as an 'attempt to ground, formalize, and institute (Tory) politics through philosophy' (Pyle 1995, 54) by establishing it as 'a governing social principle in the interests of the nation' to be developed 'through the national clerisy, through the pedagogical and administrative offices organized in the "civil service"'. (Pyle 1995, 55). And to the extent that poetry can be seen as essentially a performance of this imagination, the disguise would be effective and could therefore eventually be dropped. The fact, however, that Coleridge does not proceed to champion poets as the acknowledged legislators of the state and in his programme for the national clerisy does not even, strictly speaking, mention poetry a single time (a vague reference to 'the Literae Humaniores, the products of genial power' hidden in a footnote is the closest he gets (Coleridge 1976, 54)) suggests that literature ultimately does not live up to the prescriptive demands of Coleridge's theological ideology of the imagination and consequently fails to adequately cover his conception of the system of morals and politics. What must continue to exercise contemporary criticism, however, is the nature, or rather the culture, of this failed synthesis, and to this end Coleridge's criticism, precisely because it is informed by a frustrated totalizing desire to erase the difference between literature and its others, remains a formidable test case.

After his second lecture as Professor of Poetry in May 1858, Matthew Arnold reported in a letter to his mother on the relative dwindling of his audience – 'the theatre was, to me, depressingly too big for us' – and suggested that the very project of his lectures might have been to blame: 'the attempt to form general ideas is one which the Englishman generally sets himself against: and the one grand'-idée of these introductory lectures is to establish a formula which shall *suit* all literature: an attempt which so far as I know has not yet even been made in England' (1996, 389). Placed in its immediate context, Arnold's remark can be read as an ironic gloss on his entire critical career. There is the powerful critical ambition to suitably represent the essence of literature which is necessary for a proper perception of the literary object 'as in itself it really is' (1964, 9) which will, in turn, enable a solid evaluative classification of the entirety of literature and, eventually, of all culture in the '*disinterested endeavour to learn and propagate the best that is known and thought in the world*' (1964, 33). Unfortunately, however, this project took its most influential shape as the mere establishment of a sequence of indiscriminately repeated formulas, soundbites censoriously celebrating the virtues of 'tact' and 'taste' in discrimination but typically divorced from systematic critical analysis. And there is the characteristic blend of arrogance and melancholy in the conviction that the project of criticism is alien to English thought – a conviction condemning Arnold to a lifetime of urbane opposition from the margins of his culture in the name of the centrality of culture, trying 'to pull out a few more stops in that powerful but at present somewhat narrow-toned organ, the modern Englishman' (1964, 4), in a theatre which has become 'depressingly too big'.

It is in his oppositional mode that Arnold is at his most intriguing – not so much in his blanket condemnation of the lack of '*sanity*' he diagnoses in his modernity (1979, 673), but in his 'vivacious' attacks on Victorian complacency. A justly celebrated example from 'The Function of Criticism at the Present Time' (1864) is his juxtaposition of contemporary eulogies of the Anglo-Saxon race as 'the best breed in the world' (1964, 22) with a harrowing newspaper account of a workhouse girl called Wragg who strangled her illegitimate child and was placed in custody. As Arnold puts it, 'There is profit for the spirit in such contrasts as this; criticism serves the cause of perfection by establishing them' (1964, 24). Importantly, however, Arnold does not develop the contrast as an object lesson in social iniquity, but instead focuses on the fact that the girl's Christian name and the reference to her sex have been 'lopped off' in the article – 'Wragg is in custody' – and further abuses the name 'Wragg' to call attention to 'what a touch of grossness in our race, what an original shortcoming in the more delicate spiritual perceptions, is shown by the natural growth amongst us of such hideous names, – Higginbottom, Stiggings, Bugg!' (23). The social criticism is implied in the very introduction of the case as one of those 'inconvenient facts' which Max Weber considered it the duty of intellectuals to force on the attention of the dominant ideology; it is rehearsed in the indignant observation of the newspaper's callous clipping of the girl's name; but Arnold's idiosyncratic signature consists in his framing of the fact in a general aesthetic judgement no less aberrant for being ironical. The example captures the stark logic of Arnold's salvational critical programme: the task of criticism is to teach the English to properly recognize the imperfection of their culture, incongruously exemplified in the hideousness of their names, by introducing them to the best that has been thought and said in the world – the rest will follow, including, presumably, a better future for the children of girls like Wragg. The task of the critic is to defy the 'defiant songs of triumph' of the present 'only by murmuring under his breath, *Wragg is in custody*', 'in no other way will these songs of triumph be induced gradually to moderate themselves, to get rid of what in them is excessive and offensive, and to fall into a softer an truer key' (24).

For Arnold, that 'softer and truer key' is essentially the key of poetry, and its perplexing introduction at this point in 'The Function of Criticism' amounts to an ambivalent recognition of the sheer unlikeliness of his critical enterprise. It is this ambivalence which makes Arnold's writing still a powerful and disturbing precedent for literary studies in search of self-legitimation. When this ironical reservation all but disappears, as in his preaching promotion of poetry to the status of religion in his influential late essay on 'The Study of Poetry' (1880), with its dispiriting propagation of 'the high seriousness of the great classics' (1964, 250) as 'an infallible touchstone for detecting the presence or absence of high poetic quality' (242), the function of criticism is to refute him by kicking his touchstones back into the long grass – or into the wilderness of 'that most Arnoldian of fields, Cultural Studies' (Bell 1997, 217).

In Coleridge there is an unmistakable gravitation towards the final foundation in God, but his writing seems almost perversely driven to avoid that centre by losing itself in magnificent digressions that have saved his criticism from the fate of his theological ideology. In Arnold, the central point is invoked on almost every page, perhaps because it no longer bears the self-evidently authoritative name of God but is simply, or rather merely, called 'the best' – and in his worst moments, all he accomplishes is a tedious liturgy of Literature as the High Point of High Culture. The blatant absence of a secular notion of excellence comparable in authority to the notion of God and, perhaps more importantly, the disastrous consequences of some attempts to found such a notion in the course of the last century, still make Arnold something of a suspicious figure today. It has seemed easier to bracket Coleridge's solid theological commitment than to forgive Arnold for his ultimately far less fundamentalist commitment to the centrality of a true culture whose core is poetry. Yet as recent reinvestigations suggest, Arnold's actual criticism of culture is itself a powerful ally in the displacement of culture as the position of a stable centre of authority, towards culture as 'always already culture critique', a 'dis-position' that 'severs any attachment to the particularization and positionality of cultural identity' (Walters 1997, 364–5). Instead of forgiveness, Arnold deserves the critical reading he practised rather than preached.

Ortwin de Graef

Further reading and works cited

Appleyard, J. A. *Coleridge's Philosophy of Literature*. Cambridge, 1965.
Arnold, M. *Essays in Criticism, First and Second Series*, intro. G. K. Chesterton. London, 1964.
—. 'The Critical Prefaces of 1853 and 1854', in *The Poems of Matthew Arnold*, ed. K. Allott, 2nd edn M. Allott. London, 1979.
—. *Culture and Anarchy*, ed. Samuel Lipman. New Haven, CT, 1994.
—. *The Letters of Matthew Arnold. Volume 1: 1829–1859*, ed. C. Y. Lang. Charlottesville, VA, 1996.
Ashton, R. *The Life of Samuel Taylor Coleridge*. Oxford, 1997.
Bell, B. 'The Function of Arnold at the Present Time', *Essays in Criticism*, 47, 3, July 1997.
Butler, M. *Romantics, Rebels and Reactionaries*. Oxford, 1981.

Coleridge, S. T. On the Constitution of the Church and State, ed. J. Colmer. Princeton, NJ, 1976.
—. Biographia Literaria, or, Biographical Sketches of My Literary Life and Opinions, eds J. Engell and W. Jackson Bate, 2 vols. Princeton, NJ, 1983.
Collini, S. 'Arnold', in Victorian Thinkers, eds A. L. Le Quesne et al. Oxford, 1993.
Colmer, J. Coleridge: Critic of Society. Oxford, 1959.
Day, A. Romanticism. London, 1996.
de Graef, O. 'Congestion of the Brain in an Age of Unpoetrylessness: Matthew Arnold's Digestive Tracts for the Times'. Victorian Literature and Culture, 26, 2, 1998.
de Man, P. Aesthetic Ideology, ed. and intro. A. Warminski. Minneapolis, MN, 1996.
Eliot, T. S. The Sacred Wood. London, 1957.
Fulford, T. and Paley, M. D. (eds) Coleridge's Visionary Languages. Rochester, NY, 1993.
Gallant, C. Coleridge's Theory of Imagination Today. New York, 1989.
Gravil, R. The Coleridge Connection. London, 1990.
Hawkes, T. 'The Heimlich Manoeuvre', Textual Practice, 8, 2, 1994.
Levine, G. 'Matthew Arnold: The Artist in the Wilderness', Critical Inquiry, 9, 3, March 1983.
Orr, L. (ed.) Critical Essays on S. T. Coleridge. New York, 1994.
Pyle, F. The Ideology of Imagination. Stanford, CA, 1995.
Trilling, L. Matthew Arnold. London, 1963.
Tucker, H. F. A Companion to Victorian Literature and Culture. Oxford, 1999.
Walters, T. 'The Question of Culture (and Anarchy)', Modern Language Notes, 112, 3, 1997.

2. John Ruskin (1819–1900) and Walter Pater (1839–1894): Aesthetics and the State

Although John Ruskin and Walter Pater made their contemporaneous reputations as critics and theorists of art and are indeed virtually the only two British aesthetic (as opposed to literary) theorists of note in the nineteenth century, twentieth-century critics have read them primarily in the tradition of nineteenth-century prose, along with Coleridge, Carlyle and Arnold. From this perspective, Ruskin has had considerable importance in extending the Coleridgean idea of organic form into an organic critique of British society that influenced William Morris's socialism and through him the British labour party (Rosenberg 1961, 131). Along with Coleridge and Arnold, Ruskin continued to influence the British Cambridge critics' organicist social views (he had less influence on American New Critics and Ruskin specialists in the United States, following Rosenberg, discuss his organicism generally in connection with his social and economic theories). Both Ruskin's political heirs and his academic critics have then construed Pater's writings as an aesthetic narrowing of Ruskin, a concern for aesthetics that deliberately drained it of moral and political significance, as indeed Ruskin saw it (see Ruskin 1903–12, IV, 35). Although the view of Pater as an ahistorical relativist and quietist has been increasingly contested (see Williams 1989 and Loesberg 1991), the view of Ruskin as having turned his earlier Evangelical art theory into a secular, mostly left critique of capitalism and of Pater as resisting Ruskin's absolutist theorizing and moralist preference for the Gothic over the Renaissance (see Hill's notes to The Renaissance, in Pater 1980, 294 and Bloom 1974, xvi) remains standard.

The view of Ruskin through the lens of William Morris's socialist reading of him certainly captures an aspect of his later economic theories and there is no question that his theories of both art and society are deeply and explicitly organicist. But this version of Ruskin ignores or writes off as marginal his extremely authoritarian view of how organic relations should work in society, as well as the precise nature of his turn from art to politics and economy. It also not only falsifies the general tenor of Pater's theories but also reduces our view of Ruskin's and Pater's dialogue to one about Gothic and Renaissance or to whether art is a matter of perception or theoretical apprehension, while leaving Pater's larger social, historical and critical views to be influenced mainly by Arnold (for this influence see DeLaura (1969) and Dowling (1984)). As a corrective to these perspectives, I will look at Ruskin's and Pater's dialogue over the political significance of art in terms of the decidedly un-British idea of the aesthetic state. The idea of the aesthetic state begins with the Jena German romantics and particularly with Friedrich Schiller. Ruskin read little Schiller, barely mentions him and then only to misinterpret him (see Wilkinson and Willoughby 1967, clviii) and although Pater had read as much in Schiller as in German romanticism (see Inman 1981, 100–2), he does not seem to have particularly attended to this concept. Still, by using the idea that art, rather than being relevant as a moral activity or as a taste analogous to a moral sentiment (these are the eighteenth-century British ideas about the relevance of art to morality, as most significantly formulated by Shaftesbury and Hutcheson, and they remain largely definitive of how Anglo-American critics make the connection), is a model pattern for how a state may be formed (the best history of the idea of the aesthetic state is in Chytry 1989), we will be able to see the line from Ruskin's early aesthetic theories to his critique of laissez-faire capitalism as both insufficiently benevolent and insufficiently authoritarian. The relevance of Pater's critique of organicism, and his views on art and society from his earliest published works through *Plato and Platonism* to Ruskin's theories and the anti-statist political significance of Pater's aesthetics will also emerge.

Ruskin's theory of beauty, in its earliest articulation, attributes our sense of beauty to a recognition of God's ordering of the universe as a gift to us. Although Ruskin formulated this theory as part of an early Evangelical project to prove the divinity of art and beauty, that early articulation is already ready to be stripped of its religious elements and to serve as a general model of value for Ruskin. He starts by distinguishing between aesthesis and theoria, defining aesthesis as the pleasure afforded by the senses alone and theoria as 'the moral perception and appreciation of the ideas of beauty' (Ruskin 1903–12, IV, 35). Despite his use of the word 'moral' and his late footnote directing this passage at aestheticism, his target in this distinction necessitating an extra-sensual apprehension to appreciate beauty seems not to be theories of art that do not recognize its moral elements (as Landow 1971, 90, seems to suggest) but rather the eighteenth-century British theorists who saw the appreciation of art in terms of sense-apprehension and argued its moral relevance in terms of analogy between a moral and an aesthetic apprehension. Ruskin, in contrast, asserts an identity between moral and aesthetic apprehension.

Having set up the distinction between aesthesis and theoria, Ruskin then defines the workings of beauty on the theoretic apprehension:

> Now in whatever is an object of life, in whatever may be infinitely and for itself desired, we may be sure there is something of the divine, for God will not make anything an object of life to his creatures which does not point to or partake of Himself . . . But when instead of being scattered,

> interrupted, or chance-distributed, [pleasures of the sight] are gathered together, and so arranged
> to enhance each other as by chance they could not be, there is caused by them not only a feeling
> of strong affection towards the object in which they exist but a perception of purpose and
> adaptation of it to our desires; a perception therefore, of the immediate operation of the
> Intelligence which so formed us, and so feeds us. Now the mere animal consciousness of the
> pleasantness I call aesthesis; but the exulting, reverent, and grateful perception of it I call
> theoria. (Ruskin 1903–12, IV, 46–7)

The first thing to notice is that though this passage seems to indicate that the designed
arrangement is instrumental to producing a gratification that we desire, in fact this
distinction between instrument and end cannot be the case since Ruskin insists on a
difference between objects that instrumentally gratify us (food to satisfy our hunger) and
objects that are intrinsically gratifying in themselves. This design leads to no purpose
outside itself and it gratifies us inherently. The value of design making unity out of
scattered variety is fundamental and objective (Landow 1971, 92 and Hewison 1976, 55
note Ruskin's contestation of subjectivist theories of beauty), there in objects and thus
universally apprehensible. Even the gratitude to an external, designing intelligence cannot
really be a consequence of the perception of design since that would suggest a distinction
between purpose and object (although in this case between the divine designer's purpose
and its object) that Ruskin's theory denies. Apprehension of design contains simultaneously as equivalent elements gratification and gratitude.

As Ruskin moved from an Evangelical to a more and more explicitly humanist
justification of this theory of the intrinsic and fundamental value of mere design, he
moved increasingly to a political and economic theory from an internal necessity that made
that later political theory essentially still an aesthetic one and that also had as a
consequence the authoritarianism so many of Ruskin's critics want to downplay as an
idiosyncrasy. The first step in the movement from aesthetics to politics occurs famously in
The Stones of Venice, when he uses his qualities of beauty to judge the ethics of the society
that produced the beauty. While still tying this value to Christianity, Ruskin praises the
Gothic arrangement of labour for what amounts to an aesthetic arrangement that respects
the freedom of its labourers:

> Therefore to every spirit which Christianity summons to her service, her exhortation is: Do
> what you can, and confess frankly what you are unable to do; neither let your efforts be
> shortened for fear of failure, nor your confession silenced for fear of shame. And it is, perhaps the
> principal admirableness of the Gothic schools of architecture, that they thus receive the results
> of the labour of inferior minds; and out of fragments full of imperfection in every touch,
> indulgently raise up a stately and unaccusable whole. (Ruskin 1903–12, X, 190)

Critics have long noted the incipient social theory in this passage (see Spear 1984, 123).
The great Gothic cathedrals, using imperfect workers and finding a place for all of them
within a more perfect whole, are models of just societies. Further, if Gothic beauty
manifests this social arrangement, then the relevance of art to society is only too clear: that
which produces beauty is also just.

The problem is that, at first glance, the relationship between mode of production and
designed object seems less than perfect. Although Ruskin famously argued in *The Crown of
Wild Olives* that you could not really have Gothic architecture without living in a Gothic
society and that great works of art could only be produced by a properly organized society,
the truth of that assertion is not self-evident. Not only can one imagine justly organized

systems producing less than beautiful works of art, if only as a result of technical failure, but, precisely because beauty is an objective quality of things, its mode of production is logically irrelevant to it. Only if it is, by some natural law as rigorous as the law of gravity, impossible to produce beautiful works except through just organization will Ruskin's equivalence between Gothic labour systems and beauty hold as more than an analogy.

The answer to this problem lies in the equivalence outlined above between the apprehension of design and the experiences of gratification and gratitude. For Ruskin, the capturing of variety within unity has, as an objective part of its pattern, the recognition that the pattern was designed and the gratitude that that recognition elicits. In the discussion of aesthesis and theoria, the designed object recognized as beautiful was in the first instance natural and the designer was the divine intelligence that Ruskin, in his Evangelical period, wanted to prove necessarily connected to the appreciation of beauty. When one moves to an artificed object, a cathedral in *The Stones of Venice*, however, because human beings do the designing, the apprehension of design will equivalently include the designing system to which an experience of beauty entails a gratitude. In other words, one perceives as beautiful those objects designed by justly organized systems, where justly organized means organized to contain variety within unity (the stonecutter's freedom and imperfection within the larger purpose of the cathedral). As one can see, a justly organized society will be perceived as aesthetically valuable, then, not by a separate, non-moral judgement, but precisely by an aesthetic judgement that appraises moral arrangement.

As Ruskin secularizes his definition of aesthetic design, he must also, because of his sense of what it then means to call that design objective, both depart from nature as the model of its working and insist on authoritarian control. To understand how this change works, one must note the difference between Coleridgean organicism and explications of productive design and design in objects in both *Modern Painters II* and in *The Stones of Venice*. Coleridge's highly influential definition distinguishes natural order from artificial order in terms of the immanence of natural order and its absence of any impress of an external stamp. The extension of this definition to art is by loose analogy since art is by definition externally authored. Moreover, this argument is not friendly to the idea that natural objects show evidence of being divinely designed, since such evidence would be precisely the mark of external stamping. For Ruskin, as an evangelical, though the recognition of divine design is immanent in the design, indeed a part of it, it is still at least intellectually separable enough to mark it out as part of the definition. When Ruskin loses his belief in a divine designer, because design for him always entails gratitude to a designer, he must also give up nature as the model from which to explain design. He continues to believe in an order to the appearance of nature and he continues to describe it in terms of achieving purposes, for instance in *Modern Painters V* (published in 1860, two years after what Ruskin describes as his un-conversion and clearly with his turn to political and economic writing already in mind), but he no longer insists that nature was ordered by God for our appreciation and he constantly describes natural order with social and political analogies: 'And in the arrangement of these concessions there is an exquisite sensibility among the leaves. They do not grow each to his own liking, till they run against one another, and then turn back sulkily; but by the watchful instinct, far apart, they anticipate their companions' courses, as ships at sea' (Ruskin 1903–12, VII, 48).

But as artificed ordering replaces natural order as the model for design that both art and society share, the ramifications of its objective status shift. When Ruskin believed that natural order was the first model of beauty and that art created beauty by being true to that natural order, he also believed that all human beings were naturally disposed to appreciate that beauty (see Landow 1971, 93–4 for a discussion of this issue). Those who did not appreciate the beauty of Turner simply did not understand how nature really worked or appeared. When they were fully instructed on how storms or light worked, the beauty of both nature and Turner automatically became manifest. When humanly artificed order replaces divinely patterned nature as simultaneously artistic beauty and proper social arrangement, though, the import of the fact that evidently all humans do not perceive either beauty or social justice in the same way changes. Although Ruskin regularly claims that anyone who simply looks at the evidence straightforwardly or reads what the Bible says will understand that his claims about society or his interpretation of a text are obviously and irrefutably right, his experience of being constantly contested also clearly meant that not all humans would by themselves see beautiful art as beautiful or a just society as just. Our taste for beauty is now part of our moral make-up and cannot be easily improved by the kind of education the first two volumes of *Modern Painters* imagined. Thus Ruskin now argues that

> . . . a picture of Titian's, or a Greek statue, or a Greek coin, or a Turner landscape, expresses delight in the perpetual contemplation of a good and perfect thing. That is an entirely moral quality – it is the taste of the angels . . . it is not an indifferent nor optional thing whether we love this or that; but it is just the vital function of all our being. (Ruskin 1903–12, XVIII, 436)

Saying that taste is a moral quality is not new for Ruskin. Since he describes moral and aesthetic order with the same language throughout *Modern Painters*, taste has always been a moral quality. But since it is now so deeply imbedded in us, good taste cannot be taught in any easy way: thus Ruskin immediately goes on to say that a scavenger or a costermonger could not be taught to enjoy Dante or Beethoven without entirely changing his nature. In other words, beauty and equitable order are still equivalent and objective, but they are not dependably and universally apprehensible.

This article opened by arguing the value of the concept of the aesthetic state for explaining Ruskin's political and economic theories. We are now ready quickly to go through the features of those theories that indicate he aimed at an aesthetic order and neither a welfare state (as Rosenberg 1961, 139 argued) nor some form of organic socialism, as those following from William Morris's interpretation have argued. First, although *Unto this Last* quite famously argues for replacing competition with affection as the basis for social relation, Ruskin also states quite explicitly that he does not espouse affection as a matter of abstract justice but as a reality of organization: 'Observe, I am here considering the affections wholly as a motive power; not at all as things in themselves desirable or noble' (XVII, 30). If one takes this claim seriously and puts it in the context of the theory of artistic composition in *Modern Painters V*, the aesthetic basis of Ruskin's concept of social organization becomes clear: 'Now invention in art signifies an arrangement in which everything in the work is thus consistent with all things else, and helpful to all else . . . Also in true composition, everything not only helps everything else a *little*, but helps it with its utmost power' (Ruskin 1903–12, VII, 208–9). In other words, Ruskin argues against political economy with what he takes to be a basic law of composition, though it is also an aspect of human relationship. Moreover, although Ruskin does describe what he calls here the Law of Help as the basis of organic life, the difference between organic life and art is that if the parts do not help each other in a plant, the plant will die – the law is inescapable. In art, one can disobey the law but one will create flawed works of art. In society, one can disobey the law at least in the short run by choosing competition, but the rules of artistic composition show the ultimate mistake of doing so. Ruskin's key claim, then, 'Government and co-operation are in all things and eternally the law of life' (Ruskin 1903–12, VII, 207), literally true of organic life, becomes true of social order (and the terms 'government' and 'co-operation' have their primary meaning there and not in organic life) through the lens of artistic composition.

Although the theory of the aesthetic state has frequently had as part of its vision an ordered whole comprised of individual human actions freely chosen and Schiller, at least, was suspicious of any easy analogy between the artist and the teacher or the politician (see Wilkinson and Willoughby 1967, clxii and cxci as well as Chytry 1989, 82), the concept of an ordering and controlling artist as a model for a state leader has frequently forced its way through. In Ruskin's case, as we have seen, his theory's secularization forced the replacement of a divine designer with an artist. And his recognition that human beings did not inevitably perceive beauty or accept proper social organization meant a strong stress on authority. In *Unto this Last*, that stress is at its weakest, though one can still find him insisting on the necessity of teaching people what to desire (Ruskin 1903–12, XVII, 83). In *A Joy For Ever*, though, on a note to the need for fatherly authority in the state, Ruskin makes clear how little he values 'liberty': 'I will tell you beforehand what I really do think about this same liberty of action, namely, that whenever we can make a perfectly equitable law about any matter, or even a law securing, on the whole, more just conduct than unjust, we ought to make that law (XVI, 109). And, in an inflammatory defence of slavery that gives a dark context to his reading of Turner's painting of the slave-ship and to his statement about a worker's freedom under medieval Christianity, Ruskin makes clear his sense of the absolute necessity of compulsion: 'The fact is that slavery is not a political institution at all, *but an inherent, natural, and eternal inheritance* of a large portion of the human race – to whom the more you give of their own free will, the more slaves they will make themselves' (Ruskin 1903–12, XVII, 256). When Ruskin moved from art to society then, the model he used remained aesthetic in the sense that the state would follow rules of composition, those rules being simultaneously moral and artistic, and that that composition would come from a designing authority, the ends of whose designs would assuredly be a just and equitable ordering, but whose means would be the artist's control of the elements of his or her work.

Although Pater read Ruskin as early as 1859 (Gosse, cit. Inman 1981, 62), if he was as influenced as many argue (Bloom 1974, xvi, calls Ruskin, improbably, Pater's 'only begetter'), he buried that influence deeply. Even the seemingly obvious connections – the opening of *The Renaissance* and its rejections of abstract theory in favour of concrete experience (Pater 1980, xix), the general reversal of Ruskin's evaluations of the Gothic and the Renaissance – are at best reliable guesses since Pater almost never mentions Ruskin. In discussing Pater's response to Ruskin in terms of the latter's view of art and the state, one can hardly be sure that Pater thought he was responding directly to Ruskin, since the writers he discusses in outlining his alternative are William Morris, Coleridge, Winckelmann and Plato, among others. Still at key moments in various texts, Pater took direct aim at the idea of a state organized on organicist, or aesthetic principles, at its valuing of ideal order, at its authoritarian principles. Moreover his view of art's value and its relation to issues of moral judgement constitute one of the primary oppositions in aesthetic literature to the notion of the aesthetic state.

Pater's first three published essays, 'Coleridge's Writings', 'The Poems of William Morris' and 'Winckelmann' (in 1866, 1867 and 1868), read together rather than in their reprinted versions in *The Renaissance* and *Appreciations*, seem more like the first works of a social critic than of an art critic. Both 'The Poems of William Morris' and 'Winckelmann' end with visions of an overarching value of art that has led to the usual view of Pater as a hedonist who tries to separate art from moral significance. But what the essays share most clearly with each other is a sense that the kinds of objectivist theories we have seen Ruskin trying to formulate amount to an escape from the realities of modern life. In the case of Coleridge, Pater is at his least sympathetic, and thus most directly refutes the idealized view of nature and art as unifying forces that we have seen Ruskin articulating (he refutes Coleridge's organicism first – 1866, 55, and then his notion of a natural order that shows itself by the way it holds together disparate parts, 1866, 57). But precisely because it is more sympathetic with what we frequently take as the Ruskinian ideal of the earthly paradise, in Ruskin's clearest immediate inheritor, the opening of 'The Poems of William Morris' is more striking:

> Greek poetry, medieval or modern poetry, projects above the realities of its time a world in which the forms of things are transfigured. Of that world this new poetry takes possession and sublimates beyond it another still fainter and more spectral, which is literally an artificial or 'earthly paradise'. It is a finer ideal, extracted from what in relation to any actual world is already an ideal ... The secret of enjoyment of it is that inversion of home-sickness known to some, that incurable thirst for the sense of escape, which no actual form of life satisfies, no poetry even, if it be merely simple and spontaneous. (1868, 144)

Pater opens here an article that praises this transfiguration in Morris's poetry in the highest terms. But the passage quite clearly describes the transfiguration as an escape and the earthly paradise as the artifice of someone who cannot deal with the world before him. The first problem with an aesthetics of order proposed as a social model, then, is that it is really an escape from the demands of the world before us rather than a mode of dealing with it. In this context, the theory of art's value that closes the essay, and that became the notorious 'Conclusion' to *The Renaissance*, posits a form of aesthetic apprehension that will accept rather than turn from the world science shows us, that will learn how to value experience rather than idealize it away.

Moreover, Pater does have a view of a moral vision contained in this form of aesthetic apprehension, and again it seems to contrast almost deliberately with what Ruskin thinks art has to tell us about morality. Pater suggests that view in 'Coleridge's Writings' and in *The Renaissance*, but there he seems mainly concerned to challenge abstract and absolute codes of morality, offering the basis for the view of him as a moral relativist. In an essay on *Measure for Measure*, however, he concludes with a more positive articulation of the ethics of art:

> It is for this finer justice, a justice based on a more delicate appreciation of the true conditions of men and things, a true respect of persons in our estimate of actions, that the people in *Measure for Measure* cry out as they pass before us ... It is not always that poetry can be the exponent of morality; but it is this aspect of morals which it represents most naturally, for this true justice is dependent on just those finer appreciations which poetry cultivates in us the power of making, those peculiar valuations of action and its effect which poetry actually requires. (1910a, 183–4)

Like Ruskin, Pater here claims a morality implicit within the working of art. And their moral imperatives contrast just as do their views of art. For Ruskin, art modelled a unifying order that contained variety and led to a cohering Law of Help. For Pater, far from offering overarching orders, art shows us how to attend to our experiences in all their individual intensity, giving 'the highest quality to your moments as they pass, and simply for those moments' sake' (1980, 190). The morality that follows entails a recognition of the irreducible individuality of situations and, more significantly, human beings. This recognition does not imply that no moral judgements can be made, but that moral judgements to be just to individual human beings cannot follow abstract laws or orders.

A suspicion of social order might seem to follow naturally enough from this view and, indeed, Pater's justification of Winckelmann's insincere conversion to Roman Catholicism in terms of Winckelmann's private needs is based on the claim that 'the aim of our culture should be to attain not only as intense but as complete a life as possible' (1980, 150). Although culture here means self-cultivation, the passage also suggests that a culture in the sense of a social order also must be aimed at the development of its individuals. But Pater's explicit treatment of the concept of a state modelled on aesthetic principles is in fact more ambiguous. An aesthetic order, as opposed to other orders, after all, has an element of self-undercutting in it that always endangers its own authority. Pater can discuss Morris's earthly paradise as an aesthetic achievement precisely because his evaluation of its effectiveness as a vision entails a recognition of its artifice and its escape.

In *Plato and Platonism*, Pater carries out to the limit this sympathetic appraisal of the concept of the aesthetic state that undercuts by its very sympathy. In the discussion of Plato's *Republic*, he specifies that Platonic justice rests on 'a unity or harmony enforced on disparate elements' (1910d, 242–3). This sounds very much like Ruskin's vision at various points. But then, in the most astonishing chapter of that book on 'Plato's Aesthetics', while mentioning hardly at all and only in the most indirect way Plato's most famous and notorious ideas about art's insufficiencies, Pater finds Plato's real aesthetics precisely in his design of his state: 'We are to become – like little pieces in a machine! you may complain. – No, like performers rather, individually, it may be, of more or less importance, but each with a necessary and inalienable part, in a perfect musical exercise which is well worth while' (1910d, 273). Although this may sound like a defence of Plato's state in terms of its aesthetic order, in fact the finding of Plato's aesthetics in his statecraft soon changes the value of that theory into one that attunes us to what we find attractive in the concept of a number of ordered states – notably a Ruskinian gothic that shares with Plato's republic only its Ruskinian ordering (1910d, 279). By the end of that chapter, aesthetics becomes the central force of Plato's thinking, though, since it is an aesthetics of askesis and self-resistance, it controls its own aesthetic temperament. In becoming an aesthetics, though, Plato's state can no longer function as overarching order, but only as an order, an artifice that continues to work out Pater's aesthetic of individuation.

Pater's aestheticization of Plato's republic may seem the kind of reduction that has led to the view – held by Ruskin as well as numbers of contemporary critics – that Pater's formalism denied art any moral or intellectual content. But, in fact, it drained Ruskin's aesthetics of its moral content to use it to delineate a different moral evaluation, one that Pater wanted to find in all art – even the aesthetic states of Ruskin's gothic and Plato's republic. Bloom locates Ruskin's most threatening influence on Pater in his valuing of the ability above all to see clearly (1974, xi). If Pater did indeed see this as what he learned from Ruskin, he absorbed it so completely that he made it seem far more his own than Ruskin's dictum, so completely, finally, that he could turn Ruskin's aesthetic state into a Paterian moral moment. In so doing, he opposes to the view of the aesthetic state in both its harmony and its oppression neither a deliberately anti-aesthetic politics nor an amoral aesthetic but the opposing position always potential in any aesthetic, a scepticism about the naturalness of order.

Jonathan Loesberg

Further reading and works cited

Bloom, H. 'The Crystal Man', in *Selected Writings of Walter Pater*, ed. H. Bloom. New York, 1974.
Chytry, J. *The Aesthetic State*. Berkeley, CA, 1989.
Dale, P. A. *The Victorian Critic and the Idea of History*. Cambridge, MA, 1977.
DeLaura, D. *Hebrew and Hellene in Victorian England*. Austin, TX, 1969.
Dowling, L. *Language and Decadence in the Victorian Fin de Siècle*. Princeton, NJ, 1986.
—. *Hellenism and Homosexuality in Victorian Oxford*. Ithaca, NY, 1994.
Helsinger, E. *Ruskin and the Art of the Beholder*. Cambridge, MA, 1982.
Hewison, R. *John Ruskin and the Argument of the Eye*. Princeton, NJ, 1976.
Hunt, J. D. *The Wider Sea: A Life of John Ruskin*. New York, 1982.
Hutcheson, F. *An Inquiry Concerning Beauty, Order, Harmony, Design*, ed. P. Kung. The Hague, 1973.
Inman, B. A. *Walter Pater's Reading, 1858–1873*. New York, 1981.
Landow, G. *The Aesthetic and Critical Theories of John Ruskin*. Princeton, NJ, 1971.
Levey, M. *The Case of Walter Pater*. London, 1978.
Loesberg, J. *Aestheticism and Deconstruction: Pater, Derrida, and De Man*. Princeton, NJ, 1991.
Pater, W. 'Coleridge's Writings', *Westminster Review*, January 1866.
—. 'Poems of William Morris', *Westminster Review*, October 1868.
—. *Appreciations*. London, 1910a.
—. *Greek Studies*. London, 1910b.
—. *Marius the Epicurean*, 2 vols. London, 1910c.
—. *Plato and Platonism*. London, 1910d.
—. *The Renaissance: Studies in Art and Poetry*, ed. D. L. Hill. Berkeley, CA, 1980.
Rosenberg, J. D. *The Darkening Glass: A Portrait of Ruskin's Social Genius*. New York, 1961.
Ruskin, J. *Works*, eds E. T. Cook and A. Wedderburn, 39 vols. London, 1903–12.
Sawyer, P. *Ruskin's Poetic Argument: The Design of the Major Works*. Ithaca, NY, 1985.
Shaftesbury, A. Cooper, Third Earl of. *Characteristics of Men, Manners, Opinions, Times, Etc.* ed. J. Robertson, 2 vols. London, 1900.
Spear, J. *Dreams of an English Eden: Ruskin and His Tradition in Social Criticism*. New York, 1984.
Wilkinson, E. and Willoughby, L. A. 'Introduction' to F. Schiller, *On the Aesthetic Education of Man*, eds E. Wilkinson and L. A. Willoughby. Oxford, 1967.
Williams, C. *Transfigured World: Walter Pater's Aestheticist Historicism*. Ithaca, NY, 1989.

3. Oscar Wilde (1854–1900): Aesthetics and Criticism

Devoting most of his career to poetry, prose fiction and drama, Oscar Wilde wrote the bulk of his critical work between 1885 and 1891. Along with a number of book reviews and brief articles, this corpus consists chiefly of just six major essays: 'The Truth of Masks' (1885), 'The Decay of Lying' (1889), 'Pen, Pencil and Poison' (1889), 'The Portrait of Mr. W. H.' (1889), 'The Soul of Man Under Socialism' (1890) and 'The Critic as Artist' (1890). In May 1891, four of these six essays were published together in a volume suggestively entitled *Intentions*, although each of the six was at one time or another considered for inclusion in the book (Danson 1997, 7–8). Wilde also published in 1891 the well-known 'Preface' to his only novel, *The Picture of Dorian Gray*; a brief series of aphorisms on beauty and art, the 'Preface' serves as a pithy distillation of the paradoxical, subtly equivocal theoretical framework the essays collectively establish. In 1895, Wilde's own words would be interpreted, ironically, as utterly unequivocal evidence against him in the scandalous libel and criminal suits that eventually sent him to jail and effectively ended his career.

This tragic conclusion did not extinguish Wilde's legacy. In fact, it is safe to say that his words have graced more greeting cards and bookbags than any other author featured in this encyclopaedia – all testaments to the prominent place Wilde holds in our cultural landscape to this day. Yet such a distinction does more than indicate a unique literary and critical influence. Most obviously, it attests to the witty, epigrammatic memorability of his declarations and, moreover, acknowledges that when many people speak of Oscar Wilde, they often refer to a personality and a life as much as a collection of ideas and texts. Indeed, for a writer who famously explores the question of art's relation to life, and whose life and work together offer an uncommonly rich site for examining the overdetermined sexual and social culture of late-Victorian England, such a focus is in many ways warranted. For despite his avowed artistic detachment from the age in which he lived, Wilde was a keen social critic. In 'The Soul of Man Under Socialism', to name just one example, his description of the public's despotic potential to quash – like Mill's 'tyranny of the majority' – independently thinking, creative individuals provides an eerily prescient analysis of the fate which would befall him. Recent Wilde scholars have explored such issues in groundbreaking ways. But noting his status as cultural icon also points to a peculiar challenge his critics face, that of diffusing the still popular idea of Wilde as just a stereotype or a sloganeer.

Beyond the mannered eccentricities Wilde exhibited in his deliberate cultivation of a public persona, beyond the famous utterances that seem to serve as captions to it, lies a largely coherent and complex aesthetic theory of 'art for art's sake', derived from the aestheticism of Walter Pater, though not merely derivative of it. Morality and immorality, art and life, truth and lies – throughout his work, each of these categories garner their very particular meaning by way of Wilde's paradoxical rhetoric and self-consciously performative style. In a generically diverse body of criticism – which includes lists of cryptic or ambiguously referential aphorisms, a story of a fatally wayward critic, an appreciation of a forging and murdering artist, and two dialogues involving voices that are not merely transparent representations of Wilde's own theoretical 'intentions' – *how* he makes his arguments often matters just as much as *what*, at isolated moments, they assert. Separated from their intellectual or discursive context – on bookbags or greeting cards – these statements amuse, convey a personality and perhaps seem cleverly apt. In their discursive context, they do much more. Wilde's response to important critical thinkers who preceded him, his critique of the prevailing wisdom of his time and his relevance to theoretical debates that continue to this day are considerable and warrant serious consideration.

Wilde's insistence on the separation between art and life, and his claim for art's priority in that pairing, point significantly to questions of aesthetic representation and reception that span the history of critical discourse from the classical age to the present. The privilege he gives to the imaginative, rather than mimetic, function of art recalls the ancient poetic dispute between Plato and Aristotle and also situates him in a tradition of poetic apologies from Sidney to the romantics. As Hazard Adams explains, Wilde recognizes in his own era that 'the theory of imitation was undergoing a crucial change. The trend, at least since Kant and Coleridge, had been to emphasize art's power to *make*, not to *copy*' (Adams 1992,

657). Like Pater's, Wilde's concept of aesthetic autonomy belongs to and raises the stakes of this intellectual current. If art does not primarily 'copy' life or nature, then what does it do? Wilde's provocative response to this question at once *severs* and *reverses* this mimetic relationship, proposing instead that 'Life imitates Art' (Wilde 1989, 985). Although it is the second effect – the reversal – in Wilde's proposal that has gained the status of truism, both of the gestures have significant implications within the history of critical theory.

In the first sense, the separation Wilde imposes upon the mimetic formula, upon 'natural' order from life to art, elaborates a chief tenet of Pater's aesthetic criticism: art in its highest form is something more and other than a mere reflection of the natural world. This emphatic distinction underwrites aestheticism's notorious insistence that, in Pater's words, '[t]he office of the poet is not that of the moralist' (Pater 1986, 427). For Pater, the true source of art – its 'active principle' – corresponds to what Wilde also privileges – 'imagination' (Pater 1986, 428). What it generates, for both of them, is 'beauty' and 'pleasure'. Wilde's at times outlandish preference for the artificial over the natural – his protagonist's refusal, for instance, to go outside in 'The Decay of Lying' – are best read within this specific context. As Pater explains in his essay, 'Wordsworth' (1874), the active principle in art is not entirely natural – not 'rooted in the ground' or 'tethered down to a world' – but rather 'something very different from this' (Pater 1986, 428). In the 'Preface' to *The Renaissance*, Pater calls this 'something' Wordsworth's 'unique, incommunicable faculty, that strange, mystical sense of a life in natural things', but he implies that this 'strange ... sense' might *itself* be of another order (Pater 1980, xxii). Even this quintessential nature poet, Pater audaciously suggests, produces his greatest work not in mirroring the world around him, but in 'moments of profound, *imaginative* power, in which the outward object appears to take colour and expression, *a new nature* almost, from the prompting of the observant mind' (Pater 1986, 424, emphasis mine). In such moments, 'the actual world would, as it were, dissolve and detach itself, flake by flake, and he himself seemed to be the creator ... of the world in which he lived' (424). In Pater's figuration here, the visiting light of the imagination upon the natural object decisively transforms it. The result is a 'new nature' and a different world.

The true task of the aesthetic critic, correspondingly, consists of discovering the elemental traces of such moments in the work of art – and again, aesthetic *separation* proves a key dynamic. Pater outlines this project in the 'Preface', where he characterizes the critic's work as a subliming process of elemental 'refinement'. The 'function of the aesthetic critic' – like that of a 'chemist' – 'is to distinguish, to analyse, and separate from its adjuncts' precisely what generates beauty from what does not. Reading Wordsworth's poetry, in particular, Pater argues the aesthetic critic must 'disengage this virtue from the commoner elements with which it may be found in combination ... [and leave] only what the heat of their imagination has wholly fused and transformed', thus subtly dismissing in the domestic, earth-bound aspects of Wordsworth's poetry nineteenth-century readers typically privileged (what Paul de Man calls the 'Victorian Wordsworth') (Pater 1980, xx–xxi). Though often by exaggerating it to the point of seeming elitism, translating it into impertinent solipsism or playing it up as the stereotypical dandy's hot-house cult of artifice, Wilde adheres closely to Pater's aesthetic vision.

The effective reversal in Wilde's life-and-art formula draws less directly from Pater and has, perhaps fittingly, become Wilde's signature claim. Yet it does not just describe the uncanny way in which real events seem to offer types or act out scenarios prefigured by artistic media, as it is popularly interpreted. Nor does it simply 'refer ... to the fact that fashionable ladies in the 1880s tried to dress and look like the beautiful figures in the paintings of Rossetti or Burne-Jones' (Zhang 1988, 90–1). Rather, Wilde argues we perceive the world by means of the conceptual models provided for us by art. 'Things are because we see them, and what we see and how we see it, depends on the arts that have influenced us', explains Vivian in 'The Decay of Lying' (Wilde 1989a, 986). No perception is immediate. What *is* is culturally constructed, and in a sense interpreted for us, already, by existing forms of understanding. While by no means original to Wilde, this observation highlights a significant post-romantic intellectual undercurrent to the prevailing realism and positivism of Victorian culture; namely, a growing scepticism in the possibility of objective perception, aesthetic or otherwise. In 'The Critic as Artist' and 'The Portrait of Mr. W. H.', his insistence on implicating critical discourse itself in this constructivist condition aligns him suggestively with Nietzsche and even Freud.

For this reason and others, Wilde's reversal resonates unmistakably with concerns central to contemporary theory. If, as Jonathan Culler has recently suggested, theory characteristically involves a critique of common sense and an interrogation of what we assume is 'natural', then Wilde's work is theoretical through and through (Culler 1997, 4). The aestheticism or decadence Wilde espouses declares itself overtly 'against nature' in its emphasis both on art's autonomy and on the constructedness of 'life'. As Linda Dowling argues, the aestheticist proposal announces a specifically late-Victorian state of affairs: a linguistic and epistemological condition wherein 'nature', 'reality' and 'truth' cannot be sustained as self-evident, stable or authoritative categories, if indeed they ever could be. Both Wilde's theory of art and his often affected stylistic self-consciousness, according to Dowling, 'emerge . . . from a linguistic crisis, a crisis in Victorian attitudes towards language brought about by the new comparative philology earlier imported from the continent' and largely inherited from romanticism (Dowling 1986, xi–xii).

One benefit of Dowling's reading is that it obviates the need to reconcile the seeming inconsistency between the gravity of Wilde's ideas and the levity of their presentation. In this light, we can see the relentless play of Wilde's texts – his dizzying use of paradox, the witty exaggerations, carefully staged dialogues and complex narrative frameworks – not as the frivolous camouflage for serious ideas, but as performative demonstrations of them. What Wilde's essays so often ironically present are occasions that raise, in Dowling's words, the 'spectre of autonomous language' – that is, adumbrations that our words might not correspond to our world or, more ominously, our 'intentions' in a harmoniously referential way (xii). In this sense, there is a profound consistency between the content of Wilde's aesthetic theory and his performative style. Dowling considers the latter a strategically formulated 'counterpoetics of disruption and parody and stylistic derangement, a critique not so much of Wordsworthian nature as of the metaphysics involved in any sentimental notion of a simple world of grass and trees and flowers' (x). For this reason, Dowling suggests that aestheticism and key poststructuralist projects – Foucault's, Derrida's – share a common critical lineage, albeit on separate sides of the 'metaphysical rupture brought about by Saussurean linguistics' (xiii).

A close look at Wilde's notorious use of paradox serves as an instructive illustration of the 'counterpoetics' Dowling describes. In all of his paradoxical assertions, Wilde takes the common-sense, apparently natural order of things (the *doxa*) and reverses it, goes against it (*para*) in a way that seems initially wittily absurd, but which comes to make a certain sense upon reflection. To cite just one example, we can look at the concluding sentences of Wilde's 'Preface' to *The Picture of Dorian Gray*, written in part to counter the moral opprobrium the novel's serial appearance first precipitated. Here, Wilde offers three declarations that, taken together, form a kind of skewed syllogism:

> We can forgive a man for making a useful thing as long as he does not admire it. The only excuse for making a useless thing is that one admires it intensely.
>   All art is quite useless. (Wilde 1989, 17)

In a text purportedly defending Wilde's own work of art, it seems absurd to declare such a work 'useless'. But the paradoxical logic draws out a key cultural assumption – in this case, the presumed connection between utility and value, especially with regard to art. He also glosses the seemingly obvious truth that what is 'useful' would also have more value than what is 'useless'. Wilde's apparently self-defeating defence, that '[a]ll art is quite useless', in fact, both articulates a long-standing bias – at least since Plato – that art is not socially or morally 'useful' and thus not valuable (or conversely, that it is useful, but only to the extent that it *does* serve society or morality) and turns it on its head. In the process, Wilde dislocates utility and value, makes them opposites and then reorders them, so that what is 'useful' becomes, paradoxically, what is *not* to be 'admire[d]'. And art's 'uselessness', in turn and inextricably within these terms, becomes its unique, lofty essence. Danson stresses the importance of context, both textual and intellectual, in understanding the force of such utterances: 'In Wildean paradox . . . the ironized new meanings of words are only realizable in relation to their old meanings, which the paradox, for its subversive purpose, keeps in circulation' (Danson 1997, 150). Thus, the word 'useless' becomes a kind of portmanteau in which we may read a long history of aesthetic theory. His paradox glosses at once Plato's banishment of poetry from the republic, Kant's description of the aesthetic object's 'purposive purposelessness', the 'intense' aesthetic admiration Pater advocates, as well as the contemporary popular sentiment Wilde means to subvert.

The longer essays employ this strategy and others to enact a similar theoretical engagement. 'The Decay of Lying', the first and most anthologized essay in *Intentions*, is a not-quite Platonic dialogue considering the mimetic relationship between art and nature. The dialogue's title refers to an article Vivian (the parlour-room Socrates) reads to Cyril (his unequal foil) in the course of their discussion: 'The Decay of Lying: A Protest'. Vivian's 'protest' most pointedly objects to realism's dominance as an artistic method and aesthetic ideal in nineteenth-century art. But the protest is embedded in a larger discussion that both articulates aestheticism's central argument and situates it in long history of discourse on mimesis.

'[W]hat I am pleading for is lying in art', *not*, Vivian emphasizes, in spheres where lying merely serves venal interests – in politics, for instance. Vivian instead values the 'fine lie', informed purely by the imagination, and created solely for its own sake (Wilde 1989a, 971). This differentiation points to the first of his four 'doctrines of the new aesthetics', namely that 'Art never expresses anything but itself. It has an independent life . . . and develops purely on its own lines' (991). As does the 'uselessness' argument in the 'Preface', Vivian's doctrine calls art a distinct enterprise not properly judged according to normative, rational standards of truth. In both instances, Wilde draws on the Kantian argument that 'to judge an art object in terms of use' – or truth value – 'is not to make an aesthetic judgement' (Adams 1992, 659). Kant's separation of aesthetic from rational or practical judgement also recalls Aristotle's rescue of poetry from Plato's banishment. Wilde's dialogue subtly restages the ancient poetic debate between Plato and Aristotle, echoing Aristotle's insistence that poetry – in medium and manner – operates differently than other forms of representation and should be judged accordingly. In characteristically paradoxical fashion, Wilde has Vivian explicitly enlist Plato himself in support of this argument as much as he does Aristotle. Adopting Plato's mimetic formula – wherein poetry, at two removes from 'truth', is a 'lie' – Wilde also turns it on its head. What Plato declares poetry's ultimate weakness Wilde celebrates as its unique strength.

Vivian's second doctrine argues that realism strays from art's distinct *raison d'être*. 'As a method, realism is a complete failure [for] it forgets that when art surrenders her imaginative medium she surrenders everything' (979). His supporting argument recalls Aristotle's own mode of defence. He offers an aetiological history of aesthetic development that sees imaginative instinct as its 'first stage': 'Art begins with . . . purely imaginative and pleasurable work dealing with what is unreal and nonexistent' (978). Like Aristotle, Vivian too claims that this primal instinct is 'natural'. But even more so, Vivian's 'first stage' is self-generated, 'natural' in that it stems from human nature, from within. We 'start . . . in life with a natural gift for exaggeration', and so too does art begin with this essential element (973). The second stage in this history might surprise those who read Wilde's separation of art and life absolutely, for here Vivian makes clear that there is indeed a connection – but a very particular one: 'Art takes life as part of her rough material, recreates it, and refashions it in fresh forms' (978). Like Pater's Wordsworth, who throws the light of his imagination on nature and produces 'a new nature', Vivian's vision of art relies on nature ('life') as well, but secondarily. Realism's crucial error is to reverse this proper order, to present a 'third stage' in which 'life gets the upper hand, and drives art into the wilderness'. By Wilde's subtle redefinition of the very label his critics used to condemn his aesthetic, realism's late aberration becomes art's 'true decadence, and it is from this that we are now suffering' (978).

Mistaking the proper relation between life and art, elevating life as an 'artistic method' instead of using it as 'rough material', stems from a more comprehensive misreading of the mimetic formula. This 'third doctrine' is the familiar suggestion that 'Life imitates Art far more than Art imitates Life' (985). In its service, Wilde provides Vivian with some of his most outrageous claims: that London fogs 'did not exist till art had invented them', that 'the whole of Japan is a pure invention. There is no such country, there are no such people' (986, 988). But of course, Vivian is not negating what 'exists' and what 'is', but placing them within a specific theory of perception. The outlandishness of the examples may stem from the fact that Cyril reminds Vivian that he needs these proofs to make his theory 'complete' and challenges him to do so. Vivian's flourish demonstrates that he confidently accepts the challenge: 'My dear fellow, I am prepared to prove anything' (986).

That Vivian indeed manages to show that what seems so patently false may possess a certain kind of truth underscores a further implication of 'The Decay of Lying', as well as its fourth doctrine. The aesthetic theory Vivian proposes does not sophistically devote itself to what is merely *false*. And the 'lying' Vivian values, ultimately, does not merely oppose truth, but rather a narrow understanding of it: 'not simple truth but complex beauty' (978). Perhaps recalling Keats, Vivian supplants 'simple truth' with 'complex beauty' and thus implicitly equates the latter with some higher, 'truer' object. The paradoxical, equivocal valence of 'truth' and 'lies' throughout the essay are contained in the essay's 'final revelation', that 'lying, the telling of beautiful untrue things, is the proper aim of art' (992).

'The Critic as Artist', also a dialogue, pursues many of these same assertions. Aestheticism's spokesman here is Gilbert, who corrects a number of 'gross popular error[s]' regarding criticism's proper relation to its aesthetic object. In typical Wildean style, Gilbert presents this hypothesis by means of counter-intuitive paradoxes that Ernest, more pugnaciously than Cyril, earnestly resists. 'The creative faculty is higher than the critical. There is really no comparison between them', intones Ernest, Wilde's voice of orthodox opinion (1020). Gilbert counters that we are wrong to consider criticism merely secondary to the work of art it interprets and never creative in its own right. He argues instead that this hierarchy is unstable, indeed 'entirely arbitrary' (1020). 'Criticism is itself an art', and conversely genuinely 'fine imaginative work' is actually critical (1026, 1020). For 'there is no fine art without self-consciousness, and self-consciousness and the critical spirit are one' (1020). Like poetry, criticism too involves a working with existing materials and putting them into a new form (1027). And here Gilbert insists that not only do poets work with words and generic conventions, they draw from existing works of art as well. Like Vivian, Gilbert argues that art imitates other art more often than life: Homer retells existing myths, Keats writes poems about a translation of Homer's retelling, and so on. The work of the critic is yet one more extension of that same process, its own retelling of what has been told before. The argument glosses Arnold's claim that 'the proper aim of Criticism is to see the object as in itself it really is' and rehearses Pater's response to it (1028). Like Pater, Gilbert believes instead that the critic's 'sole aim is to chronicle his own impressions' (1028). The critic deludes himself if he believes objectivity or 'discovering the real intention of the artist' is possible (1029). Gilbert's supporting example – in which he claims 'the work of art [is] simply ... the starting-point for a new creation' – subtly suggests that Pater's much criticized, idiosyncratic reading of the *Mona Lisa* might be remarkable not for how wilfully wrong it seems, but rather for how dramatically it demonstrates this discursive and epistemological condition (1029).

In fact, one may fruitfully read Wilde's 'Pen, Pencil and Poison' by the light of this proposal as well. Written in the style of Pater's *Appreciations* and *Imaginary Portraits*, the essay studies the 'artistic temperament' of Thomas Griffiths Wainewright, a minor nineteenth-century artist who was also a notorious forger and murderer. In 'The Critic as Artist', Gilbert tells Ernest that Pater's 'imaginative insight ... and poetic aim' – indeed his very words – suffuse his own impressions of the *Mona Lisa*. 'Pen, Pencil and Poison' makes such a tongue-in-cheek avowal of influence its guiding principle. Along with details from Wainewright's life and work (which Wilde liberally embellishes), the essay is strategically laced with plagiarisms from Pater's critical work. Wilde's 'new creation' from this raw material is at once a rehearsal of the critical ideal expressed in 'The Critic as Artist' and an ingenious parody of it. Taking aestheticism's purported separation between aesthetic and moral judgements, Wilde offers hyperbolic enthusiasm for Wainewright's work, impertinently insisting that '[t]he fact of a man being a poisoner is nothing against his prose' (1007). By giving his detractors such an outrageous version of aestheticism's ills – its flirtation with danger, its complicity with violence and amorality – Wilde satirizes their censorious objections and, in the process, offers his own subtle commentary on where the real force of Pater's critical project might lie. 'The Portrait of Mr. W. H.', Wilde's story of a wayward critic, explores similar ground. Obsessed with the personally overdetermined belief that he knows the 'true secret' of Shakespeare's sonnets, Cyril Graham wanders down the garden path from creative criticism to outright forgery, manufacturing evidence when he cannot find it. The story shrewdly outlines just how much epistemological desire, perhaps at the heart of creativity, necessarily drives the critical impulse. Our own critical projects, variously aimed at uncovering Wilde's true 'intentions', would do well to remember that lesson.

Megan Becker-Leckrone

Further reading and works cited

Adams, H. (ed.) *Critical Theory Since Plato*. Fort Worth, TX, 1992.
Beckson, K. (ed.) *Oscar Wilde: The Critical Heritage*. London, 1970.
Brown, J. Prewitt. *Cosmopolitan Criticism*. Charlottesville, VA, 1997.
Culler, J. *Literary Theory: A Very Short Introduction*. Oxford, 1997.
Danson, L. *Wilde's Intentions: The Artist in His Criticism*. Oxford, 1997.
Dellamora, R. *Masculine Desire*. Chapel Hill, NC, 1990.
Dollimore, J. *Sexual Dissidence*. Oxford, 1991.
Dowling, L. *Language and Decadence in the Victorian Fin de Siècle*. Princeton, NJ, 1986.
—. *Hellenism and Homosexuality in Victorian England*. Ithaca, NY, 1994.
Ellmann, R. *Oscar Wilde*. New York, 1988.
Gagnier, R. *Idylls of the Marketplace*. Stanford, CA, 1986.
— (ed.) *Critical Essays on Oscar Wilde*. New York, 1991.
Gillespie, M. P. *Oscar Wilde and the Poetics of Ambiguity*. Gainesville, FL, 1996.
Knox, M. *Oscar Wilde: A Long and Lovely Suicide*. New Haven, CT, 1994.
Kohl, N. *Oscar Wilde: The Works of a Conformist Rebel*. Cambridge, 1989.
Pater, W. *The Renaissance: Studies in Art and Poetry, The 1893 Text*, ed. D. L. Hill. Berkeley, CA, 1980.
—. *Three Major Texts: The Renaissance, Appreciations, and Imaginary Portraits*, ed. W. E. Buckler. New York, 1986.
Raby, P. *Oscar Wilde*. Cambridge, 1988.
— (ed.) *The Cambridge Companion to Oscar Wilde*. Cambridge, 1997.
Rieff, P. 'The Impossible Culture: Wilde as Modern Prophet', *Salmagundi*, 58, 1983.
Schmidgall, G. *The Stranger Wilde*. New York, 1994.
Showalter, E. *Sexual Anarchy*. London, 1991.
Sinfield, A. *The Wilde Century*. New York, 1994.
Small, I. *Conditions for Criticism*. Oxford, 1991.
—. *Oscar Wilde Revalued*. Greensboro, NC, 1993.
Stokes, J. *Oscar Wilde: Myths, Miracles, and Imitations*. Cambridge, 1996.
Wilde, O. *The Artist as Critic: Critical Writings of Oscar Wilde*, ed. R. Ellmann. New York, 1969.
—. *The Complete Works of Oscar Wilde*. New York, 1989a.
—. *Oscar Wilde's Oxford Notebooks*, eds P. E. Smith and M. S. Helfand. Oxford, 1989b.
Willoughby, G. *Art and Christhood: The Aesthetics of Oscar Wilde*. London, 1993.
Zhang, L. 'The Critical Legacy of Oscar Wilde'. *Texas Studies in Literature and Language*, 30, 1988.

4. The Cambridge School: Sir Arthur Quiller-Couch (1863–1944), I. A. Richards (1893–1979) and William Empson (1906–1984)

In 1910, Sir Harold Harmsworth (Lord Rothermere) donated money to Cambridge for a new Chair in honour of the late Edward VII to deliver courses on English literature from the age of Chaucer onwards, and to 'treat this subject on literary and critical rather than on philological and linguistic lines' (Brittain 1947, 57). After the death of the first classicist in post, Arthur Verrall (1912), when Prime Minister Asquith wanted the Donne scholar H. J. Grierson in post, Lloyd George persuaded him to make a political appointment of a Liberal (Tillyard 1958, 39). Hence Sir Arthur Quiller-Couch ('Q'), who had been knighted in 1910, became Professor. English was then not a separate subject, but part of the Medieval and Modern Languages Tripos, founded in 1883. In association with H. F. Stewart and H. M. Chadwick, Professor of Anglo-Saxon, 'Q' aimed at making English its own full subject. Philology, Anglo-Saxon and Middle English would be optional. The English Tripos was established in 1917, within the patriotic atmosphere that the war engendered (the Germanic associations of philology soured this discipline). 'Q', an Oxford classicist, writer and novelist, anthologist, and editor of fourteen of Shakespeare's Comedies for Cambridge between 1921 and 1931, who divided his time between Cambridge and Fowey in Cornwall, held that 'Literature cannot be divorced from life, that Literature cannot be understood apart from the men who have made it, that Literature is a living art, to be practised as well as admired' (Brittain 1947, 92). The genteel amateurism is worked into the study of literature from the beginning. Oxford had begun its English School in 1893, and had appointed Sir Walter Raleigh (1861–1922) in 1904 as Professor, but the differences that Cambridge English implied were soon to be noticed. The context of the new school fitted with the Newbolt Report, 'The Teaching of English in England' (1921, commissioned 1919) which urged the teaching of the national literature at all levels of schooling and at universities as a means of uniting divided classes after the war. Whereas Oxford and London, which had begun the study of English in 1859, placed Anglo-Saxon, philology and the history of the language near the centre of their English schools, and Oxford had until recently finished its syllabus at 1830, Chadwick moved Anglo-Saxon out of English, making it a cultural field of study in itself, so that Cambridge's syllabus, beginning with Chaucer, extended to the then present and responded to the modernism of the 1920s. Early lecturers in English at Cambridge included Mansfield D. Forbes, E. M. W. Tillyard, G. R. Coulton and H. S. Bennett (Medievalists) and F. L. Lucas; after 1924, when women were allowed to lecture, Hilda Murray and Enid Welsford. Basil Willey, T. R. Henn and F. R. Leavis followed.

Perhaps the most considerable voice was I. A. Richards, who, from an undergraduate degree in Moral Sciences (i.e. Philosophy), began lecturing in 1919 on the theory of criticism. Richards collaborated with C. F. Ogden (1889–1957) to produce *The Meaning of Meaning* which worked from the arguments about language then being made current by Peirce and Saussure, and paralleled by Wittgenstein in the *Tractatus Logico-Philosophicus* which aimed at identifying a foundation in semantics for linguistic statements. Richards and Ogden, borrowing from Jamesian pragmatism and behaviourism, held that meaning was dependent upon context, that words do not correspond to things. Yet this does not imply acceptance of the Saussurian arbitrariness of the signifier, and the relativity, therefore, of all systems of meaning: instead *The Meaning of Meaning* sees 'the relationship between words and things as *the* modern problem of knowledge, judgement and culture' but which can be solved by 'not making conceptual mistakes' (Bove 1986, 51). Attention to context will make mistakes avoidable, which is the positivism in Richards' thought, and his commitment to a belief in unitary truth. Insisting on the autonomy of science, in a way which made his thought hospitable to American pragmatism, Richards's position, from a marxist perspective, still the most influential one in reading Cambridge English, 'ends up obscuring the contexts in which questions regarding purpose and human meaning, deep moving forces of human life, can be given historical, non-metaphysical answers referring to the production and reproduction of the totality of human existence. In consequence he subverts the argument that problems of meaning can be resolved only through or in relation to human praxis. He himself will seek the solution in questions of mental organization' (Fekete 1977, 271). Whereas the progress of science was advanced and unquestionable, Ogden and Richards held that language uses in other areas were held back by the hold of mystical, superstitious attitudes towards language which prevented users of language from seeing its instrumentality.

With such a sense of the possibility of controlling language-use, which would eventually find its destiny in the project for Basic English, the authors divided language-uses up into the referential and emotive, keeping the first category for science and the latter for poetry. The symbolic use of words was statement, communication, while the emotive use of words expressed or excited feelings or attitudes. Poetry did not 'mean' something objective, but it worked upon feelings, and it was this which Richards followed up in later writings. Richards took from Coleridge and John Stuart Mill and Matthew Arnold the importance of nurturing feelings, and regarded poetry as a means of providing homeostasis, equipoise (as opposed to satisfaction), a calming of subjective feelings – on the principle that 'anything is valuable which will satisfy an appetency without involving the frustration of some equal or *more important* appentency' (Richards 1924, 48). The echo of the language of Jeremy Bentham and the Utilitarian implications of this are plain and can be contextualized through Richards's adoption for himself of John Stuart Mill's challenge of 1840: 'whoever could master the premises and combine the methods of [Bentham and Coleridge] would possess the entire English philosophy of his age' (Richards 1962, 18). Mill had been brought up as a Benthamite, and had found emotional stability through reading Wordsworth: his essays on Bentham and Coleridge reflected his sense of the impossibility of putting together these two opposing voices and philosophies. Richards in the twentieth century hoped to combine Bentham's materialism and psychological determinism (he calls himself a Benthamite) with Coleridge's idealism and belief in the imagination as an integrative, unifying tendency, reconciling opposites. It will be recalled how, in Coleridge's *Biographia Literaria*, the 'secondary imagination' 'dissolves, diffuses, dissipates, in order to re-create; or, where this process is rendered impossible, yet still at all events it struggles to idealize and to unify' (Richards 1950, 516). According to Pamela McCallum, Richards 'wished to introduce to literary theory the apex of the early liberal tradition' (McCallum 1983, 88) – i.e. the moment when bourgeois ideology was not obviously wholly inflected by capitalism and its powers of destabilization – and he hoped also to incarnate a specific Englishness, identified with that liberalism. In this thinking, the limits of social, political and economic theory were defined through Bentham and the limits of thought about the individual or about imagination and the work of art were set through Coleridge. Poetry in the modern world could be justified for its contribution to feelings, but poetry in itself said nothing, its statements were 'pseudo-statements' (see Rosso 1989, 239). It had less to do with cognition than the ordering of attitudes. The crisis to do with the dominance of alienated science in modernity 'like every other problem in Richards, is interpreted as a problem of misunderstanding and hence is accessible to resolution on the level of consciousness' (Fekete 1977, 28).

At the same time, an Arnoldian stress appears in Richards in *Science and Poetry*, when he says that 'our protection [from the authority of science], as Matthew Arnold ... insisted, is in poetry. It is capable of saving us, or, since some have found a scandal in this word, of preserving us or rescuing us from confusion and frustration' (Richards 1970, 78). Salvation does not come from some act of the individual, even though the poet is 'the man who is most likely to have experiences of value to record. He is at the point where the growth of the mind shows itself ... his work is the ordering of what in most minds is disordered' (Richards 1924, 61). The modernism implicit in the sentence accounted for his essay on *The Waste Land*, just after its appearance in 1922 (Richards 1924, 289–96). The attempt to equate emotional education (ordering) with something scientific accounted for Richards's method of 'practical criticism' (Richards 1929), in *Practical Criticism*, the book which his biographer, John Paul Rosso, takes to be his 'masterpiece' (Rosso 1989, 294). The title Richards took from the opening of Coleridge's *Biographia Literaria*, chapter 15 (1950, 525). The book, comprising an examination of students and contemporaries' responses to poems including those by Leavis and Mansfield Forbes, contained approaches to thirteen undated and unsigned poems, including ones by Donne, Hopkins and Lawrence, and reads the students' responses to them. Cambridge English thus became identified with an empirical approach – in Richards's case, an empirical observation of other people working their way through the poems he had set – which presupposes an implicit refusal of theory, while not recognizing that the empirical approach was itself premised on theory. It involves a regulation of emotions, and a sense that a poem – or any literature – could be pronounced on for its worth outside of context.

In 'practical criticism', whose Benthamism is heard in Richards's will, as he puts it, to 'prepare the way for educational methods more efficient than those we use now in developing discrimination and the power to understand what we hear and read' (1929, 3) readers, whose power to respond to what they heard and read in, say, politics, was to be formed, defined and delimited on the basis of their response to the literary – had to respond to the sense of the poem and to its feeling, to its tone and to the author's intention, distinguished by Richards as 'the four kinds of meaning' (1929, 179–88). Judgement as to the worth of a poem came from attention to its details: from the idea of a union of sound and sense, the poem's aural patterning (e.g. in alliteration and assonance) corresponding to and amplifying its meaning which was immanent, immediately available and visible in the text's 'minute particulars' (Richards 1929, 302), and so ahistorical, not requiring any hermeneutic approach. By requiring the poem's rhythms and patterns of speech – matters of a reader's 'sensuous apprehension' – to follow the rhythms of everyday speech, the text allowed no space to notions of *ostranenie* (estrangement) such as Russian formalism allowed for. The result was the text's tendency towards conservatism, replicating the dominant ideology, the norms of present-day society, with no sense, for instance, of the power of alienation – this even though Richards offered the work as a study of 'comparative ideology' (1929, 6) and dwelt on the need to avoid the 'stock response' (1929, 15–16), where the reader's predisposition towards the sentiments expressed in the poem prevented a reading of what the text actually said – the phrase belonged to behaviourism and to the notion of a 'conditioned reflex'. Richards also used Freud to discuss inhibition, which he defined as a blocking off of necessary emotions, and sentimentality, which he saw as the opposite, squandering mental energy (1929, 255–70). Yet he employed psychoanalytic concepts 'without recognising their subversive, interrogative potential' (McCallum 1983, 73, compare Richards 1926, 29–30, where psychoanalytic criticism is accused of being 'unverifiable') and in doing so, implied his own delimiting of allowable emotions, whose class and gender bases and whose history were never examined.

Criticism is then an act of responding relevantly to the 'words on the page', giving an account of what the poem is doing, so that criticism becomes a means of saying more fully what the poem already said, and being passive before it requires a position on the reader's part. It is such a position which Raymond Williams finds to be a form of servility, as he also accuses Richards's position as servility to the literary establishment (Williams 1963 245; compare Fekete 1977 30). It produces, further, a pessimistic conclusion: that 'if poetry remains inscrutably impenetrable to the most suitable readers, it will be inaccessible to the majority of the population' (McCallum 1983, 74). In this sense of the near impossibility of changing the course of 'mass' culture, which in the work of Leavis and *Scrutiny*, became a full-scale cultural despair, passivity and pessimism were inseparable from a conservatism or reaction which was expressed literally, in suggesting that 'the arts are our storehouse of recorded values' (Richards 1924, 32), which means that education means passing on a received 'tradition', a term given new currency by T. S. Eliot. More subtly, the reactionary agenda appeared in that new, postwar undergraduates were being regimented towards 'right' feelings – which are also class-feelings – in a process of self-discipline, the passivity of reading being a form of depoliticization, and the intention being 'normalization' (Bove 1986, 61). On this reading, Cambridge English with Richards as its inspiration put in position a powerful set of tools to produce a new hegemonic subject, which, unlike Oxford English, would have the power of directly moulding thought through the nurture of sensibility and right feelings, and preserve a liberalism and humanism that concealed its own relationship to power. It is revealing to note how the opposition to Cambridge English from Oxford was characteristically expressed in terms of the Cambridge school's 'Puritanism' which was 'reluctant to regard literature simply as a matter for enjoyment' (Rosso 1989, 529). The Cambridge school in contrast to the Oxford – and class-distinctions are implicit in the use of the concept of the Puritan – looks to English as a means of critique, even critique of ideology. While this contains something positive, especially in its attention to 'literary language' and metaphor, its most obvious limitation is that it does not go outside the terms of the English liberal tradition in order to make that critique.

The tendency in Cambridge in the 1920s was modernist, and practical criticism may be seen as a strategy belonging to that ethos: 'practical criticism believes it can be successful if it can establish that reality is like a modernist poem: complex, ambiguous, interrelated but 'orderly' and finally 'static' in its 'organic' relationships. The poem and reality are both systems whose workings can be understood only on the model of the sublime intellectual's complex sensibility or reading skills' (Bove 1986, 54–5).

After 1929, Richards's rationalist tendencies increased in his attempts to give a utilitarian reading of Coleridge, in his attempts to classify metaphor in terms of tenor (the idea) and vehicle (what the principal subject is being compared to) in *The Philosophy of Rhetoric* (1936) and in his collaboration with Ogden on Basic English, carrying his critical belief in precise language to an experimentally reduced version of English with a vocabulary of 850 words, and intended for places where English might be a second language, especially China. In 1939 he became director of the Commission of English Language Studies at Harvard, and remained in America until 1974, returning then to Cambridge.

The Cambridge English Richards dominated through the 1920s had moved towards 'difficult' and 'strenuous' or 'muscular' poetry. The decade coincided with Cambridge's emphasis on Metaphysical poetry (and the diminution of Milton on account of his classicism): in 1926, T. S. Eliot gave the Clark lectures on 'The Metaphysical Poets' and the culmination of the decade, which saw the graduation of Muriel Bradbrook, the Cambridge Shakespeare scholar, and William Empson set its seal upon the importance of poetry held to be tough, rational, not plangent, anti-romantic, anti-Victorian and certainly anti-Georgian. Empson, who had read Mathematics before turning to English, was supervised by Richards in his final year, and produced *Seven Types of Ambiguity* the year following, as a culmination of work done with Richards (see Richards 1929, 340–5 on ambiguity as basic to language). Empson's poetry, which was praised by Leavis in *New Bearings in English Poetry* (1932) similarly showed the impact of Metaphysical poetry, its conceits, its wit, its rapid association of idea with idea.

Seven Types of Ambiguity took assorted passages of drama and poetry for analysis, and for its first six types located 'ambiguity' as a point of complexity in a text, and indicative of richness of thought in it, though even the first had the potential to explode Richards's neat sense of metaphor, for it implied that 'far from referring back to an object that would be its cause, the poetic sign sets in motion an imaging activity that refers to no object in particular. The "meaning" of the metaphor is that it does not "mean" in any definite manner' (de Man 1983, 235). It found ambiguity in Shakespeare and seventeenth-century poetry, but, predictably, given the temper of 1920s Cambridge English, much less in Victorian verse, with the exception of Hopkins. Eliot, too, as a modern displayed ambiguity. The seventh type of ambiguity, introduced by a reference to Freud's essay 'The Antithetical Meanings of Primal Words', showed 'a fundamental division in the writer's mind' (Empson 1930, 192) – ambivalence, rather than ambiguity, a contradiction that could not be resolved. Discussing Hopkins's poem 'The Windhover', a poem given some attention by Richards in 1926 (Richards 1976, 139–47) – Hopkins's verse had first appeared in volume form in 1918, and it was read as distinctively modern – Empson found in its use of the word 'Buckle', 'a clear case of the Freudian use of opposites, where two things thought of as incompatible, but desired intensely by different systems of judgements, are spoken of simultaneously by words applying to both' (Empson 1930, 226). Paul de Man, in 'The Dead-end of Formalist Criticism' (1954), writes of this seventh type in a piece on New Criticism which contrasts Empson with Richards. He finds Empson more interesting, and accuses Richards's criticism of being premised on 'the adequacy of the object itself with the language that names it' (de Man 1983, 244). This, of course, harks back to the issues that haunt *The Meaning of Meaning*. Thus, de Man says, whereas Richards 'did recognise the existence of conflicts [in poetry] . . . he invoked Coleridge, not without some simplification, to appeal to the reassuring notion of art as the reconciliation of opposites'. But in Empson's reading, 'the text does not resolve the conflict, it *names* it' (de Man 1983, 237). This reading of Empson has made him seem like a precursor of deconstruction (Norris 1985), and antagonistic to the strains in American New Criticism which see contradiction as subsumable under the formal headings of paradox, or tension or irony, an integral part of the poem's organisation: this is how de Man takes Empson. In relation to the ideology of Cambridge criticism, it will be seen that *Seven Types of Ambiguity* has the potential to undo the integrative tendencies of liberal thought, whose organicist images, in striving to idealize and unify, have the effect of insinuating the irrelevance of class difference, and impose an imaginary unity within the nation.

Empson followed *Seven Types of Ambiguity* with *Some Versions of Pastoral*, whose topic is not a separate genre called 'pastoral', since he says that the formula which applies to pastoral poetry – that of 'putting the complex into the simple' might include all literature (1965, 25). Literature here is thought of as ideology, whose pretension is that the complex – which may be indescribable, even sublime (in either the traditional or postmodern, Lyotard-derived sense of this term) may be thought of in terms of the unifying, whole terms of the text which itself may be criticized or appreciated. Richards's view of the relation of thought to expression, as de Man criticizes this, will come to mind. The consciousness in its split state invents at that stage of recognizing its condition as split (i.e. as complex) the notion of some natural, originary condition. De Man (1983, 238–45) picks on Empson's point that marxism itself is a form of pastoral to argue that the split Empson identifies is inherent to the state of Being (the Heideggerian tendency in de Man's thought), like the contradictoriness implied in the seventh type of ambiguity. By doing so, he depoliticizes and dehistoricizes Empson's text (for there is no moment when alienation has historically occurred: there is no development of a split within modern literature). The project of Richards-inspired criticism is 'to expect a reconciliation from poetry; to see in it a possibility of filling the gap that cleaves Being' (de Man 1983, 245); but Empson's criticism has the potential of showing the impossibility of doing this. Claiming Empson for deconstruction opposes one element in his thought to rationalism, but to date, the comparable project, of linking Empson's approach to language with Bakhtin on the dialogic, and thus showing how Empson's work is open to the presence of otherness, has not been undertaken.

Paul de Man comments on Empson's third book, *The Structure of Complex Words* in a later essay, 'Wordsworth and the Victorians' via Empson's essay 'Sense in [Wordsworth's] *The Prelude*' to argue that 'Empson shows that, if one follows the trace of a recurrent word in a given corpus, the emerging confusion cannot be reduced to any known model of trope that would control an identifiable semantic field; it is impossible, in other words, to make sense out of Wordsworth's "sense"' (de Man 1984, 88). 'Complex' in Empson's title derives from his definition of pastoral, and with Freud on antithetical meanings behind it contains his conviction that words are nodal points of contradictory senses which have been overdetermined historically. Empson reads literary history in words such as 'wit', 'fool' and 'folly' and 'honest' and 'sense' – terms which often enough presuppose clear distinctions between the clear and the non-clear, and finds ambiguity and complexity not at the level of a text's context, which is where Richards had started from, but in the buried history of apparently simple words. De Man reads Empson in a radical way, and derives a Wordsworth from him who is the opposite of the integrative Coleridge of Richards's arguments (and thus suggesting the possibility of rereading English romanticism) but it also as an argument runs counter to the rationalism in Empson (Fry 1991, 79) which impels a belief that 'you can decide what a piece of language conveys' (Empson 1951, 437), which allowed Empson to support Basic English (Empson 1987, 191–238), and which, more positively, structured his further study, *Milton's God*, whose target is the irrationalism of the 'neo-Christian', defined as 'those recent critics, some of whom believe in Christianity and some not, who interpret any literary work they admire by finding in it a supposed Christian tradition' (Empson 1985, 229).

Empson's direct targets are, in Milton studies, C. S. Lewis and E. M. W. Tillyard, and in the United States, Hugh Kenner's Catholic readings of Joyce (in contrast to Richard Ellmann's), Dorothy Sayers on Dante, and American New Criticism and T. S. Eliot, the argument being that English literature has become a way of presenting pseudo-metaphysics, occluding rationalism. Such a covert message in English studies promotes, for example, the pessimism of Orwell's *1984* – against which Empson contends that 'the human mind, that is, the public human mind as expressed in a language, is not irredeemably lunatic, and cannot be made so' (Empson 1951, 83). Empson's rationalism is repeated in Milton's Satan – 'a very argufying character' (1985, 62; i.e. not like a romantic poet, as in Blake) and

Empson's argument about Milton's *Paradise Lost* is that 'Milton ... positively denied [the] importance of blind obedience, and ... expressed anxiety verging upon horror lest God be found unjust' (1985, 286–7). Milton's God is not the Christian God, but an invention of Milton's, justifying an 'appalling' theology, and to read *Paradise Lost* adequately means not 'sinking [the] mind into the mental world of the author' on the assumption that such a mental world would be simply Christian. Instead, Empson assumes that Milton himself thought outside the terms of that mental world (1985, 204). The rationalism dehistoricizes, makes claims to be outside the relativity of historical systems of thought. The importance given to the story the epic tells (Empson, 1951, 36) is an example of how Empson implicitly rejects Richards's arguments for poetry as 'pseudo statements' in the sense that these in their apparent permission of illogic have allowed literature to become susceptible to religious readings (1951, 13).

Empson's rationalism means that he holds on to notions of intention, and to the author, and remains hostile to the theory with which Norris tried to identify him (1985, 20–1). Negatively it seems that Empson's agenda, by being focused on the English literature that he felt had been commandeered by neo-Christians, remained both too committed to identifying its form of rationalism with Englishness, and delimited its sense of religion in relation to middle-class views of Christianity. The paganism of Empson's thought did not extend as far as to, say, Bataille on the sacred, nor towards the transgressive. A fine reading of Cowper's poem 'The Castaway', whose theme is the subject's madness, goes through verse by verse, with detailed attention to the story, but has nothing at all to say about madness, or its existence as a limit-state; in this way, Empson, though madness had been a topic in his poetry, as in 'Let It Go' (1955, 81), and a topic for *The Structure of Complex Words*, turns away from exploring a state which would pull him away from certain conventionalities (1987, 289–96). He was caught, in his Milton discussions, by the common-sense terms with which more conventional critics than himself – such as C. S. Lewis – set the debate, and in this it seems that Empson's own thinking was more conventional than it should have been and necessarily more obsessed with issues that showed his entrapment in a subject too small for his talent. The Cambridge with which he sparred – though he never taught there – showed its continuing resistance to theory in the 'structuralist' arguments of 1979: in so doing it perpetuated its tendency to reify its institutionalized genteel amateurism in policing the bounds of the subject: a tendency which had been there from the beginning, and which played a sizeable role in limiting Empson's achievement to a certain provincialism of thought.

Jeremy Tambling

Further reading and works cited

Baldick, C. *The Social Mission of English Criticism, 1848–1932*. Oxford, 1983.
Bove, P. *Intellectuals in Power*. New York, 1986.
Brittain, F. *Arthur Quiller Couch: A Biographical Study of Q*. Cambridge, 1947.
Culler, J. *Framing the Sign*. Oxford, 1988.
de Man, P. *Blindness and Insight*. Oxford, 1983.
—. *The Rhetoric of Romanticism*. New York, 1984.
Eagleton, T. *Against the Grain*. London, 1986.
Empson, W. *The Structure of Complex Words*. London, 1951.

—. *Collected Poems*. London, 1955.

—. *Seven Types of Ambiguity*. Harmondsworth, 1961.

—. *Some Versions of Pastoral*. Harmondsworth, 1965.

—. *Milton's God*. Cambridge, 1985.

—. *Argufying*, ed. J. Haffenden. London, 1987.

Fekete, J. *The Critical Twilight*. London, 1977.

Fry, Paul H. *William Empson*. London, 1991.

Hawkes, T. *That Shakespeherian Rag*. London, 1986.

McCallum, P. *Literature and Method*. Dublin, 1983.

Norris, C. 'Some Versions of Rhetoric: Empson and de Man', in *Rhetoric and Form: Deconstruction at Yale*, eds R. Con Davis and R. Schliefer. Norman, OK, 1985.

— and Mapp, N. (eds) *William Empson: The Critical Achievement*. Cambridge, 1993.

Richards, I. A. *The Philosophy of Rhetoric*. Oxford, 1936.

— (ed.) *The Portable Coleridge*. New York, 1950.

—. *Principles of Literary Criticism*. London, 1960.

—. *Coleridge on Imagination*. London, 1962.

—. *Practical Criticism*. London, 1964.

—. *Poetries and Sciences*. New York, 1970.

—. *Complementarities*, ed. J. P. Russo. Manchester, 1976.

— with Ogden, C. K. *The Meaning of Meaning*. London, 1923.

Rosso, J. P. *I. A. Richards: His Life and Work*. London, 1989.

Tillyard, E. M. W. *The Muse Unchained*. London, 1958.

Williams, R. *Culture and Society: 1780–1950*. Harmondsworth, 1963.

5. James Joyce (1882–1941): Theories of Literature

If Joyce's central place in high modernism is undisputed today, the relationship between a masterpiece such as *Ulysses* and the literary or aesthetic theories developed in the novel and employed in its very construction is more complex, even contested. Besides, James Joyce, after a number of early experiments collected in his *Critical Writings*, soon decided not to write any self-contained aesthetic treatise and even more decidedly refused to engage at any length in the kind of critical writing that marked the works of immediate modernist contemporaries like Woolf, Pound, Lewis or Eliot.

If most readers of Joyce sense that there is something like an aesthetic theory that would be specific to his works, it is unlikely that two readers will agree as to what the term exactly covers. Rather than starting with an abstract definition of these terms, it might be more helpful to begin by surveying the available corpus. A good place to start might be Joyce's perception of his own canon in the making, as evinced by the proud assertion made to his mother (from his first Parisian 'exile') that among his projects, an aesthetic theory would have to figure prominently. In a juvenile manner, he outlines a work schedule filling up the two next decades: 'Synge says I have a mind like Spinoza! . . . I am at present up to the neck in Aristotle's Metaphysics . . . My book of songs will be published in the Spring of 1907. My first comedy about five years later. My "Esthetic" about five years later again. (This *must* interest you!)' (*L*, IV, 19) Surprisingly Joyce was in fact quite right about the first date: *Chamber Music* was actually published in 1907, while *Exiles* (if it can be called a 'comedy') was only started in 1914. But no 'Esthetic' was ever published or written – unless we count the few reviews and odd essays collected under the title of *Critical Writings* and add to them a few theoretical passages in *Ulysses* (1922), mostly culled from Stephen Dedalus's ruminations on art, paternity, creation and rhythm. Indeed, one could easily realize with Joyce's writings what Meschonnic had done with Mallarmé when he edited his 'Writings about the Book' and produced a careful selection of theoretical fragments from letters, reviews and essays that, put together, provide a strikingly coherent aesthetic. It might be harder to find a workable title in Joyce's case, although one could easily settle for a conservative subtitle such as 'post-Aristotelian poetics'. I will have to return to the philosophical lineage that Joyce had chosen for himself, and the fact that when he was supposed to follow medical studies in Paris, he spent most of his time in the Sainte Geneviève library opposite the Panthéon – not just contemplating his own inevitable immortality but reading Aristotle. This brief survey will find a focus in two main concepts that are not arranged historically but map out the entire field of what can be called a Joycean aesthetic theory: the epiphanies and mimesis.

Epiphanies

This is probably the term most lay readers will immediately associate with Joyce's aesthetics. Despite its familiarity and systematic occurrence in various contexts, its meaning and use are nevertheless quite tricky. The most detailed description is provided by Joyce in the unfinished manuscript called *Stephen Hero*. He begins with a famous example of a 'triviality' overheard as he passes through Eccles Street (the very street in which Molly and Leopold Bloom live in *Ulysses*):

> A young lady was standing on the steps of one of these brown brick houses which seem the very incarnation of Irish paralysis. A young gentleman was leaning on the rusty railings of the area. Stephen as he passed on his quest heard the following fragment of colloquy out of which he received an impression keen enough to afflict his sensitiveness very severely.
>   The Young Lady – (drawling discreetly) ... O, yes ... I was ... at the ... cha ... pel...
>   The Young Gentleman – (inaudibly) ... I ... (again inaudibly) ... I...
>   The Young Lady – (softly) ... O ... but you're ... ve ... ry ... wick ... ed.
>   The triviality made him think of collecting many such moments together in a book of epiphanies. By an epiphany he meant a sudden spiritual manifestation, whether in the vulgarity of speech or of gesture or in a memorable phase of the mind itself. He believed that it was for the man of letters to record these epiphanies with extreme care, seeing that they themselves are the most delicate and evanescent moments. (*SH*, 210–11)

What may puzzle one is the almost total lack of content in the actual words of a vignette that allegorizes a fascinating mixture of Irish paralysis and sexual banter. Moreover, this curious emptiness generates a serial concept: having captured one epiphany, Stephen decides to compose a whole book of them, showing concretely the link between two meanings of 'aesthetic *theory*': first, capturing a moment of revelation in a privileged glimpse or audition, then, through a 'procession' of these moments, the emergence of some sort of order or process underpinned by a new sense of authority. We know – and this complicates the picture – from archival evidence and the testimony of several friends and relatives that Joyce made no secret about his collecting these 'moments' in a book of epiphanies. The epiphanies appear thus as urban snapshots caught at unforeseen inter-sections, 'trivial' indeed from being generated by chance encounters with anonymous strangers seen or heard at crossroads rather than suggested by bucolic scenes remembered in romantic tranquillity.

When Robert Scholes edited all the extant epiphanies (forty short vignettes survive out of at least seventy-one according to Joyce's own numbering), he pointed out the variety of genres and scenes evoked: the short texts range between dream transcriptions and fragments of dialogues, between first drafts of relatively objective narrative passages and very autobiographical confessions. The impression left by them upon Joyce must have been very strong since these pre-written passages reappear systematically in the later fiction: *A Portrait of the Artist as a Young Man* seems to have been structured by at least twelve important epiphanies, from the first scene evoking castrating eagles (already in epiphany no. 1) to the last page with one of Stephen's diary entries saluting the 'spell of arms and voices' (which quotes epiphany no. 30). Some epiphanies recur with a curious and inexplicable insistence in all of Joyce's works, as the scene overheard at the corner of Connaught Street in epiphany no. 38 in which a male child only answers '. . . Na . . . o' to a young lady who asks him who his sweetheart may be, which is then reintroduced into the scene with Gerty MacDowell and the children who play on the beach in the 'Nausicaa' episode of *Ulysses*, to be finally reused in the Mime section of *Finnegans Wake* – this time, it is Glugg who tries to guess the name of a flower, answering negatively with a crescendo of 'Nao', 'Naoho' and finally 'Naohaohao' (*FW*, 233.21–6; see also 225.23–7).

Enigmatic as they may be, these recurrences should not veil another factor: as these pre-written fragments are reinscribed in the narrative texture, they lose their own appellation as 'epiphanies'. This is why the term is not even mentioned in *A Portrait of the Artist as a Young Man* whereas it has clearly become derogatory in *Ulysses*. (Stephen muses in ironic retrospection on his juvenile fantasy of sending copies of his 'epiphanies on green oval leaves' to 'all the great libraries of the world, including Alexandria'.) Critics like Scholes have speculated that this should be taken as a clear sign that by the late 1910s, Joyce did not believe in a theory of the epiphany any longer: the term can be employed to define a certain genre of writing, closer to his later systematic note-taking process (more recently, David Hayman has coined the category of 'epiphanoids' in *The 'Wake' in Transit* to describe the fragments collected in notebooks that cover all the personal vignettes, memories, dream fragments, bits of dialogue, passages from conversations that, till a very late stage, continue to find their way into the crowded and rather illegible pages of the archive, often to be reworked and introduced into the Wake.

One can notice that the epiphany does not aim at defining a type of object but a dialectical and temporal process linking an object and a subject in such a way that one will keep on hesitating between an objective pole (let us not forget that for the Stephen of *Stephen Hero*, 'the clock of the Ballast office was capable of an epiphany' (*SH*, 216), a fortiori, any object will be 'capable' of a similar process of inner and outer illumination) and a subjective pole (since it becomes a 'task' for the artist to 'record' these). Aesthetic pleasure might well consist in prolonging this hesitation, even more as we also hesitate between a religious and a profane sense of the term. Let us return to that famous Dublin clock in Stephen's optical and almost technological version of the theory of the epiphany – one can almost imagine a gigantic spiritual camera at work: 'Imagine my glimpses at that clock as the gropings of a spiritual eye which seeks to adjust its vision to an exact focus. The moment the focus is reached the object is epiphanised. It is just in this epiphany that I find the third, the supreme quality of beauty' (SH, 216–17). Here, the subjective pole is downplayed, a shift that is accounted for by the need for a general theory of aesthetic. Stephen follows suit with an attack on the idea of 'tradition' – 'No esthetic theory ... is of any value which investigates with the aid of the lantern of tradition' (SH, 217) – which allows him paradoxically to quote (and distort) Aquinas's three main concepts of 'integrity', 'wholeness' and 'radiance' in support of his theory:

> For a long time I couldn't make out what Aquinas meant. He uses a figurative word ... but I have solved it. *Claritas* is *quidditas*. After the analysis which discovers the second quality the mind takes the only logical possible synthesis and discovers the third quality. This is the moment which I call epiphany. First we recognise that the object is *one* integral thing, then we recognise that it is an organised composite structure, a *thing* in fact: finally, when the relation of the parts is exquisite, when the parts are adjusted to the special point, we recognise that it is *that* thing which it is. Its soul, its whatness, leaps at us from the vestment of its appearance. The soul of the commonest object, the structure of which is so adjusted, seems to us radiant. The object achieves its epiphany. (SH, 218)

If the epiphany is a manifestation of the very soul of any object chosen at random, it organizes a principle of individuation comparable to Duns Scotus's 'haecceitas' revisited by Hopkins: the absolute singularity shines forth and somehow proves the existence of a God who loves 'dappled' things. Joyce chooses Aquinas as a guide, although it has often been noted that he does this at the price of major distortions – for instance Stephen replaces the 'good' by the 'true' in his discussions of beauty, and he is very careful, as Noon has noted, to disentangle his line of reasoning from a theological system based upon the notion of divine and human love. One might say that the earlier formulations use a post-romantic opposition between the imagination and the intellect to steer away from ethical concerns, while the later rearrangements of aesthetic fragments in A *Portrait of the Artist as a Young Man* combine insights garnered from post-Hegelian philosophers of aesthetics like Bosanquet.

Joyce was not Hopkins, although he was a student in the same university – and he soon abandons the Platonician and romantic echoes of the theory when he rewrites *Stephen Hero*. In A *Portrait of the Artist as a Young Man*, all this phraseology recurs but without being underpinned by the momentous term of 'epiphany' so as to make the reader follow Stephen's 'curve of an emotion' while seeing the elaboration of the theory of epiphanies as a mere stage, a progression through juvenile neo-Shelleyian aesthetics. This seems to be confirmed by the fact that if the scene of the novella 'The Dead' in *Dubliners* takes place around the Epiphany, the usual associations of a 'manifestation' showing forth the divine nature of the divine child lead in this case to a final disclosure that appears much more negative. Gabriel does not bring any 'good news' to either the Virgin or himself, but confronts his own blindness, his selfishness and limitations. Like Stephen who brags about his new 'theory' concocted through an Aquinas he does not understand very well, Gabriel forces us to understand that there is a narrative process at work that is more crucial than the perception of the radiance of the thing qua thing. In that sense, one may say that the subjective pole has not been forgotten, it has simply been eclipsed for a while by the 'aesthetic theory' in order to return with a vengeance like the repressed of Freudian theory.

While showing us all the radiance of its manifestation, the epiphany has not concealed its part of blindness; it conveys an important connotation of 'betraying' or revealing something that had been concealed and in that sense should be connected with the loaded geometrical term of 'gnomon' offered as a hermeneutic key to the first story of *Dubliners*: a parallelogram with one corner missing. In that sense, Joyce's epiphany is never far either from the Freudian symptom or from the political drama of an Ireland systematically abused and betrayed from within and without. In Stanislaus Joyce's useful account, the 'manifestations or revelations' in which the epiphanies consist undo the very process of ideological concealment while exhibiting ironically the type of repression at work: 'Jim always had a contempt for secrecy, and these notes were in the beginning ironical observations of slips, and little errors and gestures – mere straws in the wind – by which people betrayed the very things they were most careful to conceal ... The revelation and importance of the subconscious had caught his interest' (Joyce, S. 1958, 134–5). A good exemplification would be epiphany no. 12 in which we see Hanna Sheehy, asked who might be her favourite German poet, reply sententiously after a pause and a hush: 'I think ... Goethe ...' Here, all the irony comes from the multiplication of the dots. This is an 'epiphany' because the pretensions of a shallow culture that takes itself too seriously have been caught in a moment of revelation that condenses an entire social symptom. In brief, the epiphany is not the key (given too soon in earlier drafts and then withheld for obscure reasons) of a theory of aesthetics but a bridge to a mimetic practice of language. It is therefore important to understand precisely what Joyce meant by mimesis.

Mimesis

In the Paris notebook (1903) one entry famously states: '*e tekhne mimeitaiten physin* – This phrase is falsely rendered as 'Art is an imitation of Nature'. Aristotle does not here define art; he says only, 'Art imitates Nature' and means here that the artistic process is like the natural process ...' (*CW*, 145). The replacement of the noun (*mimesis*) by a verb implies that mimesis is a process connecting art with life, and more precisely actively refusing any divorce between art and life. This seems to be a constant feature of Joyce's aesthetic theories, from the very early essay 'Drama and Life' (1900) that urges us to follow the model of Ibsen who has 'let fresh air in' (*CW*, 46) and shown us how to accept Life 'as we see it before our eyes, men and women as we meet in the real world, not as we apprehend them in the world of faery' (*CW*, 45), to a relatively late declaration made to an Irish friend, Arthur Power, a few years after *Ulysses* had been published: '... that is now what interests me most, to get to the residuum of truth about life, instead of puffing it up with romanticism, which is a fundamentally false attitude' (*CW*, 36). Here lies the source of the well-known 'classicism' of Joyce and of his resistance to a romanticism which he always associates with idealization and lyrical delusion (symptomatically, Power professed being a romantic himself). Ibsen, whom Joyce took as a literary example very early on, or Maupassant and Zola are thus superior to older models because they try to grapple with 'real life' in all its aspects.

This posture is in fact based upon Joyce's aesthetic tenets, and there again he finds Aristotle as a principal source of inspiration. If the *Poetics* define tragic drama as the 'imitation of an action' that produces pity and terror, it is because the playwright's aim is not the creation of a resembling picture of this or that man, but wishes to create emotions similar to those inspired by suffering characters like Oedipus. As Butcher's commentary on Aristotle's *Poetics* (a book upon which Joyce based his remarks, as Aubert (1992) and Schork (1998) have both demonstrated) insists, mimesis is the imitation of an action, of real 'men in action' (1895, 123). This is why music and dancing can be said to 'imitate' passions. Butcher concludes that 'imitation' is synonymous with 'producing' or 'creating according to a true idea' (1895, 153) which suggests a dynamic theory of an imitation linked with a living process and completely divorced from any preconception of the beautiful. Joyce's itinerary from Aristotle to Vico appears thus relatively direct, since both philosophers share the belief that imitation is a fundamentally human process and not based upon any notion of the beautiful or even limited to categories of aesthetics.

The concept of 'imitation' based on Aristotelian theories thus defines a psychological realism that has important consequences. As Stephen explains to a friend, 'Aristotle's entire system of philosophy rests upon his book of psychology' (APAM, 208). This position justifies an effort aiming at paralleling formal structures of the work of art with the stages of the mind's apprehension of it. Psychology and aesthetics are both underwritten by a more fundamental genetic and mimetic rationality since aesthetics cannot become a 'science of the particular' without accounting for its own genesis. Here lies the main quandary of A Portrait of the Artist as a Young Man, a Bildungsroman in which the description of aesthetic experience explains how any subject is bound to follow Stephen and apprehend the three stages of the individuating beauty in an object, and also lays the foundations of a quasi biographical narrative.

In Stephen Hero, the youthful Stephen Dedalus had been presented as a 'hero' when he managed to link the production of an aesthetic theory with an attitude of refusal or subversion of dominant values. This is accompanied by an attendant fetishization of the word 'theory', the term being a short-cut for 'aesthetic theory' but brandished in a repeated gesture of distanciation and negation, but also of ecstatic contemplation leading to a heightened sense of revelation – as when Stephen is described as exultant, under the shock of the vision of a young girl wading in the sea at the end of chapter IV in A Portrait. We have seen that the Aristotelian heritage claimed by Joyce leads him to refuse any notion of beauty as a guiding principle or Platonician essence. Does this for all that push him closer to a concept of the sublime? This is what Ginette Verstraete (1998) has argued about a Joycean 'feminine sublime' based less on Kant or Hegel than on Schlegelian aesthetics (possibly mediated by Croce). If a new 'feminine sublime' can be described, it would fundamentally encompass ugliness and ridicule. And even if Joyce was not aware of Schlegel's theses, he shares his basic insight into the duplicity, irony and reversibility of any gendered version of the Sublime.

Joyce thus soon felt the need to move beyond the confines of German romanticism, whether it be under its neo-Hegelian aspect with Bosanquet, or under a more Schlegelian guise, to engage less with offshoots of Hegelianism than with earlier forms of 'philosophy of history'. History had to embody the very site of a mimesis that did not wish to be measured by subjective psychological categories alone, or of a sublime that tended to overthrow all the older 'forms' determined by previous representations. This is why in philosophical and aesthetic terms, Joyce deliberately 'regresses' from Hegelianized theories of History to Vico's ricorsi storici in the New Science. Vico becomes his favourite source of inspiration because his aesthetics (like the investigations into the 'true Homer', or the theories of a 'poetic language' full of bodily metaphors) cannot be distinguished from his theory of the cyclical return of cultures and civilizations.

In Vico's New Science, however, Joyce also found another version of the Aristotelian notion of mimesis as a congenital property of men's activities in the world. The concept of mimesis was then be reinterpreted in the terms of what Vico calls the world of 'civil society', which is in fact (according to Vico) the only world that we can ever know since we cannot fathom the world of absolute truths that would reside in God only. It is the world of historical and social artefacts kept for us in monuments and language. For instance, in Vico's account of the genesis of language, some archaic giants who had thus far been sporting in the open evolved a mimetic response to the noise of the thunder which they took for God's angry rebuke at their sexual licence. These primitive beings then took refuge in caves where they invented marriage ceremonies, then added funerary rituals and started using language to distinguish relations of parenthood. The basic institutions of social life were thus invented: religion, marriage and burial. These first men who acted like children who imitate everything around them also gave birth to our distinctively human world – and it is the epic of this slow historical process that is being narrated in *Finnegans Wake*.

Joyce's mimetic theory – in a somewhat unexpected derivation – finally generates a theory of a universal language. As Joyce was toiling on his 'Work in Progress', a book he took seventeen years to complete and whose concept was based on the combined theories of Giordano Bruno and Giambattista Vico, he found an unforeseen help in the work of a French Jesuit, father Jousse. Jousse, who had started by investigating what he called the 'rhythmico-motric' style of a historicized Jesus whom he saw primarily as a Rabbi who wished to teach in such a way that his words would never be forgotten, and for that aim exploited all the resources of an embodied memory, must have looked to Joyce as a belated confirmation of his earlier theories about rhythm and language. Indeed, in the 1907 'Trieste Notebook', one finds under the heading of 'Esthetic' several entries that bear on this issue. The last of them is 'The skeleton conditions the esthetic image' and it comes just after: 'Art has the gift of tongues' and 'Pornography fails because whores are bad conductors of emotion'. This is echoed by Stephen in *Ulysses* where he is seen in 'Circe' entering the red light district of Dublin and exclaiming drunkenly: 'So that gesture, not music not odours, would be a universal language, the gift of tongues rendering visible not the lay sense but the first entelechy, the structural rhythm', to which his companion Lynch replies: 'Pornosophical philotheology'. We are thus sent back to much earlier discussions of the 'static' nature of beauty as opposed to a negative dynamism of desire in pornography in the Paris notebook and *Stephen Hero*. Here, Joyce reaches a satisfactory conclusion through Stephen's divagations, which also provides him with a basis for the construction of the 'tower of Babel' of the Wake. Jousse's idea of a rhythmic verbo-motricity based on the bilateral nature of the body and the brain confirms earlier speculations on the silent language of gesture and the principle of basic rhythm that would underpin Universal History. This is why one can assert that the language of the Wake is mimetic throughout (it is easy to provide examples of lisping 'baby talk' with Issy or of male Freudian symptoms betraying lust or hunger in Shaun's absurdly greedy speeches). Jousse and Vico agree with Joyce on one central point: it is the human body that becomes the foundation not only for the creation of poetic metaphors but also for the rhythmic reception of the structural 'music of time' thus produced. This is why *Finnegans Wake* avoids falling into the trap of Jungian universal archetypes, while working through bodily music and literary stereotypes based upon a synthetic universal language.

Jean-Michel Rabaté

Further reading and works cited

Aubert, J. *The Aesthetics of James Joyce*. Baltimore, MD, 1992.

Bosanquet, B. *A History of Aesthetics*. London, 1982.

Butcher, S. H. *Aristotle's Theory of Poetry and the Fine Arts*. London, 1895.

Eco, U. *The Aesthetics of Chaosmos: The Middle Ages of James Joyce*. Tulsa, OK, 1982.

Hayman, D. *The 'Wake' in Transit*. Ithaca, NY, 1990.

Jaurretche, C. *The Sensual Philosophy: Joyce and the Aesthetics of Mysticism*. Madison, WI, 1997.

Jousse, M. *The Oral Style*. New York, 1990.

Joyce, J. *Finnegans Wake* [FW]. London, 1939.

—. *Stephen Hero* [SH] London, 1956.

—. *Critical Writings* [CW] eds E. Mason and R. Ellmann. New York, 1964.

—. *A Portrait of the Artist as a Young Man* [APAM] ed. C. Anderson. New York, 1968.

—. *Selected Letters* [L, IV], ed. R. Ellmann. London, 1975.

—. *Ulysses*, ed. H. W. Gabler. London, 1986.

—. *Dubliners*, ed. T. Brown. London, 1992.

Joyce, S. *My Brother's Keeper*. New York, 1958.

McGrath, F. C. *The Sensible Spirit: Walter Pater and the Modernist Paradigm*. Tampa, FL, 1986.

Mahaffey, V. 'Joyce's Shorter Works', in *Cambridge Companion to James Joyce*, ed. D. Attridge. Cambridge, 1990.

Mallarmé, S. *Ecrits sur le Livre*, ed. H. Meschonnic. Paris, 1985.

Noon, W. T. *Joyce and Aquinas*. New Haven, CT, 1957.

Power, A. *Conversations with James Joyce*. London, 1974.

Scholes, R. (ed.) *The Workshop of Daedalus*. Evanston, IL, 1965.

— and Corcoran, M. G. 'The Aesthetic Theory and the Critical Writings', in *A Companion to Joyce Studies*, eds Z. Bowen and J. F. Carens. Westport, CT, 1984.

Schork, R. J. *Greek and Hellenic Culture in Joyce*. Gainesville, FL, 1998.

Tysdahl, B. J. *Joyce and Ibsen*. Oslo, 1968.

Verene, D. P. (ed.) *Vico and Joyce*. Albany, NY, 1987.

Verstraete, G. *Fragments of the Feminine Sublime in Friedrich Schlegel and James Joyce*. Albany, NY, 1998.

Walton Litz, A. *The Art of James Joyce*. New York, 1961.

Weir, L. *Writing Joyce*. Bloomington, IN, 1989.

6. Virginia Woolf (1882–1941): Aesthetics

Many of the fundamental ideas and debates of literary criticism and theory concerned with modernism, feminism and even postmodernism have been shaped by and with reference to the work of Virginia Woolf. Although she did not write in the style of high theoretical discourse, Woolf has been recognized for her experimentalism with, and transformation of, critical writing itself. Her avant-garde novels, essays and short stories have been read with one eye on her notoriety as a leading member of what later was called the Bloomsbury Group. Other members of this liberal, pacifist and at times libertine intellectual enclave of Cambridge-based privilege included art critics Roger Fry and Clive Bell, artists Vanessa

Bell (Woolf's sister) and Duncan Grant, economist Maynard Keynes, critic Lytton Strachey, novelist E. M. Forster and political journalist and publisher Leonard Woolf (Woolf's husband). Virginia Woolf's aesthetic understanding was in part shaped by, and at first primarily interpreted in terms of, (male) Bloomsbury's dominant aesthetic and philosophical preoccupations, rooted in the work of G. E. Moore, and culminating in a pioneering aesthetic formalism. But, increasing awareness of Woolf's feminism and of the influence on her work of other women artists, writers and thinkers has meant that these points of reference, though of importance, are no longer considered adequate in approaching Woolf's aesthetic. Woolf's writing has been of central interest to the major shifts in feminist critical debates concerning, in the 1970s, marxism, materialism and androgyny, in the 1980s subjectivity and textuality, and more recently historicist, cultural materialist and postcolonialist theories.

Woolf was not only a writer of experimental fiction but also (from a young age) a professional reviewer, publishing many anonymous reviews, for example, in the *Times Literary Supplement*; a biographer (*Roger Fry* (1940)); an accomplished and innovative essayist – she published two collections of essays as *The Common Reader* (1925 and 1932), and several collections have appeared since her death; an impressive polemicist (*A Room of One's Own* (1929) and *Three Guineas* (1938)); and not least, along with her husband, a successful and influential publisher. The Hogarth Press was responsible, for example, for the first major works of Freud in English, and published significant works by key modernist writers such as T. S. Eliot and Gertrude Stein. Since her death the publication of Woolf's private and personal writings has provided a rich and controversial literary and critical resource, which is often cited in commentaries on Woolf's fiction and on modernist writing more generally, and which has also been influential in recent theorizing on autobiography.

While her fiction has always been central to canonical high modernism, some of her work in other genres has come to dominance more recently, not least because of its transgeneric qualities (although a number of Woolf's novels also push the boundaries of genre, experimenting, for example, with elegy, journalese and academic biography). The (draft) essay-novel, *The Pargiters* (published posthumously, 1978), was an ambitious project conceived to combine critical and political argument with fictional narrative, which Woolf eventually divided for publication into two works, the epistolary anti-fascist, pacifist polemic, *Three Guineas*, and the conventional novel, *The Years* (1937). Her feminist tract, *A Room of One's Own*, undoubtedly her most important contribution to literary criticism and theory, notoriously blurs the boundaries between critical and fictional discourses. It is regarded as a founding text for feminist aesthetics, not least because it is also a source of many, often conflicting, theoretical positions. *A Room of One's Own* is cited as *locus classicus* for a number of important modern feminist debates concerning: gender, sexuality, materialism, education, patriarchy, androgyny, subjectivity, the feminine sentence, the notion of 'Shakespeare's sister', the canon, the body, race, class, and so on. Woolf's other texts of significance to literary theory include: the essays 'Modern Fiction' (1919), 'Mr Bennett and Mrs Brown' (1924) and the short story 'The Moment: Summer's Night' (c.1929), all of which have been influential in the theorizing of modernism; the essays 'Memories of a Working Women's Guild' (1930), 'Professions for Women' (1931) and the 'The Leaning Tower' (1940), which have influenced theories of feminism, class and fiction; and the posthumously published collection of autobiographical writings *Moments of Being*, which includes the memoir, 'A Sketch of the Past' (c.1939), where Woolf explains her 'philosophy' in terms of epiphanic moments. Her critical writing is discussed below in terms of modernism and feminism.

Modernism

'Modern Fiction', first published in April 1919 (as 'Modern Novels') and revised for the first *Common Reader* (it is the revised, 1925, version – often dated 1919 – that is commonly anthologized and cited here), is perhaps Woolf's most well known and most frequently quoted essay. Woolf here distinguishes between the outmoded 'materialism' of the Edwardian novelists, H. G. Wells, John Galsworthy, and Arnold Bennett, and the more 'spiritual' and experimental writing of her Georgian contemporaries. The tyranny of plot and characterization afflicts Bennett's work, she contends, along with the obligation 'to provide comedy, tragedy, love interest, and an air of probability embalming the whole so impeccable that if all his figures were to come to life they would find themselves dressed down to the last button of their coats in the fashion of the hour' (*Essays*, 4, 160). Such writing fails to capture 'life', as Woolf's most famous and most quoted passages of criticism explains:

> Look within and life, it seems, is very far from being 'like this'. Examine for a moment an ordinary mind on an ordinary day. The mind receives a myriad impressions – trivial, fantastic, evanescent, or engraved with the sharpness of steel. From all sides they come, an incessant shower of innumerable atoms; and as they fall, as they shape themselves into the life of Monday or Tuesday, the accent falls differently from of old; the moment of importance came not here but there; so that, if a writer were a free man and not a slave, if he could write what he chose, not what he must, if he could base his work not upon convention, there would be no plot, no comedy, no love interest or catastrophe in the accepted style, and perhaps not a single button sewn on as the Bond Street tailors would have it. Life is not a series of gig lamps symmetrically arranged; life is a luminous halo, a semi-transparent envelope surrounding us from the beginning of consciousness to the end. Is it not the task of the novelist to convey this varying, this unknown and uncircumscribed spirit, whatever aberration or complexity it may display, with as little mixture of the alien and external as possible? (160–1)

Woolf's story, 'The Moment: Summer's Night', offers a closer, equally lyrical, account of a luminous moment, and is often cited in conjunction with this passage, which, in advocating subjective, fleeting, interior, experience as the proper stuff of fiction along with the abandonment of conventional plot, genre and narrative structure, has become one of the standard critical sources in the discussion of modernist literary qualities – particularly 'stream-of-consciousness' – not least because it is followed by a (not uncritical) defence of James Joyce's work. Woolf cites his *Portrait of the Artist as a Young Man* (1916) and the extracts from *Ulysses* (1922) recently published in the *Little Review* (1918) to exemplify the new 'spiritual' writing. Joyce, she argues, is 'concerned at all costs to reveal the flickerings of that inmost flame which flashes its messages through the brain' (*Essays*, 4, 161). Woolf's alchemical imagery here owes much to Walter Pater's aesthetics, and her concern with subjective temporality – the epiphanic 'moment' – to the philosophy of Henri Bergson. Although Woolf identifies, in 'Modern Fiction', a fragment of *Ulysses* ('Hades') as a 'masterpiece' for 'its brilliancy, its sordidity, its incoherence, its sudden lightning flashes of significance', she nevertheless finds that it 'fails to compare' with the work of Joseph Conrad or Thomas Hardy 'because of the comparative poverty of the writer's mind' (161). Woolf is less generous to Joyce in private. On reading *Ulysses*, she notoriously captures him in her diary as 'a queasy undergraduate scratching his pimples' (*Diary*, 2, 188). 'Modern Fiction' nevertheless stands as an early and significant defence of his work, and as a manifesto of modernism.

'Mr Bennett and Mrs Brown', like many of Woolf's essays, evolved from a speech (in this instance to the Cambridge Heretics Society), and many of its rhetorical features survive into the published text. Here Woolf continues her assault on the Edwardians, Wells, Galsworthy and Bennett, for their materialist conventions, and her uneven defence of the Georgians, Joyce, Eliot, Forster, Lytton Strachey and D. H. Lawrence, whose work, she declares, must make us 'reconcile ourselves to a season of failures and fragments' (*Essays*, 3, 435). The essay's title is derived from its central, virtuoso, conceit whereby Woolf illustrates the inadequacies of the Edwardian novelists as she makes a number of attempts, using their 'tools', to construct a fictional narrative about the character of 'Mrs Brown', a stranger encountered on a train. The essay also contains one of Woolf's most famous, and most quoted, assertions: 'on or about December 1910 human character changed' (421). This has come to represent for many cultural commentators the cataclysmic moment of modernity, the inception of the avant-garde, the shock of the new. In the context of the essay, it marks the shift from the Edwardian to the Georgian era, when 'all human relations have shifted – those between masters and servants, husbands and wives, parents and children. And when human relations change there is at the same time a change in religion, conduct, politics, and literature' (422). But Woolf is not arguing that literature merely changes in terms of subject matter to reflect new, modern, experience, but that literary form itself undergoes radical and turbulent, transformation: 'And so the smashing and the crashing began ... Grammar is violated; syntax disintegrated' (434). The work of Joyce, Eliot and Strachey illustrate the point that modern literature has necessarily become caught up in the business of finding new form. Readers must 'tolerate the spasmodic, the obscure, the fragmentary, the failure' (436). The self-reflexive, fragmentary, subjective and momentary qualities of modernist writing are, of course, acknowledged and celebrated by Woolf's avant-garde contemporaries, but her own particular aesthetic was anathema to some. Woolf's 'luminous halo' metaphors, for instance, 'imply an art that rejects precise statement and moral certainty', according to M. H. Levenson, 'in favour of the sugges-tiveness and imprecision usually associated with symbolism or Impressionism. [Ezra] Pound on the other hand, opposed all "mushy technique" and "emotional slither", preferring a poetry "as much like granite as it could possibly be"' (1989, 154–5). In quoting from Pound's essay, 'The Hard and the Soft in French Poetry', and reflecting T. E. Hulme's taste for 'hard' poetry, Levenson alerts us to the critical ruptures of the period. Yet there is common ground between Woolf and Pound. Eliot, who owed much to Pound, for example, was also championed by Woolf.

Feminism

It was not only her choice of metaphor that could distance Woolf from her male contemporaries, but her feminism. 'There are spots of it all over her work,' according to her friend Forster, 'and it was constantly in her mind' (1997, 34). But even he acknowledged *A Room of One's Own* as 'brilliant' (34). The title alone has had enormous impact as cultural shorthand for a modern feminist agenda, while the book itself is widely regarded as 'the first book of feminist literary criticism' and 'the founding text of Anglo-American feminist literary theory' (Gallop 1992, 77, 145). Woolf developed the text from two lectures to Cambridge women students and an essay version on 'Women and Fiction', and although much revised and expanded, the final version significantly retains the original's sense of a woman speaking to women. Woolf again adopts fictional narrative strategies and shifting narrative personae to present her argument. She anticipates postmodernist, post-Lacanian, theoretical concerns with the constitution of gender and subjectivity in language when she begins by declaring that ' "I" is only a convenient term for somebody who has no real being ... (call me Mary Beton, Mary Seton, Mary Carmichael or by any name you please – it is not a matter of any importance)' (1992a, 5). Woolf here invokes the Scottish ballad 'The Four Marys', and ventriloquizes much of her argument through the voice of her own 'Mary Beton' (Marcus 1987a, 197). In the course of the book she encounters the other Marys – Mary Seton has become a student at 'Fernham' college and Mary Carmichael an aspiring novelist – and it has been suggested that Woolf's opening and closing remarks may be in the voice of Mary Hamilton (the narrator of the ballad). This multivocal strategy, along with the text's multitude of other citations, has encouraged later feminists to celebrate *A Room of One's Own* as a dialogical text. The intertext with the Scottish ballad feeds a subtext in Woolf's argument concerning the suppression of the role of motherhood – Mary Hamilton sings the ballad from the gallows where she is to be hung for infanticide. (Marie Carmichael, furthermore, is the *nom de plume* of contraceptive activist Marie Stopes who published a novel, *Love's Creation*, in 1928.) Woolf further insists, in her later essay, 'Professions for Women', on the woman writer's necessary suppression of a traditionally submissive – and domestic – feminine role, encapsulated in Coventry Patmore's 'Angel in the House': 'Had I not killed her she would have killed me. She would have plucked the heart out of my writing. . . . Killing the Angel in the House was part of the occupation of a woman writer' (153).

Woolf's main subject in *A Room of One's Own* is, as her earlier title indicates, 'Women and Fiction', and her main argument is that 'a woman must have money and a room of her own if she is to write fiction' (1992a, 4). Woolf's contempt for the 'materialism' of the Edwardian novelists seems forgotten here, as the narrator begins by recounting her experience at Oxbridge where she was refused access to the library, and compares in some detail the splendid opulence of her lunch at a men's college with the austerity of her dinner at a more recently established women's college (Fernham). This account is the foundation for the book's main, materialist, argument: 'intellectual freedom depends upon material things' (141). Woolf extends this line of argument in her later essay, 'The Leaning Tower', a paper she read to the Workers' Educational Association, to discuss the class alignments of writing. She claims that 'all writers from Chaucer to the present day . . . come from the middle class' and 'were educated at public schools and universities' (165). D. H. Lawrence is her only exception. She rallies her working-class audience by insisting 'we are not going to leave writing to be done for us by a small class of well-to-do young men who have only a pinch, a thimbleful of experience to give us. We are going to add our own experience, to make our own contribution' (178). If the categorization of middle-class women like herself with the working classes seems problematic here, Woolf has already proposed, in *A Room of One's Own*, that women be understood as a separate class altogether. Here is the nub of contention in feminism's encounters with marxism. Yet the alignment of women and the working class is hardly exclusive to Woolf. *A Room of One's Own* was published in the year after the full enfranchisement of women, ten years after the enfranchisement of working-class men along with middle-class, propertied women over 30 years of age. Woolf's point concerns the exclusion of women and the working classes from material resources and education. In 'Memories of a Working Women's Guild' she explores the complexities of her position as an educated and privileged middle-class woman aligned with working-class women in organized feminist politics. In *Three Guineas*,

Woolf's counterblast to fascism (which she aligns with patriarchy), she more radically separates off the category of women as, paradoxically, transcending all boundaries, including national ones: 'As a woman, I have no country. As a woman I want no country. As a woman my country is the whole world' (1992a, 313).

Woolf puts forward, in *A Room of One's Own*, a sophisticated and much-quoted simile for the material basis of literary production when she begins to consider the apparent dearth of literature by women in the Elizabethan period:

> For it is a perennial puzzle why no woman wrote a word of that extraordinary literature when every other man, it seemed, was capable of song or sonnet. What were the conditions in which women lived, I asked myself; for fiction, imaginative work that is, is not dropped like a pebble upon the ground, as science may be; fiction is like a spider's web, attached ever so lightly perhaps, but still attached to life at all four corners. Often the attachment is scarcely perceptible; Shakespeare's plays, for instance, seem to hang there complete by themselves. But when the web is pulled askew, hooked up at the edge, torn in the middle, one remembers that these webs are not spun in mid-air by incorporeal creatures, but are the work of suffering human beings, and are attached to grossly material things, like health and money and the houses we live in.

Feminist scholarship has since corrected the view of a singularly male Elizabethan literary canon, while feminist literary theory has claimed 'Virginia's web' as a defining figure for writing by women. The passage offers a number of different ways of understanding literary materialism. Firstly, it suggests that writing itself is physically made, and not divinely given or unearthly and transcendent. Woolf seems to be attempting to demystify the romantic figure of the (male) poet or author as mystically singled out, or divinely elected; but this idea is also connected to a strand of modernist aesthetics concerned with writing as a self-reflexive object and to a more general sense of the materiality of the text, the concreteness of words, spoken or printed. Secondly, the passage suggests writing as somatic process or bodily production. The material status of the body is far from stable here, and the figure of the spider suggests a gendered somatic model of writing. Thirdly, writing as 'the work of suffering human beings' suggests that literature is produced as compensation for, or in protest against, existential pain and material lack. Finally, moving from this general sense of connection with human lived experience to a more specific one, in proposing writing as 'attached to grossly material things, like health and money and the houses we live in', Woolf is delineating a model of literature as grounded in the 'real world', that is in the realms of historical, political and social experience. This latter position may be broadly associated with marxist literary theory, but Woolf's work cannot very readily be reconciled to this category *per se*, and it is possible to understand, in any case, this sense of materialism as not strictly speaking marxist. It should be noted that *A Room of One's Own*, experimental in form, appeared before the Soviet and marxist anti-modernist strictures of the 1930s after which social(ist) realism was the dominant marxist aesthetic; and this has some bearing on later feminist debate, in the 1980s, centring on this work (see Moi 1985). It is not merely Woolf's avant-garde aesthetic, however, that problematizes this work's relationship to marxism, but – more significantly – her feminism. Attempts to 'marry' marxism and feminism, in short, arose from the desire to correct and supplement a historical and class-based analysis of literature with a gender-based one, and vice versa. Materialist feminism, although sometimes a more polite term for marxist-feminism, may also be understood as the issue borne of that well documented 'unhappy marriage'. Woolf's work remains an important focus for both marxist and materialist feminist literary theory.

Interestingly, Jane Marcus has argued (with Woolf's nephew and biographer, Quentin Bell, who insisted 'Woolf wasn't a feminist and wasn't political') that Woolf's work is in fact marxist (See Homan 1993, 7). Whereas Michèle Barrett, while acknowledging in the introduction to *Virginia Woolf, Women and Writing*, that 'Woolf's writings on women and fiction constitute a sustained analysis of the historical determinants of women's literary production [which] might gladden the heart of a contemporary Marxist feminist critic' (1979, 17), nevertheless refutes the idea that 'her general "materialist" argument [in *A Room of One's Own*] could under any circumstances be regarded as a Marxist argument', but not on the grounds of her feminism. Woolf, she explains, 'explores the extent to which, under adverse conditions, art may be restrained and distorted by social conditions, but she retains the notion that in the correct conditions art may be totally divorced from economic, political or ideological constraints' (23). Woolf's theory of androgynous art, and her vision of a transcendent poetics, 'resists the materialist position she advances in *A Room of One's Own*' (22).

The narrator shifts scene, in *A Room of One's Own*, to the British Museum where she researches 'Women and Poverty' under an edifice of patriarchal texts, concluding that women 'have served all these centuries as looking glasses . . . reflecting the figure of man at twice his natural size' (1992a, 45). Here Woolf touches upon the forced, subordinate complicity of women in the construction of the patriarchal subject. Later in the book, Woolf offers a more explicit model of this when she describes the difficulties for a woman reader encountering the first person pronoun in the novels of 'Mr A': 'a shadow seemed to lie across the page. It was a straight dark bar, a shadow shaped something like the letter "I". . . . Back one was always hailed to the letter "I". One began to tire of "I" . . . In the shadow of the letter "I" all is shapeless as mist. Is that a tree? No it is a woman' (130). This displacement of the feminine in the representation and construction of subjectivity not only points up the alienation experienced by women readers of male-authored texts but also the linguistic difficulties for women writers in trying to express feminine subjectivity. It certainly explains Woolf's sliding and elliptical use of the first person throughout her argument. But Woolf's idiosyncratic narrative strategies in *A Room of One's Own* have been regarded as detracting from her feminist message. The American feminist Elaine Showalter notably takes Woolf to task for the book's 'playfulness [and] conversational surface' (1977, 282). Toril Moi, in her introduction to *Sexual/Textual Politics* (1985), claims to 'rescue' Woolf's text from such criticism by showing how its very playfulness is in fact a feminist strategy that anticipates the deconstructive and post-Lacanian work of the French feminists, Julia Kristeva, Hélène Cixous and Luce Irigaray (broadly associated with the idea of '*écriture feminine*'). Moi's reading of Woolf's writing as radically feminist by virtue of its textuality, although helpful to her basic introduction to French feminism, is dismissive of the latent humanism and marxism in much 'Anglo-American' feminist criticism and makes no account of such aspects in the argument, however circumlocutionary or playful, of *A Room of One's Own*, which nevertheless puts forward a strong materialist and historicist approach to women's writing.

In trying to discover the conditions of women's lives in, for example, the Elizabethan period, the narrator discovers a significant discrepancy between women in the real world and 'woman' in the symbolic order:

> Imaginatively she is of the highest importance; practically she is completely insignificant. She pervades poetry from cover to cover; she is all but absent from history. She dominates the lives of kings and conquerors in fiction; in fact she was the slave of any boy whose parents forced a

ring upon her finger. Some of the most inspired words, some of the most profound thoughts in literature fall from her lips; in real life she could scarcely spell, and was the property of her husband. (1992a, 56)

Woolf here points up not only the relatively sparse representation of women's experience in historical records, but also the more complicated business of how the feminine is already caught up in the conventions of representation itself; how women may be represented at all when 'woman', in poetry and fiction, is already a signifier in patriarchal discourse, functioning as part of the symbolic order: 'It was certainly an odd monster that one made up by reading the historians first and the poets afterwards – a worm winged like an eagle; the spirit of life and beauty in a kitchen chopping suet. But these monsters, however amusing to the imagination, have no existence in fact' (56).

Woolf converts this dual image to a positive emblem for a feminist writing:

> What one must do to bring her to life was to think poetically and prosaically at one and the same moment, thus keeping in touch with fact – that she is Mrs Martin, aged thirty-six, dressed in blue, wearing a black hat and brown shoes; but not losing sight of fiction either – that she is a vessel in which all sorts of spirits and forces are coursing and flashing perpetually. (56–7)

This dualistic model, contrasting prose and poetry, is of central importance to Woolf's modernist aesthetic and is encapsulated in the term, 'granite and rainbow' (*Essays*, 4, 478), which she elsewhere ('The New Biography' (1927)) uses to describe innovations in the art of biography. In the essay, 'Poetry, Fiction and the Future' (1927; also known as 'The Narrow Bridge of Art'), Woolf acknowledges the different tasks each traditionally performs, but is interested in creating a new form of writing that marries prose and poetry:

> [Poetry] has always insisted on certain rights, such as rhyme, metre, poetic diction. She has never been used for the common purpose of life. Prose has taken all the dirty work on to her own shoulders; has answered letters, paid bills, written articles, made speeches, served the needs of business men shopkeepers, lawyers, soldiers, peasants. (*Essays*, 4, 434)

She anticipates a new form of writing in a 'prose which has many of the characteristics of poetry', asking whether prose can 'chant the elegy, or hymn the love, or shriek in terror, or praise the rose' (436) and so on. This is a celebration of the new lyrical prose of modernism – and indeed of her own novel, *To the Lighthouse*, which she famously christened an elegy (see *Diary*, 3, 34). But, *A Room Of One's Own* explores the gender implications of this new form of writing and puts it forward as a feminist tool – just as *To the Lighthouse*, in exploring the social politics surrounding the execution of a painting by a woman artist, is simultaneously a high modernist and a feminist text.

Yet it is still considered controversial, in some quarters, to talk of Woolf's writing as feminist. The source of the confusion may well be the much cited passage in *A Room of One's Own* where it is declared that 'it is fatal for anyone who writes to think of their sex' (136) and a model of writerly androgyny is put forward, derived from Samuel Taylor Coleridge's work:

> It is fatal to be a man or woman pure and simple; one must be woman-manly or man-womanly. It is fatal for a woman to lay the least stress on any grievance; to plead even with justice any cause; in any way to speak consciously as a woman. And fatal is no figure of speech; for anything written with that conscious bias is doomed to death. It ceases to be fertilized ... Some collaboration has to take place in the mind between the woman and the man before the art of creation can be accomplished. Some marriage of opposites has to be accomplished. (136)

Woolf's theory of androgyny has been interpreted as positioning her argument beyond feminist concerns, yet it is conceived in the context of her analysis of women and fiction, and is proposed as a goal not yet attained by most of her contemporaries because of inequalities between men and women. Shakespeare, the poet playwright, is Woolf's ideal androgynous writer. She lists others – all men – who have also achieved androgyny (Keats, Sterne, Cowper, Lamb and Proust – the only contemporary). Carolyn G. Heilbrun (1973) and Nancy Topping Bazin (1973) were the first critics to explore Woolf's theory of androgyny. Showalter's (1977) attack on it, in her famous chapter, 'Virginia Woolf and the Flight into Androgyny', marks the start of continuing ferocious theoretical debate on the subject. For critics like Moi, Woolf's theory of androgyny anticipates the French feminist concept of '*différance*'.

A *Room of One's Own* culminates in the prophesy of a woman poet to equal or rival Shakespeare – 'Shakespeare's sister'. But in collectively preparing for her appearance, women writers need to develop in several respects. In predicting that the aspiring novelist, Mary Carmichael, 'will be a poet . . . in another hundred years' time' (1992a, 123), Mary Beton seems to be suggesting that prose must be explored and exploited in certain ways by women writers before they can be poets. She also finds fault with contemporary male writers – such as Mr A who is 'protesting against the equality of the other sex by asserting his own superiority' (132). She sees this as the direct result of women's political agitation for equality: 'The Suffrage campaign was no doubt to blame' (129). She raises further concerns about politics and aesthetics when she comments on the aspirations of the Italian fascists for a poet worthy of fascism: 'We may well join in that pious hope, but it is doubtful whether poetry can come out of an incubator. Poetry ought to have a mother as well as a father. The Fascist poem, one may fear, will be a horrid little abortion such as one sees in a glass jar in the museum of some county town' (134). Yet if the extreme patriarchy of fascism cannot produce poetry because it denies a maternal line, Woolf argues that women cannot write poetry either until the historical canon of women's writing has been uncovered and acknowledged. Nineteenth-century women writers experienced great difficulty because they lacked a female tradition: 'For we think back through our mothers if we are women' (99). They therefore lacked literary tools suitable for expressing women's experience. The dominant sentence at the start of the nineteenth century was 'a man's sentence . . . It was a sentence that was unsuited for women's use' (99–100).

Woolf's assertion here, through Mary Beton, of gendered syntax, and that 'the book has somehow to be adapted to the body' (101) (again anticipating the libidinal writing projects of French feminism), seems to contradict the declaration that 'it is fatal for anyone who writes to think of their sex'. She identifies the novel as 'young enough' to be of use to the woman writer:

> No doubt we shall find her knocking that into shape for herself when she has the free use of her limbs; and providing some new vehicle, not necessarily in verse, for the poetry in her. For it is the poetry that is still the denied outlet. And I went on to ponder how a woman nowadays would write a poetic tragedy in five acts. Would she use verse? – would she not use prose rather? (100–1)

Woolf seems to confirm this theory of gendered aesthetic form in her earlier review (1923) of Dorothy Richardson's novel, *Revolving Lights*: 'She has invented, or, if she has not invented, developed and applied to her own uses, a sentence which we might call the psychological sentence of the feminine gender. It is of a more elastic fibre than the old, capable of stretching to the extreme, of suspending the frailest particles, of enveloping the vaguest shapes' (*Essays*, 3, 367). But, acknowledging that men also have constructed similar sentences, she points out that the difference lies with content rather than form:

> Miss Richardson has fashioned her sentence consciously, in order that it may descend to the depths and investigate the crannies of Miriam Henderson's consciousness. It is a woman's sentence only in the sense that it is used to describe a woman's mind by a writer who is neither proud nor afraid of anything that she may discover in the psychology of her sex. (367)

This assertion of woman as both the writing subject and its object is reinforced in *A Room of One's Own*: 'above all, you must illumine your own soul' (1992a, 117), Mary Beton advises. The 'obscure lives' (116) of women must be recorded by women.

Mary Carmichael's novel in fact explores women's relationships with each other. *A Room of One's Own* was published shortly after the obscenity trial of Radclyffe Hall's *The Well of Loneliness* (1928), and Woolf flaunts in the face of this a blatantly lesbian narrative: 'if Chloe likes Olivia and Mary Carmichael knows how to express it she will light a torch in that vast chamber where nobody has yet been' (109). Her refrain, 'Chloe likes Olivia', has become a critical slogan for lesbian writing. Woolf's own fictive celebration of her lesbian lover, Vita Sackville-West, in the satirical novel *Orlando* (1928) escaped the censure directed at Hall's work. In *A Room of One's Own*, she calls for women's writing to more openly explore lesbianism and for the narrative tools to make this possible. Lesbian writing has certainly been widely published in the decades following, but it is only recently that lesbian criticism of Woolf's own work has flourished.

A Room of One's Own has not always been regarded positively by feminists, as Showalter's work has shown, but it has become a touchstone for most feminist debates. One of the most controversial passages, for example, concerns Woolf's positioning of black women. Commenting on the sexual and colonial appetites of men, the narrator concludes: 'It is one of the great advantages of being a woman that one can pass even a very fine negress without wishing to make an Englishwoman of her' (1992a, 65). In seeking to distance women from colonial practices, Woolf disturbingly excludes black women here from the very category of woman. This has become the crux of much contemporary feminist debate concerning the politics of identity. The category of women both unites and divides feminists: white middle-class feminists, it has been shown, cannot speak for the experience of all women, and reconciliation of universalism and difference remains a key issue. 'Women – but are you not sick to death of the word?' Woolf retorts in the closing pages of *A Room of One's Own*, 'I can assure you I am' (145). The category of women is not chosen by women, it represents the space in patriarchy from which women must speak and which they struggle to redefine. Woolf's ambition for the coming of Shakespeare's sister has been taken up by feminist critics and anthologisers. 'Judith Shakespeare' stands for the silenced woman writer or artist. But to seek to mimic *the* model of the individual masculine writing subject may also be considered part of a conservative feminist agenda. On the other hand, Woolf seems to defer the arrival of Shakespeare's sister in a celebration of women's collective literary achievement: '– I am talking of the common life which is the real life and not of the little separate lives which we live as individuals' (148–9). Shakespeare's sister is a messianic figure who 'lives in you and in me' (148) and who will draw 'her life from the lives of the unknown who were her forerunners' (149), but has yet to appear. She may be the common writer to Woolf's 'common reader' (a term she borrows from Samuel Johnson), but she has yet to 'put on the body which she has so often laid down'

(149). The sense of a collective authorial voice, here, along with the multivocal narrative of *A Room of One's Own*, has been seen to anticipate Woolf's more formally stylized and poetic, multivocal novel, *The Waves* (1931). But while writing *The Waves*, Woolf was also composing her introduction to another, more prosaic perhaps, multivocal text, *Life as We Have Known It*, a collection of letters by members of the Working Women's Guild (see Goldman 1998, 192).

Woolf puts forward a collective and non-transcendent sense of the writing subject in her memoir, 'A Sketch of the Past', where she maintains

> that behind the cotton wool is hidden a pattern; that we – I mean all human beings – are connected with this; that the whole world is a work of art; that we are parts of the work of art. *Hamlet* or a Beethoven quartet is the truth about this vast mass that we call the world. But there is no Shakespeare, there is no Beethoven; certainly and emphatically there is no God; we are the words; we are the music; we are the thing itself. And I see this when I have a shock. (72)

This epiphanic vision, more radical than Eliot's theory of impersonality, and anticipating in some respects Roland Barthes' idea of 'death of the author', seems to move beyond questions of gender and feminism to a sense of an ungendered collective aesthetic. Yet it appears in the context of Woolf's account of her experience of childhood sexual abuse by her brother and of the domestic tyranny of her father. Having recalled these unhappy autobiographical details, she goes on to consider how memory operates, and to record three particular 'moments of being'. She explains that such moments are triggered by physical shocks. Woolf's 'moments of being' have been likened to Henri Bergson's idea of the *durée* – subjective, non-spatial temporality – but they are also rooted in, record and resonate with the historical and material. Her aesthetic attempts both to record the real, including the interior, lives of women and to imagine life and art beyond such concerns.

Jane Goldman

Further reading and works cited

Auerbach, E. *Mimesis*. Princeton, NJ, 1953.
Barrett, M. (ed.) *Virginia Woolf, Women and Writing*. New York, 1979.
Bazin, N. Topping. *Virginia Woolf and the Androgynous Vision*. New Brunswick, NJ, 1973.
Beer, G. *Virginia Woolf*. Edinburgh, 1996.
Bowlby, R. *Feminist Destinations and Other Essays*. Edinburgh, 1996.
Brosnan, L. *Reading Virginia Woolf's Essays and Journalism*. Edinburgh, 1997.
Dowling, D. *Bloomsbury Aesthetics and the Novels of Forster and Woolf*. London, 1985.
Ezell, M. J. M. 'The Myth of Judith Shakespeare', *New Literary History*, 21, Spring 1990.
Forster, E. M. 'Virginia Woolf', in *Icon Critical Guide: Virginia Woolf*. ed. J. Goldman. London, 1997.
Gallop, J. *Around 1981: Academic Feminist Literary Theory*. New York, 1992.
Goldman, J. *The Feminist Aesthetics of Virginia Woolf*. Cambridge, 1998.
Heilbrun, C. *Towards Androgyny*. London, 1973.
Homans, M. (ed.) *Virginia Woolf*. Englewood Cliffs, NJ, 1993.
Hulme, T. E. *Speculations*, ed. H. Read. London, 1924.
Hussey, M. *The Singing of the Real World*. Columbus, OH, 1986.
— (ed.) *Virginia Woolf A–Z*. Oxford, 1995.
Kamuf, P. 'Penelope at Work'. *Novel*, 16, 1982.
Levenson, M. H. *A Genealogy of Modernism*. Cambridge. 1989.
Marcus, J. (ed.) *New Feminist Essays on Virginia Woolf*. Lincoln, NE, 1981.

— (ed.) *Virginia Woolf*. Lincoln, NE, 1983.

— (ed.) *Virginia Woolf and the Languages of Patriarchy*. Bloomington, 1987a.

— (ed.) *Virginia Woolf and Bloomsbury*. Bloomington, IN, 1987b.

—. *Art and Anger*. Columbus, OH, 1988.

Minow-Pinkney, M. *Virginia Woolf and the Problem of the Subject*. Brighton, 1987.

Modleski, T. 'Some Functions of Feminist Criticism, or The Scandal of the Mute Body', *October*, 49, Summer 1989.

Moi, T. *Sexual/Textual Politics*. London, 1985.

Pound, E. *Literary Essays of Ezra Pound*, ed. T.S. Eliot. London, 1954.

Showalter, E. *A Literature of Their Own*. Princeton, NJ, 1977.

Smith, S. Bennett. 'Gender and the Canon', in *Virginia Woolf: Themes and Variations*, eds V. Nevarow-Turk and M. Hussey. New York, 1993.

Woolf, V. 'Memories of a Working Women's Guild', in *Life As We Have Known It*, by Co-Operative Working Women, ed. M. Llewelyn Davies. London, 1931.

—. *The Death of the Moth and Other Essays*. London, 1942.

—. *The Diary of Virginia Woolf*, 5 vols, eds A. Olivier Bell and A. McNeillie. London, 1977–84.

—. *Moments of Being*, ed. J. Schulkind. London, 1985.

—. *The Essays of Virginia Woolf*, 4 vols. ed. A. McNeillie. London, 1986–92.

—. *The Complete Shorter Fiction of Virginia Woolf*, ed. S. Dick. London, 1989.

—. *A Room of One's Own & Three Guineas*, ed. M. Shiach. Oxford, 1992a.

—. *A Woman's Essays*, ed. R. Bowlby. Harmondsworth, 1992b.

7. T. S. Eliot (1888–1965)

From the 1920s until his death T. S. Eliot had a massive influence on literature and literary criticism in the English-speaking world. Though Eliot's modernist contemporaries – such as Ezra Pound, Wyndham Lewis, Virginia Woolf, D. H. Lawrence – also wrote criticism, they were not taken seriously as critics in the way that Eliot was. Eliot's criticism was seen as being almost equal in importance to his poetry whereas the criticism of Pound and the others was seen as very much secondary to their creative output. Eliot was also the most respected of Modernist writers – with the possible exception of Joyce, who had no aspiration to be a critic – and this gave his criticism a special status. Modernist writing had created a crisis for traditional forms of criticism since it seemed to demand a new critical approach that would be appropriate to the literary innovations ushered in by modernism. The fact that Eliot was both a high priest of modernism and a critic who seemed to take his criticism as seriously as his poetry gave him authority as a critic unmatched in the twentieth century. Over the past thirty years or so a reaction has set in and Eliot has been attacked on a number of fronts: for example, a marxist critic such as Terry Eagleton describes his criticism as a response to a 'world imperialist crisis' which led him 'to adopt the aesthetics of a late phase of Romanticism (symbolism), with its view of the individual artefact as organic, impersonal and autonomous, and then project this doctrine into an authoritarian cultural ideology' (1976, 147); it has also been suggested that his criticism as well as his poetry is contaminated by anti-Semitism (Julius 1995), and that it devalues 'minor' cultures by denying them any possibility of producing significant literature since '[n]o writer can achieve real significance, "maturity", unless he has the weight of a developed tradition on which to draw' (Craig 1996, 14). But despite such attacks, just as it is impossible to discuss twentieth-century poetry without taking account of Eliot's work, likewise the foundational force of his criticism cannot be denied even by those who may be in basic disagreement with its premises.

Though Eliot was a major innovator in literary form, in some respects his criticism is old fashioned. If one compares it with the writings of the Russian formalists or with the work of I. A. Richards or William Empson it seems to belong to a previous tradition: that of the critical essayist. He does not explore fundamental concepts in the manner of Richards, nor was he a close reader in the manner of Empson or the New Critics. Indeed, Eliot rejected the idea that there could be critical laws or even a critical method: 'there is no method except to be very intelligent' (1960, 11). However, though Eliot was not a theorist in the orthodox sense, significant theoretical assumptions and implications clearly emerge from his criticism.

Eliot's most important and influential critical study is his collection of essays, *The Sacred Wood*, first published in 1920, and the most highly regarded essay in the collection was 'Tradition and the Individual Talent' which has been reprinted in virtually every anthology of twentieth-century criticism. A major reason for Eliot's authority as a critic was that unlike major literary innovators of the past who tended to see themselves as rebels in both social and artistic terms, Eliot was a strong defender of conservative values. He had no interest in striking bohemian attitudes *pour épater le bourgeois* in the manner of such poetic predecessors as Shelley or Baudelaire or Rimbaud, and even more important: though associated with literary innovation in his poetry, in his criticism he defended tradition and regarded himself as a traditionalist. 'Tradition and the Individual Talent' is a crucial essay because it confronts this paradox and explains how Eliot can be both a practitioner of and advocate for the new while apparently being faithful to what has gone before.

T. E. Hulme in *Speculations* (1924) saw classicism and romanticism as being in fundamental conflict and Eliot's allegiance in this conflict, like Hulme's, was to classicism. Eliot's detestation of romantic subjectivism and individualism is clear all through his criticism. Instead of art being a matter of individual self-expression on the part of the artist, he claims in 'Tradition and the Individual Talent' that 'The progress of an artist is a continual self-sacrifice, a continual extinction of personality' (1960, 53). He goes on to declare that 'The emotion of art is impersonal', with the poet achieving such impersonality by 'surrendering himself wholly to the work to be done' (1960, 59). Moreover, he argues 'that not only the best, but the most individual parts of [the poet's] work may be those in which the dead poets, his ancestors, assert their immortality most vigorously', and he goes on to say that 'No poet, no artist of any art, has his complete meaning alone' (1960, 48, 49). Tradition is a force in poetry precisely because it is not inert, something passively inherited; the poet must 'obtain it by great labour' (1960, 49). The poet must acquire a historical sense so that he writes not only for readers in the present 'but with a feeling that the whole of the literature of Europe from Homer and within it the whole of the literature of his own country has a simultaneous existence and composes a simultaneous order' (1960, 49). What follows from this is the paradox that the present is as much an influence on the past as the reverse: 'what happens when a new work of art is created is something that happens simultaneously to all the works of art which preceded it. The existing monuments form an ideal order among themselves, which is modified by the introduction of the new (the really new) work of art among them' (1960, 49–50). A radical theory of intertextuality, therefore, underlies Eliot's discussion of tradition.

Eliot's concept of tradition had consequences for both literary practice and critical judgement. To make a significant literary contribution it was not enough merely to be an innovator: innovation should not ignore tradition but must seek out a relationship with it. Thus for Eliot a poet such as Blake could not be a major figure as his work was too individual. In an essay on Blake in *The Sacred Wood* he writes: 'His philosophy, like his visions, like his insight, like his technique, was his own' (1960, 155). The consequence was that Blake was 'eccentric' and his poetry 'inclined to formlessness'. In contrast, writers such as Dante or Lucretius who did not create original philosophies avoid formlessness: 'Blake did not have that more Mediterranean gift of form which knows how to borrow as Dante borrowed his theory of the soul; he must needs create a philosophy as well as a poetry' (1960, 156) This is not merely a problem for Blake but 'frequently affects writers outside of the Latin traditions' (1960, 157). Eliot asserts that 'What [Blake's] genius required, and what it sadly lacked, was a framework of accepted and traditional ideas' (1960, 157–8), and given this situation he was inevitably limited, a kind of do-it-yourself poet whom one might admire in the same way as one might admire someone who creates 'an ingenious piece of home-made furniture' (1960, 156) to which Eliot compares Blake's philosophy.

Blake could be seen as a romantic in the broad sense since he rebelled against tradition in terms both of art and of ideas. However, the modern writer could not merely emulate Dante and identify easily with tradition. The problem for the modern writer was that such a relationship with tradition no longer seemed possible. Here we see Eliot's critical concerns coming together with his concerns as a poet. It has often been pointed out that Eliot's criticism should be seen as part of a strategy to justify his own poetic practice and what is clear from that practice, especially in a poem such as *The Waste Land*, is that the modern writer must connect with tradition in new ways and this means that modern writing must adopt very different forms from those that had been dominant in the past. It seemed clear to modernists like Eliot that western culture had been fragmented by various cultural developments so that traditions based on classicism and Christianity had broken down. There was no obvious way in which such fragmentation could be overcome and some sort of unity restored; rather the modern writer had to try to construct a tradition out of fragmentation. As Eliot famously put it at the end of *The Waste Land*: 'These fragments I have shored against my ruins.' Whereas poets of the past and their readership had shared traditions, this no longer obtained for modern poets. Yet since Eliot believed that great poetry could only be written in relation to tradition, his only option was to forge the tradition necessary for himself as poet. An added incentive for doing this was that Eliot regarded the English poetic tradition as conventionally perceived, one in which Milton was a dominant figure, as an unfortunate development in the history of English poetry. Since Eliot the poet needed a tradition for himself as a modern poet and believed that a poet could achieve major status only within one of the major literary traditions, Eliot the critic set about adapting this tradition to suit his purposes.

As an American, Eliot felt he had not been born into a major poetic tradition but he believed that he and other writers in a similar situation were not necessarily at a disadvantage since it was open to writers to make a commitment to such a tradition, Eliot himself choosing to identify with an English tradition within the wider European tradition. For him, great literature could only emerge from such a tradition. In a discussion of Scottish literature, questioning whether Scottish writing could ever have major literary status, he wrote: '... when we assume that a literature exists we assume a great deal: we suppose that there is one of the five or six (at most) great organic formations of history' (Craig 1996, 14). And in *Notes towards the Definition of Culture* he claimed that 'the benefits which Scottish, Welsh and Irish writers have conferred upon English literature are far in excess of what the contribution of all these individual men of genius would have been had they, let us say, all been adopted in early infancy by English foster-parents' (Craig 1996, 15–16). In other words, writers from 'minority' cultures have to identify with the literary tradition of a major culture if they are to have any chance of achieving significant literary status, but once such identification has taken place, as with Eliot himself, the writer who comes from outside the culture may have much greater influence than native-born writers. There is reciprocity: the outsider is absorbed but in compensation may bring new life to an existing major tradition. The influence of Eliot's ideas about tradition are apparent in the work of F. R. Leavis who in *The Great Tradition* included the American Henry James and the Pole Joseph Conrad along with George Eliot in his triumvirate of the greatest of English novelists, James and Conrad in Leavis's view having chosen to situate their fiction within the tradition of the English novel.

One of the most significant elements of Eliot's critical project arising out of his belief both in tradition and in the need continually to renew it is canon formation. At the time he began writing Milton and the major romantics were seen as central to the tradition of English poetry, whereas writers he admired more and who were more useful to him as a poet were seen as marginal: the Metaphysical poets and Elizabethan and Jacobean dramatists. Tradition must therefore be reconstructed (or perhaps deconstructed) to marginalize Milton and Shelley and place Donne and Webster closer to the centre as well as being widened to take account of European literature. Even Shakespeare's status could be questioned in this reconstruction of tradition. In *The Sacred Wood*, Eliot questions whether the play generally regarded as Shakespeare's greatest, *Hamlet* – and perhaps significantly the play most revered by the romantics – could be regarded as artistically successful: 'So far from being Shakespeare's masterpiece, the play is most certainly an artistic failure' (1960, 98).

It is in 'Hamlet and his Problems' that Eliot introduces a critical concept that was to be extremely influential: the 'objective correlative'. Eliot's critique of *Hamlet* is indirectly an attack on the romantic approach to writing. The elevation of *Hamlet*, Eliot claims, is the result of critics who were also artists, such as Goethe and Coleridge, 'find[ing] in Hamlet a vicarious existence for their own artistic realization' (1960, 95). For Eliot this is artistic heresy since the critic's 'first business was to study a work of art' and to resist such subjective indulgence as identifying with characters. The problem with *Hamlet* is that it encourages this kind of subjectivist criticism because of Shakespeare's artistic failure, since '*Hamlet*, like the sonnets, is full of some stuff that the writer could not drag to light, contemplate, or manipulate into art' (1960, 100). This leads Eliot to formulate an alternative to the idea that art arises out of the self-expression of emotion:

> The only way of expressing emotion in the form of art is by finding an 'objective correlative'; in other words, a set of objects, a situation, a chain of events which shall be the formula of that *particular* emotion; such that when the external facts, which must terminate in sensory experience, are given, the emotion is immediately evoked. (1960, 100)

It is clear that this can be equated with Eliot's impersonal view of art: there is no need to discuss the artist or the artist's state of mind since the work itself, if it is successfully realized, embodies emotion dramatically, and such emotion does not necessarily need to have been experienced directly by the artist. It is also clear that the concept of the 'objective correlative' reflects the idea that the image was seen as overwhelmingly the dominant element in modernist writing. In such writing interpretation was also superfluous because one could not adequately paraphrase an image. As Eliot writes earlier in 'Hamlet and his Problems': '*Qua* work of art, the work of art cannot be interpreted; there is nothing to interpret; we can only criticize it according to standards, in comparison to other works of art' (1960, 96).

By implication, therefore, the problem for the modern artist was how to achieve form given the emphasis on the image and the loss of a coherent sense of tradition that existed for earlier poets such as Dante. One of the reasons why Eliot admired Joyce's *Ulysses* was that he saw it as offering a solution to the problem of form for the modern artist living in a contemporary reality that seemed fragmentary or chaotic. Joyce's use of myth Eliot asserts – in '*Ulysses*, Order and Myth' (1923) – 'is simply a way of controlling, ordering, of giving a shape and a significance to the immense panorama of futility and anarchy which is contemporary history' (Eliot 1997, 22). Eliot believes this 'mythical method' has general application to modern writing and can provide the superstructure, as it were, within which modern writing can establish a relation to tradition. But since the writer has to reformulate tradition rather than sharing one with the reader, tradition can enter modern writing only in a fragmentary and allusive way. It has also to be accommodated to the dominance of the image which has a further fragmentary effect. The inevitable consequence of this is a form of writing that may seem wilfully obscure. Whereas writers in the past in alluding to tradition in the form of allusions or citations from classical or Biblical texts would assume that their ideal reader would share this knowledge, modern writers could assume no such ideal reader. They wrote in the knowledge that their works might appear to be wilfully obscure not only because tradition could only exist within works in a fragmentary form but also because many works that a writer such as Eliot regarded as central to his sense of tradition, such as plays by minor – at least by conventional literary standards – Jacobean dramatists, would not have been familiar to even a well-educated readership.

Eliot's belief that conventional notions of poetic tradition needed to be undermined and that modern writing needed to relate itself to what he regarded as a more authentic tradition was based on one of his most influential critical ideas: his claim that feeling and intellect had become split off from each other because of a 'dissociation of sensibility' that took place in the middle of the seventeenth century. This idea was first put forward in Eliot's essay on the Metaphysical poets, published in 1921. He refers to the presence in Chapman of 'a direct sensuous apprehension of thought, or a recreation of thought into feeling, which is exactly what we find in Donne' (1951, 286). In contrast nineteenth-century poets such as Tennyson and Browning 'do not feel their thought as immediately as the odour of a rose' (1951, 287). They are the victims of a dissociation of sensibility, one from which, Eliot claimed, 'we have never recovered', and which 'was aggravated by the influence of the most powerful poets of the [seventeenth] century, Milton and Dryden' (Eliot 1951, 288). In later writings Eliot modified his position somewhat, absolving Milton and Dryden from responsibility and seeing it as a consequence of the English Civil War and even having wider European origins.

The historical basis of Eliot's claim has been attacked, notably by Frank Kermode in *Romantic Image*, first published in 1957. For Kermode, 'The theory of the dissociation of sensibility is, in fact, the most successful version of a Symbolist attempt to explain why the modern world resists works of art that testify to the poet's special, anti-intellectual way of knowing truth' (1966, 143). However, the idea not only allowed Eliot to discard writers who embodied a tradition that was antagonistic to his own poetic purposes – such as Milton, romantic and Victorian poetry – but to justify this in critical terms and thus deflect the claim that his preferences merely reflected his own poetic prejudices. Attacks on the 'dissociation of sensibility' on the grounds that it lacks historical objectivity are perhaps beside the point despite Eliot's attempts to argue that it did have a historical basis. It should perhaps be seen as similar to such concepts as Freud's 'Oedipus complex' or Lacan's 'mirror phase' which are beyond confirmation in empirical terms. The value of such concepts lies in their explanatory power, and the influence of Eliot's notion of a 'dissociation of sensibility' over several decades indicates that for many people it did have an exceptional explanatory power. Of course, the culture has moved on since and arguably the idea of a 'dissociation of sensibility' may now have outlived its usefulness, but it is undeniable that the concept has played a major role in twentieth-century culture.

Eliot's key critical concepts: tradition, artistic impersonality, the objective correlative, the dissociation of sensibility have had a crucial effect on twentieth-century criticism. The work of the critics and theorists who came after him: I. A. Richards and especially F. R. Leavis and the American New Critics, were fundamentally affected by these concepts. For a while the literary status of Milton and romantics such as Shelley was seriously undermined; Donne ascended the poetic hierarchy almost to the level of Shakespeare; the fusion of feeling and thought through images that could not be paraphrased became a criterion of literary value, together with its corollary that literature was a force in itself separate from history or philosophy. Even when advocates of a different critical philosophy emerged, such as Northrop Frye and Harold Bloom, one can feel the power of Eliot's thought in the background as something to be resisted. His influence has only been seriously weakened by the emergence of forms of literary criticism that have been shaped by critical and cultural theories influenced to a considerable extent by continental philosophy. Many critical questions that were not addressed for several decades during the ascendancy of Eliot and Eliot-influenced criticism have now come back onto the agenda.

Perhaps one of the most crucial of these questions is whether art and literature can be separated from the political. One of Eliot's fundamental assumptions is that the poem is a work of art and is autotelic, that is it has no purpose or end beyond itself. In the introduction to the 1928 edition of The Sacred Wood Eliot declared that 'the problem appearing in these essays, which gives them what coherence they have, is the problem of the integrity of poetry, with the repeated assertion that when we are considering poetry we must consider it primarily as poetry and not another thing' (1960, viii). He dismisses the definitions of great predecessors such as Wordsworth or Arnold, denying that poetry is 'emotion recollected in tranquillity' or a 'criticism of life', nor can it be reduced to morals, politics, religion or to 'a collection of psychological data about the minds of poets, or about the history of an epoch' (1960, ix). His conclusion is 'that a poem, in some sense, has its own life ... that the feeling, or emotion, or vision, resulting from the poem is something different from the feeling or emotion or vision in the mind of the poet' (1960, x).

The issues raised here are perhaps highlighted most powerfully in relation to Eliot's own poetry. The extent to which Eliot succeeded in dominating critical thinking up until the 1960s is indicated by the fact that certain aspects of his own poetry were hardly ever mentioned or discussed, notably the apparent anti-Semitism of certain of the earlier poems. A subject such as anti-Semitism in its twentieth-century context does powerfully raise the question as to whether Eliot's view that poetry can be discussed legitimately only as poetry and not in terms of other discourses is sustainable. If one adopts Eliot's critical philosophy there seems no way of confronting directly anti-Semitism in his poetry yet these poems are clearly embroiled in the cultural matrix that created the conditions for mass murder. During the ascendancy of Eliot and those critics influenced by him this kind of problem was ignored because Eliot had created a critical discourse that defined literature in very narrow terms and endeavoured to preserve literature from any contamination by non-literary considerations. To discuss questions of meaning was anti-literary as the literary text was a special form of discourse: in Archibald MacLeish's celebrated formulation: 'A poem must not mean / But be.' Though this view now seems highly questionable what one should put in its place still remains problematic as going to the opposite extreme and judging poetry by its content seems equally unsatisfactory. Does 'great poetry' somehow transform anti-Semitism and if so in what way, or should poetic value be simply denied to any poetry embodying such an ideology, or does the issue need to be discussed in quite different terms? These are questions that still need to be debated and perhaps the emergence recently of a theoretically sophisticated 'ethical criticism' which has redirected critical attention to the responsibility of both author and reader in the production of meaning in literary texts indicates an awareness that these sorts of questions need to be discussed.

Other related developments in contemporary criticism that have undermined Eliot's critical philosophy are the claims by feminist and gay critics that gender and sexual orientation cannot be excluded in any discussion of a literary text, and as a result of their work the textualism and anti-intentionalism of the Eliot-influenced New Critics have been seriously undermined. Although textualism still remains powerful in contemporary criticism in the work of deconstructive critics, it takes its cue not so much from Eliot as from a theorist like Derrida who comes from a quite different tradition. Also Eliot's claim that significant writers must belong to a major literary tradition can be questioned on the grounds that many of the most significant writers of the twentieth century were born outside the dominant culture and resisted identification with it, writers such as Yeats, Joyce, Beckett, MacDiarmid, Rilke, Kafka. It has been argued that, contrary to Eliot's cultural philosophy, 'peripheries' have refused to accept the dominance of the 'cultural core' as this unequal relationship between centre and margins is founded on 'a system of cultural exchange designed to enhance the core and impoverish the periphery and thereby to maintain the power relations between them' (Craig 1996, 29), and that in this changed cultural context Eliot's identification of tradition with the dominant culture has lost its force.

K. M. Newton

Further reading and works cited

Austin, A. T. S. Eliot: The Literary and Social Criticism. London, 1974.
Baldick, C. Criticism and Literary Theory from 1890 to the Present. Oxford, 1996.
Craig, C. Out of History. London, 1996.
Eagleton, T. Criticism and Ideology. London, 1976.
Eliot, T. S. The Use of Poetry and the Use of Criticism. London, 1933.
—. After Strange Gods. London, 1934.
—. Selected Essays. London, 1951.
—. The Sacred Wood. London, 1960.

—. To Criticize the Critic and Other Writings. London, 1965.

—. 'Ulysses, Order and Myth', in James Joyce: Ulysses; A Portrait of the Artist as a Young Man, ed. J. Coyle. Basingstoke, 1997.

Gray, P. T. S. Eliot's Intellectual and Poetic Development, 1909–1922. London, 1982.

Jay, G. S. T. S. Eliot and the Poetics of Literary History. Oxford, 1983.

Julius, A. T. S. Eliot: Anti-Semitism and Literary Form. Oxford, 1995.

Kermode, F. Romantic Image. [1957]. Oxford, 1966.

Leavis, F. R. Anna Karenina and Other Essays. Harmondsworth, 1967.

Lee, B. Theory and Personality. Cambridge, 1979.

Lobb, E. T. S. Eliot and the Romantic Literary Tradition. London, 1981.

Newton-de Molina, D. (ed.) The Literary Criticism of T. S. Eliot. London, 1977.

Ricks, C. T. S. Eliot and Prejudice. London, 1988.

Shusterman, R. T. S. Eliot and the Philosophy of Criticism. Oxford, 1988.

Wellek, R. A History of Modern Criticism. New York, 1986.

8. After the 'Cambridge School': F. R. Leavis (1895–1978), *Scrutiny* (1932–1952) and Literary Studies in Britain

Whether there is or was a recognizable 'Cambridge School' of English literature criticism is debatable, because the justification for recognizing such a thing would probably necessitate accepting the centrality to Cambridge of F. R. Leavis, who while fervent in support of an 'English school' at the centre of the ideal university, throughout his life polarized opinion in Cambridge, making more enemies than friends, and who now has few people speaking from something like his standpoint either in Cambridge or other universities. From the time of his first publications in 1930 and the founding of the quarterly journal *Scrutiny*, Leavis, with his students, friends and, above all, with his wife, Queenie Dorothy Leavis (who wrote powerful novel-criticism, some of which has attracted some feminist attention), in writing for *Scrutiny*, set a course for the study of English literature in the twentieth century. This was given some official backing when he took up a full-time position at Downing College, Cambridge, in 1936. Leavis retired from Cambridge in 1962, and he never held a Professorship there, though he was to go and take a Chair at York for the rest of the 1960s.

Leavis's impact worked in schools (English public schools and grammar schools: it is arguable that the timbre of his work could not work in comprehensive schools), in syllabuses and in educational theory which placed 'English' and English literature at the centre of the curriculum. It was disseminated through the employment of his ex-students in universities throughout the UK and Commonwealth countries in the 1950s and 1960s, and through such popularizations of his work as Boris Ford's edited *Penguin Guide to English Literature* (1953–62), written, mostly, by Leavis's ex-pupils. The most important influence was the writing: the books of Leavis himself, Q. D. Leavis, and such other *Scrutiny* associates as Marius Bewley, D. J. Enright, D. W. Harding, L. C. Knights, Wilfrid Mellers, H. A. Mason, John Speirs, Denys Thompson, E. W. F. Tomlin, Derek Traversi, Martin Turnell, and then by others who were too young to have contributed to *Scrutiny*, such as David Holbrook and Ian Robinson. Such books, many using *Scrutiny*-derived material, have become formative of an approach which is perhaps lamely called 'Cambridge English', as have many others on literature published by Cambridge University Press in the 1960s and 1970s, which at that stage had a pro-Leavis editor in Michael Black. Two journals at least have derived from Leavis: *Essays in Criticism*, which was begun by F. W. Bateson at Oxford in 1951 in response to *Scrutiny*, and the *Cambridge Quarterly*, begun by Leavis's ex-pupils in 1966, is similarly still recognizable in character: local judgements may be different, but the emphasis continues. The journal *New Universities Quarterly* also showed much influence from Leavis. On the Left, the work of Richard Hoggart, Raymond Williams and Terry Eagleton shows further derivations, while also remaining independent. In America, Leavis's influence has been in significant relation to 'New Criticism', and been found in such journals as *The Kenyon Review* and *The Sewanee Review*.

Influences on Leavis came from the criticism of Matthew Arnold, Henry James, T. S. Eliot and D. H. Lawrence; from Edgell Rickword and his journal *The Calendar of Modern Letters* (1925–7), from John Middleton Murray, whose *The Problem of Style* (1921) showed some Oxford competition to Cambridge, from G. Wilson Knight on Shakespeare, for an approach that was anti-A. C. Bradley, and in an immediate and important sense from I. A. Richards, with whom all his work might be seen to be in dialogue. Leavis took 'practical criticism' from him and focused on the texts he studied an intense concentration. In the belief that great writers responded to the English language as to something which created them and which survived in ordinary speech acts, and in pre-capitalist popular culture, he argued that great writing responds to speech and in it 'we read as we read the living' (1936, 18). The demonstrable features of writing that follows the creativity of the language can be pointed to in a poem or novel, or play (Leavis referred to Shakespeare's plays, and to novels, as 'dramatic poems') in a form where the critic says 'This is so, isn't it?' and gets the response 'Yes, but ...' – thus making criticism collaborative, and – based on T. S. Eliot's 'the common pursuit of true judgment' (1953, 18) – directed towards greater sensitivity, creativity and closer response to the 'life' of the poem. Leavis argued that great writers showed a sensitivity and reverence for 'life' as this surfaced within language, and their 'impersonality' demonstrated itself as they set aside their own impositions of order or rationality in favour of the life welling up in the text. Creative writing was heuristic, driven by a 'nisus' or need, and with an intuitive *ahnung* prompting it (1975, 62–3). Thus great writing had a moral import, but it would not be possible to specify the morality, nor would the writer's local allegiances (e.g. to Christianity, or to marxism) be relevant in the face of such 'impersonality' (a word taken from Eliot's 'Tradition and the Individual Talent' (1953, 21–30) but given a much stronger reading by Leavis). The enemies throughout were triviality, grossness of response and dullness, or Milton's artificiality adopted towards the language (and Leavis continued the Cambridge distancing from the classics, from histories of the language, and from Anglo-Saxon in the English curriculum).

Such readings of literary texts, religious in their intensity – Leavis frequently quoted the line from *The Rainbow* 'he knew he did not belong to himself' (1970, 270) to indicate his commitment to an individual's connectedness – though without conforming to any religion, imposed as strong inclusions as exclusions. Leavis wrote enthusiastically, and path-breakingly, on Shakespeare, Donne, Wordsworth, Blake, Hopkins, Eliot and Pound's

Hugh Selwyn Mauberley, and among novelists, on Austen, Dickens, George Eliot, James, Conrad and D. H. Lawrence, the last of whom continued to assume greater and greater importance for him. The 'essence' of Leavis's positions may be found in his essay on *Hard Times* (1948). In this essay, which specifically alludes to John Stuart Mill and which refers to his utilitarian background as crippling, Leavis attacks Benthamism, and so, implicitly, Richards, and Richards's desire to restate the romantic stress on the imagination and creativity in terms of Bentham. The heart of Leavis's position will also be found in his essay on *Macbeth* in 'Tragedy and the Medium' (1952), in the essay on *Women in Love* (1955) and in the essay on Wordsworth (1936). Examples of his close readings will be found in Leavis (1943, 1975). Negatively, Leavis rejected Milton, Sterne and Joyce (*Finnegans Wake* especially), for their playing with the language, treating it as a thing in itself, Shelley for his displays of emotion that were never criticized or distanced (likewise Swinburne and much other Victorian verse), Fielding, Thackeray and Trollope for their lack of 'serious-ness' and the Bloomsbury group likewise (so that Virginia Woolf never received recogni-tion), and the Pound of the *Cantos*. None of these rejections was innocent: all implied a hostility to the social attitudes these writers represented. A position assumed with regard to language presumed a position with regard to life.

René Wellek (see Leavis 1952, 211–22; Mulhern 1979, 163–6) addressed Leavis's readings of English poetry with the demand that he state his assumptions explicitly. Leavis's response formulated a distinction between philosophic statement and poetry which decidedly gave the edge to poetry; the point returns in a discussion of Quentin Anderson's work on the Swedenborgian influences on Henry James, where Leavis contends that 'extraneous knowledge about the writer's intentions' cannot replace 'the tests of realization' (i.e. making real – a crucial term for Leavis). The tests are 'a matter of his sense . . . of what the living thing looks like – of the difference between that which has been willed and put there, or represents no profound integration, and that which grows from a deep centre of life . . . the deep animating intention [may be] something very different from the intention the author would declare' (1952, 225). A marxist critique, such as Eagleton's, would see Leavis's refusal to see that his 'petty bourgeois non-conformist humanism' (1976, 13) was passing itself off as a source of potentially universal judgement as to what is 'the real', and refusing to notice its partiality and relativity. The implied reference to the unity of the work in the word 'integration' is non-Freudian, non-Machereyan, and distinct from deconstruc-tion, since it has no sense of texts being marked by absences, or by the symptoms of something else not present: Leavis insists on significance (rather than meaning – a word he regards as reductive) being present in the text, even if, as in D. H. Lawrence's phrase, 'Never trust the artist. Trust the tale' (1956, 297) he does not regard intention as a final decider, and so admits the complexity of the text, its disagreement with its own stated positions. Nonetheless the sense of the importance of the word 'presence' – see his essay on Wordsworth (Leavis 1936) – makes for a comparison with Paul de Man on Wordsworth (1984). It indicates why marxist, rather than deconstructive, criticism has engaged with Leavis's positions – on account of the commitment to the text making a difference, existing in a world where 'meanings still exist' (Eliot 1953, 57). Yet Leavis's 'real' is outside ideology, it is neither engendered by Lukács's 'realism', nor hospitable to the idea that all language uses may be constructed, artificial, so that no language use can be closer to the real (see MacCabe 1978). Attacks on Leavis on these lines in the 1970s and 1980s became frequent and have necessitated the question of how he may be reread after them: a task not yet addressed.

Marxist readings of Leavis have had also to face Leavis's analyses of social history. Here, reinforced by Q. D. Leavis's PhD thesis, published as *Fiction and the Reading Public* (1932), *Scrutiny* increasingly, and Leavis especially in his later writings (1969, 1970, 1972, 1975, 1976), presented a social history of cultural decline owing something to Eliot's theory of a 'dissociation of sensibility' setting in in the seventeenth century (1953, 117) and entailing the current triumph of 'technologico-Benthamitism' (Leavis 1969, 109). Inflected by the marxism of R. H. Tawney's *Religion and the Rise of Capitalism* (1926), which influenced one of the most considerable ventures into literature and sociology and social history, L. C. Knights' *Drama and Society in the Age of Jonson* (1937), Leavis tried the same with the nineteenth century, and the results were simplistic. He read the modern in terms of loss of *Gemeinschaft* (the 'organic society') and replacement by a substitute culture formed by mass-circulation newspapers, market-driven popular fiction and loss of contact with the past. Though he could have received support from Adorno on the 'culture industry', the argument ignored any marxist analysis, conveying rather an impression of hostility to industrialism (as opposed to capitalism) and to the modern. Unnuanced as far as its response to present-day popular culture was concerned (in that it hardly listened to that culture), it gave the impression that the writers Leavis praised were elitist and that education meant the education of elites. By linking arguments about literary texts to a banal sociology, conducted in the face of sociologists, Leavis became in the 1970s and 1980s a prisoner of the Right (e.g. Roger Scruton in *The Salisbury Review*) and an apparent reactionary in speaking for a 'great tradition' which must be taught, or civilization would be lost.

Critical theory of the late 1970s onwards, then, has been explicitly or implicitly anti-Leavis, from varying degrees of awareness of his work. While Leavis was of the wrong generation to respond to Barthes, Foucault or Derrida, post-Leavis writers have avoided such a confrontation, taking refuge in the general lack of responsiveness in Britain to new theory, and thereby becoming the more reactionary. The implicit drive in Leavis's work towards an assertion of the power of English could not survive Britain's multi-racialism, any more than Lawrence's reputation (and hence Leavis's) could quite survive undented the feminism of Kate Millett's *Sexual Politics*. There is no need to align Leavis with con-servatism, even though the tradition within which he worked and helped produce has remained bourgeois, humanist, Arnoldian in its appeal to 'culture' as 'the best that is thought and known in the world' (Leavis 1943, 141). It could not be simply that, as his enthusiasm for Dickens's inwardness with his own popular culture indicated to him. Nonetheless, in his own time, Leavis, for all his astonishing inwardness with regard to poetry, was also guilty of parochialism with regard to Cambridge, whose importance he inflated (the importance of teaching there) as much as it has inflated its own. If he had accepted a career outside Cambridge, he might have done something to lessen that university's grip in terms of alliance of class and culture. In accepting Cambridge, he silently underwrote its exclusiveness. While cultivated in other literatures himself, he gave the impression of seeing English literature as unique, which not only implied a cultural imperialism and developing anti-Americanism – so much that he would not even recognize the work of Lionel Trilling and Edmund Wilson with regard to Dickens (Leavis 1970) – but also an anti-marginality (see his contempt for Wilde and put-down of Proust, 1948). It produced cut-off points in his own thinking, which disappointing in him were death-dealing in some of his followers, and productive of a reaction against him. He never said much which implied attention to Freud – and so to the unconscious of the text, in a suspicion that such attention would prove reductive or predictable; nonetheless, such a refusal weakened his sense of how the text might differ from the intention behind it. Despite the evident possibility of a dialogue, and the point that there has been a whole left-Leavisism engendered by his approach, he had little to say on Marx, beyond giving a sense that the marxist stress on the economic entailed a reduction of attention to the values of the 'human world' (Leavis 1972, 61). He had even less to say on Nietzsche. *Scrutiny* never attended to European modernism (Flaubert, Kafka, Beckett, Mann). Leavis's insistence on thought being embodied in creative uses of the language might have led him to Heidegger (see Bell 1988), but instead impelled him towards the comparatively minor: Michael Polanyi, Marjorie Grene, A. N. Whitehead and R. G. Collingwood, from whom he took his philosophy. While he knew Wittgenstein, Leavis's 'anti-philosopher' stance meant that he never became a challenge to his thought. The social historians and economists he relied on in his later books tended to be narrowly anti-modern and of the Right, while the targets he selected for attack – for instance C. P. Snow, in Leavis's famous lecture of 1962 rejecting the idea that there were 'two cultures's, scientific and literary, contending only for one, that based on literature (Leavis 1972) – again now hardly make a ripple intellectually.

In the 'two cultures' debate may also be seen something of Leavis's ongoing critique of Richards, never fully articulated (see Leavis 1952, 134–5; 1975, 31). Richards's bracketing off of meaning from poetry's 'pseudo-statements', like Empson's continual finding of ambiguities, Leavis finds a form of trivialization of poetry's claims to relevance and to its discovery of 'the real'. This informs Leavis's anti-philosopher stand, and makes what he finds in 'practical criticism' different from Richards. It is here that Leavis is most vulnerable, and also, perhaps, most sensitive and interesting, in his demand that the text should become a form of cognition, and English 'a discipline of thought'. That said, the greatest criticism of Leavis would not be that his work needs rereading under the impact of critical theory, as do the writers he spoke for, because in a sense that work is clearly antagonistic to what it would see as the reductiveness implied in the very premises of such theory before the theory has begun its work. The critique would be that he fought a battle he could win too easily against English intellectual mediocrity and Cambridge parochialism, and never perceived that there were more interesting challenges to his own position. While the debates about culture that he in the twentieth century did much to initiate in Britain, and that have generated British cultural studies, have gone beyond his concern with the literary and poetic uses of language, his work there, while remaining definitive in some instances, is also end-stopped. The criticism, in its self-justifications and rebukes, comes across often as paranoid and self-protective, so that the critic's call to openness to 'life' shows also the traces of being closed-off and filled with the impulse to dominate, which itself asks to be read psychoanalytically.

Jeremy Tambling

Further reading and works cited

Anderson, P. 'Components of the National Culture', *New Left Review*, 50, May–June 1968.
Bell, M. *F. R. Leavis*. London, 1988.
de Man, P. *The Rhetoric of Romanticism*. New York, 1984.
Eagleton, T. *Criticism and Ideology*. London, 1976.
—. *The Function of Criticism From The Spectator to Post-Structuralism*. London, 1984.

Eliot, T. S. *Selected Prose*, ed. John Hayward. Harmondsworth, 1953.
Lawrence, D. H. *Selected Literary Criticism*, ed. A. Beal. London, 1956.
Leavis, F. R. *New Bearings in English Poetry*. London, 1932.
—. *Revaluation*. London, 1936.
—. *Education and the University*. London, 1943.
—. *The Great Tradition*. London, 1948.
—. *The Common Pursuit*. London, 1952.
—. *D. H. Lawrence*. London, 1955.
—. *Anna Karenina and Other Essays*. London, 1966.
— (ed.) *A Selection From 'Scrutiny'*. Cambridge, 1968.
—. *English Literature in Our Time and the University*. London, 1969.
— with Leavis, Q. D. *Dickens the Novelist*. London, 1970.
—. *Nor Shall My Sword*. London, 1972.
—. *The Living Principle*. London, 1975.
—. *Thought, Words and Creativity*. London, 1976.
—. *Collected Essays*, ed. G. Singh. Cambridge, 1983–89.
— with Leavis, Q. D. *Lectures in America*. London, 1969.
Leavis, Q. D. *Fiction and the Reading Public*. London, 1932.
MacCabe, C. *James Joyce and the Revolution of the Word*. London, 1978.
MacKillop, I. *F. R. Leavis*. Harmondsworth, 1995.
Millett, K. *Sexual Politics*. New York, 1970.
Mulhern, F. *The Moment of 'Scrutiny'*. London, 1979.
Nairn, T. 'The English Literary Intelligentsia', in *Bananas*, ed. E. Tennant. London, 1977.
Samson, A. *F. R. Leavis*. London, 1992.
Strickland, G. *Structuralism or Criticism?* Cambridge, 1981.
Thompson, D. (ed.) *The Leavises*. Cambridge, 1984.
Williams, R. *Politics and Letters*. London, 1979.

9. J. L. Austin (1911–1960) and Speech-Act Theory

Austin and the ordinary language philosophy he invented loomed large on the philosophical scene from about 1948 on; Austin was felt to be Oxford's answer to Cambridge's Wittgenstein, and one of the leaders of the movement to deny that a vast number of apparent philosophical problems had a general and coherent meaning. Roughly speaking, Austin belonged to a movement that found its earliest expositions in William James's pragmatism, a movement that included not only the later Wittgenstein but also G. E. Moore and W. V. Quine, and that opposed the high metaphysical idealism not only of Kant and Hegel, but also of Bertrand Russell, A. J. Ayer and the early Wittgenstein. This broad statement needs considerable qualification, since the arguments among the more pragmatist philosophers are as intense as their arguments with their metaphysical opponents (Austin sharply distinguishes himself from pragmatism, but it is notable that he felt he had to do so); and also because the modern metaphysics of Russell and Frege is itself based on the same kind of attentive consideration of sentences or propositions paid by the ordinary language movement Austin led. The apposition of sentence and proposition I have just made is one place to summarize the differences, however. The metaphysicians, as they might be abbreviated, sought to find the propositions named or expressed by sentences (the same proposition would be expressed by 'Snow is white' and 'Der Schnee ist weiss'), whereas Austin, Quine and the later Wittgenstein denied the reality of that abstract entity, the 'proposition' (and therefore as well the reality of that abstract entity, its 'meaning'), and concentrated instead on sentences.

In doing so, they might be said to have identified one of the great projects – and great errors – of the philosophical tradition as that of canonical paraphrase. Ever since Platonic dialectic, philosophical discourse has aimed at a clarified translation of what people say and what people think. Such translation would then have the virtue of making manifest the hidden assumptions, contradictions and begged questions of ordinary thinking, and allow for a perspicuous presentation of justified claims, possible truths and clear falsehoods. Socrates' incessant demand for definition inaugurates this sceptical demand for clarity. Get clear on the claims that people tend to make (as to what piety is, for example, or that I really am sitting at my desk writing) or the questions that they tend to ask (e.g. what is time? am I dreaming? are universals real?) and then you can begin analysing those claims and questions.

This through-line in the history of philosophy might be said to find its culmination in the attempts of Frege and his followers to invent a formalism – codified in the modern logic Frege invented – which would allow for the derivation of all true consequences from true premises. Such a project would naturally affect conceptions of truth and knowledge, and the strengths and limitations of the latter. All philosophical claims worth analysis or debate might then be paraphrased in this canonical notation for readier analysis. Unfortunately logic, at least any logic with the power to analyse general statements, itself runs up against inherent and insoluble structural difficulties, mainly through paradoxes of self-reference that cannot be avoided. The early Wittgenstein attempted to deal with these by regarding all self-reference as nonsense, although necessary nonsense, and in so doing he implicitly opened the way to his later philosophy of language, which no longer sought to purge language of what the logicians regarded as its vagueness, heterogeneity or arbitrariness.

The anti-metaphysicians (including the later Wittgenstein) might all be said to share the idea that canonical paraphrase, far from clarifying, falsifies. Its simplifications are all deceptively plausible but false renderings of the things that it claims to be setting forth. Austin was regarded by legal theorist H. L. A. Hart as having the makings of a great lawyer or judge, especially at common law, and like a lawyer Austin knew that in cross-examination (Socrates' method) skilful paraphrase could make any witness seem to be saying what a cross-examiner wanted him or her to say, and even to agree to. Resisting the force of such paraphrase as more fitted to forensics than to philosophical investigation, Austin bases his method on the idea that human language, as it has evolved down the centuries, is far more supple, fertile of distinction and expressive of subtlety than any artificial substitute:

> Our common stock of words embodies all the distinctions men have found worth drawing, and the connexions they have found worth marking, in the lifetimes of many generations: these surely are likely to be more numerous, more sound, since they have stood up to the long text of the survival of the fittest, and more subtle, at least in all ordinary and reasonably practical matters, than any that you or I are likely to think up in our arm-chairs of an afternoon – the most favoured alternative method. (1979, 182)

The relevance to literature and post-romantic literary theory should become at once evident if this passage is juxtaposed with Wordsworth's account of his own poetic ambition, in the Preface to *Lyrical Ballads*, in which he says that he wishes to write the natural language of natural men. Austin is as radical as Wordsworth in his sense of what we can learn by paying attention to the way people actually use language and what they use it for. To put the point as succinctly as possible, what people tend to use language for is something other than designating true propositions.

Austin shows that the central role of language in human life is what he calls 'performative'. To say something is always to do something. It is to do something within a social situation, in which the hearers of what you say also participate, more or less actively. Followers of Austin take promising as the paradigmatic example of what Austin called 'performative utterances' and sometimes 'speech acts' (a phrase that he seems first to have published in 1953, in 'How to Talk'). When I promise (or bet, or take in marriage, or christen, or congratulate, or bequeath) I am not saying something true or false; I am doing something and *not* describing what I am doing. Not that my act necessarily succeeds: my bet may fail to find a taker; my promise might not be heard; the person I would espouse might already be married, etc. Failures of performative utterance, however, are not failures in point of truth or falsity (I don't *lie* when I make a bet), but in point of achievement; my speech act may turn out to be unhappy in various ways. Two major rubrics group a large number of these ways: it can be void – the act can be purported but misfire, as for example if I christen the wrong ship, one which already has a name; or it can be hollow – the act can be professed but abusive, as when I promise what I do not intend to fulfil. (These are not mutually exclusive categories of infelicity: I may bequeath what I know not to be mine to give, and in that my bequest would be both hollow and void.)

These considerations have philosophical as well as sociological interest. Austin approaches the traditional philosophical questions without accepting the insidious paraphrase that goes into formulating them. A short list of those questions might include: what is knowledge? what is willing? what is the self? what is matter (or what is the world made of)? does the external world exist? do other minds exist? what are possibility, actuality, and necessity? what is truth (or by virtue of what is a proposition true)? All of these questions, for Austin, have something wrong with them, or at least very quickly give rise to misleading ways of thinking and speaking.

Consider some examples of how attention to ordinary language can make a difference here. In 'Other Minds' (1946) Austin considers the claim that there are some things that we can know with certainty and others that we can never claim to *know* at all (as, for example, what another person is feeling), and that there are very grave limitations on the extent of our possible knowledge. Austin considers the variety of contexts and of situations in which we do in fact claim to know something and suggests that in each case, or in most cases, such a claim tends to answer the question or more or less friendly challenge, 'How do you know?'

> Suppose I have said 'There's a bittern at the bottom of the garden', and you ask 'How do you know?' my reply may take very different forms:
>
> (*a*) I was brought up in the fens
> (*b*) I heard it
> (*c*) The keeper reported it
> (*d*) By its booming
> (*e*) From the booming noise
> (*f*) Because it is booming. (1979, 79)

Each reply answers a different possible doubt or inquiry: how do I come to be in a position to know about bitterns? or how do I come to be in a position to say that there's a bittern here and now? or how can I tell bitterns, or how do I tell them? or how can I or do I tell the thing here and now as a bittern? Austin's partial list of 'ordinary' answers to the question does not contemplate the idea that someone might ask me what theory of epistemology allows me to assert ideal knowledge about an empirical fact. For I am talking about bitterns and *not* about empirical facts. We rarely talk about empirical facts: we talk about goldfinches or bitterns or elections or money or restaurants or parents.

This account of how we answer the question 'How do you know?' denies the relevance of the philosophical claim that if I *know* something I can't be wrong. What if it turns out that what I heard was a recording of a bittern, or that the keeper lied to me, or was wrong, or that I had misheard? Would such events shake my theory of knowledge? Not at all: rather I would apologise for or explain my mistake. And this then leads to Austin's most characteristically important claim: when I say that 'I know' I am doing something like making a promise. I am assuring you that you can rely on my statement. My answer to the question 'How do you know?' tells you why you can rely on me. I am giving you my word that I am not merely guessing, or hoping, or betting: that I'm not merely pretty sure, nor even that I am absolutely certain. If I say I'm certain, I am telling you that *I* would act on my belief without hesitation, but I am not actually guaranteeing it. In saying 'I know' I could of course be attempting to mislead, just as I can give a false or hollow promise, and I would be open to the same opprobrium if I did so. What is important is that the use of the verb 'I know' has nothing to do with some theory of unmediated access to truth; it belongs to a social situation and refers to various issues that might arise in the context in which it is said.

In 'A Plea for Excuses' (1956–57) Austin takes on the philosophical chestnuts of selfhood and action by considering the various ways that we *explain* our actions when we feel called upon to explain them. We may apologize for them, or seek to excuse ourselves, or justify them; we may modify our descriptions of them by calling them unintentional, or accidental, or inadvertent, or clumsy, and in each case we are thinking about them differently, or explaining different kinds of actions.

Thus Austin treats explanations of action or assurances of knowledge as performative utterances or speech-acts, and in so doing he dislodges knowledge and action as the central philosophical enigmas and makes them rather counters or props within the speech act, things invoked in response to various human or social situations. Like the later Wittgenstein, Austin's method is to see the solution of philosophical problems consist in the vanishing of the problem. But he nonetheless has positive doctrine to assert as well: the doctrine of speech-acts and how they function, put forth most strenuously in *How to Do Things with Words*, the William James lectures given at Harvard in 1955, and published posthumously in 1961.

In this little book Austin catalogues a variety of speech acts and the different sorts of effects they might aim at as well as have. The most important single conclusion of the book is that all utterances are in some central way performative, that is all speech is social action, and sentences are not names or pointers to truth or falsity but parts of social interaction (something like what Wittgenstein called language-games). Austin describes himself as being inclined to 'play Old Harry with two fetishes ... viz. (1) the true/false fetish, (2) the value/fact fetish' (1975, 151). These are the fetishes of the metaphysician whose philosophy falsifies by paraphrase that might have analogous truth-value, or designate a synonymous fact, but that misses the point of utterances and their uptake:

It is essential to realize that 'true' and 'false'. like 'free' and 'unfree', do not stand for anything simple at all; but only for a general dimension of being a right or proper thing to say as opposed to a wrong thing, in these circumstances, to this audience, for these purposes and with these intentions. (1975, 145)

How to Do Things with Words inaugurated a project followed up by John Searle to come up with a kind of taxonomy of speech-acts. From a philosophical point of view, the taxonomy is wonderful and illuminating fun, but Austin's goal isn't so much a new grammar as a critique of the older philosophical one. His project is in many ways very close to William Empson's in *The Structure of Complex Words*: critical and not philological, but the criticism relies on great philological sensitivity and dexterity.

Austin has also reminded readers with a continental background of Nietzsche and the ways he derives philosophy from grammatical categories, especially in *The Genealogy of Morals*. Indeed Judith Butler makes the connection explicit in an article on hate speech, 'Burning acts, injurious speech'. She relies on another terminology established by Austin in *How to Do Things with Words*, between the locutionary, illocutionary and perlocutionary aspects of a speech act. These formidable terms are easily sketched: the locutionary aspect is something close to a statement of fact, what the utterance says. The illocutionary aspect names what act the utterer was performing *in* (in- = il-) uttering it. The perlocutionary aspect is one of effect: what the utterer did *by* (per) uttering it. I tell you 'The toast is on fire.' The locutionary aspect states a fact. The illocutionary force is to warn or admonish you to do something about it. The perlocutionary effect is to alarm you (the effect I may aim at) or to exasperate you (which I may not be aiming at).

Unfortunately Butler, like most literary theorists who make use of Austin, tends not to pay attention to his distinctions, nor to his warning that 'Our interest ... is essentially to fasten on the second, illocutionary act and contrast it with the other two. There is a constant tendency in philosophy to elide this in favour of one or other of the other two' (1975, 103). Most literary-theoretical uses of Austin, because they attempt to relate him to a continental or Nietzschean version of the philosophical matrix he is subverting, tend to fall into this elision. Even the best of them – Shoshana Felman – assimilates Austin to Nietzsche and thereby assimilates also the illocutionary to the locutionary or constative: she wants what Austin calls a happy performative to be true in virtue of the fact that it is self-describing. 'I beg you to believe me' would be a successful instance of begging, and therefore a true statement, even as its perlocutionary effect might be an implicit but false promise. But Austin firmly declines to make the happy performative into an instance of, say, analytic or tautologous truth. And he also firmly declines to make the perlocutionary effect the same thing as the utterer's independent action, as Butler would have it. The logic of her argument would allow injury to be an illocutionary aspect of the utterance (as though one could say, 'I hereby injure you') and not its perlocutionary effect (as one may indeed say, 'Your words injured me').

This misreading of Austin probably results from the fact that literary theorists have tended to come to Austin through Derrida's 'Signature Event Context' (1988) which Butler cites approvingly, an essay in which Derrida himself calls Austin's procedure 'nothing less than Nietzschean' (1988, 13). His most telling critique of Austin is that Austin tends to describe literary uses of language as *aetiliolated, non-serious, parasitic* (1975, 104, for example). As Stanley Cavell points out, in the most important critical account of Derrida's essay (in *A Pitch of Philosophy*, 1994), Austin's view of ordinary language effectively excludes such deeply human and characteristic uses of language as writing poetry and telling jokes (104); both of these feature on Wittgenstein's list of language-games in *Philosophical Investigations*, a list Austin took to task in his unscripted 1956 radio talk 'Performative Utterances', where he rebukes 'philosophers' but quotes Wittgenstein for talking 'about the *infinite* uses of language' (1975, 234: cf *Philosophical Investigations*, 1972, part I, section 23: where he says there are '*unzählige*' – 'countless' different kinds of use of what we call 'symbols', 'words', 'sentences'). In general, however, Derrida's critique of Austin is misguided, since he imagines that Austin's theory of performative utterance relies on some relic of the correspondence theory of truth, namely an *adequation* between performance and a conspectual system guiding that performance. But like Wittgenstein, Austin is deeply sceptical of the notion of 'rule-following' as involving correspondence or reference to the rule being followed, and thirty years later it is Derrida who seems to have been caught in a metaphysical trap in 'Signature Event Context'. Derrida there insists on the iterability of the sign as its shimmering foundation, but Austin and Wittgenstein are not interested in the semiotic questions of signification or representation at all, but in what people do.

Nevertheless, Derrida's generally high praise of Austin had the effect of introducing him to a broad range of literary theorists. That praise is not surprising since Austin too tends to have a bracing view of binary opposition; see, for example, his 1947 account of the way binary oppositions distort the phenomena they are meant to clarify:

> One of the most important points to grasp is that these two terms, 'sense-data' and 'material things', live by taking in each other's washing – what is spurious is not one term of the pair, but the antithesis itself. The case of 'universal' and 'particular', or 'individual', is similar in some respects though of course not in all. In philosophy it is often good policy, where one member of a putative pair falls under suspicion, to view the more innocent-seeming party suspiciously as well. (1964, 4; the last two sentences footnote the first)

Austin's policy of inversion leads to his demonstration that the things metaphysicians take as the real puzzle – direct perception, or knowledge, or intention – are actually only terms that would come up to name a contrast that might be relevant to a real situation: seeing your shadow, and so perceiving you, but *not* directly, or hearing a recording and so being wrong when I said that I knew a bittern was there because I heard it booming, or shooting your donkey *un*intentionally, because I was aiming at my own. Direct perception, knowledge, intention: Austin calls it glib to make these into philosophical problems as though they name some central issues about our relation to the world or to being, when in their usage down the generations what they really *do* is act as assurances in some case where there might be a reason to wonder about how something happened.

Paul de Man also helped interest American theorists in Austin, since he used the distinction between performative and constative as a parallel or at least homology to his distinction between grammatical and rhetorical structures of language. Like Derrida, de Man saw that a writer of fiction might suffer some interesting anxiety about whether a fictional sentence were performative or cognitive (as he called it), and if performative in what way. De Man's students (including Felman) extended his interest in Austin, and made one received version of him a kind of staple in deconstructively oriented literary theory in America. But there is some irony in the fact that American readers of Austin have tended to come to him through Derrida and de Man, since Derrida himself was reading Cavell's essay on Austin in 1970. Cavell is the literary theorist who understands Austin best, or who has thought about Austin most clearly and profoundly in a literary context (and thereby in a philosophical context as well). Not the least of Derrida's contributions will have been the fact that he has sent readers back to Austin, and onwards to Cavell.

William Flesch

Further reading and works cited

Austin, J. L. *Sense and Sensibilia*. New York, 1964.
—. *How to Do Things With Words*. Cambridge, MA, 1975.
—. *Philosophical Papers*. Oxford, 1979.
Benveniste, E. *Problems in General Linguistics*. Coral Gables, FL, 1971.
Butler, J. 'Burning Acts, Injurious Speech', in *Performativity and Performance*, eds A. Parker and E. Kosofsky Sedgwick. New York, 1995.
Cavell, S. *Must We Mean What We Say?* Cambridge, 1976.
—. *The Claim of Reason*. Cambridge, MA, 1979.
—. *A Pitch of Philosophy*. Cambridge, MA, 1994.
de Man, P. *Allegories of Reading*. New Haven, CT, 1979.
Derrida, J. *Limited Inc.*, ed. Gerald Graff. Evanston, IL, 1988.
Felman, S. *The Literary Speech Act*. Ithaca, NY, 1983.
Gould, T. 'The Unhappy Performative', in *Performativity and Performance*, eds A. Parker and E. Kosofsky Sedgwick. New York, 1995.
Parker, A. and Sedgwick, E. Kosofsky (eds) *Performativity and Performance*. New York, 1995.
Searle, J. *Speech Acts*. London, 1969.
Wittgenstein, L. *Philosophical Investigations*. Oxford, 1972.

10. Richard Hoggart (1918–), Raymond Williams (1921–1988) and the Emergence of Cultural Studies

The term 'culture' has become virtually ubiquitous in our society. In certain circumstances and on certain occasions it still retains some of its elitist and exclusive connotations, and yet we also talk frequently enough of popular culture, of black or gay cultures – even of business or management cultures – terms which might once have been considered antithetical. All such phenomena might – indeed have – come within the purview of contemporary cultural studies. Yet, in Britain, the emergence of cultural studies as a project or discipline was very much bound up with the work of figures such as Richard Hoggart and Raymond Williams, and therefore with a fairly specific history and debate which requires us to understand the significance of the term 'culture' as it circulated during the nineteenth and early twentieth centuries. Indeed, a great deal of Williams's work in particular is explicitly concerned with the genealogy and connotations of the term 'culture', culminating in a particular theoretical position, cultural materialism, which emerged out of this lengthy engagement.

As Williams argues in his important early work, *Culture and Society*, the term becomes increasingly important in the nineteenth century, denoting a broadly humanistic rather than merely formal education. This sense of the term is most closely associated, though it did not originate with Matthew Arnold for whom the dissemination of culture represented the best hope for achieving national unity in the face of contemporary class divisions between barbarians (the dissolute gentry and aristocracy), philistines (the puritanical and determinedly uncultured bourgeoisie) and a potentially unruly populace (the working class). Arnold's was therefore an organic ideal, as indeed is implied by the term's origins in an analogy with the development of the land, 'cultivation'. In his supposed class neutrality and undogmatic appeal to 'the best that has been thought and said' Arnold believed he was promoting a form of education which would develop our essential *humanity* – in the sense that humanity is not merely another species but one characterized by intellectual, imaginative and, crucially, moral faculties which are capable of various degrees of development: the value of culture was therefore potentially universal. Moreover, the principal opposition which culture formed for Arnold was with 'machinery', in its literal and metaphorical senses. Machinery was, of course, the vehicle of economic power for the dominant class of the period, the bourgeoisie, but Arnold expanded the term's significance, using it to refer to those institutions, laws and principles in which the bourgeoisie placed its faith for the improvement of civilization. By contrast, culture was 'a study of perfection and of harmonious perfection, general perfection, and perfection which consists in becoming something rather than in having something, in an inward condition of the mind and spirit, not in an outward set of circumstances' (Arnold 1966, 48). It is significant—and a feature of the conservatism of Arnold's thought – that he did not provide a precise definition of culture, and his sense of what constitutes culture is based on supposedly self-evident criteria. His strategy was rather to say 'look at this particular product of philistine civilization and compare it with this example of true culture'. But Arnold's lack of specificity in this respect emerges with an ideological consistency from his own ideals, since to provide a definition of culture would be to establish a new set of machinery, an 'external' set of guidelines akin to the rule-bound thinking of the middle classes which so offended Arnold's humanism.

The most prominent twentieth-century advocate of Arnoldian ideals was F. R. Leavis, and the timing of his writing in defence of a culture which he perceived to be under threat from the forces of modernity also serves to highlight one of the conditions for the emergence of cultural studies: Leavis polemicized against the effects of a developing 'mass culture', including, crucially, an expansion of the various media and new levels of popular consumerism. In his famous, perhaps notorious, essay 'Mass Civilization and Minority Culture', Leavis focuses his attack on the standardization and mass production which characterized modern capitalism – once again, machinery acts as a metonym for dehumanization – and which were increasingly setting the values by which things other and more sacrosanct than commodities were to be judged. Leavis argued for a renewed defence of culture against the encroachment of such values. This, he claimed, would necessarily be the task of an elite which would include, most prominently, university lecturers such as himself. Again, as with Arnold, nowhere does he make explicit the values he is defending, but merely holds up for ridicule the judgements and values of those who typify contemporary degenerate principles (Leavis's chief instance in this respect is Arnold Bennett, whom Leavis derides in rather patrician fashion for being both provincial and middle class and therefore an enemy of the supposedly universal culture Leavis aims to restore).

We need to note two things in particular about this version of 'culture', since, for those who still give voice to Arnoldian and Leavisite principles, 'cultural studies' is anathema. First, despite its supposed universalism, what counted as 'culture' was clearly informed by educational traditions which, though not specifically 'aristocratic', were certainly the province of an elite centred on Oxbridge. Second, 'culture' was a specifically untheorized and, for ideological reasons, untheorizable phenomenon, since to theorize culture – that is, to take it as an object of study, rather than as a means of transmitting desirable qualities – would be to betray its essentially humanistic, non-mechanistic and unstandardizable values. These are key features of older ideas of 'culture', then, and it is instructive to contrast them with certain typical features of cultural studies. Hoggart's work – and also that of the historian E. P. Thompson, whose *The Making of the English Working Class* played a significant role in the discipline's emergence – took as their object the lived values – the *cultures*, in a different sense, that is – of the English working class, ascribing to them a significance and validity which the Arnoldian tradition would deny. The work of Williams, while less descriptive of particular class lifestyles, nonetheless explicitly repudiates Leavisite elitism and is informed by socialist convictions. The trajectory of cultural studies, moreover, has largely been to focus on popular culture: it is more likely to consider *Coronation St* than *Coriolanus*, and therefore to 'collude' with that standardization so despised by Leavis. Finally, cultural studies has been keenly receptive to what we tend to refer to rather homogenizingly as 'theory', and in this respect also offends against the Arnoldian distrust of 'machinery'.

Richard Hoggart

Richard Hoggart's principal contributions to the development of cultural studies are twofold: his publication of an innovative analysis of the changing patterns of working class life, *The Uses of Literacy*, and his role in the development of the School for Contemporary Cultural Studies at Birmingham University in the 1960s.

The significance of *The Uses of Literacy* is that it was probably the first book written from a 'cultured' – in the Leavisite sense – perspective which sought to analyse in a serious way not merely the publications which were then being consumed in working-class circles, but also the ways in which these related to the dominant values of working-class life. Hoggart's intimacy with the context he describes results from his own working-class background in Leeds, though, as was the case with Raymond Williams, he was educated at grammar school and university in ways which produced a sense of separation, even alienation, from that background. This is something which is self-consciously dealt with in the book's description of 'the scholarship boy' who 'has left his class, at least in spirit, by being in certain ways unusual; and he is still unusual in another class, too tense and over-wound' (1992, 302). The consequence of this is that in his analyses Hoggart tends to combine an insider's knowingness with an outsider's judgements, and, in this respect, it would be easy to accuse him of developing a merely snobbish relationship to working-class life, most notably in his disdain for the vulgarity of modern developments (notoriously, for instance, in his characterization of 'juke-box boys' who frequent 'milk-bars [which] indicate at once, in the nastiness of their modernistic knick-knacks, their glaring showiness, an aesthetic breakdown so complete that, in comparison with them, the layout of the living-rooms in some of the poor homes from which the customers come seems to speak of a tradition as balanced and civilized as an eighteenth-century town house' (1992, 247–8)). However, there is a critical emphasis in his work which, though it often incorporates disdain, is arguably not reducible to this.

Leavis's attack on modernity was, as we have seen, directed at machinery and mass standardization and focused in particular on the development of a mass media. Hoggart was influenced by Leavis's critique and is also concerned with this phenomenon and with the effects of mass consumerism in disrupting, transmuting or corrupting working-class attitudes. Invariably, change is for the worse. The 'popular publicists' he denounces disseminate an unquestioning belief in progress which is more or less synonymous with the spread of materialism (in its pejorative sense). I want to focus here on the four general tendencies Hoggart discerns since these are perhaps more important than any specific manifestation of them as described in the book:

1. Principles of tolerance and freedom rooted in the pragmatic working-class senti-ment of 'live and let live' have acquired a different inflection, enabled by – or perhaps the consequence of – the sensationalism of contemporary publications: the unwillingness to admit that freedom should have its limits. For Hoggart, 'The tolerant phrases have been joined by others in similar dress; the new depreciate the old, and together they become the ritual uniform of a shared unwillingness to admit that freedom can have its punishments. Anything goes and there is no scale' (1992, 178).

2. Similarly, Hoggart discerns a shift in the established principle of working-class solidarity – which enjoins a suspicion of outsiders ('them and us') – since this has been debased and transformed into a form of intolerance. The popular press, in identifying themselves with 'the people', promote the sense that the people's ideas are not only as good as anyone else's, but are even superior because they are more representative. Hoggart illustrates this with a still recognizable pseudo-democratic phenomenon: 'The popular press … conduct polls on this matter and question-naires on that matter among their readers, and so elevate the counting of heads into a substitute for judgement' (1992, 179–80).

3. Materialism goes together with, and is encouraged by, an unquestioning belief in progress, which is partly bound up with the kudos of science. The consequence of this is a historical amnesia and 'glorification of youth' (Hoggart 1992, 193). Hoggart's image of this process invokes explicitly Arnoldian language: 'the wagon, loaded with its barbarians in wonderland, moves irresistibly forward: not forward to anywhere, but simply forward for forwardness's sake' (1992, 193–4).

4. Finally, all of these processes together have produced an 'indifferentism' (another Arnoldian term) and relativism by contributing 'to an endless flux of the undistinguished and the valueless, to a world in which every kind of activity is finally made meaningless by being reduced to a counting of heads' (1992, 194–5). Moreover, this process is paradoxically accompanied by an abdication of respon-sibility and a pervasive surrendering to authority on the part of the working class.

Though Hoggart's account of these developments involves some perceptive commentary on the transformations being wrought by mass consumerism, it is manifestly the case that his work is tinged with nostalgia and conservatism. His role in the institutionalization of cultural studies, however, was of more radical and lasting significance. Some years after being appointed Chair of English at Birmingham University, Hoggart decided to continue the work he had begun with *The Uses of Literacy* by setting up a Centre for Contemporary Cultural Studies in 1964, the first of its kind, though subsequently there were to be numerous university centres in related fields. Stuart Hall, who took up the directorship following Hoggart's departure in 1968, records that it was regarded contemptuously by other cognate disciplines who considered themselves under threat, and this is indicative of the status of cultural studies as neither 'science' (sociology) – a status it would be even more keen to repudiate in these poststructuralist times – nor belletristic humanism (literature):

> On the day of our opening, we received letters from the English department saying that they couldn't really welcome us; they knew we were there, but they hoped we'd keep out of their way while they got on with the work they had to do. We received another, rather sharper letter from the sociologists saying, in effect, 'We have read *The Uses of Literacy* and we hope you don't think you're doing sociology, because that's not what you're doing at all.' (1990, 13)

As Hall also points out, though, the CCCS was not bound by any particular consensus about what it was its staff were up to, and, in political terms, Hall was significantly to the left of Hoggart in his thinking. Hall's directorship of the Centre saw a change in orientation away from the focus on working-class lived experience towards the study of 'the relations between media and ideology ... through the analysis of signifying systems in texts' (Turner 1996, 72). Indeed, Hall is more of a representative figure than Hoggart in terms of the contemporary practice of cultural studies, and his work has largely eclipsed the outdated approach of Hoggart himself. The same, however, cannot be said of Raymond Williams, whose influence remains considerable.

Raymond Williams

Williams's relationship to the English tradition of thinking about 'culture' is both more sustained and, ultimately, more critical than that of Hoggart. As a statement of his early position, we might consider his 1958 essay 'Culture is Ordinary'. Here he acknowledges two intellectual debts in particular, marxism and Leavis, which perhaps inevitably produce tensions and contradictions in the essay which remain characteristic of his work up to his elaboration of cultural materialism in the 1970s. But even in this essay, we find a discernibly leftist version of the organicism which is integral to the Arnoldian ideal of a common culture, and also a recognition of the disdain which has characterized other versions of that ideal of culture. Williams, for instance, refuses simply to indulge in any blanket condemnation of modernity, citing the real improvements to working-class life which have been made by mechanization and industrialization. More to the point here, he is also contemptuous of the minoritizing, elitist view of culture, of culture as 'the outward and emphatically visible sign of a special kind of people, cultivated people'. But if Williams wants to rescue culture from the minority, he also wants to defend it against those who, because of its elitist aura, would make it 'a dirty word' (1958, 5). Implicitly, he is referring to marxists at this point, those who have argued that the cultural ideal was ultimately 'bourgeois'. Williams rejects this, claiming not only that there is 'a distinct working-class way of life, which I for one value', but also that 'the arts and learning. .. are in a real sense a national inheritance, which is, or should be, available to everyone' (1958, 8). In this sense, while Williams is clearly writing with the grain of postwar democratization – and, indeed, much of his work in texts such as *The Long Revolution* has been directed not merely at analysing culture, but in arguing for an expansion of democracy, even to those areas of our lives dominated by the undemocratic writ of the market – there is still an acceptance of culture's organic credentials as rooted in essentially human values (see especially Eagleton 1976, 21–42). Only much later, and after a rapprochement with marxist thinking, did Williams fully recognize that culture can be marked by relations of conflict.

Williams's trajectory through the 1960s led him away from an engagement simply with literature to a consideration of other media, including television. This, indeed, represented the logical extension of his concern that the study of culture should not be rooted in an idealization of the pre-industrial past or in a disdain for its popular forms, including those governed by capitalist organization and directed towards 'the masses' (who, crucially, Williams consistently argues, only have an existence in the constructions of them made by those who disdain them while actually having a design on them – newspaper proprietors and the like). The first movement in this direction was with *Communications* in 1962 which, though now outdated in its approach, is significant precisely because of its attempt seriously to analyse modern media, rather than reject them as part of the dehumanizing tendency of modernity. Williams's later book *Television: Technology and Cultural Form*, published in 1975, once his theoretical orientation had moved significantly leftwards, is a much more sophisticated work while maintaining his established emphasis on cultural *production*, that is with culture as something which is bound up both with material processes and broader values. It is impossible to do justice here to the reach of Williams's argument which involves consideration of the historical development of television technology as a consequence of specific social and commercial pressures as well as a consideration of the specific forms television adopts. It ends, characteristically, with speculation on the possibility of democratizing televisual technology.

This final point is also indicative of another aspect of Williams's career as an intellectual, since he was not the kind of academic figure so familiar today whose academic work is merely coterminous with their political interventions. He was, for instance, an activist in the Labour Party up to 1966 – when he rejected it because of its lack of radicalism on key issues and because of 'the ruling-class style of the Wilson government' (O'Connor 1989, 21) – as well as in CND and the anti-Vietnam war movement. His later intellectual development emerged out of a re-engagement with marxist thought after the revolutionary protests of 1968 and following the translation and promotion of Western European marxist thought – particularly that of Gramsci – by the New Left. His key theoretical statement, an elaboration of what he called 'cultural materialism', came with the publication of the somewhat misleadingly named *Marxism and Literature* in 1977, a work which elaborates and extends the arguments made in an earlier essay originally published in *New Left Review*, 'Base and Superstructure in Marxist Cultural Theory', which, for reasons of space, I will focus on here. The essay is very much concerned with theorizing possibilities for change.

Most marxist cultural theory has concentrated on refining and complicating the determining relationship between base and superstructure in the classical model in which the base refers to the forces and relations of production and the superstructure to just about everything else – law, philosophy, religion, art, for instance. Williams, though, argues for a reconsideration of the whole set up:

> We have to revalue 'determination' towards the setting of limits and the exertion of pressure, and away from a predicted, prefigured and controlled content. We have to revalue 'super-structure' towards a related range of cultural practices, and away from a reflected, reproduced or specifically dependent content. And, crucially, we have to revalue 'the base' away from the notion of a fixed economic or technological abstraction, and towards the specific activities of men [sic] in real social and economic relationships, containing fundamental contradictions and therefore always in a state of dynamic process. (1980, 34)

In this respect, while recognizing the fundamental importance in our society of specifically capitalist economic production – the production of commodities – Williams argues for a recognition that cultural productivity is itself part of 'the material production and reproduction of real life' (1980, 35), hence the term 'cultural materialism'.

Not that Williams wants to do away with the concept of determinism; hence his resort to the Gramscian concept of hegemony. But here again, Williams is keen to emphasize the complexity of this term which he takes to refer to 'the central, effective and dominant system of meanings and values, which are not merely abstract but which are organized and lived' (1980, 38). Crucially, though, to say that these meanings and values are dominant is to imply nothing about their *value*. However, for Williams, hegemony is also to be considered as a dynamic *process*, always in need of renewal in one way or another, hence the complex relations between these *dominant* meanings and values and those which are either *residual* or *emergent*, that is bound up with a prior or developing historical moment. The crucial point is that residual or emergent meanings and values are rarely treated with indifference by those who seek to defend dominant ones – unless those residual or emergent values are simply *alternative*, or content to remain marginal, rather than truly *oppositional* – hence the importance, even urgency, for the dominant order of *incorporating* these areas of experience. In this way, Williams is able to suggest a more sophisticated, more historically nuanced form of marxist cultural analysis which moves beyond those abstract epochal designations such as 'feudal' or 'capitalist' – invaluable, but unwieldy – which have characterized marxist cultural analysis.

The development of Cultural Studies

Williams's recognition that conflict, rather than consensus, was characteristic of culture is *the* important break in his thought, and the terms dominant, residual and emergent have continued to be invoked in literary and cultural analysis. However, cultural studies have also been increasingly influenced by other traditions, both within and external to western marxism: while retaining its leftist leanings, cultural studies has arguably increasingly privileged analyses emerging out of what used to be known as the 'new social movements' – feminism, racial politics, the lesbian and gay movements, for instance – over the kinds of class and economic concerns which dominate Williams's thinking (though it should also be said that Williams's political engagements both in his work and in practice were not bound up with the labour movement in any narrow sense).

In some cases the shift of focus has been the consequence of explicit disagreement with the work of Williams, as in Paul Gilroy's critique of the impression given by Williams that the culture and society tradition was one which was generated through purely indigenous English processes. Gilroy argues that 'the New Left heirs to the aesthetic and cultural tradition in which Turner and Ruskin stand. .. reproduced its nationalism and its ethnocentrism by denying imaginary, invented Englishness any external references whatsoever. England ceaselessly gives birth to itself, seemingly from Britannia's head' (1993, 14). The force of Gilroy's argument is that Williams's work itself constitutes a selective tradition – a term originally invoked by Williams in *The Long Revolution* and reinvoked in 'Base and Superstructure' to describe 'that which, within the terms of an effective dominant culture, is always passed off as "*the* tradition", "*the* significant past"' (1980, 39) – in occluding the influence of colonial matters in the development of the culture and society tradition as well as the contributions which black writers and activists have made to supposedly indigenous radical traditions. Gilroy's critique, then, is both a contribution to and symptomatic of the broadening of cultural studies. Indeed, cultural materialism has itself evolved and integrated such concerns into its purview, with one of its most prominent contemporary advocates providing the following gloss (albeit principally in relation to literary analysis): 'Cultural materialists say that canonical texts have political projects, and should not be allowed to circulate in the world today on the assumption that their representations of class, race, ethnicity, gender and sexuality are simply authoritative' (Sinfield 1994, 38).

   Moreover, the impression should not be given that cultural studies has remained in thrall to the theoretical approach elaborated by Williams. As with modern literary studies, or indeed most disciplines which have opened up to the influence of 'theory', cultural studies routinely engages with a number of other theoretical models, from the Frankfurt School to the ideologically liberal influences of postmodernism and poststructuralism. Nonetheless, given that, in Britain at least, the term 'culture' remains peculiarly bound up with a specific and politically charged history of debate about education, class and value, Williams's contribution will remain central.

David Alderson

Further reading and works cited

Arnold, M. *Culture and Anarchy*. Cambridge, 1966.
Eagleton, T. *Criticism and Ideology*. London, 1976.
Gilroy, P. *The Black Atlantic*. London, 1993.
Hall, S. 'The Emergence of Cultural Studies and the Crisis of the Humanities', *October*, 53, 1990.
— et al. *Policing the Crisis: Mugging, the State, and Law and Order*. London, 1978.
Hoggart, R. *The Uses of Literacy*. Harmondsworth, 1992.
Hebdige, D. *Subculture: The Meaning of Style*. London, 1979.
Inglis, F. *Cultural Studies*. Oxford, 1993.
Leavis, F. R. 'Mass Civilization and Minority Culture', *Education and the University*. London, 1948.
O'Connor, A. *Raymond Williams*. Oxford, 1989.
Sinfield, A. *Cultural Politics – Queer Reading*. London, 1994.
Thompson, E. P. *The Making of the English Working Class*. Harmondsworth, 1968.
Turner, G. *British Cultural Studies*. London, 1996.
Williams, R. *Culture and Society 1780–1950*. London, 1958.
—. *The Long Revolution*. London, 1961.
—. *Communications*. Harmondsworth, 1962.
—. *Television*. New York, 1975.
—. *Marxism and Literature*. Oxford, 1977.
—. *Problems in Materialism and Culture*. London, 1980.
—. *Towards 2000*. London, 1983.
—. *Resources of Hope*. London, 1989.

11. Raymond Williams (1921–1988)

Raymond Williams is widely regarded as the most significant 'left-wing' figure in late twentieth-century British intellectual life, or in Cornell West's forgivable hyperbole 'the last of the great European male revolutionary socialist intellectuals' (1995, ix). His various contributions, as a creative writer, as a central source of inspiration for the proto-discipline of cultural studies, as a key figure in the New Left intelligentsia, have all been variously acknowledged. Much less common, however, is a serious acknowledgement of his role as a critical theorist. Yet Williams himself increasingly came to characterize his work as a distinctive kind of theory, that is as a kind of 'cultural materialism'. He had first used this term in a short essay published in the hundredth issue of the journal *New Left Review*, to which he had been a long-standing contributor. Cultural materialism, he explained, 'is a theory of culture as a (social and material) productive process and of specific practices, of "arts", as social uses of material means of production'. He added that the position would be 'spelled out more fully' in *Marxism and Literature* and in the book that would eventually be published as *Culture* (1980d, 243). There is an important sense in which these two books do indeed 'spell out' the theory, and they will therefore command our attention here. But we should note also Williams's own insistence, in the 'Introduction' to *Marxism and Literature*, that cultural materialism had been 'a position which, as a matter of theory, I have arrived at over the years' (1977, 5). Its pre-history, as part of a much longer intellectual evolution, demands our attention also.

Trained in English at Cambridge, Williams derived much of his initial critical vocabulary from the Leavises and *Scrutiny*. Formed by the biographical experience of Welsh working-class life, he was also a lifelong socialist, with an enduring interest in marxist and quasi-marxist cultural theory. At one point in his 1977 interviews with the *New Left Review*, he recalls the establishment of *Politics and Letters*, which he had co-edited at Cambridge during 1947 and 1948: 'Our intention was to produce a review that would ... unite radical left politics with Leavisite literary criticism. We were to be to the left of the Labour party, but at a distance from the CP. Our affiliation to *Scrutiny* was guarded, but ... nevertheless quite a strong one' (1979a, 65). An understanding of Williams's intellectual evolution will require some appreciation of how he variously negotiated this doubly ambivalent relationship to Leavisism on the one hand, marxism on the other. From Leavis, he inherited organicist and holistic conceptions of culture and methods of analysis, a strong sense of the importance of the particular, whether in art or in 'life', and an insistence on the absolute centrality of culture. But he rejected *Scrutiny*'s cultural elitism, especially as displayed in the mass civilization versus minority culture topos. From marxism, he inherited both a radically socialistic critique of ruling class political, economic and cultural power and a strong sense of 'materiality'. But he rejected the economic determinism of the so-called 'base/superstructure' formula and the structural determinism of later Althusserian and quasi-Althusserian theories of ideology.

It is possible to identify three main 'phases' in Williams's thought, each explicable in terms of its own differentially negotiated settlement between Leavisism and marxism, and each characterizable, in perhaps overly political terms, in relation to a relatively distinct, consecutive moment in the history of the British New Left. In the first such phase, that of the moment of '1956' and the foundation of the first New Left, Williams addressed himself very directly to the definition of a third position, simultaneously dependent upon but in contradictory relation to Leavisite criticism and orthodox marxism. He thus played a central role in the development of a peculiarly 'culturalist' post-Communist marxism, a kind of indigenously British 'Western Marxism'. The key texts from this period are without doubt *Culture and Society* and *The Long Revolution*. The central procedure of *Culture and Society* could not be more Leavisite: to move by way of a series of close readings of particular texts to the account of a distinctively 'English' national 'tradition'. Moreover, Williams's sense of the intellectual content of this tradition had much in common with Leavis and Eliot. And for Williams, as for Leavis, the tradition developed in more or less explicit antagonism to utilitarianism (though this remained in many respects a surprisingly underdeveloped theme). Williams's strategic purpose was nonetheless radically opposed to the explicit cultural and political conservatism displayed by Eliot and increasingly by the Leavises. To the contrary, he sought to demonstrate that, in its very complexity, the 'culture and society' tradition remained, not only finally unassimilable to any obvious conservatism, but also often openly amenable to radical, indeed socialistic, interpretation. Quite fundamentally, Williams rejected the Leavisite notion of 'mass civilization', and with it the notion of 'masses': 'There are in fact no masses; there are only ways of seeing people as masses' (1963, 289) He rejected also the notion of a distinctively valuable minority culture, but did so nonetheless in distinctly Leavisite terms. A culture, Williams wrote, 'is not only a body of intellectual and imaginative work; it is also and essentially a whole way of life' (1963, 311). In principle, this is little different from Eliot or Leavis. But in the practical application of the principle, Williams so expanded its range as to include within 'culture' the 'collective democratic institution', by which he meant, primarily, the trade union, the cooperative, and the working-class political party (1963, 313).

Thus redefined, the notion of a common culture became supplemented, and importantly qualified, by that of a plurality of class cultures. Yet, despite such qualification, the normative ideal remained central: 'We need a common culture, not for the sake of an abstraction, but because we shall not survive without it' (Williams 1963, 304). This ideal provided Williams, as it had Leavis, with the ground from which to mount an organicist critique of utilitarian individualism. But a common culture could never be properly such, he argued, if established on the basis of the merely vicarious participation Eliot and Leavis had sanctioned. 'The distinction of a culture in common', he wrote, 'is that . . . selection is freely and commonly made and remade. The tending is a common process, based on a common decision' (1963, 322). In a characteristically leftist move, Williams thus relocated the common culture from the idealized historical past it occupied in Eliot and Leavis, to the not too distant, still to be made, democratically socialist future. If the common culture was not yet fully common, then it followed that the literary and cultural tradition should be seen, not so much as the unfolding of a group mind, as in Eliot, but as the outcome, in part at least, of a set of interested selections made in the present. A 'tradition is always selective,' wrote Williams, 'and . . . there will always be a tendency for this process of selection to be related to and even governed by the interests of the class that is dominant' (1963, 307–8). Where Leavis had revered a 'Great Tradition', Williams would thus detect a selective tradition. But even as he insisted on the importance of class cultures, he was careful also to note the extent to which distinctions of class are complicated, especially in the field of intellectual and imaginative work, by 'the common elements resting on a common language' (1963, 311). For Williams, any direct reduction of art to class, such as is canvassed in many versions of marxism, remained unacceptable. 'The area of culture', he observed, 'is usually proportionate to the area of a language rather than to the area of a class' (1963, 307). This argument is repeated and significantly elaborated upon in the opening theoretical chapters of *The Long Revolution*:

> The selective tradition creates, at one level, a general human culture; at another level, the historical record of a particular society; at a third level ... a rejection of considerable areas of what was once a living culture ... selection will be governed by many kinds of special interest, including class interest ... The traditional culture of a society will always tend to correspond to its *contemporary* system of interests and values ... (1965, 68)

Once again the stress falls on selection according to class-specific criteria, but once again also on the reality of a truly general human culture.

It is here too that Williams proposed an initial theorization of the concept of structure of feeling, a term actually coined in the much earlier *Preface to Film* (Williams and Orrom 1954), but not hitherto given any extensive theoretical articulation. 'In one sense', he wrote, 'this structure of feeling is the culture of a period: it is the particular living result of all the elements in the general organization' (1965, 64). He continues: 'in this respect ... the arts of a period ... are of major importance ... here ... the actual living sense, the deep community that makes the communication possible, is naturally drawn upon' (1965, 64–5). A structure of feeling, Williams makes clear, is neither universal nor class specific, though it is 'a very deep and very wide possession' (1965, 65). Nor is it formally learned, he speculates, and thence follows its often peculiarly generational character: 'the new generation will have its own structure of feeling, which will not appear to have come "from" anywhere' (1965, 65). This concept of 'structure of feeling' was to prove quite extraordinarily fruitful. In *The English Novel*, for example, Williams would attempt to show how, from Dickens to Lawrence, the novel became one medium among many by which people sought to master and absorb new experience through the articulation of a structure of feeling the key problem of which was that of the 'knowable community' (1974a, 14–15). In *Drama from Ibsen to Brecht* he would produce an account of the development of naturalism and of expressionism in the modern theatre organized around precisely 'the history and significance of the main dramatic forms – the conventions and structures of feeling' (1973a, 14). The concept would also occupy a commanding position in his later cultural materialism.

In *The Long Revolution* Williams sought to chart the long history of the emergence of modernity and of the interrelationships within British society between the democratic revolution, the industrial revolution and the 'cultural revolution' embodied in the extension and democratization of communications (1965, 10–12). The book's central novelty lies in its form, in its peculiar combination of theoretical discussion, substantive 'sociological' analysis and expressly political argument. The opening theoretical discussions, in which the concept of a structure of feeling is elaborated, are both dense and original. The book's second part moves to supplement the more conventional procedures of Leavisite textual criticism with a sociological account of the historical development of a number of major British cultural institutions: there are pioneering analyses of the education system and the growth of the reading public, the popular press and the development of 'Standard English'; followed, in turn, by chapters on the social backgrounds of a selection of canonical English writers and on the social histories of dramatic forms and the contemporary novel. The concluding third part, in effect an exploratory inquiry into the structure of feeling of the early 1960s, critically addresses the politico-cultural problems of the apparent moral decline of the labour movement (1965, 328–9). The combination of a sharply analytical intelligence and an at times near-utopian radical vision, which informs much of this last essay, spoke powerfully and provocatively to a society slowly shrugging off the moral and political conservatism of the 1950s.

What holds the book together, however, is its very strong underlying sense of the materiality of culture, at once a restatement and a transcendence of the position originally outlined in *Culture and Society*. 'It was certainly an error', Williams wrote against Leavisite humanism, 'to suppose that values or art-works could be adequately studied without reference to the particular society within which they were expressed' (1965, 61). But, 'it is equally an error', he wrote against marxism, 'to suppose that the social explanation is determining, or that the values and works are mere by-products' (1965, 61). He moves thence to what might well be the book's central set of propositions:

> If the art is part of the society, there is no solid whole, outside it, to which … we concede priority. The art is there, as an activity, with the production, the trading, the politics, the raising of families … It is … not a question of relating the art to the society, but of studying all the activities and their interrelations, without any concession of priority to any one of them we may choose to abstract … I would define the theory of culture as the study of relationships between elements in a whole way of life. (1965, 61–3)

Here, then, was the prospectus for what would become a thoroughgoing cultural materialism.

In the interim between the first publication of *The Long Revolution* in 1961 and that of *Marxism and Literature* in 1977, Williams's work proceeded by way of a series of often radically innovative encounters with an extremely diverse set of substantive issues, ranging across the whole field of literary and cultural studies: the mass media (Williams 1974b, 1976a), the novel (Williams 1974a), the drama (Williams 1973a, 1979b) and the pastoral (Williams 1973b). In the work on theatre and on television a new awareness of the social conventionality of form and of the interrelationship between technology and form is increasingly brought to bear. Williams's coupling of the problem of cultural form to that of cultural technology clearly drew attention in each case to the materiality of what were in orthodoxly marxist terms 'ideal' superstructures. This led him, in turn, to a simultaneous rejection of both technological determinism and the notion of a determined technology (1974b, 12–13), and thence to a much more complex understanding of the notion of determination itself. The chronological overlap between Williams's work in theatre studies and that on the mass media is thus by no means merely 'coincidental'. Disparate though the work might appear, it proceeds along clearly connected lines of inquiry. And these connections are empirical and substantive as well as theoretical and methodological. As Williams had noted in the 'Conclusion' to his *Drama from Ibsen to Brecht*: 'drama is no longer coexistent with theatre … The largest audience for drama, in our own world, is in the cinema and on television' (1973a, 399).

The cumulative effect of these apparently diverse lines of inquiry would finally be registered in *Marxism and Literature*. In Williams's earlier 'left culturalist' writings the 'deep community' that is culture had been understood as simultaneously transcendent of class and yet irredeemably marked by it. For all the eloquence with which this position had been argued, it remained quite fundamentally incoherent: the competing claims of commonality and difference, culture and class, Leavisism and marxism, formed a circle which stubbornly refused to be squared. But in the second phase of his work, that of the moment of '1968' and the emergence of a second New Left, it finally became possible for Williams to explain, to his own satisfaction at least, how it could be that structures of feeling are common to different classes, and yet nonetheless represent the interests of some particular class. In this second phase, his engagement with a series of continental European western marxisms, each only very recently translated into English (Lukács, Goldmann, Althusser, Gramsci), and with various forms of Third Worldist political radicalism, clearly paralleled, but nonetheless neither reduplicated nor inspired, that of the younger generation of radical intellectuals associated with Perry Anderson's *New Left Review*. The radicalism is readily apparent in *The Country and the City*, where a developing critique of various mythological accounts of rural life (including Marx's own dismissal of 'rural idiocy') eventually culminated in a defence of Third World insurrectionism (Williams 1973b, 304). The theoretical encounter with western marxism initially entailed little more than a recognition that not all marxisms were necessarily economically determinist and a corollary discovery of preoccupations similar to his own in the work of individual western marxist writers. Williams's response to Goldmann, for example, had centred on the recognition that they were 'exploring many of the same areas with many of the same concepts' (1980b, 20). The response to Gramsci, however, was of an altogether different order, precipitating a much more positive redefinition of Williams's own theoretical stance. As he would insist in *Marxism and Literature*: 'Gramsci's ... work is one of the major turning-points in Marxist cultural theory' (1977, 108).

Williams was impressed both by Gramsci's work on intellectuals, which seemed to him an 'encouraging' and 'experimental' model for work in the sociology of culture (1977, 138), and by the wider implications of the theory of hegemony. The significance of the latter had registered initially in an essay written in 1973, entitled 'Base and Superstructure in Marxist Cultural Theory' (1980c, 37). But in *Marxism and Literature* the argument is elaborated upon at much greater length. Here, as before, Williams argued against the base/super-structure model for cultural analysis, on the grounds that culture is both real and material: 'From castles and palaces and churches to prisons and workhouses and schools; from weapons of war to a controlled press ... These are never superstructural activities. They are necessarily material production within which an apparently self-subsistent mode of production can alone be carried on' (1977, 93). Here, though, this more general materialism is decisively articulated to the theory of hegemony. The first and last chapters respectively of the book's first part are devoted to two key concepts and two keywords, deriving respectively from Leavisism and marxism, 'Culture' and 'Ideology'. In a subsequent chapter, Williams argues for the theoretical superiority over each of these of the Gramscian notion of hegemony:

> 'Hegemony' goes beyond 'culture' ... in its insistence on relating the 'whole social process' to specific distributions of power and influence ... Gramsci therefore introduces the necessary recognition of dominance and subordination in what has still, however, to be recognized as a whole process. It is in just this recognition of the *wholeness* of the process that the concept of 'hegemony' goes beyond 'ideology'. (1977, 108–9)

For Williams, Gramsci's central achievement consisted in the articulation of a culturalist sense of the wholeness of culture with a more typically marxist sense of the interestedness of ideology. Thus, hegemony is 'in the strongest sense a "culture", but a culture which has also to be seen as the lived dominance and subordination of particular classes' (1977, 110). Understood thus, culture is no longer either 'superstructural', as the term had been defined in the marxist tradition, or 'ideological', in either the more generally marxist or the more specifically Althusserian definition. On the contrary, 'cultural tradition and practice . . . are among the basic processes', which need to be seen 'as they are . . . without the characteristic straining to fit them . . . to other and determining . . . economic and political relationships' (1977, 111). Whether all of this remains exactly faithful to Gramsci's own intent seems open to some doubt. But whatever the original authorial intention (and this is by no means at all self-evident), Williams's appropriation of Gramsci finally delivered that resolution of Leavisite and marxist thematics hitherto denied him.

In one respect, Williams's reading of Gramsci remains clearly faithful to its object: for both, the counter-hegemonic moment is what truly matters, hence Williams's own attempt to distinguish between practices, experiences, meanings and values that are part of the effectively dominant culture and those that are not. The dominant or hegemonic culture, he reminds us, 'is always an active process', an organization of often quite disparate meanings, 'which it specifically incorporates in a significant culture' (1977, 115). Rehearsing an argument first broached in *Culture and Society*, he points once again to the decisive importance of 'selective tradition' in the effective operation of such processes of incorporation (1977, 115). In *Marxism and Literature*, however, the selective tradition is also seen as necessarily dependent both upon identifiable institutions and what Williams terms 'formations', that is intellectual or artistic movements and tendencies (1977, 117–120). This double stress is explored at greater length in *Culture*, where he advanced a preliminary historical typology of institutions and formations (Williams 1981, 35–86). For all this attention to the hegemonic, however, Williams remained insistent that, at the level of 'historical' as distinct from 'epochal' analysis, that is at the level of movement rather than system, there is much in any lived culture that cannot be reduced to the dominant (1977, 121). Here, he dissents sharply from the implied consensualism of Althusserian theories of ideology: '*no mode and therefore no dominant social order*', he wrote, '*and therefore no dominant culture ever in reality includes or exhausts all human practice, human energy, and human intention*' (1977, 125, emphasis in original).

Williams's initial theorization of the alternatives to hegemony had been broached in the 'Base and Superstructure' essay, where he had sought to distinguish between 'alternative' and 'oppositional', 'residual' and 'emergent' cultural elements (1980c, 39–42). The terminology recurs both in *Marxism and Literature* and in *Culture*. By 'residual' Williams means, not the simply 'archaic', defined as 'that which is wholly recognized as an element of the past', but rather those cultural elements external to the dominant culture which nonetheless continue to be lived and practised as an active part of the present 'on the basis of the residue . . . of some previous social and cultural institution or formation' (1977, 122). Unlike the archaic, the residual may be oppositional or at least alternative in character. Thus he distinguishes organized religion and the idea of rural community, which are each predominantly residual, from monarchy, which is merely archaic. But it is the properly 'emergent', that is those genuinely new meanings and values, practices, relationships and kinds of relationship, which are substantially alternative or oppositional to the dominant culture (1977, 123), that most interest him. For Williams, as for Gramsci, the primary source of an emergent culture is likely to be the formation of a new social class. But there is also a second source of emergence: 'alternative perceptions of others, in immediate relationships; new perceptions and practices of the material world' (1977, 126). For Williams, as for Gramsci, the exemplary contemporary instance of a new social class is that of the development of the modern working class. At the second level, however, which Williams termed 'the excluded social [human] area' (1977, 126), a level often peculiarly pertinent to the analysis of artistic and intellectual movements, the situation is much less clear. As Williams writes in *Culture*: 'No analysis is more difficult than that which, faced by new forms, has to try to determine whether these are new forms of the dominant or are genuinely emergent' (1980d, 205). This testimony to complexity is no mere rhetorical gesture on Williams's part. Quite the contrary: his work both in drama studies and in media studies had made him all too aware of the difficulties entailed in distinguishing the properly emergent from the merely novel.

In *Marxism and Literature*, Williams was able to offer an unusually interesting formulation of this problem, if not necessarily of the ways in which it might be resolved. Here he redeployed and significantly redefined the concept of 'structure of feeling'. An emergent culture, he argued, unlike either the dominant or the residual, requires not only distinct kinds of immediate cultural practice but also and crucially 'new forms or adaptations of forms'. Such innovation at the level of form, he continued, 'is in effect a *pre-emergence*, active and pressing but not yet fully articulated, rather than the evident emergence which could be more confidently named' (1977, 126). It is at this level of the pre-emergent, then, that the concept of structure of feeling is brought back into play. From *The Long Revolution* onwards, Williams had used the term to denote both the immediately experiential and the generationally specific aspects of artistic process. In *Marxism and Literature* both emphases are retained, but are conjoined to a quite new stress on cultural pre-emergence. In this reformulation the experiential remains at odds with official, 'formal' culture precisely in so far as it is indeed genuinely new: 'practical consciousness is what is actually being lived, ... not only what it is thought is being lived' (1977, 130–1). And similarly the generationally-specific remains different from the experience of previous generations precisely in so far as it too is indeed genuinely new. Structures of feeling writes Williams in an unusually arresting formulation

> can be defined as social experiences *in solution*, as distinct from other social semantic formations which have been *precipitated* and are more evidently and more immediately available ... The effective formations of most actual art relate to already manifest social formations, dominant or residual, and it is primarily to emergent formations ... that the structure of feeling, *as solution*, relates. (1977, 133–4)

Structures of feeling are no longer, then, in any simple sense 'the culture' of a period: they are, rather, precisely those particular elements within the more general culture that most actively anticipate subsequent mutations in the general culture itself; in short, they are quite specifically counter-hegemonic.

At one level, this distinctly Gramscian reformulation merely recaptures something of what Williams had all along intended: the problem of the knowable community in the English novel and the naturalistic revolution in the modern theatre each delimit a distinct structure of feeling only in so far as they are indeed genuinely innovatory. But in each case these respectively pre-emergent qualities are never fully theorized. It is as if the concept itself was still pre-emergent and required the encounter with Gramsci for precipitation. Moreover, the substantive question of the precise interplay between the emergent or pre-emergent on the one hand, and novelty within the dominant on the other, in both mass media and modernist avant-garde forms, was to become especially pressing in Williams's later work. In the third and final phase of his work, that produced during the 1980s, the developing globalization of corporate capitalism and the promise of a postmodern radicalism centred around the new social movements each obliged Williams to think through the theoretical and practical implications of an apparent decentring of the British nation state on the one hand, class politics on the other. The key texts here are the 1983 reworking of the long revolution analysis, *Towards 2000*, and the posthumously published and sadly unfinished *The Politics of Modernism*. Both books attempt to reformulate the earlier aspiration to community and to culture as a whole way of life by way of a critique of 'postmodern' appropriations both of modernism and of the popular mass media.

In *Culture and Society* and *The Long Revolution*, Williams had respectfully but determinedly aired his differences with the guardians of Leavis's minority culture. In *Towards 2000*, however, he set out to show how late capitalism had itself effectively collapsed the distinction between minority and mass arts: 'There are very few absolute contrasts left between a "minority culture" and "mass communications"', he wrote; 'many minority institutions and forms have adapted, ... with enthusiasm, to modern corporate capitalist culture' (1983, 134, 140). The older modernisms, which had once threatened to destabilize the certainties of bourgeois life, have been transformed, he argued, into a new '"postmodernist" establishment' which 'takes human inadequacy ... as self-evident' (1983, 141). The deep structures of this now dominant postmodernism are present, moreover, in effectively popular cultural forms like film, television and fiction: 'these debased forms of an anguished sense of human debasement ... have become a widely distributed "popular" culture that is meant to confirm both its own and the world's destructive inevitabilities' (1983, 141–2). The 'pseudo-radicalism' of 'the negative structures of post-modernist art' (1983, 145) is thus neither pre-emergent nor emergent, but rather a moment of novelty, indeed perhaps the institutionalization of novelty itself, within the already dominant culture. As Williams would observe in *The Politics of Modernism*, the dominant institutions 'now incorporate or impose' such 'easy labels of radicalism' (1989, 176). But if the dominant culture had indeed so mutated, then Williams was also able to detect a more properly innovatory, pre-emergent 'structure of feeling' (though the term itself is not actually used) in the politics of the new social movements. He would thus seek to claim the peace movement, the ecology movement, the feminist movement and what he termed the movement of 'oppositional culture' as 'resources of hope' for a journey beyond capitalism (Williams 1983, 250). Yet, even as he invoked the new movements, he would insist that only a 'misinterpretation' could see them as 'getting beyond class politics'. Rather, these 'new' issues, followed through, 'lead us into the central systems of the industrial-capitalist mode of production and ... into its system of classes' (1983, 172–3). The specifically 'cultural' corollaries of this analysis are quite explicitly anti-postmodern:

> If we are to break out of the non-historical fixity of *post*-modernism, 'then we must search out and counterpose an alternative tradition taken from the neglected works left in the wide margin of the century, a tradition which may address itself not to this by now exploitable because quite inhuman rewriting of the past but, for all our sakes, to a modern *future* in which community may be imagined again. (1989, 35)

If Williams's early 'left Leavisism' was in the most obvious of senses a 'culturalism', then the later cultural materialism might best be understood as a kind of 'post-culturalism'. This is so in more than a simple chronological sense. Before Williams, the culturalist tradition had typically subscribed to a kind of 'objective idealism' in which truth is seen as inhering in the cultural tradition itself. Williams's deconstruction of this notion, through the idea of the selective tradition, effects a relativizing turn similar to that of poststructuralism in relation to structuralism. It does so by virtue of an appeal to the role of the (collective) reader. It more than gestures in the direction of a recognition of the intrication of power within discourse such as the later Foucault acknowledged, and of the materiality, historicity and arbitrary variability of the linguistic sign similar to that in both Derrida and Foucault. And all this remained coupled to a sense of genuinely free communicative action – a truly common culture – as normative, of which even Habermas might approve. Hence, perhaps, Terry Eagleton's judgement that: 'Williams's work has prefigured and pre-empted the development of parallel left positions by, so to speak, apparently standing still' (1984, 109).

Andrew Milner

Further reading and works cited

Dworkin, D. L. and Roman, L. G. (eds) *Views Beyond the Border Country*. London, 1993.
Eagleton, T. *The Function of Criticism*. London, 1984.
— (ed.) *Raymond Williams: Critical Perspectives*. Cambridge, 1989.
Eldridge, J. and Eldridge, L. *Raymond Williams*. London, 1994.
Higgins, J. *Raymond Williams*. London, 1999.
— (ed.) *The Raymond Williams Reader*. Oxford, 2000.
Inglis, F. *Raymond Williams*. London, 1995.
Milner, A. *Cultural Materialism*. Melbourne, 1993.
O'Connor, A. *Raymond Williams*. Oxford, 1989.
Pinkney, T. *Raymond Williams*. Bridgend, 1991.
West, C. 'In Memoriam: The Legacy of Raymond Williams', in *Cultural Materialism*, ed. C. Prendergast. Minneapolis, MN, 1995.
Williams, R. *Culture and Society 1780–1950*. Harmondsworth, 1963.
—. *The Long Revolution*. Harmondsworth, 1965.
—. *Drama from Ibsen to Brecht*. Harmondsworth, 1973a.
—. *The Country and the City*. New York, 1973b.
—. *The English Novel*. St Albans, 1974a.
—. *Television*. Glasgow, 1974b.
—. *Communications*. Harmondsworth, 1976a.
—. *Keywords*. Glasgow, 1976b.
—. *Marxism and Literature*. Oxford, 1977.
—. *Politics and Letters*. London, 1979a.
—. *Modern Tragedy*. London, 1979b.
—. 'Notes on Marxism in Britain Since 1945', in *Problems in Materialism and Culture: Selected Essays*. London, 1980a.
—. 'Literature and Sociology: In Memory of Lucien Goldmann', in *Problems in Materialism and Culture: Selected Essays*. London, 1980b.
—. 'Base and Superstructure in Marxist Cultural Theory', in *Problems in Materialism and Culture: Selected Essays*. London, 1980c.
—. *Culture*. Glasgow, 1980d.
—. *Towards 2000*. London, 1983.
—. *The Politics of Modernism*, ed. T. Pinkney. London, 1989.
— and Orrom, M. *Preface to Film*. London, 1954.

12. Stuart Hall (1932–)

Stuart Hall is a central figure in the history and the continuing evolution of cultural studies and marxist intellectual thought in Britain. He came to Britain from Jamaica as a Rhodes scholar in the early 1950s, and since then he has played a key role in the development of 'New Left' political thinking, in the foundation and institutionalization of the discipline of cultural studies, and in contributing to, and promoting, marxist cultural and sociological analyses of contemporary Britain. His work since the 1950s has been engaged chiefly in marxist debates about the role of ideology in popular culture, but this has taken a wide variety of forms, from his neo-Leavisite examination of popular cultural forms in the book he co-authored with Paddy Whannel, *The Popular Arts* (1964), to his Althusserian studies of the ways in which 'Thatcherism' had become embedded as an ideology in media and cultural forms in the 1980s. His most important achievement is to have successfully engineered a central place for cultural studies in the academy in Britain, and to have demonstrated its usefulness as a discipline for investigating a broad range of sociological, political and economic issues, as well as the more obvious cultural expressions, such as the jazz and rock 'n' roll music which he wrote about in *The Popular Arts*. Alongside Raymond Williams and E. P. Thompson, Hall is also the most prominent marxist academic in Britain of the postwar period, and his work is central to debates about the relevance and function of marxist and post-marxist thought in contemporary British culture.

Hall became part of the intellectual left in Britain at a time of profound change in left-wing politics. Prior to the Second World War British marxists tended to look towards Russia as a model for Marxist social and economic revolution, but in the 1950s Russia's aggressive interventions in East Germany (1953) and particularly in crushing the popular uprising in Hungary (1956) led many British marxists to criticize the forms which marxism had taken in Russia. Hall writes that he was not a marxist prior to the Hungarian uprising: 'I came into marxism backwards: against the Soviet tanks in Budapest, as it were' (Morley and Chen 1996, 264). For British marxists, the events in Hungary effected a dramatic shift away from the notion that marxism need only transfer the economic means of production to the proletariat in order for a revolution to succeed. The fact that a post-revolutionary state could become as imperialist as the capitalism which it had defeated signalled to intellectuals such as Williams and Hall that marxism had to counter the ideology of capitalism much more effectively. The New Left which emerged in the 1950s thus emphasized the role played by ideological forms – culture, media, education, religion – in bolstering the power of capitalism, and in harnessing the working class within capitalist hegemony.

Hall pioneered marxist analyses of culture, firstly in his role as editor of the *Universities and Left Review* (*New Left Review* after 1959) between 1957 and 1961, and later when he played a central role in the evolution of cultural studies. Initially, Hall's conceptions of culture owed much to the work of F. R. Leavis, even though he disagreed with Leavis's politics. Hall believed that Leavis's discussions of the nineteenth-century novel in particular could be appropriated for a socialist-humanist criticism, especially in the way in which Leavis believed that literature could represent 'experience', morality and 'a whole way of life'. Hall understood from Leavis that literature had much to offer a political study of society 'as a whole', as he argued in 1958:

> The political intellectual is concerned with the institutional life of the society: the creative artist with the attitudes, the manners, the moral and emotional life which the individual consummates within that social framework. It seems to me that the beginning of a common socialist humanism is the realisation that these are not two distinct areas of interest, but the complementary parts of a complex, common experience. (1958b, 87)

In the *Universities and Left Review*, Hall promoted the study of 'lifestyles' with a view to integrating insights into culture with a broad-based socialist political analysis, and thus shared in common with the emerging generation of working-class writers an interest in the ways in which literature and politics intersected. Hall persevered with this interest when he co-authored a book with Paddy Whannel, *The Popular Arts*, which took as its subject the cultural politics of mass culture. The book distinguished between 'popular' and 'mass' culture in useful ways, but it also entailed a Leavisite focus on the 'quality' of popular culture. Hall and Whannel replicated the Leavisite bias towards 'complexity' and 'richness', arguing that jazz was preferable to rock 'n' roll because it was as creative as classical music, just as film was preferable to television. The criteria by which Hall and Whannel judged popular music – such as rhythmic variety, musical diversity, personal expression and imagination – borrowed heavily from Leavis, and ultimately failed to analyse the possible relationships between popular culture and social struggle, partly because it did not extend its analyses sufficiently far to take into account the ways in which popular music was appropriated and used by its audiences. Hall's first book-length study of popular culture thus replicated the terms of Leavisite analysis, and contained little of the political engagement which a marxist cultural studies seemed to promise.

This changed radically in the course of Hall's career, however. After lecturing at Chelsea College, University of London, for three years, Hall was appointed a Research Fellow at Richard Hoggart's Centre for Contemporary Cultural Studies at the University of Birmingham in 1964, and he became its Acting Director in 1968. The Centre was first formed as an annex to the English department at Birmingham university and its original goal, outlined and defended by Hoggart in his inaugural address in 1964, was to apply the traditional methods of literary criticism to the new domains of popular and mass culture. Admittedly, this also entailed a recognition that new criteria would have to be found for the evaluation of specific texts, but their early judgements tended to parallel normative standards, those standards which were always already set by high culture. Hall became the Centre's Director from 1972 to 1979, and, as Andrew Milner argues, 'displayed a remarkable flair for academic entrepreneurship' (Milner 1993, 76). He founded a house journal, *Working Papers in Cultural Studies*, and published several volumes of collected work on culture, society and politics in Britain. Under Hall's influence, the work of the Centre increasingly moved away from the influence of Leavis towards marxist analysis of the role of culture in ideology, and in the 1970s the work of the Centre in general attempted to fuse the socialist humanism of the early writings of Raymond Williams and Richard Hoggart with the influential structuralism of continental marxism. Hall's own writings also moved from the essentially culturalist analysis of Leavis to studies which were focused more specifically on ethnographic issues and which increasingly borrowed from the work of Gramsci and Althusser. Thus, Hall's work made the paradigm shift in cultural studies which he himself described as moving between culturalism and structuralism (Hall 1980).

If in *The Popular Arts* Hall had attempted to locate cultural forms which might be resistant to capitalism *per se*, such as jazz, and thus recapitulated culturalist solutions to the problem of ideology, in *Resistance Through Rituals*, the book he edited with Tony Jefferson, he and his co-authors explored the ways in which youth subcultures emerged as structural effects of capitalism, and yet embodied some degree of oppositional content. For Hall and the Centre for Contemporary Cultural Studies in general, the study of youth subcultures was a way of focusing on the relationship between class and culture without returning to absolute distinctions between the proletariat and the bourgeoisie. The emergence of teenage subcultures in the 1950s and 1960s was a product of market capitalism in the sense that teenagers were created for the first time as a specific section of consumers with their own tastes and spending habits, but they also symbolized a threat to the social order by identifying with radical subcultural elements. This threat was represented throughout the postwar period in a series of moral panics and crises which revolved around notions of delinquency, mugging, drugs, sexual licence and deviancy. *Resistance Through Rituals* included studies of skinheads, teds, mods, rockers, junkies, Rastafarians and hippies, and there lurked a series of assumptions throughout the anthology that these subcultures existed within a parent culture defined by class. As Robert Hewison has argued, however, 'the issue that remained unresolved ... was to what extent the "magical" resolutions that these different ritualistic assertions of identity represented were truly capable of resisting domination' (1994, 190). Hall argued that such subcultures were the products of specific socio-economic circumstances, and therefore were determined by capitalist structures of power, but so too the structural position of subcultures enabled them to expose the contradictions of the parent culture. Hall thus located the agency for exposing ideological contradictions in contemporary society in youth subcultures, even if their capacity for developing effective forms of resistance remained underexamined.

But Hall's work was increasingly turning away from a 'simple' search for agencies of resistance to a thorough examination of forms of domination. *Policing the Crisis*, which he co-wrote with Chas Critcher, Tony Jefferson, John Clarke and Brian Roberts, was a study of 'mugging' as a social phenomenon in contemporary British society. Hall and his co-authors were not interested particularly in 'mugging' from criminological perspectives, nor were they interested in the 'revolutionary' aspects of mugging. Instead, the book was a study both of the 'social causes' of mugging and 'why British society reacts to mugging in the extreme way it does'. Mugging had become 'an index of the disintegration of the social order' in political and media discourses:

> The book is ... about a society slipping into a certain kind of *crisis*. It tries to examine why and how the themes of *race, crime* and *youth* – condensed into the image of 'mugging' – come to serve as the articulator of the crisis, as its ideological conductor. It is also about how these themes have functioned as a mechanism for the construction of an authoritarian consensus, a conservative backlash. (Hall et al. 1978, viii)

Policing the Crisis is almost Foucauldian in its analysis of 'mugging' as a discursive formation which is produced within political and media discourse as 'panics' and 'crises' in order to entrench further the authoritarian values of law and order. It borrowed extensively from marxist studies of ideology, specifically from Althusser's 'ideological state apparatus' and Gramsci's hegemony, but also developed earlier anthropological work, such as Stan Cohen's *Folk Devils and Moral Panic* (1972). As such, it is as much an examination of the rising 'new right' ideologies in the 1970s as it is an attempt to grapple with the complex and ambiguous relationship between mugging and forms of class resistance.

The next phase of Hall's work developed the former strand more than the latter. It became clear to him that the election to government of the Conservative party under Mrs Thatcher's leadership in 1979 was the obvious manifestation of a political and cultural shift which had been taking place in Britain throughout the 1970s. 'Thatcherism', as Hall termed it in 1983, was a new development in right-wing ideology in Britain, which significantly departed from the establishment conservatism of the early postwar decades. Hall examined the phenomenon of Thatcherism in three books in the 1980s: *The Politics of Thatcherism* (1983), *The Hard Road to Renewal* (1988) and *New Times* (1989). Hall sought to explain and understand why Thatcher's policies were so popular among the working classes in Britain in the 1980s, and recognized that the attraction of her particular brand of politics – what Hall called 'authoritarian populism' – could not be explained only in economic terms. Thatcher's populism was based on ideologies of patriotism and national identity (the Falklands War in particular), 'family values', 'traditionalism', 'authority' (standing up to the miners), all of which are consonant with traditional 'one nation' Toryism. But it coupled these with 'the aggressive themes of neoliberalism – self-interest, competitive individualism, anti-statism' (Hall 1988, 48) and material social relations, including the use of new media forms (such as the marketing strategies of Saatchi & Saatchi and the dominance of the tabloids). Initially, Hall's overtly Gramscian conclusions on the success of Thatcherism as an ideology found its marxist detractors. In a famous series of articles in the *New Left Review*, Jessop and others argued that Hall's analysis of Thatcherism failed to grasp the real economic shifts and social reconstructions it effected (Jessop et al. 1984, 1985, 1990). As Thatcherism continued without serious ideological challenge, however, Jessop and his colleagues began to admit the importance of ideology in securing the support of the working class within a conservative economic and social politics.

Hall became an important critic and analyst of the new right ideologies which dominated Britain in the 1980s, but while his publications and research focused largely on Thatcherism, he was also busily engaged in consolidating cultural studies in his new post as Professor of Sociology at the Open University, which he took up in 1979. He was a key contributor to the module on 'Popular Culture' which ran at the Open University between 1982 and 1987, which Antony Easthope has described as 'the most ambitious, serious and comprehensive intervention in cultural studies in Britain and, apart from the work of the Birmingham Centre, the most important' (1991, 74). In addition, he has continued to publish important essays which have defined and delimited the values, methods and problems of cultural studies through the 1980s and 1990s. He remains committed to marxist analyses of culture and society, but Hall's marxism is one which registers the interplay between many competing, shifting ideologies and cultural differences. Thus Hall characterized the relationship between marxism and cultural studies not in terms of a theory or an application, but as a struggle. Cultural studies, for Hall, was 'working within shouting distance of marxism, working on marxism, working against marxism, working with it, working to try to develop marxism' (Morley and Chen 1996, 265), never quite inside it or produced by it. Hall's concerns with race, ethnicity, feminism and youth subcultures throughout his work prompted a number of speculations that Hall was indeed more a post-marxist than a marxist proper, but this is to ignore the ways in which Hall has himself insisted on marxism as a shifting set of questions and concerns, not as an orthodox theory or doctrine:

> I am a 'post-marxist' only in the sense that I recognize the necessity to move beyond orthodox marxism, beyond the notion of marxism guaranteed by the laws of history. But I still operate somewhere within what I understand to be the discursive limits of a marxist position ... So 'post' means, for me, going on thinking on the ground of a set of *established problems*, a problematic. It doesn't mean deserting that terrain but rather, using it as one's *reference point*. (Hall, in Morley and Chen 1996, 148–9)

Stuart Hall remains active in writing and thinking about the politics of contemporary Britain, and in contributing to debates about the evolution and current practices of cultural studies. Although it could be argued that cultural studies as a discipline has moved away from the marxism of Hall and its other founders, it has remained closer to Hall's persistent concern with the politics of identity and difference, and to the methodological combination of ethnographic study with discursive analysis. The establishment of the discipline of cultural studies, and his contributions to its methods and modes of analysis, is Hall's most important achievement to date, but, as Morley and Chen argue, he has also attracted the admiration of his peers as a role model of intellectual practice:

> Hall has demonstrated his commitment to living out the contradictions of the role of the 'organic intellectual' identified by Gramsci – the commitment to being at the very forefront of intellectual, theoretical work and, simultaneously, the commitment to the attempt to transmit the ideas thus generated, well beyond the confines of the 'intellectual class'. (1996, 20)

John Brannigan

Further reading and works cited

Cohen, S. *Folk Devils and Moral Panic*. London, 1972.
Dworkin, D. *Cultural Marxism in Postwar Britain*. Durham, NC, 1997.
Easthope, A. *British Post-Structuralism since 1968*. London, 1991.
Hall, S. 'A Sense of Classlessness', *Universities and Left Review*, Autumn 1958a.
—. 'In the No Man's Land', *Universities and Left Review*, Winter 1958b.
—. 'Cultural Studies: Two Paradigms', *Media, Culture and Society*, 2, 1980.
—. *The Hard Road to Renewal*. London, 1988.
—. 'The Emergence of Cultural Studies and the Crisis of the Humanities', *October*, 53, 1990.
— and du Gay, P. (eds) *Questions of Cultural Identity*. London, 1996.
— and Jefferson, T. (eds) *Resistance Through Rituals*. London, 1976.
— and Jacques, M. (eds) *The Politics of Thatcherism*. London, 1983.
— and Jacques, M. (eds) *New Times*. London, 1989.
— and Whannel, P. *The Popular Arts*. London, 1964.
— et al. *Policing the Crisis*. London, 1978.
— et al. (eds) *Culture, Media, Language*. London, 1980.
— et al. (eds) *State and Society in Contemporary Britain*. Cambridge, 1984.
Hewison, R. *Culture and Consensus*. London, 1994.

Jessop, B. et al. 'Authoritarian Populism: Two Nations and Thatcherism', *New Left Review*, 147, 1984.
— et al. 'Thatcherism and the Politics of Hegemony', *New Left Review*, 165, 1985.
— et al. 'Farewell to Thatcherism?', *New Left Review*, 179, 1990.
Milner, A. *Cultural Materialism*. Victoria, 1993.
Morley, D. and Chen, K.-H. (eds) *Stuart Hall*. London, 1996.
Storey, J. (ed.) *Cultural Theory and Popular Culture*. Hemel Hempstead, 1994.
— (ed.) *What is Cultural Studies?* London, 1996.

13. Terry Eagleton (1943–)

> If criticism is no more than a knack, like being able to whistle and hum different tunes simultaneously, then it is at once rare enough to be preserved in the hands of an elite, while 'ordinary' enough to require no stringent theoretical justification. (Eagleton 1983, 214)

The greatest part of Terry Eagleton's career has been devoted to attacking the 'genteel amateurism' of literary criticism in English departments, by which literary study was only ever a form of 'appreciation'. His publication of *Literary Theory: An Introduction*, first published in 1983 and reprinted thirteen times between then and its second edition in 1996, reflected the increasing interest in theory among literary critics, but it also popularized theory for a generation of subsequent students and teachers. That for Eagleton this was always a political manoeuvre is evident in the quotation above, for behind this comment lie the debates concerning how we might define culture and the literary canon, and how we might explode the idea that aesthetics is a matter of fine, refined feeling, with all the class bias which such feeling invokes. The connections between Eagleton's introductory guide of literary theory and his marxism are, of course, obvious. *Literary Theory* was never going to be an explanatory book in the sense of an impartial consideration of the theories discussed. In describing and explaining New Critical, hermeneutic, structuralist, poststructuralist and psychoanalytical theories, Eagleton was also intervening in the debates about theory and from an explicitly marxist position. Rather than a neutral survey of literary theories, the book's aim is to reveal the ideological underpinnings of modern literary theories. Eagleton himself calls for a new 'rhetorical' practice, a theory which would acknowledge its own interested status, its own political commitment. Marxism and feminism, then, are celebrated as theoretical practices which do not hide behind the pretence of theoretical and political neutrality. Many teachers now refuse *Literary Theory* because of its obviously polemical stance. But Eagleton is fair to the strengths of the approaches he discusses, while admitting his own dissension from them. And this dissension is seen as inevitable. Eagleton refuses the idea that such issues could be adjudicated with 'impartiality'. Such thinking is a part of the very liberal humanism which his work so strenuously resists.

To begin thus is to suggest that Eagleton's significance as a theorist is as a popularizer and a polemicist. But the opening quotation also suggests a third, equally important aspect of Eagleton's work: the way in which Eagleton's own style is intrinsically a part of his theoretical work. Lucid, witty and combative, Eagleton's writing style is frequently a provocation as well as entertainment. Theoretical excurses are discussed through frequently extravagant hyperbole, comic irony (what Stephen Regan has described as 'deflationary humour') and the use of such rhetorical devices as alliteration, parallelism, zeugma (as, for example, in saying 'language lies at the root of human identity and to tamper with that is either poetry or treason'; Regan 1998, 149). His is an anecdotal, epigrammatic wit ('Shakespeare still embodies timeless value; it's just that you can't produce his stuff without the sponsorship of Prudential Insurance', Regan 1998, 147), whose literary antecedents might be Wilde or Swift, as Stephen Regan has noted:

> A favourite Swiftian technique is to construct some plausible, sophisticated argument with meticulous care, only to knock the skids from under it and watch it topple to oblivion. Conversely, we are just as likely to be presented with a set of seemingly ridiculous, far-fetched assumptions, and then discover in the course of argument how just and reasonable they are. (1998, viii)

Eagleton himself cites Benjamin's comment that 'there is no better starting point for thought than laughter' (1990, 337). Although this kind of flippant wit often means that Eagleton raises more hostages to fortune than he can afford to, it also illuminates a real desire to communicate. Many readers have been introduced to the finer details of aesthetic philosophy through the use of exactly such humour.

While the examples of Eagleton's style given above are to be found in the transcript of his inaugural lecture as Warton Professor of English at Oxford, entitled 'The Crisis of Contemporary Culture' (1992; rpt. Regan 1998), this kind of mordant wit is also to be found in Eagleton's most difficult, but arguably also his best, work – *The Ideology of the Aesthetic* (1990). In this work, as in *Literary Theory*, the ideological motivation of that which is apparently 'ideology-free' is revealed: here, the aesthetic in place of literary criticism or theory. Eagleton demonstrates how the aesthetic has been appropriated as 'Culture' to serve bourgeois individualism, but counters this orthodoxy by reading the aesthetic through the figure of the oxymoron and by insisting on the intrinsically contradictory nature of the aesthetic, as of other things. Embedded in the tradition of the aesthetic is a contradictory clash between an impulse to freedom and a complicity with power, which only a dialectical thought can both trace and interrogate. Such rhetorical strategies as comic irony and serious flippancy are then related to Eagleton's commitment to dialectical thinking, or the attempt to hold oppositions in a productive tension.

This kind of attention to dialectical thinking is the most frequently overlooked aspect of Eagleton's work. The most frequent criticism of Eagleton's marxism, usually from non- or anti-marxist critics, is that of a determinism in his theoretical thinking which any close reading would show is just not there. Instead, I would argue, Eagleton's theoretical marxisms have been thoroughly self-reflexive and revisionary. Indeed, the very course of marxist literary theory in Britain might be traced through Eagleton's publishing career. After *The New Left Church* (1966), the closest we get to a 'vulgar' deterministic marxism, Eagleton proceeds through such successive influences as Raymond Williams (*Shakespeare and Society*, 1967), Lucien Goldmann and an emerging Althusserianism (*Myths of Power*, 1975), Pierre Macherey (*Criticism and Ideology*, 1976), Benjamin and Brecht (*Walter Benjamin*, 1981), strands of feminism, psychoanalysis and poststructuralism (*The Rape of Clarissa*, 1982) and, in the insistence on contradiction in *The Ideology of the Aesthetic* (1990), Adorno. These studies have introduced the work of other theorists to new audiences but they have also reflected critically upon that work. Eagleton's absorption of Machereyan ideas in *Criticism and Ideology,* for example, is also a critique of their latent aestheticism, their continuing allegiance to 'Literature' as an ideological construction. And Eagleton's debt to Lucien Goldmann's theory of 'categorial structures' as key mediations between literary form, textual ideology and social relations is criticized in the later edition of *Myths of Power* as a kind of theoretical 'over-totalisation' (1988, xiii).

His own work has also been open to this kind of revisionary analysis, with much of Eagleton's later career commenting obliquely on earlier work. The most significant turn comes with the publication of *Walter Benjamin* (1981), when Eagleton leaves the more theoreticist models of Althusserianism behind. Such high theoreticism was most acutely evident in the schemas of *Criticism and Ideology* (1976a), with its 'science of the text'. Here the literary text is situated within a range of contexts: the general mode of production (the dominant form, such as late capitalism); the literary mode of production (such as print-capitalism, or distributing cheap broadsides in the street); authorial ideology (not an 'expression' of the author's beliefs, but that which is produced by a combination of the general ideology and biographical factors); and aesthetic ideology (the specific, aesthetic region of the general ideology). The literary text is then seen as produced by an interaction of these structures, but it is not the passive product of such formations, since the text also 'determines its own determinants' (1976a, 63). Eagleton's attention to the specificity of different formations, and the many individual examples cited in support, are more nuanced than might be anticipated from such a scheme. The relationship between the literary text and ideology is not a determined one: not all texts, for example, work 'against' ideology, in being able to reveal it just by their 'literariness' (1976a, 68). And the relationship between literary text and ideology can be dialectical once the 'literary' is itself analysed as ideological. (The later work on the aesthetic sketched one such philosophical context for this kind of approach.)

However, this kind of explicitly marxist science is abandoned thereafter. In retrospect, then, *Walter Benjamin* (1981) marks the moment at which Eagleton turns to Brechtian praxis rather than some kind of pure marxist theory. This is reflected too in *Literary Theory: An Introduction,* in which the concluding chapter 'Political Criticism' intentionally disappoints expectations in providing no account of 'Marxist literary theory'. Instead throughout the book, and in later work too, other theoretical ideas are shamelessly appropriated for marxist ends. Derrida, Kristeva, Lacan – all are used as tools for political analysis. In *Walter Benjamin,* the practice of the socialist worker is defined not only as 'projective', in its gestures towards an alternative, and 'polemical', in its challenge to inequality, but also 'appropriative' (1981, 113). Such work might include 'encouraging others to reap pleasure from the beauty of religious imagery, encouraging the production of works with no overt political content whatsoever, and arguing in particular times and places for the "greatness", "truth", "profoundly moving", "joyful", "wonderful" qualities of particular works ...' (1981, 113). These literary qualities are, of course, also those celebrated by liberal humanism and defenders of traditional canonicity, but liberal humanist ideas of 'Literature' are called upon here in ways which democratize while also questioning these values. Similarly, while deconstruction is one of the many theoretical influences at work in *The Rape of Clarissa* (1982) and in *William Shakespeare* (1986a), other work in this period argues that deconstruction unallied with political feminism or marxism cannot fulfil its radical claims. (Such work would include the chapter 'Marxism and Deconstruction' in *Walter Benjamin,* 1981 and the essays on poststructuralism in *Against the*

Grain, 1986, originally published in 1984.) The consequence of a deconstructive style divorced from a politicized historicism is read into William Warner's masculinist celebration of Richardson's Lovelace (1979):

> Clarissa … holds to a severely representational ideology of writing, trusts in the stable sign and the unitary self, and subscribes to the values of truth, coherence and causality; Lovelace, by contrast, is a proto-Nietzschean who celebrates plurality, groundlessness and *jouissance.* It seems logical, then, that a contemporary deconstructionist should find Lovelace the hero and Clarissa the villain, without allowing a little matter like rape to modify his judgement. (Eagleton 1982, 65–6)

Eagleton's engagement here is to defend a materialist feminism, but this does not mean that poststructuralist ideas are not part of his own writing. There is a recognition here that Clarissa and Lovelace embody different attitudes towards textuality, but Eagleton's own reading of the novel is alert to the kinds of indeterminacies which Lovelace exploits, and in the distinction between awareness and political misuse lies Eagleton's frustration with much contemporary poststructuralist theory. Two years later, *The Function of Criticism* (1984) returns to the eighteenth century, a time which Eagleton argues preceded the separation of literature from its culture, when literature was 'foregrounded as the medium of vital concerns deeply rooted in the general, intellectual, cultural and political life of an epoch' (107). The eighteenth century then becomes a surprisingly traditionalist model for contemporary criticism. But it is also a return to the kinds of Enlightenment values which Eagleton would come to defend in his attacks on postmodernism in the 1990s: the stubborn insistence on our need for truth, reason, justice, without the fastidious distancing of scare quotes.

Eagleton's immensely prolific career, then, illustrates the changes within marxist approaches to literature over the past thirty years as it is also a continuing engagement and revision of his own practice as critic and theorist. Indeed, in more recent writings, Eagleton appears to be increasingly aware of criticism in advance. For example, in the final essay of *Crazy John and the Bishop* (1998a), there is an attempt to disarm criticism by anticipating it. There is a strength here, in so far as it recognizes that one's own work is inevitably a part of other debates and even suggests an ability to see from other positions. But there is also a tendency to caricature such criticisms, which comes to take the place of an engagement with them.

Many perceived a turn to Irish Studies in Eagleton's career with the publication of *Heathcliff and the Great Hunger* (1995), *Crazy John and the Bishop* (1998a) and *Scholars and Rebels* (1999). But Eagleton's interest in Ireland had certainly been apparent not only in such works of the later 1980s as the Field Day pamphlet on 'Nationalism: Irony and Commitment' (1988) and his own creative writing (*Saints and Scholars,* 1987; *Saint Oscar,* 1989), but in an interest in Yeats and Joyce evident as early as *Criticism and Ideology* (1976a, 151–7). While it is easy to deride Eagleton's gestures towards his own 'Irishness', more potent is the argument that Irish culture is and has been politicized in a more overt way than is the case in Britain. When thought of in these terms, Eagleton's turn to Irish studies is hardly surprising.

Concurrent with these works have been continuing attacks on theoretical postmodernism (*The Illusions of Postmodernism,* 1996 and *The Idea of Culture,* 2000), but there are important ways in which these interests overlap. If the pressing political issue is now that of an international conflict between advanced capitalism and postcolonial emergent economies, then for Eagleton, Ireland is particularly situated, 'cusped ... between modernity and postmodernity', poised at the moment at which it decides whether to 'continue to cast its fortunes with a global capitalism' or to 'draw upon the resources of its own history of dispossession in order to align itself with the coming epoch' (Regan 1998, 327). But the specific economic conditions of contemporary Ireland, which resemble the high-tech and service-sector economies of advanced capitalism, are absent from Eagleton's account, where contemporary Ireland is primarily the site of continued ethnic conflict. There's a sense here in which Eagleton's argument is ill served by the specificities of his example, and this is a more general problem in Eagleton's career overall.

Eagleton's polemical stances are crucial in that they bring a lively and honest engagement to debates which are often arcane and politically unaware (perhaps deliberately so). But what Eagleton gains in wit and force, he often loses in subtlety. His is not the work of the miniaturist. Instead there's a kind of deliberate ham-fistedness throughout all his work, an almost inevitable tendency for wit and provocation to become forms of reductiveness. Eagleton's work raises the temperature of literary and cultural analysis with its provocation, its frequent sarcasm and combative manoeuvres. The example from *The Rape of Clarissa* above is, then, an important one. In discussing the 'rape' of Clarissa, Eagleton chooses a topic where the ethical responsibility is high indeed, and unavoidable. Eagleton's cultural work insists that textual interpretation matters, that we have a responsibility to connect our political aspirations with our reading practices.

Eagleton's significance on literary theory, the philosophy of aesthetics and cultural politics in Britain has been immense, his work already equalling that of Raymond Williams in its influence. He has been, and continues to be, an immensely prolific and wide-ranging writer, whose interests have included Shakespeare, Yeats, 1890s Britain, Samuel Richardson and so on. Indeed, the bibliography included here can only cite major monographs. As the most distinguished British writer working within marxist cultural politics, he has continued to provoke and inspire in equal measure. Through the growing acceptance of theory within British universities, Eagleton's interventions have maintained a marxist dimension – often adapting, often refusing and always engaging with contemporary and competing theories.

Moyra Haslett

Further reading and works cited

Eagleton, T. *The New Left Church*. London, 1966.
—. *Shakespeare and Society*. London, 1967.
—. *Exiles and Émigrés: Studies in Modern Literature*. London, 1970.
—. *Criticism and Ideology*. London, 1976a.
—. *Marxism and Literary Criticism*. London, 1976b.
—. *Walter Benjamin, or Towards a Revolutionary Criticism*. London, 1981.
—. *The Rape of Clarissa*. Oxford, 1982.
—. *Literary Theory*. Oxford, 1983.
—. *The Function of Criticism*. London, 1984.
—. *William Shakespeare*. Oxford, 1986a.
—. *Against the Grain*. London, 1986b.
—. *Saints and Scholars*. London, 1987.
—. *Myths of Power*. London, 1988a.

—. *Nationalism*. Derry, 1988b.
—. *Saint Oscar*. Derry, 1989.
—. *The Ideology of the Aesthetic*. Oxford, 1990.
—. *Ideology: An Introduction*. London, 1991.
—. *The Crisis of Contemporary Culture*. Oxford, 1993.
— (ed.) *Ideology*. London, 1994.
—. *Heathcliff and the Great Hunger*. London, 1995.
—. *The Illusions of Postmodernism*. Oxford, 1996.
—. *Crazy John and the Bishop and other Essays on Irish Culture*. Cork, 1998a.
—. *Scholars and Rebels in Nineteenth-Century Ireland*. Oxford, 1999.
—. *The Idea of Culture*. Oxford, 2000.
— and Milne, D. (eds) *Marxist Literary Theory*. Oxford, 1996.
Regan, S. (ed.) *The Eagleton Reader*. Oxford, 1998.
Warner, W. B. *Reading Clarissa*. New Haven, CT, 1979.

14. *Screen* (1971–)

During the 1960s a strange outbreak of Francophilia associated with the journal, *New Left Review*, took off from Louis Althusser's marxist ideas. Although the immediate consequences were mainly political, the long-term effect, one still working its way through English culture, was to inject an almost unprecedented form of rationalism into the pervasively empiricist tradition.

In 1964, for example, Tom Nairn argued that the history of the English working class, cut off from the Enlightenment, could be explained by the degree to which it was 'immunized against theory' yet needed it 'like no other' comparable proletariat. Nairn's essay concludes, 'It still does' (1964, 57). Around 1970 a small group linked with the New Left was encouraged to develop work in the area of art and aesthetic practice. Since at that time literary study was hermetically sealed in a concern with 'authors' and 'imagination' they decided to attempt theoretical work in a relatively untheorized domain, cinema. The vehicle chosen for this intervention was the film journal *Screen*, published from 1971 by the Society for Education in Film and Television funded by the British Film Institute. Following an idea taken up from the Left Book Club in the 1930s *Screen* sponsored reading groups throughout the country. At one point in 1977 *Screen* had nearly 1,200 subscribers. Two other factors shaped its trajectory. One was the degree to which, like the contemporary *Tel Quel* group in France, *Screen* succeeded as a collective endeavour with a number of people learning from and playing off each other. A second spur was the seemingly endless stream of new names that arrived across the Channel each month. Moving out from a basis in Russian formalism, Brecht and Althusser, *Screen* progressively took on board Metz, Bellour, Lacan, Kristeva, Foucault (but not, significantly, Derrida: see Easthope 1996).

In distinction to the other arts, cinema seems to have a particular relation to the real. Film is both caused by the real (light rays reflected from an object being recorded on light-sensitive material) and resembles the real by looking like it. From its origins in the 1920s film theory could be divided into two contrasted positions, those of 'realists' (typified by André Bazin) and 'creationists' (Rudolf Arnheim). While the realist view valued cinema because of its purchase on the real, creationists insisted that cinema did not just record but was *also*, in addition, artistically significant. Both positions share the view that cinema has a privileged relation to the real. *Screen* broke with any such 'naturalist' or 'reflectionist' assumptions. It was helped along the path because film theory in the 1960s had already developed from *auteur* theory into a formalism concerned with genre and iconography. *Screen* developed this approach by joining it to structuralism, largely retrieved from French sources, which supported a general assumption that any form of meaning must be understood as the effect of a system producing it. In the place of a notion of film as reflection of the real, *Screen* asserted in 1976 that 'no one has yet seen a signified without a signifier' (Heath 1981a, 44), and that 'a text is structured primarily at the level of the signifier' since 'it is the order of the signifiers which determines the production of the signifieds' (Wollen 1976, 19). It was consistently argued that film, including documentary film, should be approached as an act of representation and not as a record of the real, an achievement of culture, not nature.

This premise was powerfully confirmed by Christian Metz. He had already claimed that in a film 'the image of a house does not signify "house", but rather "Here is a house"'' (1974, 116). His 'The Imaginary Signifier' was published in Paris in May 1975 and translated for *Screen* later that summer. It draws on psychoanalysis and the theory of the fetish to argue that in cinema, the more vividly present the image seems to make its object, the more it insists the object is actually lacking, 'made present', as Metz says, 'in the mode of absence' (1982, 44).

Starting from this basis the *Screen* project came to be defined in an essay of 1976 as the attempt to theorize 'the encounter of Marxism and psychoanalysis on the terrain of semiotics' (Heath 1981b, 201). The aim was to think together cinema overdetermined semiologically, ideologically, subjectively. In concluding I shall offer some comments on the limitations of this endeavour; here I need say no more about the diachronic construction of the project except that just at the point when the hoped-for synthesis trembled on the edge of dissolution, after the mid-1970s it found a new impetus in relation to feminist theorizations of film.

Dovetailed with Althusserian marxism *Screen's* formalist emphasis imported a striking novelty. Most traditional marxist analysis of art and literature shared with conventional criticism a main concern with 'content' though differed in thinking of this as an expression of ideology. *Screen* was determined to understand film not just in terms of thematic content and ideology at the level of the signified – what was referred to dismissively as 'the province of a traditional "content analysis"'' – but on the basis of its 'ideological *operation*' (Heath 1981b, 201). That concern is taken over from the work of the Russian formalists who directed attention towards the *differentia specifica* of literature, its particular 'literariness'. With close attention to the formal properties of cinema *Screen* undertook a detailed and thorough investigation of deep focus, lighting, the point of view shot. These constituted its 'ideological operation', at the level of the signifier. Film was to be understood as 'a *specific signifying practice*':

> 'Signifying' is the recognition of a language as a systematic articulation of meanings; 'practice' refers to the process of this articulation, to the work of the production of meanings, and in so doing it brings into the argument the problem of the relations of the subject within that work; 'specific' gives the necessity for the analysis of a particular signifying practice in its specific formations. (Heath 1974, 128)

This needs a little unpacking. The concept of a 'signifying practice' picks up the claim that film makes rather than reflects meanings; 'specificity' refers back to the Russian used by Sklovsky and the others but has acquired a decisive connotation from Althusser's analysis of 'practice'.

The concepts *Screen* borrowed from Althusser were the political, the economic and the ideological. Marx can be accused of thinking that the structure of society was mechanically determined as a fixed shape, with the economic structure forming 'the real foundation' on which rises a 'political superstructure' and to which correspond forms of ideology (Marx and Engels 1950, I, 328). It's not hard to spot here that Marx's thinking is *spatial*. Althusser rethinks structure as *temporal*, a process of transformation, and therefore a practice. Accordingly, each practice has a relative autonomy in relation to the others; it operates as itself, not something else, but it is simultaneously determined by its place in a totality. This account underpinned *Screen*'s conception of cinema as a signifying practice. The New Left took great encouragement from this view because it made it possible to argue that marxism did not entail a mechanical sense of determination but rather recognized the 'specific effectivity' of each practice. It was left for others later to ask if a practice is autonomous, exactly how can it be relative? if relative, how can it be autonomous?

Given his commitment to thinking of society as a 'social formation' constantly in process, Althusser was compelled to rethink inherited ideas about science. He would not consider it as a static knowledge, achieved once and for all, but rather as a form of practice, *theoretical* practice. In doing so, he contrived to maintain a traditional marxist contrast between 'science' and 'ideology' since theoretical practice was defined as a transformation and refinement of ideology. These ideas empowered the *Screen* project. If as an object cinema was ideological practice, the theoretical work of the journal could construct a knowledge of it. Moreover, Althusser's willingness to think of practices in terms of 'different times' (Althusser and Balibar 1975, 96) lets him embrace the possibility that subjectivity unfolds according to its own temporality. Althusser contends that the subject of ideology is constructed through a process of *interpellation*, that is ideology 'hails' the subject into position, rather as someone in the street calls 'Hey, you there!' and you have to recognize that it is really you who is being addressed.

In a recent revitalization of the concept Judith Butler suggests that for Althusser interpellation 'precedes and forms the subject' and 'appears to constitute the prior condition' of 'subject-centred speech acts' (1997, 24). I think Althusser indeed supposes that the subject is exclusively constituted by interpellation, of which subjectivity is an effect. But here Althusser's understanding departs from that of Jacques Lacan (on whom he initially drew in his formulation of subjectivity) which defines the signifier as that which 'represents a subject not for another subject but for another signifier' (1972, 194); subjectivity and desire always *exceed* any position into which the subject is hailed. A rather formal distinction but, as we shall see, this bad weld leads to a fissure that runs through the whole project. *Screen* follows Althusser in treating the subject as *only* the effect of interpellation. Interpellation constitutes or produces the subject to imagine itself as constitutive, a free agent (a duality deriving from Lacan's theory of the mirror stage). Interpellation therefore comprehends both the opposed accounts of the subject traditional in philosophy, '(1) a free subjectivity, a centre of initiatives, author of and responsible for its actions; (2) a subjected being, who submits to a higher authority' (Althusser 1977, 169). In this view ideology functions through a pervasive naturalization. Developing from Althusser *Screen* works out a number of propositions for the analysis of film.

Mainstream cinema is, in Althusser's terms, an ideological state apparatus (the fact that Hollywood is an extreme expression of private capital is not thought to damage the argument that it nevertheless serves the state). As such it constructs forms of subjectivity, as Metz described: 'the cinematic institution is not just the cinema industry (which works to fill cinemas, not to empty them), it is also the mental machinery – another industry – which spectators "accustomed to the cinema" have internalized historically' (1975, 18). *Screen* proceeded, though with a certain unease, on the assumption that cinema as a 'mental institution' produced a position for the reader. This was 'inscribed in the film' (MacCabe 1975, 61), bringing about an 'implicit reader', one who 'conforms to the supposed intentions of the text' (Brewster 1977, 162).

Over the question of position *Screen* leans on the work of Julia Kristeva and her concept of the subject (*Screen* also borrowed the idea of 'signifying practice' from her, see: 1976, 60–75). In *Revolution in Poetic Language*, Kristeva affirmed that the 'realm of signification' is always 'a realm of *positions* . . . establishing the identification of the subject' (1984, 44). The avant-garde work of Mallarmé, Lautréamont and others is potentially radical because it threatens to break the unity of the subject. Yet there is a difference here. Kristeva offers a history of literary texts analysed in terms of subject and position while *Screen* sees position as an effect of the text on its reader.

A characteristic of what I have been calling 'the *Screen* problematic' is its readiness to incorporate a range of theorizations, some of which have already been addressed. *Screen* contrasted two forms of subject position as afforded by the conventional realist text on the one hand and the modernist or experimental text on the other. In working this out *Screen* referred back to the 1930s and Brecht's critique of theatrical form. Brecht argued that realist theatre produced empathy in the spectator. Non-naturalist theatre, using 'alienation-effects', brought about a critical attitude. Thus realism led to passive identification, non-realism to active criticism.

After 1968 *Cahiers du Cinéma* amplified Brecht's formal account of spectator reactions by linking it with Althusserian analysis. In addition to the intervention between the work of Brecht and that of Althusser, Russian formalism, the *Cahiers* manifesto and the work of Kristeva were fed into the *Screen* problematic. The novel move, however, was to rethink cinema within the framework of psychoanalysis. Since cinema is a visual signifying practice *Screen* turned to Lacan's theory of vision. The topic needs some care.

In *Seminar 11* of 1964 Lacan discusses the development of modern 'perspective' representation in the art of the Quattrocento (see 1977b, 65–119). He was out fishing when a small boy in the group pointed to a sardine tin on the surface, glittering in the sun: '*You see that can? Do you see it? Well, it doesn't see you*' (95, emphasis in original). The can does not see you but someone situated there might, since whatever I can see constitutes a point from which I could be seen. Lacan says 'That which is light looks at me' (96): I think I see the sardine tin but the same light is the grounding condition of possibility for someone else to look at me from there. In supposing I see – as though I alone could see – I disavow the point of view I myself can never see from since it belongs to the Other, the order of the symbolic. Next issue: 'I see only from one point, but in my existence I am looked at from all sides' (72); to look and 'see the world' comes within the dominion of the conscious I and what Lacan terms 'the imaginary'. To 'be the object of the gaze' represents the operation of the unconscious, the domain of the Other on which I depend for my being but which I can never lay claim to. In Quattrocento painting the aim has been for the look to overcome the gaze in *dompte-regard*, 'a taming of the gaze' (109), the imaginary to appear fully present to itself by containing the symbolic. Perspective would ensure that I see and possess the represented image while the inescapable possibility of the gaze, looking back, is controlled and effaced. By rendering the image as an object for my eye Quattrocento painting techniques try to exclude the gaze of another.

In its engagement of marxism and psychoanalysis *Screen* was willing to map the gaze and the look, the gaps and fissures introduced by the symbolic and the seeming plenitude fantasized by the imaginary onto Althusser's account of the process of ideology as operating to produce 'a subjected being' who imagines itself as 'a free subjectivity, a centre of initiatives', and these in turn onto modernist and realist cinema and the positions into which each interpellated the viewer. Thus the textual operation of modernist and avant-garde film, exhibiting the signifiers it relied on, had a radical force because it would confront the reader with his or her construction within ideology, denaturalizing, opening up the possibility of social change. The operation of the signifiers in the realist text produce a position for the viewer but deny the fact of that production. In situating the viewer as a subject for the look, outside, as it were, and looking on, realism tends to confirm the subject as self-sufficient, a 'transcendental ego', a master, not wanting a world different from the one there appears to be.

In an essay on 'Narrative Space', Stephen Heath analyses 'classical', that is conventional, realist cinema. Film depends upon photography, which in turn depends on the Quattrocento tradition developed to depict three-dimensional objects on a flat surface. Quattrocento space relies not only on linear perspective but various strategies for placing the viewer at the centre of an apparently all-embracing view. But cinema consists of 'moving pictures'. This process constantly threatens the fixity and centring aimed for by the tradition of the still image. Figures and objects constantly move, moving in and out of frame, likely therefore to remind the spectator of the blank absence which surrounds the screen. Classical cinema would make good this dangerous instability through a narrativization which 'contains the mobility that could threaten the clarity of vision' (Easthope 1992, 76); its narrative constantly renews a centred perspective for the spectator. Heath cites the procedures advised by the film manuals – use of master-shot, the 180-degree rule, matching on action, eyeline matching, avoidance of 'impossible angles' and so on – and affirms these are designed to ensure that 'the spectator's illusion of seeing a continuous piece of action is not interrupted' (Heath 1977a, 80).

An example of 'narrative space' is the beginning of *Jaws*:

> a beach party with the camera tracking slowly right along the line of faces of the participants until it stops on a young man looking off; eyeline cut to a young woman who is thus revealed as the object of his gaze; cut to a high-angle shot onto the party that shows its general space, its situation before the start of the action with the run down to the ocean and the first shark attack. (Heath 1981b, 80)

Classical cinema always operates like this: 'in its movement, its framings, its cuts, its intermittences, the film ceaselessly poses an absence, a lack, which is ceaselessly recaptured for – one needs to be able to say "for in" – the film, that process binding the spectator in the realisation of the film's space' (88). Through such narrativization conventional cinema seeks to transform process into fixity in an ideological operation which promotes the imaginary over the symbolic.

It is just here, when the *Screen* project achieves what is probably its most complete statement, that the attempted totalization begins to fall into crisis. In the mid-1970s the air round the journal was thick with epistemological anxiety: by trying to make its theoretical project work in practice *Screen* inadvertently articulated doubts about the conception of knowledge as 'theoretical practice'. However, *Screen* adroitly changed position, propelled by an article published in 1975.

While many feminists had written against psychoanalysis, Juliet Mitchell's *Psychoanalysis and Feminism* argued that a theorization of the unconscious was necessary to understand why so many women seem to submit to patriarchy. Laura Mulvey followed this lead in 'Visual Pleasure and Narrative Cinema' by appropriating psychoanalysis 'as a political weapon' (1992, 111), extending the *Screen* analysis of the reader as an effect of the text to show that in mainstream cinema gender positions are assigned according to the principle '*Woman as image, man as bearer of the look*' (116, emphasis in original). Through this, cinema gives pleasure and that pleasure must be contested. What pleasure though? Early in the *Three Essays on the Theory of Sexuality* Freud introduced *Schaulust* or 'looking pleasure' ('scopophilia') as one expression of desire. Looking is obviously central to the pleasures of cinema. Taking up Freud's distinction between object libido and ego libido, Mulvey argues that scopophilia has both a sexual component, which Freud describes, but also a narcissistic aspect, investigated by Lacan in his analysis of the mirror stage. The first leads to looking at someone as an erotic object, the second to identification with an image seen. In principle one might expect these two contradictory forms to find equal expression in culture; in practice, they do not.

Mainstream cinema invites men to imagine identifying with men on the screen and, with them, look at women; women to identify with the women looked at:

> In a world ordered by sexual imbalance, pleasure in looking has been split between active/male and passive/female. The determining male gaze projects its fantasy onto the female figure, which is styled accordingly. In their traditional exhibitionist role women are simultaneously looked at and displayed, with their appearance coded for strong visual and erotic impact so that they can be said to connote *to-be-looked-at-ness*. (Mulvey 1992, 116)

The visual regime promotes men as active instigators of narrative while women are more often placed in a static position as an object of the look.

The same organization also mobilizes male homophobia: if in present society men in the audience do not look with desire at male objects on the screen it is because a man, says Mulvey, 'is reluctant to gaze at his exhibitionist like' (117). Elsewhere she suggests that for women 'trans-sex identification is a *habit* that easily becomes *second nature*' (129). If a woman enjoys conventional films it is because they revive a memory of her early 'masculine' or phallic phase (133).

Lacan speculates that having the phallus is masculine, being the phallus feminine (see 1977b, 289). Mulvey takes this up as an analysis of phallocentric society. The image of woman is bound into the structure twice over, both exciting the threat of castration and becoming fixed in place of that lack. She opens the wound her passivity is meant to close. On this basis, reintroducing the distinction between ego and object libido, Mulvey typifies two different kinds of film narrative. One offers mastery when a woman's mystery is investigated and she is punished or saved; in the other her imputed castration is disavowed as she is turned into a fetish. All these procedures depend upon classic realism and coherent narrative in order to establish identification as well as hold objects for the look (the public images in a modern city – advertisements and so on – provide overwhelming empirical support for Mulvey's discussion). Mulvey avoids the problem of an essentialist definition of gender by moving from signified to signifier, from the obvious maleness represented by on-screen heroes to formal operations of the 'look' of the camera and point-of-view shots. Problems remain, which I shall come back to.

The closer the *Screen* project approached to a worked-out synthesis between marxism, psychoanalysis and semiotics, the more the joints began to leak. When Stephen Heath asserted that the two processes of history and the unconscious form a 'necessary simultaneity – like the recto and verso of a piece of paper' (1976, 62) he implicitly concedes that they cannot be theoretically integrated. If so, it would not be possible to amalgamate an Althusserian theory of ideology with Lacan's account of the subject constructed in discourse. Associated doubts spilled onto *Screen*'s claim that its study of cinema was historical. At best its perspective on history was epochal, the history of the Quattrocento and realist visual representation, the capitalist institution of cinema and the 'mental machinery' that went with it. This provoked Terry Eagleton's charge against *Screen* that its formalism evaporated history so 'the historical specificity of the ideological codes' examined was merely a 'gesture' (1978, 23).

More troubles presented themselves. A major worry for *Screen* grew over Althusser's opposition between science and ideology. Sympathizers began to doubt that theory could produce a knowledge of cinema and this led to a more general failure of nerve, a situation exacerbated when Althusser himself conceded that the science/ideology opposition could not be regarded as absolute (see 1976, 106). Much more than a local difficulty peculiar to *Screen* the misgiving was part of a widespread intellectual phenomenon ensuing from Derrida's critique of logocentrism.

In 1978 an article in *Screen* pointed out what had always been disavowed:

> There remains an unbridgeable gap between 'real' readers/authors and inscribed ones ... Real readers are subject in history, living in given social formations, rather than mere subjects of a single text. The two types of subject are not commensurate. But for the purposes of formalism real readers are supposed to coincide with constructed readers. (Willemen 1978, 48)

There are all kinds of problems with 'real readers', mainly that analysis of them is only as good or bad as the theoretical model according to which their reality is interpreted. Willemen's brutal frankness demonstrates how far the *Screen* theory had been a structuralism all along. For Althusser, subjects are the effect of interpellation; for *Screen*, readers are the effect of the position provided by a textual organization. The problem extends to Mulvey's analysis as well. She assumes that the process of desire means that neither men nor women ever overshoot any fixity assigned to them. Adequately grasped, Lacan's teaching shows they always do. Nevertheless, Mulvey's classic article has led to a shelf of books concerned with the question of gender and the cinema, and particularly the issue of the feminine look at film, and it is not an exaggeration to say that today the prevailing though certainly not exclusive mode for feminist analysis of cinema has become psychoanalytic.

The importance of an attempted theoretical totalization is not measured by its theoretical cohesion. *Screen* has had a lasting effect on English intellectual life, and this is explicitly acknowledged in innovative versions of cultural studies, social psychology, art history and literary criticism the were published during the 1980s (see Easthope 1988). The subsequent influence of a generation of teachers on the students they taught is hard to calculate. Although few people today would give the same answers as *Screen* to the questions it posed, the debate resulting from them remains fully active or is overlooked only at a price.

Antony Easthope

Further reading and works cited

Althusser, L. *Essays in Self-Criticism*. London, 1976.
— 'Ideology and Ideological State Apparatuses', in *Lenin and Philosophy*. London, 1977.
— and Balibar, E. *Reading Capital*. London, 1975.
Brecht, B. *Brecht on Theatre*, ed. John Willett. London, 1964.
Brewster, B. 'Notes on the Text of John Ford's *Young Mr Lincoln* by the Editors of Cahiers du Cinéma', *Screen Reader 1*, ed. J. Ellis. London, 1977.
Butler, J. *Excitable Speech*. London, 1997.
Eagleton, T. 'Aesthetics and Politics', *New Left Review*, 107, January/February 1978.
Easthope, A. *British Post-Structuralism since 1968*. London, 1988.
— (ed.) *Contemporary Film Theory*. London, 1992.
Heath, S. 'Lessons from Brecht', *Screen*, 15, 2, Summer 1974.
—. 'Anata mo', *Screen*, 17, 4, Winter 1976.
—. *Questions of Cinema*. London, 1981a.
—. 'Jaws, Ideology and Film Theory'. *Popular Film and Television*, eds A. Bennett et al. London, 1981b.
—. *Revolution in Poetic Language*. New York, 1984.
Kristeva, J. 'Signifying Practice and Mode of Production'. *Edinburgh Magazine*, 76, 1976.
Lacan, J. 'Of Structure as an Inmixing of an Otherness Prerequisite to Any Subject Whatever', in *The Structuralist Controversy*, eds R. Macksey and E. Donato. Baltimore, MD, 1972.
—. *The Four Fundamental Concepts of Psycho-Analysis*. London, 1977a.
—. *Ecrits, A Selection*. London, 1977b.
MacCabe, C. 'The Politics of Separation', *Screen*, 16, 4, Winter, 1975.
Marx, K. *Capital*. London, 1970.
— and Engels, F. *Selected Works*. London, 1950.
Metz, C. *Film Language*. Oxford, 1974.
—. 'The Imaginary Signifier', *Screen*, 16, 2, Summer 1975.
—. *Psychoanalysis and Cinema*. London, 1982.
Mulvey, L. 'Visual Pleasure and Narrative Cinema', in *Contemporary Film Theory*, ed. A. Easthope. London, 1992.
Nairn, T. 'The English Working Class', *New Left Review*, 24, March/April 1964.
Willemen, P. 'Notes on Subjectivity', *Screen*, 19, 1, Spring 1978.
Wollen, P. '"Ontology" and "Materialism" in Film', *Screen*, 17, 1, Spring 1976.
—. 'Derrida and British Film Theory', *Applying: to Derrida*, eds J. Brannigan, R. Robbins and J. Wolfreys. London, 1996.

15. Structuralism and the Structuralist Controversy

Imagine if cultural phenomena could be broken down and analysed with all the precision of a chemistry experiment – this was the structuralist dream. Its most intense phase (in the English-speaking West) was a ten-year period from towards the end of the 1960s to the late-1970s, when the study of culture was felt by many to have been transformed from an art into a science. That feeling did not, of course, go unchallenged, and for a brief while all hell broke loose.

However much they may have since mutated, the reverberations emanating from the controversy – indeed the scandal – structuralism caused in the 1970s, especially although not exclusively in the UK, are ongoing. At their heart lies a dispute (no doubt an incommensurable disputation) over competing concepts of culture. But no less important – now as then – is a certain Anglo-American suspicion, if not hostility, towards continental thought.

For literary studies, the controversy took the form of criticism versus theory. By the end of the 1970s, literary theory had attained 'quite suddenly', in the words of British literary critic and essayist Frank Kermode, 'a central importance it had not possessed since Aristotle' (1983, 1). At that time literary theory was dominated by a structuralist approach to the study of narrative; hence the resistance to theory was in large measure a reaction against the perceived threat to literary studies posed by the scientific presumptions of structuralism. Yet it would be wrong to see it only as a professional demarcation dispute, for the resistance to theory – so often vehement if not violent in expression – was also energized by a culturally patrician attitude on the part of many English-speaking literary critics towards what they saw as the philosophical and scientific pretensions of European theorists.

We will come back to that controversy in a moment. But for now we need to ask, what are some of the key concepts and principles of structuralism? As would be expected, the importance of a certain concept of *structure* underpins the dream of a science of culture: just as the objects of scientific investigation are understood to be explicable in terms of chemical, mathematical and other measurable relations, so too, for structuralism, cultural phenomena are taken to be reducible to the hidden structures that generate and sustain them. Here the work of Ferdinand de Saussure is of crucial importance. Indeed it was Saussure himself who first projected (or dreamt of) a new mega-discipline he proposed to call semiology (or semiotics), based on his radical overturning of received ideas on language, whose proper object of study would be no less than the social life of signs in general (Saussure 1974, 16). Saussurean linguistics, then, was but a branch of the much larger, if not all-encompassing, discipline of semiotics whose object was to be the whole field of cultural practices and meanings, the totality, as it were, of sign usage in every conceivable occurrence and context.

As the inheritor of that dream, or the realization of the promised science of culture in general, structuralism has to be seen as having thought big! Consistent with that ambition, its objects of analysis are typically macrological in scale (not, for example, individual works of literature but literature as a *system*), where the aim is to identify the underlying rules and constraints that form the structural basis of particular meanings. Following Saussure, structuralism is concerned with *langue* (a rule-governing system, like language) rather than *parole* (particular cases of a general type: individual speech acts, for example, which are made possible by language as a system). In the extreme, this can lead to grandiose generalizations that overlook all manner of stubborn details; in practice, though, a good deal of structuralist work is concerned not to locate meanings as effects of universal conditions but as the property of particular sign-using communities. These communities may of course exist within the 'same' culture; hence the meanings and values accorded, say, to a Primal Scream CD will vary, often quite dramatically, from the contemporary dance scene to the hip hop crowd to fans of Guns n' Roses, and so on.

This is to encounter a key structuralist principle, once again deriving from Saussure: meanings are effects of differential relations; 'in language [or any system] there are only differences *without positive terms*' (1974, 120). The meanings attributed to a Primal Scream CD are produced therefore out of differences between communities (and not only music-based communities) as well as being an effect of internal differences from and affinities to other forms of music (by the Rolling Stones, the Chemical Brothers, the Stone Roses, etc.) within the system of popular music at large. On its own – outside these differences or sets of differential relations – there could be no sense in which, for structuralism, the music of Primal Scream could be said to mean in any positive or meaningful way at all.

Structuralism, then, goes looking for these sets or, as the French structural anthro-pologist Claude Lévi-Strauss called them, 'bundles' of relations, which it takes for the base units of meaning in any system. Lévi-Strauss's analysis of the structure of the Oedipus myth is the most famous case in point (1968, 213–18; Lucy 1997, 7–11). Here we must be brief: the analysis proceeds according to the method of laying out the myth's constituent elements (in the form of bundles of relations or 'mythemes') along horizontal (diachronic) and vertical (synchronic) axes. The story of the myth is read off from the horizontal axis, the structure from the vertical axis. Arranged as four columns, the mythemes encapsulate (1) excessive blood relations, (2) undervalued blood relations, (3) monster slaying and (4) problems in walking upright. Columns one and two are inversions of each other (Oedipus marries his mother; Oedipus kills his father), but the relation between the second pair of columns is not as seemingly straightforward. According to Lévi-Strauss, though, Oedipus's name (meaning 'swollen foot') recalls the story of our rising out of the primordial mud, laming ourselves in the process; column four refers then to the myth of auto-generation. Column three denies the myth, because monsters like the Sphinx would keep us from being born. Hence the relation between these columns is one of a tension between origin myths: are we born of one (sameness) or two (difference)? Can I, in other words, be wholly at one with myself (self-same) if who I am depends on an originary and ineluctable difference from myself, in the form of the two others (who are not me but not not-me) who brought about my conception?

From this we can see that binary relations (between pairs of columns, in the present case) are crucial to a structuralist method of analysis. Once again *difference*, in the form of these binary relations or oppositions, is seen to *structure* meaning. Rather than inhering in 'positive terms', meaning is produced out of *structures of difference*. Yet – and this is to raise a serious question for structuralism – are not these very structures of difference themselves required to function as if in fact they were positive terms? What price, after all, the scientific credibility of Lévi-Strauss's analysis of the Oedipus myth if the structures of difference he identifies as underpinning it (in all its manifold forms) were open to endless disagreement or simply to counter-claims? This amounts to saying that the structure of 'structure', as it were, has to be seen as positive – the abstract equivalent of a natural or found object, over whose identity and constitution nothing has to be decided – or the whole structuralist enterprise would be in danger of collapsing back from 'science' into a simplified and familiar hermeneutics.

This point has been made most famously by Derrida (1978). In a nutshell, it accounts for the poststructuralist critique of structuralism, which is not the concern of the present essay. Nevertheless it should be noted that poststructuralism is not in a relation of *opposition* to structuralism, as might be said to characterize the response of many Anglo-American literary critics in the 1970s to what they saw as structuralism's scandalous affront to prevailing views on literature. The principal 'enemy' was not so much, however, Lévi-Strauss as a younger generation of European theorists associated with the Parisian journals *Communications* and especially *Tel Quel* in the 1960s. Of the many key figures – including Italian semiotician Umberto Eco, French narratologists A. J. Greimas, Claude Bremond and Gérard Genette, Bulgarian feminist psychoanalyst Julia Kristeva and French film theorist Christian Metz – whose work appeared in those journals, helping to refine and also (via Marx's influence on some of them) to politicize the nature of the structuralist enterprise, we will look briefly here at some of the ideas of Tzvetan Todorov and Roland Barthes.

For Todorov, a deep 'universal grammar' underlies all languages and indeed all signifying systems of every description across cultures. 'This universal grammar is the source of all universals and it gives definition even to man himself. Not only all languages but all signifying systems obey the same grammar' (cit. Scholes 1974, 111). Like Lévi-Strauss, then, whose structural anthropology dared to dream of revealing the deep structure of 'the' human mind, Todorov believed that cultural and historical phenomena could be made to give up the transcendental laws of structuration underpinning all signifying systems and defining 'our' very being as a species. While this can be seen as hubris, nevertheless it is an ambition that promotes a radical concept of 'man himself' as the product of a transcendental grammar (or *langue*) of structuration, as opposed to the conservative idea of individual men and women of genius whose special talent for creatively manipulating a particular grammar (or *parole*) justifies the hermeneutic and appreciative tasks of literary criticism.

Since the all but infinite grammatical possibilities enabled by a language render almost impossible the work of analysing the universal grammar of all languages, Todorov turns instead to the linguistic subset of narrative fiction for evidence of who 'we' are (albeit 'our' identity turns out to be inseparable from the political and cultural histories that shape it). His most famous case study is of the *Decameron* by the fourteenth-century Italian poet Giovanni Boccaccio. Not surprisingly, given that in 1965 he had produced a French translation of many of the key texts of Russian formalism from the 1920s, Todorov's analysis is strongly influenced by a formalist approach and elaborates especially on methods developed by Vladimir Propp whose *Morphology of the Folktale*, first published in 1928 but virtually unknown outside the former Soviet Union until much later, represents one of the earliest extended attempts to find a *langue* of narrative. Briefly, Propp maintained that behind the confusing mass of *parole* forms of Russian fairy tales lay a systematic organizing principle in the form of characters' *functions*. Variables such as age, height, hair colour and the like aside, each character performs one or more of a total of 31 functions (the hero leaves home, the villain is punished, etc.) and, although Propp found no tale to contain all of these at once, he argued that the order by which functions appear in any tale is always the same. From this he drew four laws, the most striking being that 'All fairy tales are of one type in regard to their structure' (1968, 63).

Building on Propp's method, Todorov saw in the one hundred tales of the *Decameron* the manifestation of a set of underlying grammatical rules, of which the two most important concern *propositions* and *sequences*. As syntactical units equivalent to a sentence, propositions consist of irreducible actions (X does Y); sequences then are strings or micro-systems of propositions equivalent to a paragraph. More structurally basic still, however, are the *parts of speech* that Todorov identifies in every tale as follows: characters function as proper nouns; actions as verbs; attributes as adjectives. Hence each proposition (or sentence) comprises a noun in juxtaposition with either a verb or adjective. The complexity of Todorov's analysis cannot be fully accounted for here; what needs to be stressed, though, is that he draws from it not a lesson in literary style or genre, but a lesson in political economy. Noting that the text privileges a 'daring personal initiate', Todorov sees this as expressing extra-textual values in support of an emerging 'ideology of the new bourgeoisie' that fostered an ideal of individualism as a liberating triumph over the 'restrictive' forces of an older, more apparently interventive political and economic system (cit. Scholes 1974, 116). In celebrating individuals' 'free action', then, the *Decameron* is consistent with the new 'liberal' ideology of the time, 'which could make believe, at the beginning at least, that it amounted to the total disappearance of system' (116).

The suggestion, by Todorov and other European structuralists of the 1960s who were broadly marxist in outlook, that literature could be understood as an ideological expression of political and economic interests rankled with many Anglo-American critics in the following decade, by which time a significant body of so-called 'French' theory had been translated into English. What rankled most, it seemed, was the structuralist insistence on regarding those liberal attitudes, which Todorov and others saw as having begun to reshape European cultural codes and values in the fourteenth century, as a formation born of ideology instead of nature.

There were several consequences of this new and (from an Anglo-American view) provocative approach to literature, but none more controversial than – to give the English title of a famous essay by Barthes that appeared in 1968 in the journal *Mantéie* – 'the death of the author'. Challenging the humanist belief in the self-expressive individual, Barthes argued that in works of literature 'it is language which speaks, not the author' (1977, 143) – a variation on the structuralist idea of man himself as a *subject* of semiotic systems. For literary criticism, every instance of writing is understood as the expression of an authorial 'voice'; for Barthes, though, 'writing is the destruction of every voice, of every point of origin' (142). This is to say that no instance of writing can be separated from the general structure of writing as a system, or indeed from the entire field of signifying systems at large. On this radical view, a work of literature is not an inspirational but a structural or (con)textual phenomenon: as writing, it cannot be said to 'speak' at all (hence 'the destruction of every voice') and cannot be seen as the exclusive property of an individual or era (hence 'the destruction ... of every point of origin'). Set loose from the tyranny of the author-centred model, Barthes' theory of literature acknowledges the creative work of reading as the only condition by which a semblance of 'unity' might be said to hold for any text: 'a text's unity lies not in its origin [the author] but in its destination [the reader]' (148). It must be stressed, however, that this is not to affirm the biological fact of the reader (in substitution for the humanist author), especially given Barthes' insistence that 'the reader is without history, biography, psychology; he is simply that *someone* who holds together in a single field all the traces by which the written text is constituted' (148). Far more radically, Barthes approaches writing as an affirmation of *the semiotic act of reading*. Hence it is only in the process of being read that a work of literature can be said to signify, and to do so over and over again across 'the space of writing' (147). From this it follows that, instead of saying *literature*, 'it would be better from now on to say *writing*' (147) because this concept remains relatively unaffected by a theological (and ideological) notion of literary works as repositories of 'secret' or 'ultimate' meanings put there by authors, according to which the task of criticism is to find them. The effect of such a task is 'to close the writing' (147). But the task of reading is to keep the writing open, on the understanding that, '[i]n the multiplicity of writing, everything is to be *disentangled*, nothing *deciphered*' (147).

In granting such privilege to the reader (as a structural function of texts and not, to repeat, as an embodied subject sitting in an armchair reading a book), Barthes threatened the very enterprise of literary criticism by challenging the commonsensical or natural – in a word, the 'disinterested' – status of its assumptions. At first, in books such as *Mythologies* (1957), *On Racine* (1963) and *Elements of Semiology* (1964), his critique of common sense keeps faith with the structuralist dream of creating a science of forms. Its fullest expression is realized in the essay 'Introduction to the Structural Analysis of Narratives', published in *Communications* in 1966, which had some impress on North American structuralism in the 1970s through its influence on Jonathan Culler's *Structuralist Poetics* (1975), a book, albeit, that was written while Culler was teaching at Oxford and Cambridge. Representing what might be called his 'high' structuralist moment, Barthes' essay on narrative draws on the work of Propp, Lévi-Strauss, Todorov, Roman Jakobson (a leading light of the Prague Circle of linguists in the 1950s), Russian formalism and of course Saussure. Hence it develops an analytical method which is classical in its reliance on language as the model *par excellence* of all signifying systems and its declaration of 'structuralism's constant aim to master the infinity of utterances [*parole* forms] by describing the "language" [the *langue* or deep structure] of which they are the products and from which they can be generated' (Barthes 1977, 80).

If, however, Barthes still holds to an ideal of scientific observation in the 1966 essay, his methods aimed only at better *description*, his thinking can be seen to shift by 1968 with the 'The Death of the Author'. What marks the shift (aside from flashes of a certain speculative and stylistic bravura that came to 'tag' his later work as poststructuralist) is a more open or less positive concept of structure than the dream of a science of culture relies on. Instead of functioning as the bedrock of signification, structure comes to be conceived as a kind of groundless ground of signifying effects which are *produced* in acts of reading; hence the attention in his later work to the 'space' or 'surface' of writing in contrast to the idea of particular works of literature having an essential 'core' or 'depth' of meaning, whether thought to originate authorially or structurally. By 1970, in his widely read and much debated *S/Z*, this formative affirmation of the signifier develops into Barthes' distinctive theory of literature as an ongoing process of reading rather than a finished product of writing: 'the goal of literary work (of literature as work) is to make the reader no longer a consumer, but a producer of the text' (1974, 4; see also Eagleton 1996, 116–23, and Lucy 1997, 75–7). Rather than what has been written, literature is what always remains *to be read*. All the properties of writing (in the standard sense of a creative practice associated with genius authors) are given over therefore to this new sense of reading conceived as productive activity rather than passive reception. This, for Barthes, is the condition of literature in general, and it is precisely this condition to which literary criticism remains blind. For literary criticism, works of literature are always (as Barthes terms it) 'readerly': they are always already unified in advance of any act of reading them, having to be conceived as finished (albeit complex) products waiting to be read in the sense of being passively consumed. But understood as demanding and defining *work* in the sense of interpretative activity, literature can be reconceived in terms of the 'writerly' text which always remains to be written (and rewritten) in acts of reading (and rereading) because its semiotic potential is always in excess of literary criticism's delimiting concepts of genre, authorship, unity, style and the like. Hence the writerly is 'the novelistic without the novel

..., writing without style, production without product, structuration without structure' (Barthes 1974, 5). Although for Barthes all literature is writerly (as his brilliantly destabilizing reading of a classical readerly text, 'Sarrasine' by Honoré de Balzac, shows in *S/Z*), writerliness seems more pertinent to some forms of literature than others. This is true especially of the *nouveau roman* in France (the 'new novel' associated most famously with the work of Allain Robbe-Grillet in the 1950s and 1960s) and what came to be known as 'metafiction' in the US, or a kind of writing practised by the likes of John Barth, Donald Bartheleme and Robert Coover in the 1960s that draws attention to itself *as writing* rather than attempting to represent 'reality' as prior and external to it. Even so, while writerliness is arguably a conspicuous feature of so-called avant-garde literature, it is important to stress that the writerly text is irreducible to a style or genre: it is rather *an effect of reading* understood in terms of a theoretical approach to writing as a dynamic process, a process which cannot be contained or explained by what Barthes calls 'the law of the Signified' (1974, 8) that sets the limits and determines the goal of literary criticism both as a professional enterprise and an ideology.

This point was not always well taken by Barthes' earliest admirers and critics in the UK. Much of the controversy over structuralism in the 1970s – its newsworthiness deemed to be important enough for coverage in such outlets as *The Times Literary Supplement*, *The Times Higher Education Supplement* and *The London Review of Books* – concerned the mistaken belief that Barthes and other continental thinkers were calling for a kind of 'anything goes' approach to the evaluation of culture generally, but especially to the interpretation and appreciation of literature. Somewhat later, this belief would come to be associated (mistakenly again) with poststructuralism, but at that time 'structuralism' was the preferred term of the British press and tended to be used as the marker both of 'ideological' and 'relativistic' approaches to literature and culture. Since it enflamed so much passion at the time, British literary theorist Colin MacCabe's work is central to the controversy surrounding 'structuralism' in the UK. As late as 1983, indeed, in an essay by the conservative British critic Iain Wright, MacCabe was still being scolded (albeit by inference) for espousing a so-called 'doctrinaire a-historical relativism' associated with 'doctrinaire anti-realists' whom Wright chose not to name (1983, 60, 66). A year earlier, the British philosopher Roger Scruton had put the case against structuralism and its reliance on 'Saussurean jargon' in no uncertain terms: acknowledging that structuralist studies were 'by now widely accepted as part of the academic repertoire', Scruton himself chose not to imitate them 'out of respect for a concept – that of truth – which many of those studies seem to overlook' (1982, 86)!

Simply for daring to want to find, or to dream of finding, what Culler called 'a poetics which strives to define the conditions of meaning' (1975, viii), structuralism was unfairly hectored by many conservative critics in the UK in the 1970s and beyond. While the case against it could, however, have been put more graciously, that does not mean that structuralism has no case to answer at all. But its problem is not the patrician accusation that it ignores 'truth'; the problem for structuralism, rather, is that it thinks truth can be found in a stable concept of structure.

Niall Lucy

Further reading and works cited

Barthes, R. *On Racine*. New York, 1964.
—. *Elements of Semiology*. New York, 1968.
—. *Mythologies*. New York, 1973.
—. *S/Z*. New York, 1974.
—. *Image Music Text*. London, 1977.
Culler, J. *Structuralist Poetics*. London, 1975.
—. *Saussure*. London, 1976.
Derrida, J. *Writing and Difference*. London, 1978.
Eagleton, T. *Literary Theory*. Oxford, 1983.
Eco, U. *A Theory of Semiotics*. Bloomington, IN, 1976.
Genette, G. *Narrative Discourse*. Oxford, 1980.
Greimas, A. J. *Sémantique structurale*. Paris, 1966.
Hawkes, T. *Structuralism and Semiotics*. London, 1977.
Jameson, F. *The Prison-House of Language*. Princeton, NJ, 1972.
Kermode, F. *Essays on Fiction*. London, 1983.
Lévi-Strauss, C. *The Savage Mind*. London, 1966.
—. *Structural Anthropology 1*. Harmondsworth, 1968.
Lucy, N. *Postmodern Literary Theory*. Oxford, 1997.
MacCabe, C. *James Joyce and the Revolution of the Word*. London, 1978.
Macksey, R. and Donato, E. (eds) *The Structuralist Controversy*. Baltimore, MD, 1972.
Propp, V. *Morphology of the Folktale*. Austin, TX, 1968.
Robey, D. (ed.) *Structuralism*. Oxford, 1973.
Saussure, F. de. *Course in General Linguistics*. London, 1974.
Scholes, R. *Structuralism in Literature*. New Haven, CT, 1974.
Scruton, R. 'Public Text and Common Reader', *Comparative Criticism*, 4, 1982.
Todorov, T. *Grammaire du Décaméron*. Paris, 1969.
Wright, I. ' "What Matter Who's Speaking?": Beckett, the Authorial Subject and Contemporary Critical Theory', *Comparative Criticism*, 5, 1983.

16. The Spread of Literary Theory in Britain

By the late 1990s literary theory had become the most compulsory topic on English degree courses in Britain. Of the seventy-six university institutions which responded to a questionnaire on the syllabus sent out in 1998 by 'CCUE' (the Council for College and University English) forty listed it as an obligatory topic of study. (The study of Victorian fiction – the second most compulsory topic on the syllabus – is obligatory at thirty of the responding institutions.) How did this spectacular rise come about? What follows is a kind of ethnographic 'thick description' of the institutional assimilation of literary theory (hereafter referred to just as 'theory') into English studies in Britain.

It is usually suggested that before the outbreak of continental theory in the 1970s an unbroken liberal-humanist quietus completely dominated literary studies in Britain, but it should be emphasized that there already existed currents of 'native' dissent from the

Leavisite consensus, and that these provided fertile ground in which imported theories could later take root. In the late 1950s, for instance, Richard Hoggart's *The Uses of Literacy* (1957) and Raymond Williams's *Culture and Society* (1958) offered broader notions of culture than Leavisite approaches allowed, and these concerns became the focus of the influential Centre for Contemporary Cultural Studies at Birmingham University, which had been founded by Hoggart in 1963 and was directed by him till 1968, and then by Stuart Hall from 1968 to 1979. Perry Anderson's 'Components of the National Culture' (1968, 3–57), was an influential full-frontal attack on the residual dominance of Leavis, and this was broadly aligned in spirit with that of several other prominent UK critics of the time, including Alan Swingewood (of the LSE), whose book *The Sociology of Literature* (written with Diana Laurenson) was published in 1972 by Paladin (an imprint which would become an important progressive force in the 1970s), and David Craig (of Lancaster University), author of *The Real Foundations: Literature and Social Change*, another key work which challenged Leavis's resistance to the broader social contextualization of literature. This kind of material overlaps chronologically with the arrival of the work of continental theorists in the early 1970s, and the Birmingham CCCS under Stuart Hall increasingly made use of these newly available perspectives. Theory, then, did not take root by magic in a liberal-humanist desert, but in ground which was ready to nourish such a crop.

The growth of 'theory' proper in the UK falls into four distinct phases, each of about five years' duration. Phase one covers the first half of the 1970s, roughly 1970 to 1975. The Oxbridge–London University triangle was the early centre of 'theory' in the UK. The Cambridge wing included Stephen Heath and his student Colin MacCabe, both of whom had studied structuralism in Paris. An important early text, from Oxford, was David Robey's edited collection *Structuralism: An Introduction*. Roland Barthes' work was promulgated by the London Graduate Seminar started by Frank Kermode after he became Professor of English at University College, London. This seminar was a significant moment in the importation of structuralism into Britain, briefly described by Bernard Bergonzi in his 1990 book *Exploding English*: the seminar, he says, 'discussed the literary implications of structuralism, semiotics, and emergent poststructuralism ... establish[ing] a useful informal link with the work going on at Cambridge, and participants included Stephen Heath, Jonathan Culler ... Veronica Forrest-Thomson ... Christine Brooke-Rose, Christopher Norris, and Shlomith Rimmon' (99). 'Theory', then, was well under way by 1973, when the *TLS* devoted the major part of two issues to a 'Survey of Semiotics', with articles by Eco, Todorov and Kristeva, and others, and in the same year a translation of *Mythologies* appeared, also in the trend-setting Paladin imprint, this being the work which established the popularity of Roland Barthes in Britain. (A little later Stephen Heath edited and translated a selection of Barthes's essays under the title *Image-Music-Text*. This became the standard 'portable Barthes' for British readers, and was published by Fontana – another important progressive paperback imprint – in 1977, in the 'Communications' series which had Raymond Williams as its general editor.) The culmination of the first phase of theory is marked by Jonathan Culler's *Structuralist Poetics*, based on his Oxford doctoral dissertation, a book which was one of the crucial mediating texts of theory. Culler had substantial Oxbridge affiliations, having taken a doctorate at Oxford and then taught for four years at Cambridge. It should be added that the 'mediatory' books mentioned here (Heath/MacCabe, Robey and Culler) which were the keystone of the first phase of 'theory' in Britain, were often obliged to discuss and summarize 'primary' theoretical (mainly French) texts which had not yet been translated into English.

The uncompromising central point of Culler's book is its insistence that the proper object of literary study is not the appreciation and enjoyment of individual works of literature, but the quest for an understanding of what constitutes 'literariness'. He writes:

> The type of literary study which structuralism helps one to envisage would not be primarily interpretive; it would not offer a method which, when applied to literary works, produced new and hitherto unexpected meanings. Rather than a criticism which discovers or assigns meanings, it would be a poetics which strives to define the conditions of meaning. (1975, viii)

On the face of it, this proposal for a change of direction in literary studies did not seem terribly promising, for it is difficult to imagine undergraduates enrolling in large numbers on a course which 'strives to define the conditions of meaning'. But the appeal of such an approach to postgraduates and to younger academics was considerable, for in Britain, to a great extent (and more so than in America), general ideas had been artificially suppressed in English studies for a long time, thereby inevitably creating a strong appetite for them. Thus a whole range of questions were never touched upon at all, questions, for instance, concerning the purpose and potential of literature itself, the nature of literary language and literary representation, the role of the reader and of the academy in the creation of literary canons, and so on. Theory offered to release this hidden, repressed subconscious of English studies, to break the taboo on ideas and generalizations which many decades of practical criticism had effectively imposed.

The characteristics of this first phase of theory in Britain, then, are, firstly, that there is relatively little availability of the primary texts of theory, and consequently a high degree of dependency on works like those just mentioned which are 'summative' or 'mediatory' in character: where primary materials were available it was mostly in the form of single chapters or articles only, like those in Jacques Ehrmann's *Structuralism*. Secondly, 'theory' at this stage was more genuinely cross-disciplinary than it later became – Culler, for instance, taught in a French department, not an English department, and there was as much interest in linguistics as in structuralism. Thirdly, theory at this time had very little impact on the undergraduate syllabus; it was the concern of 'faculty' and of graduate-school members, and finally, it had a markedly restricted geographical and 'social-academic' spread, being confined mainly to the most privileged university centres in southern England.

The second phase of theory covers the latter half of the 1970s (roughly 1976–80), when its influence spread to English departments across the whole higher education system, but still predominantly at graduate level. The definitive milestone of this phase was the founding in 1977 of Methuen's 'New Accents' series of introductory books on aspects of theory, beginning with *Structuralism and Semiotics* in that year by Terence Hawkes, the General Editor. At this stage there was still a prominent belief (characteristic of the time, and now somewhat dated) in the radicalizing potential of linguistics: the General Editor's Preface to 'New Accents' remarks that modern linguistics has 'provided a basis for the study of the totality of human communication, and so ultimately for an analysis of the human role in the world at large'. The prominence of linguistics reflected the prestige of Noam Chomsky's theories of generative grammar, and the widespread reverence for the work of Roman Jakobson and the Prague Linguistic Circle, but it also drew on the fact that literary linguistics (later called 'stylistics') had in the 1960s offered an overt challenge to the 'liberal humanist' consensus in literary studies (albeit from a very different starting point from that of the emergent New Left critics), as instanced by the polemical exchanges between F. W.

Bateson and the linguist Roger Fowler in Bateson's journal *Essays in Criticism* (see 1967, 332–47, and 1968, 164–82). Unsurprisingly, therefore, the second 'New Accents' volume was Fowler's *Linguistics and the Novel*. This second phase of theory in Britain ends with the publication of Catherine Belsey's highly successful and influential New Accents book *Critical Practice* in 1980. 'Critical practice' became the catchphrase denoting a newly theorized way of reading literature which would replace the old consensus method of practical criticism. The book insisted that there is a single system of representation, with no privileged literary realm (an assertion directly analogous to Fowler's view that there is, in effect, no such thing as literary language, no distinct linguistic entity working to different rules from language in general). Thus high literary works like *Middlemarch*, on the one hand, and advertisements for cosmetics, on the other, use the same signifying system, and draw on similar images, archetypes and signifying systems. It is, for Belsey, merely bourgeois mystification to suggest that language and representation work in a special way in literature. All the same, a particular kind of writing, literary realism, is especially to be condemned since it is of its very nature an act of collusion with a conservative status quo in society. In reading such realist works, which fraudulently attempt to efface their own status as representation, the task of the reader is constantly to resist the illusion of reality they create, avoiding, for instance, any discussion of 'characters', imagined as if they were real people. Instead, the book urges us to concentrate on the techniques and structures of representation which are seen at work in the text under consideration. Thus, *Critical Practice* reflects the strong influence of Althusser on key British theorists during this phase, for the book expresses the view that as soon as a novelist signs the realist 'contract', providing characters who are presented through the medium of psychological realism, set within a detailed and recognizable social setting, then inevitably there is a fatal collusion with the reader's 'common sense' expectations and beliefs about the world. As she puts it: '[The realist text] however critical of the world it describes, offers the reader a position, an attitude which is given as non-contradictory, fixed in "knowing" subjectivity.' Hence, the realist literary text inevitably becomes an aspect of what Althusser called the 'ISA', the ideological state apparatus by which we are rendered subject.

As this second stage progresses, theory begins to popularize its basic beliefs, starting to establish them as the taken-for-granted postulates on which further argument can be built. At this stage, therefore, the balance of pedagogical interest within theory began to shift from graduate schools to the undergraduate literature courses which would become the next frontier for the dissemination of theory. The other distinctive point about the end of this second phase is that already interest was shifting from structuralism to poststructuralism, from Barthes to Derrida, from linguistics to philosophy. Thus, if phases one and two of theory are mainly about structuralism, then the next two phases centre on poststructuralism. Deconstruction and poststructuralism became a major force in Britain with the publication of another key book, *Deconstruction and Criticism* in 1979, a book with five authors, the so-called 'Yale Mafia' of Harold Bloom, Paul de Man, Jacques Derrida, Geoffrey Hartman and J. Hillis Miller. It was harshly reviewed in both the *New York Review of Books* and the *London Review of Books*. In the former, Denis Donoghue, using the title 'Deconstructing Deconstruction', wrote that it had 'more to do with the rhetoric of power in American universities than with its ostensible subject'. These hostile reviews, however, were but a foretaste of the polarization and acrimony which are the dominant characteristic of phase three, the period of the 'theory wars in English'.

This third phase, then, comprising the first half of the 1980s, is that of head-on conflict between theory and 'liberal humanism'. This is the period of the 'theory wars', of bad-tempered semi-private rows at department meetings and graduate papers, and of more public ones at conferences, on television and radio programmes, and in the columns of national newspapers and academic journals. It was a strangely fraught time, with the frustrations induced by what was happening on the national political scene spilling over into the academic sphere. The Labour Party had collapsed into seemingly terminal in-fighting and the long ascendancy of Thatcherism began in 1979 with the first of four successive Tory election victories. The crude Thatcherite extremism encapsulated in the slogan 'There is no such thing as society' generated its reversed counter-image in English studies, which, in its high Althusserian phase, increasingly seemed to maintain that 'there is no such thing as the individual'. The cultural situation was rendered even more unstable because for over a year, from 1979, the *Times* newspapers, having moved to a new high-tech plant in Wapping, fought to the death with the print unions. For that period the *TLS* and the *THES* disappeared, leaving a spate of new journals – Richard Boston's *Quarto*, Ann Smith's *The Literary Review* and the *London Review of Books* under Karl Miller – to debate structuralism and poststructuralism. All these were sceptical, at best, about the new theories, but they were willing to devote a great deal of space to them, and for a time there seemed to be polemical pieces in almost every issue. These were days when the review of a new work of literary theory could be followed by up to two years of irate correspondence, sometimes with complaints and accusations spilling over into the correspondence sections of other journals. The effect of these new journals, then, was to heat up the temperature by breaking away from the residual politeness and gentility of the *TLS* and giving overt expression to the internal tensions which many English departments suffered in the 1980s between traditionalists and theorists. On the return of the *Times* and its stable, the *TLS* caught up by publishing a symposium entitled 'Professing Literature' (December 1982) and the *THES* had a similar 'Perspective' compilation on 11 February 1983, as indeed did the journal *PN Review* (1985). These symposia, each with its train of embattled correspondence, give a powerful insight into the polarized opinions of the time.

One of the most notorious of these public controversies followed the publication in 1982 of a New Accents book called *Re-Reading English*, edited by Peter Widdowson. Roger Poole was commissioned by the *TLS* to review the book, but his broadly favourable review was rejected by the editor, Jeremy Treglown (on grounds of 'style'), and another and highly critical one commissioned (from Claude Rawson). Here, allegedly, was proof of the Establishment's ruthless hold on the channels of cultural dissemination. The matter came to light in a letter to *PN Review* (1984, 40, 4) by Antony Easthope, responding to a piece in issue 37 earlier in the year on 'The Politicisation of English'. Treglown was invited to respond to the accusation of cultural bias in the same issue (40), and did so. Poole put his side of the case (42, 6), and Rawson his (43, 5), to which Poole responded (1985, 44, 7), and Rawson added a riposte (45, 4). In the *London Review of Books* the reviewer of the same book was the poet and critic Tom Paulin (17–30 June 1982). Paulin was even more scathing than Rawson had been, and his article generated a vicious and bitterly divided correspondence which ran – in this fortnightly journal – until February 1983, under the appropriate title 'Faculty at War'. (Paulin's piece was reprinted in his collection *Ireland and the English Crisis*, 1984.) The crisis in English studies was, he said, partly a reflection of 'that futureless and pastless sense of blankness which distinguishes the present generation of students'. Partly, too, it was the result of the vacuum left by the period of critical exhaustion which followed the overthrow of the revolution brought about by 'that sour puritan' F. R.

Leavis and his disciples many years before. English ought to be happy enough to let everybody get on with doing their own thing, since its characteristic quality as a subject is that it is 'about everything and nothing, and so is endlessly plastic'. It seemed difficult for Paulin to understand why the subject was suddenly riven with schism, since unlike a religion, or even a social club, it had never had a set of agreed aims and principles and had always been only the loosest of coalitions. Paulin did not attempt to explain why the non-aggression pacts had suddenly broken down, but his wrath was directed against *Re-Reading English* which he saw as attempting to exploit the looseness of the subject's boundaries, demystifying the notion of literary value, developing instead a 'politics of reading' and extending the word 'text' so that it could include newspaper reports, popular songs, political speeches and so on. Paulin feared that English was becoming 'a nightmare of subsidized nonsense, an arid wilderness of combative attitudes, deconstructed texts, abolished authors and demonic critical technicians'. These technicians, he said, could make the experience of reading the poetry of Philip Sydney sound like 'a spell in a forced labour camp'. These quotations illustrate the extreme heat generated in these polemical exchanges. One such – a later flare-up in the *London Review of Books* between Graham Hough and Terence Hawkes – ended with the latter inviting the former to 'piss off' (21 November 1985).

Aside from broader political considerations, the great rancour of these exchanges is partly the result of frustration at the fact that during phase three, theorists were still usually in a minority in their own departments, unable to take a decisive grasp on the reins of power (this was the lesson of the so-called 'MacCabe Affair' at Cambridge in February 1981) so that the public sphere became (in the much-used phrase) a 'site of contestation'. But a strong counter-network of conferences, organizations and sympathetic journals had grown up, which was in effect a government-in-exile which would come into its own when the theory revolution had run its course later in the decade. The network included the Sociology of Literature conferences at the University of Essex, organized by Francis Barker and Peter Hulme from 1977 to 1981 (and later the 'Essex Symposia'). Also significant was the Literature, Teaching, Politics group ('LTP'), which met annually at different venues. Between 1980 and 1986 there were annual meetings at Cardiff, Cambridge, Birmingham, Sunderland, Ilkley, Bristol and Glasgow, attracting well over a hundred delegates at their height. There were also regional 'LTP' groups, each taking responsibility for the printing, publication and distribution of an issue of the journal *Literature Teaching Politics*, including Cardiff (1980), Sussex (1981), Cambridge (1982), Leeds (1983), Birmingham (1984), Bristol Polytechnic (1985) and Glasgow (1986). Another such group set up the 'UTE' conferences (University Teachers of English), later 'HETE' (Higher Education Teachers of English), which went on throughout the 1980s, meeting at Reading (1984), Liverpool (1985), Sussex (1986), Kent (1987), Glasgow (1988), Birkbeck College (1989) and Strathclyde (1990). Events like these were attended by commissioning editors and new titles were commissioned in the several series of books which were now spreading the message of theory. In this troubled and excited climate a new left-wing theoretical/cultural consensus had begun to take shape, led by a number of vigorous and prolific academic writers and polemicists: these included Terry Eagleton, at Wadham College, Oxford; Jonathan Dollimore and Alan Sinfield at Sussex University; Catherine Belsey, Christopher Norris and Terence Hawkes at the University of Wales, Cardiff; Isobel Armstrong, Maud Ellmann and Robert Young at Southampton University; Peter Widdowson at Thames Polytechnic; John Drakakis at Stirling University; Antony Easthope at Manchester

Polytechnic; and Colin MacCabe, now at the University of Strathclyde, after his much-publicized 'Last Exit' from Cambridge.

The great success of the pioneer 'New Accents' series continued: Christopher Norris's *Deconstruction: Theory and Practice* (1982) was the definitive phase-three title, doing for poststructuralism what Culler's *Structuralist Poetics* had earlier done for structuralism. Two other key publishing events of this phase were the publication of ground-breaking general accounts of the whole field of modern literary theory, both making a serious attempt to 'package' theory for an undergraduate rather than a graduate audience, namely Terry Eagleton's *Literary Theory: An Introduction* (1983) and Raman Selden's *A Reader's Guide to Contemporary Literary Theory* (1985). The characteristics of phase three of theory, then, are firstly, prolonged and bitter hostilities between traditional approaches to literary study (usually called 'liberal humanism') and 'theory'; secondly, the continuation of the shift from structuralism to poststructuralism; thirdly the growing confidence of theorists through a vigorous culture of conferences and dedicated journals, leading to the spread of theory across the whole range of traditional universities, and throughout the so-called 'public sector' of polytechnics and colleges of higher education; and finally, its shift from being a mainly postgraduate preoccupation to its becoming established at the heart of the undergraduate syllabus.

Phase four, roughly 1985 to 1990, is marked by an abrupt and at first puzzling outbreak of peace, for the theory wars seemed suddenly to disappear. On reflection. however, the marked change in the academic climate is readily understood. *Firstly*, the attempt to teach theory at undergraduate level threw up a major problem, which was the challenge of showing that theory could be *used* in the practical study of literature. Wherever it was taught, students wanted to know what they could *do* with theory, and it was always implausible to pretend (aping the high disdain of Paul de Man for any descent from the lofty plateau of Ivy League Graduate School debate) that making such a demand was simply a form of 'resistance to theory'. Trying to meet the demand from students for clear exposition and plausible applications absorbed much of the energy which would otherwise have been available for peer-group polemic. The pioneer book of 'applied theory' was Douglas Tallack's edited collection *Literary Theory at Work: Three Texts* (1987). New series of books aimed at undergraduates also began to appear, like Blackwell's 'ReReading Literature', under the general editorship of Terry Eagleton. Extracts from the primary texts of theory were packaged into 'readers' for undergraduate courses, including Rick Rylance's *Debating Texts* (1987), David Lodge's *Modern Criticism and Theory: A Reader* (1988), K. M. Newton's *Twentieth Century Literary Theory: A Reader* (1989) and Philip Rice and Patricia Waugh's *Modern Literary Theory: A Reader* (1989). The pattern of coursebook provision in phase four is that the three different kinds of book – the discursive general account of the field (like Eagleton's and Selden's), the 'reader' of primary materials (like Lodge's and Rylance's) and the 'applied theory' text (like Tallack's) – existed as separate entities. Later on, in the 1990s and beyond, the trend would be to combine two or three of these into a single integrated theory coursebook.

As this implies, another reason for the ending of the theory wars in phase four is that theory had made such sweeping gains. Theory books sold extremely well, and commissioning editors attended the theory-based conferences, eager to sign up new authors to fill these series, and the balance of power began to tip very rapidly in theory's favour as many young academics quickly built up the kind of publication lists which lead to promotions and professorships. The shift of power away from the more conservative forces in the discipline was further accelerated by the arrival, in 1986, of Research Assessment, which is the system whereby the research and publication output of university-level departments is formally assessed and graded by quasi-governmental bodies. The grade attained determines the amount of research funding received from the public purse. The exercise was repeated in 1988, 1992, 1996 and 2001, becoming a major part of institutional and disciplinary culture. Consequently, prolific theorists became highly desirable properties. Suddenly, theory had landed and theorists were in charge, and by 1990 it had become the norm for under-graduate degrees to include compulsory literary theory.

In the 1990s and beyond, the major task of theory was to make up its 'pedagogical deficit', so that progressive teaching methods appropriate to progressive content could be developed. Hitherto, as Ben Knights had put it, 'the change of mind-set at the level of theory ha[d] grafted itself upon a very traditional pedagogy, and one which reproduce[d] the hierarchical model of transmission which theory might have been supposed to subvert or replace' (1995, 64–5). Making up the deficit may well have been accelerated by another of the new forms of assessment to which universities are subject, for since 1994 English departments, like all others, have undergone 'TQA', Teaching Quality Assessment, in which each department's teaching is assessed and given a public rating. Since theory now forms a major part of the syllabus, teaching it effectively has become a vital matter, of major importance, not just to postgraduates and young lecturers, as it was during the 'theory wars' of the early 1980s, but to heads of department, faculty deans and vice-chancellors. Theory in Britain has not just come of age, then, it has entered middle age, and carries with it the cares and responsibilities of office. Indeed, the 'Copernican revolution' of theory (to use Catherine Belsey's term) may already have passed its perihelion, for there are now likely to be younger members in most departments who question the need for and the usefulness of theory. Again, too, this shift is partly driven by changing patterns of funding, for the sabbatical leave, fellowships, research readerships and research professorships which are offered each year by governmental and charitable bodies (and which carry greater personal and institutional prestige even than publication itself) seem more likely to be awarded for traditional archival research and for major labour-intensive scholarly projects than for the production of new deconstructive or postcolonial readings of literary texts. As theory itself would tell us, theory is socially and politically constructed, and is 'always already' part of some such broader institutional picture. Inevitably so.

Peter Barry

Further reading and works cited

Anderson, P. 'Components of the National Culture'. *New Left Review*, 50, 1968.
Barry, P. *Beginning Theory*. Manchester, 1995.
Barthes, R. *Image-Music-Text*, ed. S. Health. London, 1977.
Belsey, C. *Critical Practice*. London, 1980.
Bergonzi, B. *Exploding English: Criticism, Theory, Culture*. Oxford, 1990.
Bloom, H. et al. *Deconstruction and Criticism*. London, 1979.
Bradford, R. (ed.) *The State of Theory*. London, 1993.
Craig, D. *The Real Foundations*. London, 1973.
Culler, J. *Structuralist Poetics*. London, 1975.
Eagleton, T. *Literary Theory: An Introduction*. Oxford, 1996.
Ellis, J. M. *Against Deconstruction*. Princeton, NJ, 1989.

Essays in Criticism, 16, 1967.
Essays in Criticism, 17, 1968.
Evans, C. *English People*. Buckingham, 1993.
— (ed.) *Developing University English Teaching*. Lampeter, 1995.
Hawkes, T. *Structuralism and Semiotics*. London, 1977.
Knights, B. 'The Text and the Group', *Developing University, English Teaching*. London, 1995.
Lodge, D. *Modern Criticism and Theory*. London, 1988.
Newton, K. M. *Twentieth Century Literary Theory*. Basingstoke, 1997.
Norris, C. *Deconstruction: Theory and Practice*. London, 1982.
Parrinder, P. *The Failure of Theory*. Brighton, 1987.
Pope, R. *The English Studies Book*. London, 1998.
Rylance, R. *Debating Texts*. Milton Keynes, 1987.
Selden, R. et al. *A Reader's Guide to Contemporary Literary Theory*. Prentice Hall, 1996.
Sim, S. (ed.) *The A to Z Guide to Modern Literary and Cultural Theorists*. Hemel Hempstead, 1995.
Tallack, D. (ed.) *Literary Theory at Work: Three Texts*. London, 1987.
Tredell, N. *The Critical Decade*. Manchester, 1993.
Widdowson, P. (ed.) *Re-Reading English*. London, 1982.
Wolfreys, J. (ed.) *Literary Theories*. Edinburgh, 1999.

17. Feminism and Poststructuralism

In their introduction to the recent anthology of *Feminisms*, the editors consider the current trend in feminist academic practice to 'denounce totalizing theories, to celebrate difference, recognize "otherness", and acknowledge the multiplicity of feminisms' as directly undermining any attempt to define or represent 'feminism' itself as a coherent discipline (Kemp and Squires 1997, 4). At the same time, Second Wave feminism has a long pre-academic history and originated in grass-roots activism by women's campaigning groups and consciousness-raising techniques. I understand British and American academic (and hence largely theoretical) feminism to be a development of the practice(s) and impetus of the Second Wave Women's Movement in the context of academic conditions. So rather than bewailing a severance of academic and grass-roots feminisms, we might understand academic/theoretical feminism as simply what happens to feminism when it enters the academy, or indeed what happens to the academy/theory when feminist academics enter the scene.

Poststructuralism is a composite term drawing on a number of influential theoretical methodologies developed in late 1960s and 1970s France. While a comprehensive list of theorists contributing to poststructuralist ideas is too long for the purposes of this study, in the context of encounters between feminism and poststructuralism three figures in particular seem to have attracted significant and enduring attention (Derrida, Foucault and Lacan). So while Chris Weedon identifies Althusser at the centre of the feminist-poststructuralist project, his name does not feature at all in the index to the recent *Feminisms* anthology which charts pretty comprehensively contemporary academic feminist concerns (1987, 13). The most influential French feminist-poststructuralists (Cixous,

Irigaray, Kristeva, et al.) have been drawn on in a variety of ways in the development of what has come to be called 'Sexual Difference' feminism, active mostly outside the UK in the work of Moira Gatens, Rosi Braidotti, Michelle Boulous Walker, Elizabeth Grosz as well as current in Italian feminist theory more generally. British feminism, on the other hand, with its history of engagement with a tradition of British socialism, tends to be turned off by ideas of 'Sexual Difference', but has taken up aspects of poststructuralist methodologies as conducive to an extended materialist analysis of gender, power and representation. However, the British feminist encounter with poststructuralism is largely – if not exclusively – the result of an ongoing feminist critique of the implications and pitfalls of poststructuralist methodologies for women inside and outside the academy, a response to poststructuralism that is a direct result of British feminism's largely socialist roots. At one extreme of the range of views in play poststructuralism is considered to be a threat to the very terms in which a feminist politics is grounded, characterized by Kate Soper's announcement that 'feminism as theory has pulled the rug from under feminism as politics' (Soper, in Squire and Kemp 1997, 289). At the other extreme we can find feminist-oriented theoretical work in the British journal *m/f* intent on deconstructing gender in a way that calls feminist politics *as a practice* into question. This essay will offer a frame in which to consider what is at stake in the feminist-poststructuralist affair at large, and how it has developed in British academia more specifically.

Patricia Waugh identifies the core issue in any discussion of feminism and poststructuralism when she writes:

> Those excluded from or marginalized by the dominant culture – for reasons of class, gender, race, belief, appearance, or whatever – . . . may *never* have experienced a sense of full subjectivity in the first place. They may never have identified with that stable presence mediated through the naturalizing conventions of fictional tradition. Such Others may, indeed, *already* have sensed the extent to which subjectivity is constructed through institutional dispositions of relations of power, as well as those of fictional conventions. (1989, 2)

Waugh's comment highlights the degree to which the affair which has developed between feminism and poststructuralism since their meeting in the mid–1970s has been marked by a simultaneous convergence and breach. Both positions share a general concern with, and critical undermining of, the dominant 'Subject' of Euro-western culture since the Enlightenment. Yet the specificity of the feminist position is characterized by the degree to which this 'Subject' is understood to map onto an inherently male/masculine model, as well as the consequences and implications of its/his destabilization in theory and practice.

Whereas classical (European) poststructuralists 'deconstructed' the Enlightenment 'Subject' through a series of radical theoretical displacements (Lacanian emphasis on the structure of unconscious processes producing an illusion of conscious subjectivity; Derridean decentring of the unitary and coherent 'subject' of philosophy; Foucault's emphasis on the discursive and disciplinary practices producing the experience of subjectivity; and Barthes' displacement of the authorial control of meaning in writing), feminists begin from the radical displacement of dominant subjectivity put in motion by their embodied existence as women (the feminine Other embodied). Hence feminism arises in the first instance from an experiential (rather than theoretical) context of the common ground of the female-embodied subject's situation as *already* fragmented, dispersed, self-contradictory, etc., and the history of feminism has hitherto been dominated by women's struggle to overcome this marginalized, fragmented and Othered status. Feminism, then, recognizes that the 'Subject' under deconstruction by poststructuralist meth-odologies was never more than an epistemic fiction, but brings to the debate the understanding (largely absent elsewhere) that its/his erection was (and continues to be) established on the grounds of their/her exclusion, containment, marginalization, fragmentation and Othering. Hence feminism generally, and British feminism particularly, responds to poststructuralism with dismay (because women have never had the chance to experience the kind of stable subject position currently being theoretically dismantled) as well as familiarity (because the conclusions reached by poststructuralist methodologies echo something of the status of female-embodied subjectivity). We must also consider, following Morris (1993), to what extent we misrepresent and/or overdetermine feminism as a purely academic-theoretical practice when we consider it analogous to poststructuralism, as this encyclopaedia invites us to. For this reason I have tried in the following discussion to offer a historical as well as theoretical situating of the feminism/poststructuralism affair in British universities over the last twenty years or so.

The questions raised by the coincidence in academic practice of feminist and post-structuralist methodologies have produced a heated and productive international and interdisciplinary debate (Weedon 1987; Alcoff 1988; Adams 1978; Nicholson 1990; Riley 1988 – to name but a few). While this debate spans the western academic world, the burden of discussion has been carried by feminist theorists. Poststructuralism is a key issue in feminist theory, but feminism tends to be avoided by poststructuralist theory not self-identified as feminist. Much of the ongoing debate concerns an inherent tension within the feminist movement between praxis and principle, or between grass-roots activism and academic argument, or between experience and theory. Feminism has a long and varied history preceding the incorporation of poststructuralist theory, yet it often appears that only since feminism began to think in and through the diction of 'theory' has it been noticed outside its own domains and integrated within academic disciplines more generally. Feminism over the last 20 years has become of the order of things to be included in an encyclopaedia of criticism and theory, but – perhaps – only as an 'and' category (see Spivak 1993, 188).

To make sense of the persistent but explosive relationship between feminism and poststructuralism (by which I understand the bearing of poststructuralism on feminism *and* the bearing of feminism on poststructuralism as well as the critical area in which these become integral and mutually-informing practices) we need to understand something of the history of feminism in Britain and in particular its entry into the academy in the 1970s. This is the story of the political evolution of feminism as much as of the politicizing of the academy since the late 1960s. Prior to its engagement with feminism, poststructuralist theory was sex-blind in the sense that, whatever their theoretical sophistication, the core figures associated with this term appeared to feminist academics in the familiar guise of a new – but all too familiar – 'male pantheon' (Morris 1993, 380). The work of the poststructuralist triumvirate in particular might be characterized by a general gender aphasia: Lacan's inability/refusal to see agency beyond the phallic (Irigaray 1985; Grosz and Probyn 1995; Fraser 1997); Foucault's inability/refusal to see sexed embodiment as a factor in the production/experience of subjectivity (Sawicki 1991; McNay 1992); Derrida's claim to the disembodied 'feminine' as if female-embodiment (being a woman rather than writing like a woman) remained irrelevant to the question (Whitford 1991, 50; Morris 1993, 379). Yet feminism and poststructuralism maintain an important and active symbiosis of concerns and strategies including: recognition of the partial nature of Enlightenment claims to the universal; a desire to find ways of describing the world that aim to recreate the world; a concern over difference and the politicization of the personal (local, interior, marginal); radical attention to the determinacy of structure and process in the making of meaning; a willingness to take seriously the aesthetic/semiotic realm as a site of massive political and social stakes, and so forth. But the differences and arguments remain. Feminism as understood by poststructuralist purists stands accused of essentialism in its claims to the significance of sexual difference, and of clinging to the fictional metanarrative of patriarchy (Adams 1979; Walby 1990, 33). Conversely, poststructuralism is suspected by much of feminism to have de-essentialized sexual difference to the point of absurdity and political redundancy (Braidotti 1991; Spivak 1988; Alcoff 1988). There is the added, but important, complication that 'theory' only perceives 'feminism' *as* 'feminist theory (the structuralist/poststructuralist variety)' (Smith 1987, 34 and 267 n. 2, cit. Morris 1993, 374). Somewhere in the (con)fusion committed feminists/poststructuralists continue to adapt, develop and subvert the poststructuralist canon in the ongoing struggle to undermine patriarchy/phallocentrism in the name of 'woman'. The slippage between patriarchy and phallocentrism marks the feminist/poststructuralist exchange: the former indicates an analysis of a network of social and economic institutions while the latter focuses on the symbolic as the privileged locus of power and sexed identities. The two terms are neither entirely analogous nor exclusive (phallocentrism can be understood as the symptoms of patriarchy in processes of symbolization, patriarchy as phallocentrism materialized). As Sadie Plant observes: 'the text itself is patriarchy' (1997, 503). Perhaps the most radical and potent feminist theory today is that which has integrated, but significantly problematized, poststructuralist methodologies and which then makes use of these to analyse the phallocentric tendencies at the heart of poststructuralism itself. More recent British poststructuralist-feminist work tends to draw from and develop the insights of the first-generation French poststructuralist-feminists (Irigaray, Cixous, Kristeva) as well as developing Foucauldian, Derridean, Barthesian and/or Lacanian problematics (for example Whitford 1991; Waugh 1989; Battersby 1998). French poststructuralist-feminism, however, remains a highly charged area for British feminism, due to the ongoing and heated essentialism argument. It is argued (by Felski 1989 among others) that the biologism inherent in theoretical claims to a 'feminine' writing (for example Cixous's *écriture féminine* or Irigaray's *parler-femme*) returns women to the 'anatomy as destiny' conundrum feminism has for so long been struggling to overcome. But see also Margaret Whitford's shrewd and fruitful analysis of Irigaray's work, or Elizabeth Grosz's feminist philosophy for less defensive and more strategically minded accounts which perceive a strong political manoeuvre in the reiteration of otherwise essentialist arguments by feminist theorists.

Feminism entered the British academy as a serious critical position in the 1970s, almost simultaneously with the advent of French poststructuralism. British women's desire for access to the academy is enshrined in the history of feminist writing and activism (as documented in Virginia Woolf's *Room of One's Own* in 1929), and included as one of the four original demands of the Women's Liberation Movement in Britain agreed by the first national Women's Conference held – significantly – at Ruskin College, Oxford in 1970. Since then feminist academic activism has taken root in every discipline of British academia, as well as establishing at least one of its own in 'women's studies'. While branches in the humanities have flourished and born fruit, some in the sciences (particularly the 'masculinist' disciplines of mathematics and chemistry) have yet to bud. As arguments continue in Britain regarding the demise of grass-roots feminist activism in the face of an increasing professionalization of feminism, the development of a self-conscious and active (as well as funded, resourced and globally networked) feminist practice in academic theory, research and teaching continues apace (Radstone, in Squire and Kemp 1997, 105). Academic feminism, which is driven by but not reducible to feminist theory, remains informed by feminist academics' (as well as students') extra-curricular as well as professional struggles, and can be understood as an 'unobtrusive mobilization' of the political Women's Movement at the heart of the institutions through which our culture produces, maintains and transmits 'Truth' and 'Knowledge' (Katzenstein 1990, 27; Morris 1993, 374–5). Feminist theory is not reducible to poststructuralist-feminism (see, for example, materialist feminism), but one of the key questions engaging feminist theory over the last twenty years has been the 'equality or difference' debate sparked by poststructuralism's apparent 'deconstruction' of the term 'woman' in whose name feminism had been claiming equality. Linda Alcoff summarizes what is at stake in this debate in her question: 'How can we ground a feminist politics that deconstructs the female subject?' (1988, 419). Partly the debate rests on the notion that pre-poststructuralist – or at least liberal feminist – claims to 'equality' simply reinforced the primacy of male-masculine cultural positions, by demanding access without considering the need fundamentally and irreversibly to transform the institutions and models at which these claims were aimed. Academia itself offers a strong example: women have achieved access to universities at every level, although in relatively small numbers and against institutional resistance (women academics are still 550 per cent less likely to become professors according to the latest HESA statistics, collected by the government about British universities). To achieve this level of access and promotion women have to show they can do the job as it stands, 'passing' as normative academic subjects. In the process women become homo-genized in the institution, and are no longer in a position to notice, let alone critique and undermine, its masculinist assumptions. Equality in this instance might be understood as integration: the incorporation of the (feminine) Other which answers her critique, but only at the expense of neutralizing her in the process. 'Sexual difference' feminist theory tends to raise immediately the question of the phallocentrism of dominant cultural institutions and models (including writing/consciousness/subjectivity), and has developed a number of textual and representational strategies for undermining the inherent mascu-linism at play in these processes. The academic-theoretical wing of feminist activism, then, largely associated with poststructuralist methodologies, is perhaps best understood as a strategic and adaptive response to, or counter-colonization of, the context in which arguments concerning sex, gender and power are increasingly conducted: between aca-demic disciplines, between colleagues within academic disciplines, between teaching staff and students, and between feminists working in interdisciplinary research and women's studies generally. We might like to think of feminist-poststructuralist theory generally as consciousness-raising writ very large indeed.

British academic feminism's first encounter with poststructuralism appeared in Juliet Mitchell's *Psychoanalysis and Feminism* (1974) and almost simultaneously via the *Screen* phenomenon of radical film theory which made full use of post-Lacanian tools (described by Mulvey as 'political weapons') and feminist methodologies when Sam Rhodie retitled and reconceived the journal in 1971 (Mulvey 1975). Mulvey's paradigm for considering cinema as constitutive of gendered subjectivity (the 'male gaze' and the woman's 'to-be-looked-at-ness') has had a particularly wide and international influence on subsequent feminist work in cinema and representation generally (see *Screen*, 1992), although she has subsequently revised the argument established in her *Screen* debut in a later reflective piece

(Mulvey 1989). Mitchell's work was largely a response to Kate Millett's influential rejection of (particularly Freudian) psychoanalytic methodologies in feminist work as inherently reactionary and patriarchal constructs, originally published in 1969 (Millett 1977). Mitchell's book reclaimed a post-Lacanian psychoanalysis for feminist critical methodology: 'However it may have been used, psychoanalysis is not a recommendation *for* a patriarchal society, but an analysis *of* one. If we are interested in understanding and challenging the oppression of women, we cannot afford to neglect it' (Mitchell 1975, xv). Both Mulvey and Mitchell were influenced by radical French feminist theory which was aiming to bring psychoanalytical analysis to a marxist framework, particularly in the 'Psych et Po' (Pyschoanalysis and Politics) collective. After Mitchell and Mulvey, poststructuralist-feminist film theory and (particularly psychoanalytic) poststructuralist-feminist theory in general began to dominate feminist theoretical and philosophical work, if not in the form of an agreed and coherent methodological frame then in the form of a preoccupation with arguments over 'equality or difference' the deconstructive tendency in poststructuralist thought had provoked.

There are, broadly, two quite distinct ways to consider the enduring and evolving association between British academic feminism and poststructuralist theory since Mitchell's and Mulvey's ground-breaking studies appeared. To consider feminism's appropriation and revision of poststructuralist thought we might follow the popular understanding set out by Michèle Barrett in terms of a poststructuralist-led theoretical exposure of the essentialist and universalist bias hidden in the pre-poststructuralist feminist position (Barrett, in Barrett and Phillips 1992, 201–2). In this version the poststructuralist revolution produces a feminist fragmentation into what Moi has characterized as 'Anglo-American' and 'French' schools (all sophisticated word-play with the latter and all naive socio-politics with the former) (1985; see Todd 1988; Caine 1997, 255–71). This fragmentation, while sparked by the catalyst of poststructuralist theory, was heralded by – and answered – deep criticisms of the class, race and sexuality biases embedded in 1970s feminist thought. Black and lesbian feminists argued convincingly throughout the 1970s that 'feminist' definitions of the 'woman' in whose name the feminist agenda was developing was a fiction, and a racist and homophobic one at that (Carby 1982; *Women's Liberation Newsletter*, 1974). Poststructuralism – in this version – comes to the rescue of an untheorized feminism petrified by the horror of internal racism and homophobia. The convenient ready-made analytical tools provided by the poststructuralist canon offered the means to 'deconstruct' the reified notion of 'woman' that had been the (mis)leading light in the feminist project, with the concomitant effect of destabilizing and fragmenting the project itself. The journal *m/f* was established in 1978 to address precisely these concerns through a development of poststructuralist-feminist theory.

Conversely we might consider the *affinities between* feminism and poststructuralism in such a way as to understand the latter as symptomatic of a defence mechanism on the part of the patriarchal British academy to the influx of feminist activism in its midst, such that feminist-poststructuralist theory constitutes a counter-colonization of the newly arising dominant discourse by ever-inventive feminist academic activists. The first narrative, while historically accurate, seriously misrepresents pre-poststructuralist feminist thought through the theoretical grid of poststructuralism, and results in the perception of a 'gulf between 1970s and 1990s' feminisms (Barrett and Phillips 1992, 2) – a gulf hollowed out by poststructuralism's scornful judgement of the 'naive' feminist demand for explanations of origins and causes to the oppression of women (i.e. pre-poststructuralist feminism's investment in questions of the diachronic as well as the synchronic) (Fraser 1997). I'd like to propose and develop the second understanding here – by approaching poststructuralism from the perspective of a poststructuralist-feminist analysis of institutions of power (of which the academy we must always remember is a less than shining example) which function through the exclusion and/or containment of the feminine (Irigaray 1985). This narrative might go something as follows. Academia had been a privileged arena in which the ever-more-detailed but never-changing story of the history and significance of a universalized 'Man' was formalized, documented and perpetuated for so many hundreds of years. The Women's Liberation Movement impacted that institution in Britain via student politicization and the emergence of a new generation of politically astute and academically armed feminist activists (see Jardine on the two waves of feminist academic generations since 1968, in Squire and Kemp 1997, 80–1). Exclusion of the female-embodied Other was no longer an overt institutional option, particularly since the newly educated feminism achieved sexual discrimination legislation through parliament in 1975 (although we might wonder at the slow pace of change, given that women still constitute only a third of lecturers in the UK). Furthermore, the female-embodied Other now in the midst of the academy rapidly made use of – and developed for her own uses – the new-found institutional facilities and networks (not to mention policy-making power, budgets, research funding, archives, equipment and pedagogical processes) to question fundamentally and on its own terms the universal status of the ontological subject in whose name the entire edifice has been running since anyone cared to remember. At this moment (mid–1970s) there emerged from France into the very disciplines in which these questions are raised the loudest (humanities, sociology, philosophy, literature) a 'new' approach to knowledge that: (a) appropriated the (disembodied) feminine as a key theoretical tool; (b) hastily announced the 'death' of the subject and the agentic position to which feminist-inspired legal reform was beginning to make a powerful claim; (c) decreed that all metanarratives (including that of the 'oppression of women') are naive and unsustainable; (d) resulted in a witch-hunt on 'essentialism' which – at its purest – rules out any claim made by feminist academics to speak in the name of women (Walby 1990, 35–6). The fragmentation of the term 'woman' that is the key to poststructuralist engagements with feminism, however, does not necessarily result in a weakening of the feminist position. As Squire and Kemp remind us in their anthology, '[t]he development of multiple feminist theoretical perspectives and the painful splintering of the women's movement occurred almost simultaneously with the growth of second-wave feminism, despite its oft-presumed unity. Today such fragmentation is largely viewed as symptomatic of, rather than problematic for, feminist endeavours' (Squire and Kemp 1997, 4).

Morris considers the self-perpetuating theoretical machinery of a subsequent postmodernism which continues to exclude and marginalize women theorists as 'a twilight of the gods [. . .] the last ruse of the patriarchal University trying for power to fix the meaning, and contain the damage, of its own decline' (Morris 1993, 380). Poststructuralism, in this rather simplified narrative, offered a lateral theoretical defence formation against the feminist challenge to a self-perpetuating male-masculine ontology in all its manifestations. Hence poststructuralist theoretical tools have been deployed to argue 'that the categories of men and women have no use in a social analysis' because these constitute 'essentialist' concepts, thereby removing the ground of a feminist critique just at the moment that it was beginning to gather steam (Walby 1990, 35; see Adams 1979). Feminist-poststructuralist work has subsequently developed modes of argument and analysis which reintroduce sexed embodiment and sexual difference to the debate with full consciousness of the heavy charges of essentialism at risk in such a project, producing subtle and increasingly adept interventions in the discussions that have come to dominate British academic research in the humanities since the 1980s (see especially Coward 1984; Rose 1986; Walby 1990; Whitford 1991; Barrett and Phillips 1992; Morris 1993; Radstone 1997; Battersby 1998).

It is probably worth distinguishing here between feminist theory which takes up the methodological questions of poststructuralism and their effectiveness for feminist politics, from feminist work which applies poststructuralist theory within the terms of a given discipline. Catherine Belsey's *The Subject of Tragedy* was an important instance of applied poststructuralist literary criticism (Belsey 1985), whereas Rosalind Coward's *Female Desire* (1984) was a theoretical analysis of women in popular culture which made use of poststructuralist theory without making a great fuss of it, and Walby's *Theorizing Patriarchy* (1990) deploys the problematics of feminist-poststructuralist methodologies to articulate an account of patriarchal forms which answers adeptly the criticism of an untheorized metanarrative at the heart of feminist thought. Jacqueline Rose's work on psychoanalysis, sexuality and visuality (Rose 1986) makes a strong case for poststructuralist psychoanalytic theory in critical and theoretical feminist practice, while Whitford's highly engaging and intelligent critical encounter with Irigaray (Whitford 1991) offers both a serious and challenging account of Irigaray's work, and an argument for the strategic deployment of feminist-poststructuralist methodologies more generally. Barrett's turn from marxism to poststructuralism has produced some of the clearest expositions of the questions posed by poststructuralism to feminist thought, as well as arguing for a new materialism which avoids an excessive mechanistic simplicity and reintroduces female experience as a critical category. Barrett's essay on 'Words and Things' (in Barrett and Phillips 1992) strikes me as the best place to start in any attempt to understand what is at stake in British feminism's encounter with, and transformation by, poststructuralist methodologies. It offers a full and thoughtful account of her own 'turn to theory' in the context of a more general 'turn to culture' in feminism during the 1980s.

Barrett notes that feminist theory's incorporation of poststructuralism tends to cluster around identifiable areas and has resulted in a general 'turn to culture' as the primary site of contestation. The 'turn to culture' signals a heightened concern with representation in reaction to some of the mechanistic excesses of a materialist methodology (Barrett, in Barrett and Phillips 1992, 208–11). The feminist debate, then, has shifted from a sociological focus towards the semiotic (cultural feminism). In this context Foucault's 'analysis of the exclusions and prohibitions of discourse' is easily assimilable to 'a feminism that has pioneered understanding of the power of naming and the efficacy of language' (211). Derridean deconstruction, Lacanian psychoanalysis and Foucauldian discourse analysis and foregrounding of the body as a critical locus are the favoured poststructuralist tendencies of feminist work, offering as they do a means to address 'sexuality, subjectivity and textuality' – themes already high on the pre-poststructuralist agenda (215). However, it remains a mistake to consider poststructuralism as the theoretical arm of an otherwise largely untheorized feminism – as Weedon's influential study of *Feminist Practice and Poststructuralist Theory* tends to do (Weedon 1987) – and there remain serious theoretical feminist concerns with the implications of poststructuralism, especially as this tends towards a postmodernist emphasis. As Rita Felski has argued strongly: 'the question of the politics of feminist reading or writing is not a question which can be resolved at an aesthetic level alone; it is inextricably linked to the fate of the women's movement as a whole' (Felski, in Squire and Kemp 1997, 429). In other words, the British feminist encounter with poststructuralism remains consistently anxious about poststructuralism's elision of the marxist concern with materiality. Similarly Linda Alcoff has argued that the tendency in poststructuralism to designate particularities as subjective and fictional constructs alongside a destabilization of the authority of the subjective position 'coincides neatly with the classical liberal's view that human peculiarities are irrelevant' (1988, 420). As Soper reminds us:

> The paradox of the poststructuralist collapse of the 'feminine' and the move to 'in-difference' is that it reintroduces – though in the disguised form of an aspiration to no-gender – something not entirely dissimilar from the old humanistic goal of sexual parity and reconciliation. And while one can welcome the reintroduction of the goal, it may still require some of the scepticism which inspired its original deconstruction. (1990, 243)

Perhaps the most compelling and distinctive aspect of British feminist-poststructuralist work derives from British feminism's long history of and investment in a committed socialism and a related cultural materialism. Mitchell's work was steeped in a British marxist tradition, and her argument was challenging in its appropriation of psychoanalytic critical tools in this context. Hence poststructuralist critical apparatus tends to have been subjected to a rigorous and highly critical scepticism in British academic feminism, rather than ingested whole and unaltered. The resulting arguments have a refreshing absence of jargonese, tend towards a careful self-examination of concepts and position, and are usually successful in avoiding narcissistic theoretical loops. The British encounter between feminism and poststructuralism, then, has resulted in recent years in an internalization by feminist theorists and practitioners of the serious questions raised by poststructuralist methodologies, and these questions in themselves have become integral to – rather than undermining of – the larger feminist academic project. So while Radstone identifies 'insecurities and doubts which currently shake feminist theory to its core, producing a range of questions concerning the status of the category "woman"' leading to the fundamental question: 'is a politics grounded in women's *collective* experience still desirable, given poststructuralism's deconstruction of binary oppositions?', feminist theory continues to produce a range of committed feminist theoretical and pedagogic practices which incorporate poststructuralist questions and methodologies without conceding the political efficacy and importance of the notional 'woman' in whose name the feminist project acts (Radstone, in Squire and Kemp 1997, 106–7). Elizabeth Grosz understands this process well at the level of political intervention when she notes that some anti-poststructuralist critics radically miss the point when they assume that 'feminists take on essentialist or universalist assumptions … in the same way as patriarchs, instead of attempting to understand the ways in which essentialism and its cognates function as unavoidable and therefore possibly strategically useful terms'. For Grosz, the anti-poststructuralist-feminist position 'silences and neutralises the most powerful of feminist theoretical weapons, the ability to use patriarchy and phallocratism against themselves, to take up positions ostensibly opposed to feminism and to use them for feminist goals' (Grosz and Probyn 1995, 57). Feminism remains undeniably – and some might say gloriously – parasitic on the academy in British universities, surviving and in some areas flourishing by its radical and unsettling mimeticism, a transmuting ability to reproduce itself in forms ostensibly designed or appropriated to undermine it (poststructuralism included).

Ashley Tauchert

Further reading and works cited

Adams, P. 'The Subject of Feminism', *m/f*, 2, 1978.

—. 'A Note on Sexual Divisions and Sexual Differences', *m/f*, 3, 1979.

Alcoff, L. 'Cultural Feminism Versus Post-Structuralism: The Identity Crisis in Feminist Theory', *Signs*, 13, 1988.

Barrett, M. and Phillips, A. (eds) *Destabilizing Theory*. Cambridge, 1992.

Battersby, C. *The Phenomenal Woman*. Cambridge, 1998.

Belsey, C. *The Subject of Tragedy*. London, 1985.

Braidotti, R. *Patterns of Dissonance*. Oxford, 1991.

Brennan, T. (ed.) *Between Feminism and Psychoanalysis*. London, 1989.

Caine, B. *English Feminism 1780–1980*. Oxford, 1997.

Carby, H. 'White Woman Listen! Black Feminism and the Boundaries of Sisterhood', in *The Empire Strikes Back*. London, 1982.

Coward, R. *Female Desire*. London, 1984.

Docherty, T. (ed.) *Postmodernism*. London, 1993.

Felski, R. *Beyond Feminist Aesthetics*. London, 1989.

Fraser, N. 'Structuralism or Pragmatism? On Discursive Theory and Feminist Politics', in *The Second Wave*, ed. L. Nicholson. London, 1997.

— and Nicholson, L. 'Social Criticism Without Philosophy: An Encounter Between Feminism and Postmodernism', in *The Second Wave*, ed. L. Nicholson. London, 1997.

Gatens, M. *Imaginary Bodies*. London, 1996.

Grosz, E. and Probyn, E. (eds) *Sexy Bodies*. London, 1995.

Irigaray, L. *Speculum of the Other Woman*, trans. G. C. Gill. Ithaca, NY, 1985.

Jardine, A. 'The Demise of Experience', In *The Second Wave*, ed. L. Nicholson. London, 1997.

Katzenstein, M. 'Feminism Within American Institutions: Unobtrusive Mobilization in the 1980s', *Signs*, 16, 1, 1990.

Kemp, S. and Squires, J. (eds) *Feminisms*. Oxford, 1997.

McNay, L. *Foucault and Feminism*. Cambridge, 1992.

Millett, K. *Sexual Politics*. London, 1977.

Mitchell, J. *Psychoanalysis and Feminism*. Harmondsworth, 1975.

Moi, T. *Sexual/Textual Politics*. London, 1985.

Morris, M. *The Pirate's Fiancée*. London, 1993.

—. 'Feminism, Reading, Postmodernism', in *The Second Wave*, ed. L. Nicholson. London, 1997.

Mulvey, L. 'Visual Pleasure and Narrative Cinema', *Screen*, 16, 3, 1975.

—. *Visual and Other Pleasures*. Bloomington, IN, 1989.

Nicholson, L. (ed.) *Feminism/Postmodernism*. New York, 1990.

Nicholson, L. (ed.) *The Second Wave*. London, 1997.

Plant, S. '"Beyond the Screens": Film, Cyberpunk and Cyberfeminism', in *The Second Wave*, ed. L. Nicholson. London, 1997.

Radstone, S. 'Postcard From the Edge: Thoughts on the "Feminist Theory: An International Debate" Conference Held at Glasgow University, Scotland, 12–15 July 1991'.

Riley, D. *Am I That Name?* Basingstoke, 1988.

Rose, J. *Sexuality in the Field of Vision*. London, 1986.

Sawicki, J. *Disciplining Foucault*. New York, 1991.

Screen. The Sexual Subject, ed. Mandy Merck. London, 1992.

Smith, P. and Jardine, A. (eds) *Men in Feminism*. New York, 1987.

Soper, K. *Troubled Pleasures*. London, 1990.

Spivak, G. C. *In Other Worlds*. New York, 1988.

—. *Outside in the Teaching Machine*. New York, 1993.

'Straight Women', *Women's Liberation Newsletter*, 63, 1974.

Todd, J. *Feminist Literary History*. Cambridge, 1988.
Walby, S. *Theorizing Patriarchy*. Oxford, 1990.
Waugh, P. *Feminine Fictions*. London, 1989.
Weedon, C. *Feminist Practice and Poststructuralist Theory*. Oxford, 1987.
Whitford, M. 'Introduction', *The Irigaray Reader*, ed. M. Whitford. New York, 1991.
Woolf, V. *A Room of One's Own*. London, 1929.

18. Cultural Studies

Originating with a series of 1950s investigations of the 'commonality' and 'ordinariness' of culture, and gradually institutionalized as a key element of British academic and intellectual life, the set of postwar scholarly practices identified as British cultural studies has passed through two major subsequent phases: a 1960s and 1970s moment primarily concerned with the ideological structuring of the public media, mass cultural communicative forms and working-class culture, and a post-1980s investigation of the significance of racial, gender and imperial histories to contemporary British cultural life.

Marx writes that 'Men make their own history, but they do not make it just as they please; they do not make it under circumstances chosen by themselves, but under circumstances directly encountered, given, and transmitted from the past' (1977, 15). Substitute the word 'culture' for the word 'history' in this sentence and you will have a fair outline of the history of British cultural studies from its mid-1950s 'founding' in the works of Richard Hoggart, Raymond Williams, and E. P. Thompson, to its quasi-institutionalization in the 1960s, 1970s and 1980s (in both a series of university spaces – most prominently the Centre for Contemporary Cultural Studies at Birmingham University (CCCS) – and a range of academic journals and enterprises, including the *New Left Review*, *Screen*, *Cultural Studies*, *New Formations* and the Open University's Course 'Mass Communication and Society'), to its internal post-1980s interrogation by an assortment of scholars who, while indebted to cultural studies and working within its general paradigms, have questioned its initial blindness to questions of race, gender and a range of other problems haunting the contemporary circumstances of British cultural life.

To suggest a rough analogy between Marx's dictum and the history of British cultural studies is, as this tripartite history implies, to suggest that British cultural studies may be loosely periodized into three 'moments' – each characterized by a dominant logic or problem – in much the fashion that Marx's statement may be divided into three primary claims. Thus, by this paraphrase, the key problem of the first, 1950s, moment of British cultural studies was the problem of coming to understand what it meant to conceive of culture as something 'made' rather than something simply 'found' or 'revered'. In the 1960s and 1970s, the problem was coming to understand what it meant for culture to be the product not of the autonomous will of its agents and artisans but of a range of enveloping, ideological 'circumstances' within which the subjects of culture 'find' themselves and by whose constraining force they discover themselves limited or determined. And the problem of the post-1980s immanent critique of British cultural studies has been that of demonstrating that the contemporary circumstances of British life are circumstances the nation 'inherits' from its imperial and patriarchal past, circumstances carried over into the present from a 'past' that is not, after all, past.

To gloss a complex history so is of course to oversimplify, and to exclude developments of research and thought and trajectories of inquiry that cannot be so neatly contained by a single descriptive framework. While this is, then, a framework that I think has some value, developing it also implies attending to at least some of what it leaves out. But before doing either of those things, the very terms of this history of British cultural studies require some interrogation. For whatever else they have been and whatever else they have accomplished, the set of postwar intellectual enterprises contained within the rubric of British cultural studies have demonstrated a persistent questioning of the status of the concept with which I began, a persistent investigation of just what we mean by 'culture', a questioning that has, indeed, been so constant that the history of British cultural studies might equally well be said to be the history of the attempt to unlock the riddle of this word.

Raymond Williams' *Culture and Society, 1780–1950* (1958; which, together with Richard Hoggart's *The Uses of Literacy* and E. P. Thompson's *The Making of the English Working Class*, is regularly identified as one of the founding texts of British cultural studies), provides the first key to the logic by which that riddle has been unlocked. Playing itself off Matthew Arnold's *Culture and Anarchy* – which had insisted on an essentially aestheticist conception of culture, on a notion of culture as a high sphere set apart from the ordinary transactions of life, as 'the best that has been thought and known' – Williams's text argued both for a massive expansion of those forms of human activity and production that we think of as cultural and a consequent abandonment of the notion that 'culture' names the rarefied, the exceptional, the exquisite. 'Culture', Williams insisted in one of the most famous formulations of this earliest phase of cultural studies, 'is ordinary', a suggestion whose implications Stuart Hall glosses so:

> The conception of 'culture' is itself democratized and socialized. It no longer consists of the sum of the 'best that has been thought and said', regarded as the summits of an achieved civilization – that ideal of perfection to which, in earlier usage, all aspired. Even 'art' . . . is now redefined as only one, special, form of a general social process: the giving and taking of meanings, and the slow development of 'common' meanings – a common culture: 'culture', in this special sense, 'is ordinary' . . . If even the highest, most refined of descriptions offered in works of literature, are also 'part of the general process which creates conventions and institutions, through which the meanings that are valued by the community are shared and made active', then there is no way in which this process can be hived off or distinguished or set apart from the other practices of the historical process. (1986, 35)

As Hall's reading of Williams's argument indicates, to conceive of culture as 'ordinary' is simultaneously to think of it as 'common' (in both senses of the word, i.e. as everyday and as a shared possession rather than the exclusive property of a privileged few); as eternally unfixed, constantly caught in the give and take of its collective making; and, perhaps most significantly for the consequent development of a cultural studies epistemology, as something not 'set apart', something not identical with an exclusive set of aesthetic, idealizing practices, but, rather, something fully present within that 'social' domain no longer conceivable as distinct from the cultural sphere.

This last suggestion – by which Williams not only 'democratizes and socializes' culture but also, it is frequently remarked, 'anthropologizes' it, correlates it, as another of his well-known formulations has it, with 'lived experience' – was to have major implications for the consequent study of culture and the development of a cultural studies methodology. Detached from an exclusive association with the museum, the opera house and the 'literary' canon, 'culture' was freed to name a massively proliferating array of sites and of texts. For the cultural studies methodologies that emerged in the wake of Williams's intervention, the study of culture was to imply as fully the study of television, fashion, educational curricula, mechanisms of policing, habits of working-class life and the ritualized practices of 'youth' subcultures, as it was the close analysis of painting, ballet or the romantic lyric. Hoggart's *The Uses of Literacy* (1958) demonstrated what this new kind of study might look like as Hoggart applied his Leavisite training in literary study (his 'literacy' in textual analysis) to a broad range of working-class 'texts'. In doing so, Hoggart was able not only to apply 'the analytical protocols of literary study to a wider range of cultural products: music, newspapers, magazines, and popular fiction in particular', but, as significantly, and much like Williams, to demonstrate 'the interconnections among various aspects of public culture – pubs, working-men's clubs, magazines, and sports – and the structures of an individual's private, everyday life – family roles, gender relations, language patterns, the community's "common sense" ... a complex whole in which public values and private practices are tightly intertwined' (Turner 1990, 44).

If 'culture', for Hoggart, as for Williams, is thus democratic, social, common, ordinary, then it is equally important to note that as culture is thus 'anthropologized', the anthropological is simultaneously 'textualized', treated as that which can be read much as a literary text can be read, as that which can be decoded by readerly protocols developed for the analysis of the 'literary'. Cultural studies, from its earliest moment, thus names not so much the absolute abandonment of the literary, or a simple substitution of an anthropological for an aesthetic conception of culture, as a re-deployment of textual literacy to a massively expanded field of inquiry. Cultural studies, then, is at its heart a double-order procedure, one which simultaneously 'anthropo-logizes' culture and textualizes the field of study it has thus enlarged. In the process, the literary is not so much overthrown as distributed across the entire social and historical terrain. Through this act of double expansion cultural studies not only reveals its debts to the institutional history of literary study but offers less to abolish this earlier mode of study (as is so often claimed) than to establish its readerly protocols at the centre of an expanded universe of inquiry.

'Expanded', may, however, not be the most precise word with which to characterize cultural studies' re-understanding of the domains of the literary, the cultural and the anthropological and its new mode of studying its renovated objects of inquiry. In his influential essay on the development and fundamental paradigms of British cultural studies, Stuart Hall indicates that 'convergence', 'conjunction' and 'intersection' may be better terms for both the new, post-Williamsite, conception of culture and the new methods of critique this reconceptualization has demanded. On this understanding it is not so much that 'culture' has expanded to become coextensive with the entire field of lived human experience as that culture names a new practice of study by identifying the site where the historical, the political, the social, the aesthetic, the economic, et al. intersect or converge. Hoggart's densely particular, concrete study of some aspects of working-class culture and Thompson's historical reconstruction of the formation of a class culture and popular traditions in the 1790–1830 period formed, between them, the break and defined the space from which a new area of study and a new practice opened. Culture was the site of the convergence (Hall 1986, 34–5). Hall's point, though plainly stated, is a complex one. For there are at least three 'convergences' at work here, all named by, and complicatedly contained within, the notion of culture.

The first convergence is between the work of Williams, Hoggart and Thompson whose writings are connected by their common interest in something called culture. The second convergence is that articulated by the concept of culture itself, or, somewhat tautologically, by the rearticulation of culture as the site of the convergence of what had previously been held to be separate (economic, historical, aesthetic) phenomena. Cultural studies' new 'area of study' is thus an area constituted by, and as, the conjunction of all the (no longer) disparate materials of a total 'historical process'. If such convergences are, thus, *what* 'cultural studies' studies then the third convergence pertains to *how* this 'new practice' articulates a method by which to examine this new field of study. As 'culture' itself is seen to be the site of complex convergences, so its study demands the conjunction of previously separate methodologies, not just the conjunction of methodologies developed by the disciplines of literature and anthropology but, increasingly, as this new practice invented itself, the convergence of methods derived from the fields of politics, economics, philosophy, media-studies, semiotics and ideological analysis. A revolution in the conception of 'culture', cultural studies thus equally announces a revolution in critical method, a revolution in which the new, hybrid, method developed for the study of 'culture' imitates the hybrid form of the culture it studies by making itself out of a broad array of interpretive protocols which can no longer be 'set apart' from one another.

This brief outline of some of the problems and possibilities opened by a critical interrogation of the concept of 'culture' summarizes much of the work of the first phase, the 1950s, of British cultural studies, a phase commonly, and unsurprisingly, referred to as the 'culturalist' moment of British cultural studies – generally in contradistinction to the 'structuralist' moment that was to follow in the 1960s and 1970s as various cultural studies practiners, Stuart Hall prominent among them, began the work of consolidating Williams's insights, developing institutional centres for a cultural studies practice and, fairly rapidly, reversing one of the claims central to the work of Williams, Hoggart and Thompson. But to get some sense of what was at stake in this 'structuralist' critique of Williams, Hoggart and Thompson's 'culturalism', one last thing needs to be said about this first phase.

I have suggested that the 1950s moment of cultural studies might be typified as a moment in which a range of scholars began to consider what it meant to say that 'men make their own culture', and thus far I have concentrated on what this has implied for a reconceptualization of culture as a collective, complex work, as something collaboratively fashioned by the everyday subjects of history. The phrase implies more, however, than a notion of collectivity more than an understanding of culture as a 'commonly' fabricated work. It also suggests a fairly substantial exercise of agency on the part of those making this common culture, a relatively high degree of freedom to, in fact, fashion a collective 'lived experience'. As such, this understanding of culture-making sits rather uneasily with both a classical marxist 'base and superstructure' paradigm and with marxian readings of the relatively high degree to which human activity is not autonomous or free but largely constrained or determined by the material conditions of worldly existence (the 'circumstances' not of our 'own choosing' in the second clause of Marx's formula).

The first problem could be fairly easily resolved by suggesting, as Williams and Thompson in different ways did, that 'culture' does not belong to some 'ideal' domain 'superstructural' to the material 'base' of society but is itself an element of our phenomenological materiality. The critique of Matthew Arnold's aestheticist, and separatist, notion of culture is thus, equally, a critique of the base/superstructure paradigm and indicates why cultural studies is also often referred to as a form of 'cultural materialism'. The second problem (one commonly glossed as the problem of 'agency and determinism') was not so easily resolved. Indeed, at the last, it was not resolved. Instead, Williams, Thompson, and to a lesser extent Hoggart, implicitly defined their projects as resistant to a strong theory of determinism, as something like one or other species of marxist humanism. For Thompson this implied, as *The Making of the English Working Class* makes clear, that 'class consciousness' is not the automatic and inevitable by-product of economic conditions but is something a human collectivity fashions ('makes') for itself from the brute materials of experience, indeed something out of whose making this collectivity 'makes' itself. For Williams this marxist humanism finds perhaps its most crystalline, and its most enigmatic, form in his concept of the 'structure of feeling', a phrase which admits the idea that experience is to some extent structured by an array of determinants (rather than purely self-fashioned) but limits the determining power of such structuration by suggesting that structure must work its way through, and find itself reworked by, 'feeling': a word which, in this context seems to imply the affective consciousness, desire, will and disposition of a collection of human actors.

The structuralist critique of culturalism (the critique which I am suggesting loosely corresponds to Marx's interest in the ways in which historical and cultural 'making' occurs within, and is determined by, circumstances not of our own choosing) coincided, ironically enough, with a proto-institutionalization of cultural studies within British university and intellectual life. That institutionalization took a variety of forms, perhaps the most significant of which were the establishment of the Centre for Contemporary Cultural Studies (CCCS) at Birmingham University (first directed by Richard Hoggart and then, beginning in 1970, by Stuart Hall), the emergence of a series of cultural studies journals, and, as the name of the Birmingham Centre indicates, a turn from the sort of long histories of British life that had occupied much of Williams and Thompson's attention to a primary interest in the contemporary, particularly the contemporaneous nature of British education, media and urban culture. With both a field and a method of study roughly in place, British cultural studies began, with these steps, to define a project for itself, and it seems fair to say that while this second phase of cultural studies derived its field and its method from Williams and Thompson, it inherited its project from Hoggart.

For all its methodological originality, Hoggart's *The Uses of Literacy* was, as has been widely remarked, a deeply nostalgic text, an elegy of sorts to a working-class culture Hoggart took to be vanishing under the assault of a new, commercialized, homogenized, hyper-mediated social order. Hoggart saw the rich particularities of working-class culture giving way to a generalized mass culture disseminated by television, radio and the magazines. While Hoggart's nostalgia was not a marked feature of the second moment of British cultural studies, his interest in the power of the media to penetrate and shape a social order was. Indeed this interest in the power of the media to order and construct social and cultural life and, somewhat later, in the means by which media consumers adopt, interpret or resist media representations of their 'realities', was, to a large extent, to define the 1960s and 1970s project of British cultural studies. Unsurprisingly, then, many of the more influential works of this period took an analysis of television and film as their central objects of inquiry (though, it must be noted, a cultural studies analysis of the 'media' does not imply simply an attention to such technologies of communication; education, among other things, certainly falls within the field of media studies, one perhaps more accurately identified as communication studies). Raymond Williams, still an active participant in the unfolding history of cultural studies, published *Television* (1974); Stuart Hall wrote a number of important essays on television and the media; John Fiske and John Hartley's *Reading Television* (1978), Judith Williamson's *Decoding Advertisements* (1978) and Terence Hawkes' *Structuralism and Semiotics* (1977) were among the field-defining works of the new media-oriented cultural studies; and the film journal *Screen*, established itself as a major influence in British intellectual life.

Screen was more than a journal, it became the byword for a form of theory and the central exponent of the structuralist critique of some of cultural studies' founding assumptions. The structuralist 'turn' was not, however, just a turn against Williams and Thompson's marxist humanism, it was also a turn to a body of philosophical and critical writings on semiotics, post-Freudian psychoanalysis and structuralist marxism and anthropology that had become widely influential on the European continent in the postwar years. Hall, in his years as director of the CCCS, and, through him, the Centre itself, were enormously important in introducing many of the strands of postwar continental theory to the British cultural studies debates. (Graeme Turner (1990) identifies Hall's two 1971 essays on 'Television' and the 'Media' as watershed moments in this process). But it was *Screen* that most insistently 'structuralized' a cultural studies epistemology. And the major influence on *Screen*, and the major force behind 'Screen theory', was undoubtedly Louis Althusser, his theory of 'ideology' and his notion of 'interpellation'.

Through the 1970s, *Screen* became something like the party organ of an Althusserian structuralism, the hard centre of a bleakly determinist reading of film, television and the other media's power to order cultural life. The *Screen* writers were not alone in pursuing such theories, but their Althusserian orthodoxy inspired resistance among other scholars who, while wanting to take such 'ideology critique' seriously, also sought a more flexible solution to the general problem of agency and determinism. The key to that solution came via the work of another continental thinker, Antonio Gramsci, whose theories entered the British cultural studies debate through the writings of scholars at the Birmingham Centre, centrally, once more, Stuart Hall. The Gramscian response to Althusser (and, in effect, the CCCS critique of 'Screen theory') was developed around the Italian philosopher's notion of hegemony. For Gramsci 'hegemony' defined the means by which state apparatuses of power maintain themselves in all those ordinary moments in which entrenched power formations cannot secure their existence through the direct application of violent force but must, much as Althusser suggested, convince a subordinate or subaltern group of the rightness of their oppression. The difference between this reading of hegemony and an Althusserian reading of ideology is, to simplify matters entirely, that while for Althusser ideology is largely irresistible (and the possibilities and realities of historical change thus inexplicable), for Gramsci 'hegemony' defines a set of limits and pressures, a series of dominant representations of the real, but, crucially, also a set of occasions for contestation, an array of representations not so much to be passively 'consumed' as decoded, resisted, subverted. For Gramsci, then, ideology is less an irresistible than an invitation: to resistance, to critique, to a reimagining of our relation to the 'real'.

The Althusserian and Gramscian poles of ideology critique defined the limits within which much of the 1970s cultural studies work in Britain operated, thus effecting a displacement whereby 'ideology' took the place of 'culture' as the central term on which British cultural studies went to work. The writings to emerge from this period were rich and varied, too various to catalogue. I will therefore mention just two works which, while representative of this moment, also anticipated crucial elements of the phase that was to follow. Stuart Hall and Tony Jefferson's edited collection of essays *Resistance through Ritual* was emblematic in this regard. If the Althusser/Gramsci opposition is understood as a contest of sorts, then *Resistance*, through its very title, signals its Gramscian partisanship and also the eventual outcome of that contest. While Gramsci has clearly outlasted Althusser as a central influence on British cultural studies it has partially been because in texts such as *Resistance*, Hall, Jefferson, and others were able to discover in the 'subculture' (the minor, antagonistic, counter-culture within a larger cultural formation) a series of localized, individuated practices of cultural re-invention by which minoritarian collectivities refashion inherited cultural codes. Subcultural 'resistance' is thus not simply a possibility, a standing invitation to contestation latent within the master texts of hegemonic cultural formations, but an alternative or oppositional cultural ensemble, a coherent and specific set of cultural practices, active within a social totality. The attention paid to particularized, realized, subcultural 'practices' of contestation in texts such as Hall Jefferson's *Resistance* and Hebdige's *Subculture* was eventually to develop into a more general theoretical interest in 'practices' most influentially worked out in the writings of the French philosopher Michel de Certeau. As de Certeau suggests, to speak of practices is to speak of a theory of 'consumer reproduction', a theory of the ways in which subordinate groups productively consume 'legitimate culture', making of the 'rituals, representations, and laws imposed on them something quite different from what their conquerors had in mind ... using them with respect to ends and references foreign to the system they had no choice but to accept' (de Certeau 1984, xiii).

The second text to mention from this 1970s moment is another co-edited by Hall, *Policing the Crisis* (1978), less significant for its methodological originality than for its introduction of a hermeneutics of race to the ongoing cultural studies enterprise. In this respect, *Policing the Crisis* anticipates the shift to a third moment of cultural studies work in Britain but it does not quite define it. It addresses the construction of a criminalized concept of race but does so largely within the by now dominant paradigms of a communications-theoretical cultural studies project. To put things another way, *Policing the Crisis* poses race as a problem for the British state and British society, it does not yet think race as a crisis within and a problem for cultural studies. That critical move (and with that move the shift to a third phase moment willing, once again, to subject some of the governing assumptions of British cultural studies to a thorough going critique) was to come a few years later and was most notably signalled by *The Empire Strikes Back* (1982).

By 1982, the British empire, while not quite dead, was largely, or so many Britons had taken to believing, a thing of the past. *The Empire Strikes Back* suggested otherwise, suggested, in effect, that the empire had less collapsed than collapsed inward, returned 'home' to the scene of its founding. In the decades since the end of the Second World War, ex-colonial subjects from India, Pakistan, Africa and the Caribbean had emigrated to Britain in significant numbers, at first encouraged by 1950s governments in search of labour power to reconstruct the immediate postwar economy, but then, increasingly, as a black British community expanded and consolidated itself, treated with bureaucratic and juridical hostility by the British state. Many of the authors of *The Empire Strikes Back* were members of that black British community and the letter their text returned to Britain signalled not only the arrival of an increasingly active generation of black British intellectuals and the persistence of an imperial 'past' in the nation's putatively 'post-imperial' present, but a strong rejoinder to a 'British' cultural studies enterprise that had never quite detached itself from a quasi-nationalist investment in the logics of a 'common' culture whose bonds of commonality were geographically and racially exclusive.

The problem with British cultural studies, Paul Gilroy indicated in the introduction to *The Empire Strikes Back*, was, in a word, its Britishness or, somewhat more complexly, its closet identification of 'Britishness' with 'Englishness', its exclusive interest and investment in an English national culture that constitutes only one element of a far more diverse, and entangled, national and imperial cultural formation. Even when produced as an oppositional intellectual practice, politically committed to articulating a working-class critique of the nation's dominant culture, British cultural studies, Gilroy and his co-authors suggested, implicitly confirmed the centrality of English culture to British national and imperial history. The very notions of a 'common culture' and of a 'lived' and 'long' experience functioned, they suggest, as codes that effectively defined the 'field' of cultural studies as insular, nationalist and white. If, as the title of Gilory's subsequent book *There Ain't No Black in the Union Jack* (1987) indicated, the conservative guardians of the British state had envisioned themselves as the wardens of a racially homogeneous polity, then so too had the leftist critics of that polity constructed a 'radical' cultural studies project unable to address the 'lived experience' of those British subjects whose most common experience of a 'common' culture was the experience of being told that this was a culture to which they did not belong. Two main strands of work have followed from this field-altering critique: one, typified perhaps by Kobena Mercer's *Welcome to the Jungle* (1994), has retained an interest in 'British' cultural life as its prime object of inquiry but has done so in order to examine the ways in which black cultures are constitutive of a hybrid British cultural ensemble; the other, for which Gilroy's *The Black Atlantic* (1993) is undoubtedly the central text, has sought to reposition cultural analysis outside the defining parameters of the nation, in Gilroy's case by mapping the counters of a cross-Atlantic black cultural ensemble.

The racial critique of contemporary British culture and British cultural studies was not, however, unique. Four years before the publication of *The Empire Strikes Back*, the Women's Studies Group at the CCCS had published *Women Take Issue* (1978), a collection which launched a similar critique of British cultural studies, though here, as the title of the volume suggests, it was the ways in which cultural studies work had systematically excluded women's histories from its accounts of British cultural life, indeed the implicit masculinization of both a 'common culture' and a common field of cultural study, that is at stake. Like *The Empire Strikes Back*, which helped generate a great deal of subsequent work in black British cultural studies, *Women Take Issue* introduced an ongoing feminist critique, and reinvention, of cultural studies that has helped define the third phase of the British cultural studies enterprise.

At the heart of that third moment, as I have suggested, is something like a theory of the cultural uncanny, an analysis of the ways in which 'prior' modes and experiences of repression return to assert their priority in any account or critique of the contemporary, an examination of the ways in which the current 'circumstances' of British cultural life *and* the circumstances from which British cultural studies 'makes' its project are directly encountered, given or transmitted from an imperial and patriarchal 'past' that is not, in fact, past. A moment of critique, reorientation and redefinition, this third phase should, however, be understood less as a moment of departure than as a moment of re-creation. Like the stages that have preceded it, this third moment of cultural studies has not so much dissolved the field of study from which it originates as expanded the parameters of that field, redeployed its strategies and practices of reading to an enlarged field of investigation, multiplied both its sites of analysis and its modes of enquiry. Perhaps, to conclude, it is best to say that what this third 'phase' demonstrates is that the history of British cultural studies has been not simply a dialectical history but, as Stuart Hall has it, the history of a series of convergences, the history of an ever more complex mode of studying an ever more complex object, the history, indeed, of a collective project that has proven itself capable of conjoining an ever more various range of discourses, experiences, practices, representational codes and histories under the sign of that *not* after all 'common' word, 'culture'.

Ian Baucom

Further reading and works cited

Arnold, M. 'Culture and Anarchy', in *Poetry and Criticism of Matthew Arnold*, ed. A. Dwight Culler. Boston, 1961.
Ashcroft, B. et al. (eds) *The Empire Writes Back*. London, 1995.
Brantlinger, P. *Crusoe's Footprints*. London, 1990.
Davies, I. *Cultural Studies and Beyond*. London, 1995.
de Certeau, M. *The Practice of Everyday Life*. Berkeley, CA, 1984.
Dworkin, D. *Cultural Marxism in Postwar Britain*. Durham, NC, 1997.
Fiske, J. and Hartley, J. *Reading Television*. London, 1978.
Franklin, S. et al. (eds) *Off-Centre*. London, 1991.
Gilroy, P. *There Ain't No Black in the Union Jack*. London, 1987.
—. *The Black Atlantic*. Cambridge, MA, 1993.
Hall, S. 'Deviancy, Politics and the Media', CCCS Stencilled Paper 11, 1971
—. 'Television as a Medium and its Relation to Culture', CCCS Stencilled Paper 34, 1975.
—. 'Cultural Studies: Two Paradigms', in *Media, Culture and Society*, eds R. Collins et al. London, 1986.
— and Jefferson, T. (eds) *Resistance Through Rituals*. London, 1976.
— et al. (eds) *Policing the Crisis*. London, 1978.
Hawkes, T. *Structuralism and Semiotics*. London, 1977.
Hebdige, D. *Subculture*. London, 1979.
Hoggart, R. *The Uses of Literacy*. London, 1958.
Marx, K. *The Eighteenth Brumaire of Louis Bonaparte*. New York, 1977.
Mercer, K. *Welcome to the Jungle*. London, 1994.
Rose, J. *Sexuality in the Field of Vision*. London, 1986.
Thompson, E. P. *The Making of the English Working Class*. London, 1963.
Turner, G. *British Cultural Studies*. London, 1990.
Williams, R. *Culture and Society, 1780–1950*. London, 1958.
—. *The Long Revolution*. London, 1961.
—. *Television*. London, 1974.
Williamson, J. *Decoding Advertisements*. London, 1978.
Women's Studies Group, Centre for Contemporary Cultural Studies, University of Birmingham. *Women Take Issue*. London, 1978.

19. Cultural Materialism

Cultural materialism emerged in Britain in the 1980s as a critical approach to literature which understood and read literary texts as the material products of specific historical and political conditions. Its central concerns are in the ways in which literature relates to history, and what interpretations of a literary text might result from analyses which privileged historical contexts as the key to understanding the meanings and functions of literature. An important realization of cultural materialism is that texts produce different meanings and interpretations when read in different times and in different locations. Shakespeare's *The Tempest* might have been understood in very different ways in late sixteenth-century England than it has been read and performed in the Caribbean in the twentieth century, for example. The most prominent practitioners of cultural materialism – Alan Sinfield, Jonathan Dollimore, Catherine Belsey – share much in common with new historicists in the USA, particularly in treating literary texts as agents in making sense of a culture to itself. They also share with new historicists a common preoccupation with the Renaissance period, and with the roles which literature and theatre played in interpreting and explaining Renaissance society to itself. Cultural materialists participated with new historicist critics in the radical reinterpretation of Shakespeare and his contemporaries, shifting the focus of Shakespeare studies away from traditional emphases on the bard's universalism and humanism and towards a study of how Shakespeare's texts functioned in Elizabethan society to articulate specific cultural, gender or sexual identities, or indeed to highlight the ways in which power was deployed, distributed and manipulated in sixteenth-century England. But cultural materialists have also gone further than new historicists in emphasizing the political functions of literary texts in our own time, and in critiquing the ways in which literature is often appropriated in conservative political discourses to shore up notions of national heritage or cultural superiority. Accordingly, cultural materialists tend to read literary texts in ways which frustrate conservative interpretations, either by interpreting texts as the vehicles of radical critiques of conservative politics, or by exposing the means by which texts do serve the interests of conservatism.

The roots of cultural materialism lie in the work of prominent left-wing academics of the 1960s and 1970s who challenged 'traditional' approaches to literature by, firstly, contesting the ways in which certain kinds of texts were privileged as 'literary' and others dismissed as 'popular', and secondly, debating the validity of the idea of literature as embodying timeless, universal human values. The work, for example, of Stuart Hall, Raymond Williams and Richard Hoggart in extending literary analyses to the broader domain of 'culture' exposed the ways in which literary criticism had conventionally scorned the value of popular forms of entertainment and reading as tasteless, mass consumption and privileged the reading of a select canon of 'literary' texts as an index of sophistication.

Hall, Williams and Hoggart, each in their own ways, suspected that what lay behind such distinctions between the popular and the literary was a class distinction whereby the working classes were conveniently represented as slavishly following mass-market trends while the middle and upper classes were seen to be improving their minds and morals by reading 'high' literature. Culture was, however, shown to be more complex than this in the work of these left-wing critics, for whom examples abounded of the ways in which popular expressions could mean as much, and function in similar ways, as a literary text. 'We cannot separate literature and art from other kinds of social practice', wrote Raymond Williams, because those who enjoyed classical music and Shakespeare's plays were no more sophisticated, privileged or special than those who preferred The Beatles or Mills & Boon novels (Williams 1980, 43). Cultural studies was not so interested in making the icons and fashions of popular culture equivalent to high art and literature, however, as it was preoccupied with studying the ways in which cultures told stories about themselves through all forms of media and artistic representation. It was predominantly marxist in its critique of the ideological functions of 'culture', and suggested that culture was inseparable from politics. Walter Benjamin had argued in his definition of *historical* materialism that since history was written by the rulers and conquerors, accordingly the 'cultural treasures' of the world were the spoils of conquest and oppression, remarking: 'There is no document of civilization which is not at the same time a document of barbarism' (1992, 248), which in practice means that we must take care when we encounter stories of genius writers and great art to analyse the material circumstances which enable art and literature to be so highly acclaimed. Thus, in cultural materialist terms, the claim that Shakespeare is a universal writer is also a claim that English literature can make sense of and explain the world to itself, a claim which is then uncomfortably close to the boast of English imperialism. That Shakespeare's reputation as a universal genius gained considerable ground in the eighteenth and nineteenth centuries, when English imperialism reached its height, should alert us to the historical circumstances in which 'greatness' is celebrated and promoted.

Implicit in Benjamin's explanation of historical materialism is a radical reversal of the assumption of progressive humanism that the road to civilization leads away from the barbarism of the past. Benjamin proposes instead that civilization depends on barbarism, that in order for the middle classes to become civilized the working classes must be made barbaric, or in order for the English to be civilized, there must be a barbaric 'other' in the colonies against whom the English can define themselves. One can see in Benjamin's thinking the significance which he attributes to 'representation'. Conventional marxist analyses emphasized the economic means of control which the middle classes exerted over the working classes, but for Benjamin, as for Antonio Gramsci, the ideological or representational means of control were even more important. The 'bourgeois' class may dominate the workers by economic means, but their dominance is made plausible and is perpetuated at the level of representation. For Gramsci the task of marxist criticism is then to engage with capitalism on an ideological level, representing the interests of the working and peasant classes and exposing the contradictions and 'false consciousness' of the bourgeoisie. Indeed the possibility of all social and political change relies upon the outcome of this ideological struggle; as Gramsci explains in his *Prison Notebooks*, 'men acquire consciousness of structural conflicts on the level of ideologies' (Gramsci 1971, 365). According to the view which sees economics as the sole determining factor, ideology is a delusion which conceals the real, and therefore need only be dismissed as false while the real task of transferring the means of economic production to the proletariat is conducted. But this is to miss the point that bourgeois ideology succeeds in holding the captive attention and support of all classes. Gramsci referred to this condition as hegemony.

The influence of marxist ideas and approaches is one of the key factors in distinguishing between the practices of cultural materialism and those of new historicism, for new historicists were more influenced by Michel Foucault's historicist model of power relations than by marxist cultural studies. For Sinfield, Dollimore and other cultural materialists, however, the emphases which marxists such as Gramsci, Benjamin and Williams placed on the function of literature as an agent of bourgeois ideology and power suggested the need for an interpretative approach to literature which could accommodate marxist analyses of the politics of representation. Dollimore and Sinfield published what amounted in effect to a manifesto of cultural materialism as a foreword to an edited collection of essays entitled *Political Shakespeare* in 1985, a collection which represented and celebrated the arrival of radical new historicist perspectives in Renaissance studies. In their preface, the editors acknowledged a debt to Raymond Williams for the term 'cultural materialism' which he had used to describe his own work in *Marxism and Literature*:

> It is a position which can be briefly described as cultural materialism: a theory of the specificities of material cultural and literary production within historical materialism ... it is, in my view, a Marxist theory, and indeed ... part of what I at least see as the central thinking of Marxism. (1977, 5–6)

In acknowledging the debt to Williams, Dollimore and Sinfield were declaring that cultural materialism was in many senses the progeny of marxist literary and cultural studies. It shared with marxism the notion of history as perpetual struggle between social and cultural factions, and it shared too the idea that representations of all kinds played a part in the cultural politics of their time. Dollimore and Sinfield set out the key principles of cultural materialism in the foreword to *Political Shakespeare*:

> Our belief is that a combination of historical context, theoretical method, political commit-ment and textual analysis offers the strongest challenge and has already contributed substantial work. Historical context undermines the transcendent significance traditionally accorded to the literary text and allows us to recover its histories; theoretical method detaches the text from immanent criticism which seeks only to reproduce it in its own terms; socialist and feminist commitment confronts the conservative categories in which most criticism has hitherto been conducted; textual analysis locates the critique of traditional approaches where it cannot be ignored. We call this 'cultural materialism'. (1985, vii)

The four key principles in this statement are not particularly descriptive of the method or critical practice of cultural materialism, but they are general indications of the conditions in which cultural materialists see themselves operating. The principles proposed by Dollimore and Sinfield are designed to displace what they call 'traditional' approaches, the main features of which are implied in the definition of each of the principles. Cultural materialism, accordingly, is defined as a reaction against criticism which treats texts as possessing 'transcendent significance', which interprets a text 'in its own terms' and within 'conservative categories', and which grounds its understanding of a text solely within close textual analysis. In contrast to the liberal and conservative critical approaches suggested in this foreword, cultural materialists registered a new phase of political and ideological conflict, in which literary criticism could not remain neutral. While the liberal political beliefs and practices of postwar Britain, realized in the form of the welfare state, the NHS (National Health Service), scholarships, nationalized industries and local government, were steadily, often swiftly, eroded by the new right-wing ideologies of Thatcherism, literary critics like Dollimore, Sinfield, Belsey, Barker and Holderness scrutinized how literary texts played their part in sustaining and perpetuating conservative ideologies. Sinfield, for example, has shown how Shakespeare has been pressed into service to teach reactionary social norms, to justify imperialist ideology, even to sell military weapons, but in reply Sinfield has offered dissident readings of Shakespeare's texts which challenge traditional conservative and humanist readings. Cultural materialists have sought to change the terms in which writers such as Shakespeare are read and interpreted. Instead of the humanist focus on issues of character, morality and 'timeless' human values, cultural materialists have asked questions of texts which are concerned with power and resistance, race and gender, ideology and history.

Jonathan Dollimore's *Radical Tragedy* is exemplary of cultural materialist approaches. Dollimore analyses Jacobean tragedies for the ways in which they relate specifically to two major ideological constructs – establishment providentialism (which held sway in Renaissance times as the explanation of monarchical power as the product of divine will, therefore justifying the union of church and state, and discouraging possible rebellions or criticisms of either institution), and the autonomous, essential individual (which posits the idea of an unchanging human nature, symbolized in the individual soul). Dollimore's study is partly recovering the ideological contexts in which Jacobean texts were produced and read, but partly also a self-consciously twentieth-century return to those contexts to challenge humanists ways of reading them. So, for example, in the case of providentialism, Dollimore shows how texts such as Marlowe's *Dr Faustus* and Jonson's *Sejanus* not only foreground providentialist explanations of Renaissance politics and society but also provoke disquieting and challenging questions about the limits and contradictions of providentialism. At stake in his analyses is not just a concern to discover how such texts interacted with their own historical contexts, but Dollimore is also keen to show that literature acts in subversive as well as conservative ways, that literary texts can expose the limitations and faults of conservative political orthodoxies as it can reinforce them. Thus Dollimore's book demonstrates the value of analyses of historical context, as well as highlighting the political commitment of cultural materialism to discovering the ways in which texts go against the grain of conservative interpretations and values.

In *Political Shakespeare*, Dollimore and Sinfield brought together the work of new historicist critics like Leonard Tennenhouse and Stephen Greenblatt and the work of cultural materialists, largely, although not exclusively, represented by themselves. The title is polemical to begin with, advertising the commitment to politicizing literature which has become characteristic of cultural materialism. In the foreword the editors articulated their dislike of criticism which disguises its political agenda and which pretends to be politically neutral:

> Cultural materialism does not, like much established literary criticism, attempt to mystify its perspective as the natural, obvious or right interpretation of an allegedly given textual fact. On the contrary, it registers its commitment to the transformation of a social order which exploits people on grounds of race, gender and class. (Dollimore and Sinfield 1985, viii)

This is quite different to the work of new historicism, almost invariably focused on the past as belonging to a different epoch, ideologically and politically, to our own. Cultural materialists are committed to interpretations and investigations which have overt political ends in the contemporary world. Perhaps the best example of this commitment is Sinfield's synthesis of literary analysis, historical investigation and political engagement in *Literature, Politics and Culture in Postwar Britain*, in which he traces the emergence of consensus politics in postwar England, with its promises of full employment, comprehensive free education, and welfare and healthcare for all, and charts also the destruction of the welfare state under Mrs Thatcher's governments in the 1980s. Sinfield studies the ways in which the literature of the period foregrounds and contributes to these historical shifts, finding in the working-class writing of the 1960s, for example, that such writers as Alan Sillitoe, John Braine and John Osborne did not represent the genuine interests and aspirations of the working class, but instead reflected the process of embourgeoisement which the consensus politics of the 1950s and 1960s seemed to effect. The emergence of working-class writing does not indicate for Sinfield an improvement in the lot of the working class, merely that the working class have become the object of closer cultural scrutiny, in which service a handful of writers came to prominence. However authentic the class credentials of the writers, the fate of the working class cannot be changed, according to Sinfield, if the oppressed social position of the writers has no effect on the form in which they are working. Sinfield argues that writing itself was an inherently conservative act: 'There were writers of lower-class origin, it was acknowledged, but in the very act of becoming writers they were co-opted to middle-class forms' (Sinfield 1989, 40). The premise of Sinfield's argument is that the act of writing itself in the 1950s was a middle-class act, and that the readers and audiences for literature in the 1950s were largely middle class. The representation of working-class life apparently achieves no dramatically radical position when performed to a middle-class audience already hungry for representations of 'the other' anyway. Such an analysis of the conservative cultural politics of working-class writing is offered up in Sinfield's study as part of an explanation for the state of Britain in the 1980s, which for left-wing intellectuals was a dramatic shift away from the promises of the Labour government of 1945 to provide for the poor and disenfranchised of British society. Sinfield has been the most prominent cultural materialist to engage so actively in diagnosing contemporary political problems in the course of interpreting and explaining literary texts and their functions within society. Reading literature for cultural materialists is a political activity. It reflects and shapes the meanings which we as a society assign to texts and cultural practices, and it is therefore also a site of contest between competing political ideologies.

This sense of reading as political conflict can also be seen in Sinfield's *Faultlines*, in which he states that his intention is 'to check the tendency of *Julius Caesar* to add Shakespearean authority to reactionary discourses' (1992, 21). Literary texts acquire and are assigned cultural authority to different degrees and at different times in each society, and can be appropriated and co-opted to speak for one or more political ideologies. The meanings of these texts will always be contested, but what cultural materialists are interested in showing is that where meanings are contested there is almost always more at stake than insular aesthetic or artistic principles. Sinfield summarizes his argument in *Faultlines* as the following: 'dissident potential derives ultimately not from essential qualities in individuals (though they have qualities) but from conflict and contradiction that the social order inevitably produces within itself, even as it attempts to sustain itself' (1992, 41). In new historicist accounts of the operations of power, power seems to function as a flawless, perfectly efficient and effective machine. Sinfield disputes this, however, and offers a reading of power which reveals its faults, or more correctly, the conflicts and contradictions within power which may reveal dissident perspectives and which Sinfield calls 'faultlines'. It is through these 'faultlines', Sinfield claims, that we can read the alternative identities and values, and dissident ideas, of a given society.

In *Faultlines* Sinfield argued that the motivation for cultural materialist readings lay in the conservative and reactionary uses to which literary texts had been put. Cultural materialism as a practice necessarily reacts against the appropriation of literature in conservative political discourses:

> Conservative criticism has generally deployed three ways of making literature politically agreeable: selecting the canon to feature suitable texts, interpreting these texts strenuously so that awkward aspects are explained away, and insinuating political implications as alleged formal properties (such as irony and balance). (1992, 21)

In order to counter these conservative readings, and in order to make texts politically *dis*agreeable, cultural materialists can adopt the same strategies, or turn them against traditional or reactionary texts. If, as cultural materialist critics assert, Shakespeare is a powerful ideological tool in our society, there are ways of reading which can counter the authority which Shakespeare lends to reactionary discourses.

In an essay published in 1983 Sinfield explained that there were four principal ways of dealing with a reactionary text:

> [1. Rejection] of a respected text for its reactionary implications ... can shake normally unquestioned assumptions ... [2.] Interpretation ... so as to yield acceptable meanings ... is, of course, available to the socialist critic ... [3.] Deflect into Form(alism): One may sidestep altogether ... the version of human relations propounded by the text by shifting attention from its supposed truth to the mechanism of its construction ... [4.] Deflect into History: The literary text may be understood not as a privileged mode of insight, nor as a privileged formal construction. Initially, it is a project devised within a certain set of practices (the institutions and forms of writing as currently operative), and producing a version of reality which is promulgated as meaningful and persuasive at a certain historical conjuncture. And then, subsequently, it is re-used – reproduced – in terms of other practices and other historical conditions. (Sinfield 1983, 48)

The last method is a preferred method of cultural materialists in general, of putting the text in its contexts, whether the contexts of production or the contexts of reception, so as to expose the process by which it has been rendered in support of the dominant culture. Once this process has been exposed then the text can be interpreted by dissident critics 'against the grain'. Examining literary texts in their historical contexts is, for cultural materialists, a process of estranging those texts from the naturalized conservative readings to which they have been routinely treated. To show that Shakespeare's plays were inseparable from the ideological struggles of their time is, firstly, to dismiss the idea that his plays are timeless and universal, but it is also to alert us to the ways in which Shakespeare serves ideological functions in our own time too. In this case, historically situated and contextualized readings taught cultural materialists that the past could lend radically different meanings to canonical literary texts.

In the 1980s both new historicism and cultural materialism were interested in stressing the extent to which the past differs from contemporary uses of the past, the extent to which the past is alien or 'other' to our own modern episteme, and, borrowing from Michel Foucault and Clifford Geertz, they were at the same time aware of the structural similarities between this historical difference and the cultural differences being emphasized by postcolonial critics, feminists, gay theorists and race theorists. Increasingly in the late 1980s and throughout the 1990s, cultural materialist critics extended their analyses into the domains of 'queer' theory, postcolonialism and feminism. Jonathan Dollimore published *Sexual Dissidence* in 1991, while Alan Sinfield examined the representations and figures of effeminacy in twentieth-century culture in *The Wilde Century* in 1994. Both studies extended and deepened the ways in which cultural materialist critics read literature and culture through concepts of 'difference', focusing in particular on the cultural politics of sexual difference. Do gay and lesbian sexualities pose a radical challenge to the prevailing norms and values of our societies, or are they merely the same as 'straight' sexualities? This is a question which concerns both Sinfield and Dollimore in their respective studies, and it indicates the extent to which their recent work builds on their early work as cultural materialists. Both critics have extended the analyses of earlier concepts of dissidence, faultlines and deviance by focusing more particularly on the specific cases of sexual dissidence, and the dissident strategies of lesbian and gay subcultures.

Cultural materialism, like new historicism, has succeeded in literary studies in displacing earlier formalist concerns with textual unity and humanist concerns with character and authorship, and changing the ways in which we approach literary texts and their meanings. Although there are very few critics who identify themselves explicitly as 'cultural materialist', the influence of cultural materialism on literary studies in Britain has been pervasive, most notably in the current centrality of historicist approaches, the suspicion of texts with 'canonical' or cultural authority, and the importance of concepts of 'difference' in analyses of the cultural politics of texts. Arguably too, cultural materialism has been instrumental in encouraging self-reflexivity in our critical practices, and a wider concern for the way in which literary studies interacts with, and learns from, the study of culture, society, history, politics and other disciplines. Cultural materialism has enriched literary studies by probing the relationship between literature and social, cultural, political and sexual power, and giving literary criticism a sharper political focus on the present as well as the past.

John Brannigan

Further reading and works cited

Barker, F. *The Tremulous Private Body*. London, 1984.
Belsey, C. *The Subject of Tragedy*. London, 1985.
Benjamin, W. *Illuminations*, ed. H. Arendt. London, 1992.
Brannigan, J. *New Historicism and Cultural Materialism*. Basingstoke, 1998.
Dollimore. J. *Radical Tragedy*. Hemel Hempstead, 1984.
—. *Sexual Dissidence*. Oxford, 1991.
— and Sinfield, A. (eds) *Political Shakespeare*. Manchester, 1985.
Drakakis, J. (ed.) *Alternative Shakespeares*. London, 1985.
Gramsci, A. *Selections from the Prison Notebooks*. London, 1971.
Hawkes, T. (ed.) *Alternative Shakespeares Vol. 2*. London, 1996.
Hawthorn, J. *Cunning Passages*. London, 1996.
Holderness, G. (ed.) *The Shakespeare Myth*. Manchester, 1988.
Milner, A. *Cultural Materialism*. Carlton, Victoria, 1993.
Prendergast, C. *Cultural Materialism*. Minneapolis, MN, 1995.
Ryan, K. (ed.) *New Historicism and Cultural Materialism*. London, 1996.

Sinfield, A. *Literature in Protestant England 1560–1660*. London, 1982.

—. 'Four Ways with a Reactionary Text', *Journal of Literature Teaching Politics*, 2, 1983a.

— (ed.) *Society and Literature 1945–1970*. London, 1983b.

—. *Alfred Tennyson*. Oxford, 1986.

—. *Literature, Politics and Culture in Postwar Britain*. Oxford, 1989.

—. *Faultlines*. Oxford, 1992.

—. *The Wilde Century: Effeminacy, Oscar Wilde and the Queer Moment*. London, 1994a.

—. *Cultural Politic – Queer Reading*. London, 1994b.

Williams, R. *Marxism and Literature*. Oxford, 1977.

—. *Problems in Materialism and Culture*. London, 1980.

Wilson, S. *Cultural Materialism*. Oxford, 1995.

20. Postcolonial Studies

In his critique of postcolonial theory in the 1980s, Arif Dirlik answers Ella Shohat's question 'When exactly . . . does the "post-colonial" begin?' with the barbed comment that the discipline is in part to do with the arrival of 'Third World intellectuals' into the 'First World academe'. Although this should not lead to a knee-jerk dismissal of the subject on grounds of complicity and elitism, postcolonial critical discourses, perhaps more than most academic discourses, crosses national boundaries; they are products of transnational intellectual activity within the institutional framework of the academy, although not entirely in the way Dirlik imagines. Historically, this is particularly true of a context where the emergence and development of discipline is bound up with Empire, and the anti-colonial and nationalist movements that have ensued its demise; for postcolonial studies is, above all, concerned with the historical, political, cultural, social, aesthetic and philo-sophical structures of colonial and neocolonial power. Postcolonial studies in Britain is shaped firstly by the movement of peoples and theory that is the result of the educational, literary and cultural links that are formed firstly between Britain and the newly indepen-dent colonies, and then latterly as part of a network of transnational academic links. Individuals from different parts of the globe such as Wole Soyinka, Ngũgi Wa Thiong'o, Edward Brathwaite, George Lamming, Homi Bhabha, Gayatri Spivak, Stuart Hall, Benita Parry and David Dabydeen have been – or are – based in the UK, moving between metropolitan 'centre' and colonial 'periphery'. But in tackling diverse topics like the legacy of empire, colonial historiography and literature, global capitalism and neocolonialism, nationalism, cultural identity, diaspora, aesthetics, language and the place of literature in society, their contributions have shaped the very contours of modern literary studies in Britain.

The history of 'British' postcolonial studies can perhaps be divided into distinct but overlapping periods and movements. Postcolonial studies is often spoken of as having been inaugurated with Edward Said's *Orientalism* (1978) and the methodological innovations that came in the wake of a discourse theory model of representation and power. Yet critics like Bart Moore-Gilbert, Stephen Slemon, Alan Lawson and Helen Tiffin have also made a case for an alternative genealogy in relation to the UK – one which is indebted to stronger creative and literary affiliations. Hence, Moore-Gilbert speaks of 'postcolonial literary criticism' while Tiffin, Lawson, Leigh Dale and Shane Rowlands, write of early 'Commonwealth post-colonial critics' who wrote initially within a discipline that was deeply moulded by the assumptions, values and precepts of English studies. Yet these early works on colonial writing and the literatures of the British Commonwealth also register critical resistance to, and a 'guerrilla war' against, the Anglo-centric domain of English literature. Among the early works here, one can list Susan Howe's *Novels of Empire* (1949), which looks not only at the colonial literature of Empire but also settler fiction of Australia and New Zealand, and John Matthews' *Tradition in Exile* (1962), which offers a comparative approach to Australian and Canadian poetry. Matthews' preoccupations with a common imperial legacy, the impact of location and environment on creating new different national literatures will be taken up by a succeeding generation of literary critics that work under the umbrella term of 'Commonwealth literature'. A. L. McLeod's *The Commonwealth Pen* (1961), John Press's edited conference proceedings taken from the 1964 inaugural conference on Commonwealth literature at Leeds in Britain, *Commonwealth Literature: Unity and Diversity in a Common Culture* (1965), and introductory companions such as William Walsh's *Commonwealth Literature* (1973) and Bruce King's *Literatures of the World in English* (1974) fall into this category. Here the creation of the disciplinary term 'Commonwealth literature' is somewhat ambivalently located within the paradigm of English that would reinscribe a network of exchanges which would still underscore the importance of the English literature model. But ambivalence should be stressed even in this early period, for the centrality of British literature and educational establishments in the developing empire of literary studies is assumed by some and actively contested by others. 'Commonwealth literature' as a disciplinary field is recognized as problematic even in the disciplinary standard bearer for the 1960s, the *Journal of Commonwealth Literature*. Interestingly, Press's proceedings also echo some of the basic concerns of contemporary postcolonial studies like identity, nationality, language, space/place, the relationship between literature, politics and history, interdisciplinary approaches to literary/textual study, the difficulties of reading texts from other cultures and so on. The volume includes Chinua Achebe's much cited lecture 'The Novelist as Teacher' on education and the need for the regeneration of African literature; Achebe was at this point already serving as Editorial Advisor to the newly formed African Writers Series produced by Heinemann Educational Books, whose subsidiary companies in Africa and the Caribbean did much to nurture indigenous publications. The African Writers Series, and later the Caribbean Writers Series, did much during the succeeding decades to make diverse African and Caribbean writers such as Ngũgĩ Wa Thiong'o, Cyprian Ekwensi, Bessie Head, Michael Anthony, Beryl Gilroy among others widely available nationally and internationally. The educational connections between the University of London and its external colleges, especially in Africa and the Caribbean, the programmes of exchanges funded by the British Council and the contacts made by its overseas branches, and the curriculum innovations at Universities of Leeds and Kent in the 1960 and 1970s have also facilitated the movement of writers and intellectuals between Britain and the (then) developing world. Reminders of such mundane traffic between 'centre(s)' and 'peripher(ies)' are necessary for they offer a materialist dimension to literary study and highlight the institutional dimensions of postcolonial intellectual activity.

The freedom of movement between the Commonwealth and Britain and labour shortages in Britain coupled with economic depression in the West Indies were factors that led to the recruitment of West Indian labour in the postwar period. The arrival of the *Empire Windrush* in 1948 heralded a generation of West Indian migration into Britain; a number of Caribbean novelists, poets and critics who came to live and work in Britain, notably George Lamming, Andrew Salkey, Wilson Harris, Sam Selvon and – as students – V. S. Naipaul, Edward Kamau Brathwaite and Stuart Hall, made a significant impact on the cultural and literary scene. George Lamming's *The Pleasures of Exile* (1960) explores diverse issues, notably what it means to be a writer from the Caribbean, racism, the state of literacy and publishing, the links between Africa and the Caribbean. *Exile* is an early productive example of using the Prospero–Caliban coupling from Shakespeare's *The Tempest* as a political metaphor for colonial relations, power and representation, although the trope is present as early as Octave Mannoni's *Prospero and Caliban: The Psychology of Colonialism* (1950). Brathwaite's importance as a founding member of the Caribbean Artist Movement cannot be overstated. CAM, formed in 1966, provided a London-based forum (especially in its early years) for debates on the nature of a Caribbean aesthetic, the role of the intellectual, the problems of writing and publishing in the Caribbean and the oral and literary traditions in Caribbean writing. CAM's members comprise not only writers, artists and critics who were concerned with the independent islands of the Caribbean but also student activists concerned with a more assertive grass-roots politics and a Black British identity in a country that had already seen the 1958–9 race riots, the 1962 Commonwealth Immigration Act and Enoch Powell's infamous 1968 incitement to racial hatred, the 'rivers of blood' speech. These CAM student activists were influenced by the Civil Rights campaigns in the US and the Black Power movements that followed in its wake. Brathwaite's distinctive contributions have been to explore the specific African (and Amerindian) ancestry of Caribbean identity, and the use of folk and performative elements in Caribbean poetry which has its roots in black musical rhythms. His concern with creolization (*The Development of Creole Society*, 1971) explores not only the poetics but also the politics of Caribbean hybrid artistic forms. He calls creole English 'nation language'; it is the 'language of the slaves and labourers' with African and Amerindian rhythms, syllables and idioms that by-pass the English pentameter in verse forms (*History of the Voice: the Development of Nation Language in Anglophone Caribbean Poetry*, 1984). Brathwaite's theorization of folk is continued by David Dabydeen's more recent interventions on the use of dialect in poetry, 'On Not Being Milton', which raises important questions about language and audience. Wilson Harris's famous *Tradition and the West Indian Novel* (1964) was given as a lecture to the West Indian Student Union in London; he argues against the widespread generic use of realism in terms of plot, characters and theme prevalent in a number of Caribbean novels, a form that stems from the legacy of nineteenth-century European novels. Harris offers instead a transformative and changing mytho-poetic 'vision of consciousness' (*History, Fable and Myth in the Caribbean and Guianas*, 1970); he argues for a radical openness to a creolization of an intuitive and buried archive of folk beliefs, rituals, superstition, myths and practices. These provide a unique and rich resource for the native writer that moves the novel along very different avenues. As both Andrew Bundy and Bart Moore-Gilbert note, there are strong similarities between Harris's work and that of more contemporary poststructuralist and postcolonial theorists of hybridity and difference such as Homi Bhabha. Derek Walcott's later Nobel prize acceptance speech also picks up the theme of the Antillean experience as a unique 'shipwreck of fragments' of histories, languages and 'remembered customs'. Orlando Patterson was a founding member of CAM and his history of slavery, *The Sociology of Slavery* (1967), complements the literary, sociological and philosophical texts that were produced from these productive exchanges. Although C. L. R. James was not part of the active CAM network, he represents a towering figure for these generation of writers and for Caribbean writing in general; his seminal history of the slave revolt that led to the founding of Haiti, *The Black Jacobins* (1938), is still an influential text.

Chinua Achebe's collected essays, *Morning Yet on Creation Day* (1975), posed fundamental questions about eurocentric criticism, colonialist discourse, universalism, the function of art, the responsibilities of the artist and the use of English language, and addresses literature and the curriculum in newly independent nations. These debates were continued by Wole Soyinka's *Myth, Literature and the African World* (1976), the *bolekaja* critics, Chinweizu and Madubuike's, *Towards the Decolonization of African Literature* (1983) and also Ngũgĩ Wa Thiong'o's *Homecoming* (1972), and *Decolonising the Mind: the Politics of Language in Africa* (1986). In particular, the desire to reclaim African art and writing for Africa triggered debates about what was authentically African, and how literary criticism was to come to terms with the difference of African oral performative traditions. Chinweizu, Jemie and Madubuike argued against comparing African writers against a European literate tradition and complaining about their differences; such 'pseudo' universalism is nothing but European ethnocentrism in disguise. Yet the *bolekaja* critics' talk of a separate and autonomous development of the African novel based on indigenous oral antecedents, 'African reality', traditions and 'authentic African imagery' is problematic given the historical experience and legacy of colonialism. Soyinka contests the claims of Negritude and rejects any prescriptive approach to literature, especially those that do not take into account the complexities of modern Africa; *Myth, Literature and the African World* attempts to forge a distinctive Africanist literary discourse that takes seriously the aesthetic, philosophical, religious and cultural basis of African art. Concern about the reach and penetration of global capitalism, neocolonialism and elitism led Ngugi to argue passionately, *pace* Fanon, that the task of decolonization has yet to be accomplished despite the political transition to independence. In *Decolonising the Mind*, he tackles the issue of continued European hegemony in Africa especially in relation to expressive forms of art and culture, and addresses – pointedly – the issue of African writing in European languages (an issue first broached by Achebe). His interventions reminds us that the politics of national and international publishing remains unresolved, and issues concerning audiences, literacy, uneven development and access are still very much alive today.

In the late 1970s and 1980s, postcolonial theory was dominated on both sides of the Atlantic by three major figures – Edward Said and Gayatri Spivak, based in the US but also giving important lectures in Britain, and Homi Bhabha, based initially at the University of Sussex in the UK. The publication of Edward Said's *Orientalism* (1978) represented a real watershed for postcolonial studies. *Orientalism* sought to fuse two distinctive sets of interests – a poststructuralist interest in textuality and rhetoric, and a humanist, ethical and marxist interest in the workings of power and domination. In discourse theory, Said found a way to recognize and address the network of power that is articulated through a particular way of seeing the world, the geopolitical division of the West and the East, the Occident and the Orient. The expression, sedimentation, reinforcement and overdetermination of this division across history, culture and politics is the focus of a somewhat sweeping, Foucauldian and Gramscian influenced reading of colonial power and representation. Said's later *Culture and Imperialism* (1993) attempts to think 'contrapuntally' and opens out into an ambitious study of an 'intertwined' global history of imperialism for both colonizer and colonized, metropolis and periphery, that is missing from *Orientalism*'s focus on colonial discourse. If his utopian investment in the idea of the (cosmopolitan) secular intellectual goes against the grain of an at times modern cynicism about the function and significance of the academy, it cannot be easily dismissed. His commitment to theory is matched by equal attention to the worldly question of politics in volumes such as *After the Last Sky*, *The Question of Palestine*.

Gayatri Spivak's work has been immensely influential in the field of colonial historiography, feminist studies, cultural studies and postcolonial studies. Her writing has always sought to bring together the insights of poststructuralism, deconstruction, marxism, psychoanalysis, feminism and colonial discourse theory, pointing out not only their usefulness but also their limitations. In 'The Rani of Simur', originally given as a lecture to the 1984 Essex Sociology of Literature conference, 'Europe and its Others', Spivak extends Said's investigations into colonial discourse and its contributions to the shaping of the modern world. She argues that Europe consolidated its sovereignty and subjectivity through the epistemic violence of othering. This 'worlding' forces the 'native' to see himself as 'other'; colonial discourse obliges 'the native to cathect the space of the Other on his home ground' (Barker et al. 1985, 133). Spivak's concern with the epistemic violence has also led her to (re)consider the role of elites, intellectuals, institutional power and privilege that have always haunted the project of speaking for/to oppressed groups ('Subaltern Studies: Deconstructing Historiography', 1985; 'Can the Subaltern Speak?', 1988; *Outside in the Teaching Machine*, 1993). Critical of western feminism's humanist credentials, she poses the question of what it means to address woman (femininity, sexual difference) as a unifying universal analytic category, given that different cultures, histories, mythologies, political and legal contexts have produced very different notions of the 'sexed subject' ('French Feminism in an International Frame', 1981; 'Three Women's Texts and a Critique of Imperialism', 1985; *In Other Worlds*, 1988; 'The Political Economy of Women as seen by a Literary Critic', 1989).

Homi Bhabha's work is informed by psychoanalysis, enunciation theory, poststructuralism, deconstruction and also postmodernism. 'The Other Question' (1983) emerged initially to redress Said's emphasis on knowledge and information production, by suggesting that Orientalism is also a site of fantasy, desires and anxieties. The essay explores racism and racial stereotyping though a psychoanalytic lens; here the dynamics of sexual fetishism in Freud are used to understand racism as a kind of fetishistic disavowal of (racial rather than sexual) difference. Because fetishistic disavowal is based both on a recognition and a negation that must be repeatedly re-enacted, Bhabha can claim that colonial discourse is split, ambivalent and vacillates between control and paranoia. In 'Of Mimicry and Man' (1984), and the influential and widely reproduced 'Signs Taken for Wonders' (1985), he extends the idea of ambivalence by suggesting that colonial authority should not be reified as totalizing in its effectivity and reach. Instead, colonial discourse can be read as more fractured and contradictory, seen especially in its troping on mimicry (attempts to reproduce a reformed Other mirrors or mimics the colonial self). Here colonial discourse can produce an Other that mocks or menaces precisely through its resemblance – 'almost the same but not quite', 'almost the same but not white'. It is this ambivalence, hybridity, indeterminacy and self-contradiction that unsettles or disturbs the presence of colonial authority. Bhabha's later essay 'Dissemination' develops the implicit conceptual critique of origins in the direction of national identities and narratives of the nation. Others like 'The Postcolonial and the Post-modern' propose a problematic, unstable, intersubjective poststructuralist theory of agency away from consciousness, individuation, intentionality, simple causality and control.

The Essex Sociology of Literature conference proceedings, *Europe and its Others* (1985), can be situated in the conceptual paradigm opened up by the expanded notion of rhetoric, textuality and 'worlding' initiated by Said, Spivak and Bhabha. Diverse essays on orientalist painting, Islam and the idea of Europe, travel writing, multiculturalism in Australia, Indian historiography and European and American literature from a variety of disciplines address the textual weave of European (and American) subject formation through its many socio-political, historical cultural and psychosexual strands. The influence of European theory (epitomized by the intellectual exchanges at the Essex conference) made for a flowering of literary theoretical activity particularly in the area of colonial history and literature, for example Peter Hulme's *Colonial Encounters* (1986) which addresses the discovery and settlement of the New World through different generic texts (from poetry to memoirs, log books and official documents). Hulme's exploration of historical and mythical encounters such as that between Columbus and the indigenous peoples of the Caribbean, John Smith and Pocahontas, and fictive encounters such as those between Prospero and Caliban, Crusoe and Friday, Inkle and Yarico, unearth the language of savagery and cannibalism that was used to manage the dispossession of the Amerindians and to justify the exploitation of the Americas. The *Oxford Literary Review's* special issue on colonialism in 1988 included work by Gauri Viswanathan on the political uses of English in India (later published in her *Masks of Conquest*) and Benita Parry's important critique of Spivak and Bhabha. Parry's turn to the revolutionary Fanon, as opposed to Bhabha's turn to the psychoanalytic Fanon, is part of the debate over the legacy of the revolutionary theorist, activist and psychoanalyst, Frantz Fanon. Such debates reflect the intense contestation over the Fanon who wrote *Black Skins/White Masks* and the Fanon who wrote *The Wretched of the Earth*.

Robert Young's *White Mythologies* (1990) explores postwar theories of history in relation to imperialism but is perhaps more noted for its lucid exposition of the difficult and complex work of Spivak and Bhabha. Young's commentary signals a moment in which postcolonial theory reaches a critical mass and marks its institutionalization in the teaching machine. A number of anthologies follow in quick succession, notably *Colonial Discourse and Post-colonial Theory* (1993), *The Post-Colonial Studies Reader* (1995) and *Contemporary Postcolonial Theory: A Reader* (1996). Bill Ashcroft, Gareth Griffiths and Helen Tiffin's *The Empire Writes Back* (1989) offers a survey of postcolonial literatures (and theories) in English and, with such a synoptic introduction, a user-friendly, teachable text for the higher educational curriculum. The increasing attention to what seems a veritable industry in postcolonial intellectual commodities sounds a necessary note of caution. Parry's recuperation of nationalism, 'Resistance Theory/Theorising Resistance or Two Cheers for Nativism', Neil Lazarus' 'National Consciousness and the Specificity of (Post)colonial intellectuals' and Anne McClintock's much cited critique of 'postcolonialism' collected in *Colonial Discourse/Postcolonial Theory* (1994) are early essays that mark a disenchantment with the drift of postcolonial theory. Vijay Mishra and Bob Hodges's 'What is Post-colonialism?' on the significance of the hyphen in post-colonial (1991), Ella Shohat's 'Notes on the Post-colonial' (1992), the *Oxford Literary Review's* 1991 issue on neocolonialism, Spivak's continuing interventions on the role of intellectuals, Aijaz Ahmad's *In Theory* (1992) and Arif Dirlik's *The Postcolonial Aura* (1997) are critical interventions against the complacency which sometimes characterizes the celebratory assumption of ethical and political effectivity that accompanies such academic discourses. More recently, Bart Moore-Gilbert's excellent stock-taking survey and critical assessment of postcolonial theory, *Postcolonial Theory* (1997), and Ato Quayson's *Postcolonialism* (2000), mark a point whereby postcolonial studies have (ironically) come of age. If the debates surrounding effectivity show no sign of going away, and the issues surrounding the global capitalism and neocolonialism are still as prevalent today as they were decades ago, the battles over their place in the curriculum have mostly receded. But this only begs the question not only of what is postcolonialism, but who and what postcolonial studies are for.

With the interventions of Ashcroft, Tiffin and Griffiths (academics based in Australia) and Moore-Gilbert, Said, Bhabha and Spivak's later work, there is a diminishing sense of the divide between theory and (untheorized) literary criticism. The division is perhaps artificially created with the predominance of European theory and the almost exclusive focus on colonial literature and documents (hence the term colonial discourse) in the early years following *Orientalism*. As Alan Lawson, Leigh Dale, Helen Tiffin and Shane Rowlands point out, the suspicion with which the study of Commonwealth literatures was held related to its potential for 'imperial sentimentality' and its English literary focus. Furthermore, creative writers were 'ignored' for their 'collusion' with a 'Euro-modernist project' and their determined production of 'realist', anti-colonial and nationalist narratives. But over the last two decades there has been a willingness to read literature informed by the developments of theory and to consider creative writers and their work as interventions in theoretical debates. Just as Helen Tiffin and Stephen Slemon's *After Europe* (1989), Ian Adam and Helen Tiffin's *Past the Last Post* (1991) and Bruce King's *New National and Post-Colonial Literatures* (1996) show the distance travelled from the early days of *Commonwealth Literature* (1973) and *Literatures of the World in English* (1974), 'theorized' studies like *Culture and Imperialism* (1993) consider creative writers and thinkers from the developing world. In the meantime, the dividing line between creative and conceptual/theoretical work and theory fades with writers like Wilson Harris, Amitav Gosh, Salman Rushdie and David Dabydeen.

Crossover with the field of cultural studies and cultural theory, particularly with regard to diasporic culture and Black British identity in the work of Stuart Hall and Paul Gilroy, has also been enormously productive. Hall's much anthologized essays, 'Cultural Identity and Diaspora' (1990) and 'New Ethnicities' (1989), have paved the way for a more complex understanding of cultural identity as a shifting and ongoing process of identification rather than a finished product that is inherited, and a theorized black British cultural politics that 'engages rather than suppresses difference'. Hall's earlier collection of essays *Policing the Crisis* (1978) examined the media's management of race relations in the wake of racial disturbances and *The Empire Strikes Back* (1982), produced by the Centre for Contemporary Cultural Studies, is equally critical of 'race relations' sociology in Britain. Paul Gilroy's influential *There Ain't No Black in the Union Jack* (1987) looks at the cultural politics of race and nation beyond ethnic absolutism and explores urban black expressive culture and community. His recent study of the African diasporic connections between Europe and America, *The Black Atlantic* (1993), argues for an ethnohistorical approach to modernity. His charting of the transnational and intercultural flow of ideas that are present in black vernacular culture and nationalist thought develops the trope of the ship as one of the key figures of the history of black migration. Such a trope is also part of Gilroy's general attempts to forge a new language of cultural identity that is non-organic, hybrid and non-essentialist. Hall and Gilroy's work on black British cultural politics must also be read in conjunction with feminist work on the area, particularly Pratibha Parmar's cinematic and conceptual work on gender and cultural identity and Avtar Brah's reassessment of Asian diasporic identities in the light of contemporary theories of diaspora, locations and borders, *Cartographies of Desire* (1996). One should also not forget the three important early collections of essays, stories, interviews and creative work by black and third world women, *Watchers and Seekers* (1987), *Charting the Journey* (1988) and *Let it be Told: Black Women Writers in Britain* (1988), that made such communities visible. The enduring challenge and rewards for postcolonial intellectuals is to 'think concretely and sympathetically, contrapuntually, about others' (Said 1993, 408).

Gail Ching-Liang Low

Further reading and works cited

Achebe, C. *Morning Yet on Creation Day*. London, 1975.
Ashcroft, B. et al. (eds) *The Empire Writes Back*. London, 1995a.
— et al. (eds) *The Post-colonial Studies Reader*. London, 1995b.
Barker, F. et al. (eds) *Europe and its Others*, 2 vols. Colchester, 1985.
— et al. (eds) *Colonial Discourse/Postcolonial Theory*. Manchester, 1994.
Bhabha, H. *The Location of Culture*. London, 1994.
Brathwaite, E. *History of the Voice*. London, 1984.
Bundy, A. (ed.) *Selected Essays of Wilson Harris*. London, 1999.
Chinweizu, O. J. and Madubuike, I. *Towards the Decolonisation of African Literature*. Washington, DC, 1983.
Dirlik, A. *The Postcolonial Aura*. Boulder, CO, 1997.
Fanon, F. *The Wretched of the Earth*. Harmondsworth, 1983.
—. *Black Skins, White Masks*. London, 1986.
Gilroy, P. *There Ain't No Black in the Union Jack*. London, 1987.
—. *The Black Atlantic*. London, 1993.
Hulme, P. *Colonial Encounters*. London, 1992.
King, B. *New National and Post-Colonial Literatures*. Oxford, 1996.
Lamming, G. *The Pleasures of Exile*. London, 1960.
Lawson, A. et al. (eds) *Post-Colonial Literatures in English*. New York, 1997.
Moore-Gilbert, B. *Postcolonial Theory*. London, 1997.
Quayson, A. *Postcolonialism*. Oxford, 2000.
Rutherford, J. *Identities*. London, 1990.
Said, E. *Orientalism*. London, 1978.
—. *Culture and Imperialism*. New York, 1993.
Slemon, S. 'The Scramble for Post-colonialism', in *De-Scribing Empire*. eds C. Tiffin and A. Lawson. London, 1994.
Soyinka, W. *Myth, Literature and the African World*. Cambridge, 1976.
Spivak, G. Chakravorty. 'Three Women's Text and a Critique of Imperialism', *Critical Inquiry*, 12, 1, 1985a.
—. 'Can the Subaltern Speak?', *Wedge*, 7/8, 1985b.
—. *Outside in the Teaching Machine*. London, 1993.
Wa Thiong'o, N. *Decolonising the Mind*. London, 1986.

21. Gay/Queer and Lesbian Studies, Criticism and Theory

One could chart the beginning of British queer literary criticism in the 1890s with Edward Carpenter's celebration of the writings of Walt Whitman, offering a model of masculine love and classless affiliation as a counter to the Oscar Wilde model of the indolent, upper-class, dandified, effeminate homosexual. The diaries and writings of twentieth-century writers like Siegfried Sassoon, J. P. Ackerley, E. M. Forster, even T. E. Lawrence, show that there was some notion of a gay literary canon, shared by an intellectual subculture, even if there was no openly gay critical writing (much like the contrast between the private and public writings of American critic F. O. Matthiessen). However, what can be called a body of gay and lesbian literary criticism and theory began in Britain in the 1970s.

Two crucial but radically different works were published in 1977, Jeffrey Meyers's *Homosexuality in Literature*, and Jeffrey Weeks's *Coming Out*. Though limiting himself to non-dramatic prose, Meyers's work demonstrates one of the important tactics of early gay criticism, canon formation. His first footnote lists 'the most important homosexual writers of the last hundred years', and the volume itself focuses on the prose works Meyers thinks are most indicative of the homosexual aesthetic he describes and celebrates. Unfortunately what Meyers admires are the tactics of subterfuge of an earlier, more repressive era separate from any critique of the social policing of homosexuality and homosexual discourse.

> Homosexual novels are characteristically subtle, allusive and symbolic – the very qualities we now admire in Yeats and Eliot, and the novels of Flaubert and Henry James – and form an eighth kind of literary ambiguity. For the ambiguous expression of the repressed, the hidden and the sometimes secret theme suggests a moral ambiguity as well. If a specifically homosexual tone, sensibility, vision or mode of apprehension exists, then it would be characterized by these cautious and covert qualities, and by the use of art to conceal rather than to reveal the theme of the novel ... (1977, 1–2)

The converse of Meyers's fascination with the subterfuges of the closet is his distaste for the new generation of openly gay writers. For him, 'the emancipation of the homosexual has led to the decline of his art' (Meyers 1977, 3). Though Meyers claims that he has 'no desire to praise or condemn homosexuality', he ends his long introductory essay with James Baldwin's negative vision of the gay subculture of his time. Meyers's study was the sort of work gay readers once accepted as affirming in merely taking up the subject, but actually negative in its view of homosexuality.

Jeffrey Weeks's work is another matter altogether. Though neither literary criticism or theory, his first volume, which offers a careful history of the emergence of gay self-consciousness and politics, would be important to later critics. *Coming Out: Homosexual Politics in Britain from the Nineteenth Century to the Present* begins from the premise established by Michel Foucault, that the word 'homosexual' 'is itself a product of history, a cultural artefact designed to express a particular concept' (Weeks 1977, 3). For Weeks, the concurrent rise in hostility toward homosexuality with emerging new definitions of homosexuality found in the late nineteenth century 'can only be understood as part of the restructuring of the family and sexual relations consequent upon the triumph of urbaniza-tion and industrial capitalism' (Weeks 1977, 2). Like much of the major work in British queer studies that followed, Weeks's first major volume is a work of cultural materialism, which Alan Sinfield, building on the pioneering work of Raymond Williams, concisely describes as

> analytic work which sees texts as inseparable from the conditions of their production and reception in history; as involved, necessarily, in the making of meanings which are always, finally, political. (Sinfield 1994b, vii)

Within this framework, our sense of homosexuality becomes historically shaped and ever changing. As Weeks puts it:

> There is no *essence* of homosexuality whose historical unfolding can be illuminated. There are only changing patterns in the organization of desire, whose specific configuration can be decoded. This, of course, propels us into a whirlwind of deconstruction. (Weeks 1985, 6)

This is the primary assumption of Week's work and much of what follows in British queer studies – the careful historicizing of a dynamic subject, considered static and unnatural – which historians, psychoanalysts, sexologists, queer historians and critics resist. If homo-sexuality is itself a contingent cultural construction, what of supposedly 'natural' hetero-sexuality, or of any essentialist gender definitions? On that question rests the wider claims of queer studies to be central to current critical discourse beyond its own anti-homophobic agenda.

Weeks's three major volumes were written between the enactment of legislation legalizing same-sex acts, and Margaret Thatcher's attempt to silence anti-homophobic education and art through Clause 28. His first volume, a history of British lesbians and gay men's acceptance, evasion and resistance of definitions imposed by their society from the supposedly scientifically neutral 'homosexual' to the more self-affirmative 'gay', *Sex, Politics and Society* (1981) elaborates on the relationship of regulation of sex in general and homosexual acts in particular with the growth of industrial capitalism. *Sexuality and Its Discontents* (1985) is a close investigation of the literature on sex, sexology and homo-sexuality from the nineteenth century to the present. While Weeks's work is historical, it is also focused on the power of language to regulate and resist. For some, Weeks's work may seem more in the realm of social sciences than literary studies, but in Britain, the two were linked as what was called gay studies was, as Alan Sinfield puts it, 'unthinkable outside a general left-wing orientation' (Sinfield 1995b, 73).

Weeks distilled his ideas in an essay which appears in the volume *The Making of the Modern Homosexual*, edited by Kenneth Plummer (1981), which is a kind of prolegomena for further research in the social sciences. This collection of essays by sociologists and anthropologists includes Mary McIntosh's classic 1968 essay, 'The Homosexual Role'. McIntosh's assertion, now taken for granted, is that 'it is not until he sees homosexuals as a social category, rather than a medical or psychiatric one, that the sociologist can begin to ask the right questions about the specific content of the homosexual role and about the organization and functions of homosexual groups' (McIntosh, in Plummer 1981, 43), and a social role is dynamic, not static. In an afterword included in the volume, McIntosh in essence critiques and updates her essay, asserting as Weeks had done that 'you can't understand homosexuality without locating it in sexuality in general' (McIntosh, in Plummer 1981, 46). In the same volume, Annabel Faraday, in 'Liberating Lesbian Research', attacks the notion that one can study lesbianism and male homosexuality as if they were the same phenomena: 'heterosexuality itself is a power relation of men over women; what gay men and lesbians are rejecting are essentially polar experiences' (Faraday, in Plummer 1981, 113). Faraday's essay, the only one to address lesbian issues in Plummer's volume, introduces a problem in early British queer studies, the relative absence of the lesbian voice.

Few books have had as much impact on gay literary studies as Alan Bray's *Homosexuality in Renaissance England* (1982). At the time a high-ranking civil servant and an independent scholar (a category more respected in England than in the US), Bray took the work of Foucault and Weeks and applied it to the English Renaissance. More importantly, he raised questions regarding the proper historical methodology for gay scholars. What interested Bray was the fact that 'there was an immense disparity in this society between what people said – and apparently believed – about homosexuality and what in truth they did' (Bray 1982, 9). Bray deals with this disparity in three related essays. The first deals with the way sodomy and buggery (the word homosexuality, of course, did not exist, nor the assumptions about identity it defines) were symbolized in literature as symptoms of 'the disorder in sexual relations that could, in theory at least, break out anywhere' (Bray 1982, 25). If the worldview suggested a tenuous cosmic order that could be shaken by any individual disorderly act, sodomy could have catastrophic consequences. Yet it is clear from court records that homosexual activity took place and was not always punished when it was discovered. More importantly, given the close knit social structure, such activity usually transpired between people who knew each other, often members of the same household. As in earlier societies, those relations were determined 'by the prevailing distribution of power, economic power and social power, not the fact of homosexuality itself' (Bray 1982, 56). Bray's main question is how, given the universal excoriation of homosexual acts, there could be what he calls a 'cleavage between an individual's behaviour and his awareness of its social significance' (Bray 1982, 68). The answer, in short, is that there was little or no social pressure for one to define one's sexuality, to connect one's actions with the state described in the anti-sodomy literature. So there was a reluctance on the part of the actors and of society at large to see specific actions as examples of the 'fearful sin of sodomy' (Bray 1982, 76). Bray characteristically frames his most succinct response as a question: 'Was society any more likely than the individual to recognize in the everyday reality of homosexuality the figure of the sodomite when this figure was spoken of in imagery so divorced from the social forms homosexuality actually took?' (Bray 1982, 77). Bray's final chapter moves to the eighteenth century and the institution of Molly houses to contrast the incoherences of homosexuality in the previous two centuries with a social context (London in the eighteenth century) in which there was clearly an organized homosexual subculture. The success of Bray's book on both continents (it was one of the most influential British works of gay studies in the United States) is due not only to the material and convincing argument, but to the authorial voice. The reader is aware of a constantly questioning presence, realizing that every question leads to another and that every conclusion is provisional. For some, Bray became a model of the postmodern gay scholar. It is not surprising that his next essay on homosexuality and male friendship in the English Renaissance took issue with some of his own previous conclusions as it analysed documents of same-sex affection.

Because of the British investment in cultural studies, some of the ground-breaking gay work was in film rather than literature. *Gays and Film* (1977, rev. edn 1984), edited by Richard Dyer, was a crucial starting point. Dyer's own essay, 'Stereotyping', categorizes modes of representation of gay men in mainstream gay cinema. Caroline Sheldon's 'Lesbians and Film: Some Thoughts' begins with what appears now as a theoretically simplistic description of the 'lesbianfeminist' point of view ('lesbianfeminism implies a certain analysis of the power structure in which sexism is the primary oppression and lesbianism is defined as a political and emotional choice' (Sheldon, in Dyer 1984, 5), and moves on to a consideration of lesbian representations in film. For Sheldon, 'films are often tools to maintain depoliticization' (Sheldon, in Dyer 1984, 5). Like Weeks, she sees capitalism and the modern bourgeois family as the forces both shaping and opposing homosexuality. Jack Babuscio's seminal 'Camp and the Gay Sensibility' is a fundamental attempt to move beyond Susan Sontag's classic essay on camp and create a stronger link between gayness and camp, which describes 'those elements in a person, situation or activity which express, or are expressed by, a gay sensibility' (Babuscio, in Dyer 1984, 40). While Babuscio's essentialist view of 'the gay sensibility' seems outmoded, the essay has been a crucial starting point for further inquiry.

Dyer has gone on to write some of the most important gay-oriented film criticism. Particularly important is his book-length analysis of gay-oriented film, *Now You See It* (1990). For Dyer, these films, from Germany in the 1920s through Genet to independent film of the 1970s, represent 'what could be done within actual social and historical reality' (Dyer 1990, 1):

> It is this interaction, this within and against, of historically specific lesbian/gay subcultures and particular filmic traditions, as worked through in the texts of the films, that is the subject of this book. (Dyer 1990, 2)

In the 1990s, the two major figures in queer criticism in Britain were Jonathan Dollimore and Alan Sinfield, co-founders of the graduate programme in Sexual Dissidence and Cultural Change at the University of Sussex.

Dollimore's *Sexual Dissidence: Augustine to Wilde, Freud to Foucault* (1991) is nothing if not ambitious. Dollimore begins with the meeting of André Gide and Oscar Wilde who become representatives of essentialist and constructionist attitudes toward homosexuality. Both became avatars of sexual transgression, but saw their transgressiveness in diametrically different ways:

> For Gide, transgression is in the name of a desire rooted in the natural, the sincere, and the authentic; Wilde's transgressive aesthetic is the reverse: insincerity, inauthenticity, and unnaturalness become the liberating attributes of decentred identity and desire ... (Dollimore 1991, 14)

As he does for other British queer critics (Neil Bartlett, Alan Sinfield, Joseph Bristow), Wilde becomes the postmodern queer, reversing false binaries (nature/culture, depth/surface). For Dollimore, the prerequisite to admitting transgressive desire is 'an erasure of self, a decentring' (Dollimore 1991, 17). Gide foolishly and stubbornly maintained his belief in the centred, essential self. While Gide, who survived Wilde by over half a century, has been relegated to minor status as an artist, 'decentred' Wilde is still central to literary studies and is the true father of queer theory. He understood that 'there is no freedom outside of history, no freedom within deluded notions of autonomous selfhood' (Dollimore 1991, 33).

Dollimore's principal project is a history of sexual dissidence, which unsettles the opposition between dominant and subordinate cultures. That opposition is fought through 'those conceptions of self, desire, and transgression which figure in the language, ideologies and cultures of domination and in the diverse kinds of resistance to it' (Dollimore 1991, 21). The form of sexual dissidence of most interest is, of course, homosexuality: 'It is perhaps as something under erasure, even in its emergence, that homosexuality provides a history remarkably illuminating for the issues of marginality and power upon which contemporary debates, cultural, psychoanalytical and literary, have been converging' (Dollimore 1991, 32). Two terms are of particular importance in Dollimore's argument: the 'perverse dynamic' ('that fearful interconnectedness whereby the antithetical inheres within, and is partly produced by, what it opposes' (Dollimore 1991, 33)), and 'transgressive reinscription'. If homosexuality is not actually the 'other' to heterosexuality, but rather its 'proximate', related temporally and spatially, then what is called the other can easily 'track back' into the dominant. Transgressive reinscription, then, is 'the return of the repressed and/or the suppressed and/or the displaced via the proximate' (Dollimore 1991, 33).

These terms become the foundation for Dollimore's survey of dissidence from early Christianity through psychoanalysis and literary criticism to postmodernism. Ultimately the book celebrates the perverse dynamic, which 'reidentifies and exploits the inextricable connections between perversity, proximity, paradox, and desire'(Dollimore 1991, 230). *Sexual Dissidence* provides a merger of British cultural materialism with the work of the central figures in United States queer theory, particularly Eve Kosofsky Sedgwick.

Alan Sinfield's volumes written during the 1990s (*The Wilde Century, Cultural Politics – Queer Reading, Gay and After*), while remaining firmly entrenched in cultural materialism, demonstrate three different approaches to queer studies.

In *The Wilde Century* (1994), Sinfield explores the ways in which the persona of Oscar Wilde came to link the new notion of homosexuality with effeminacy, aestheticism and aristocratic decadence, states which heretofore had no association with homosexuality. For Sinfield, 'Wilde and his writings look queer because our stereotypical notion of male homosexuality derives from Wilde and our ideas about him' (Sinfield 1994a, vii). Wilde's person and writings comprise what Sinfield calls a 'faultline story', a narrative that exposes a culture's 'unresolved issues'. Given a society's desire to silence homosexuality, one needs to examine secrets and silences as carefully as speech. It is through understanding those silences that we come to better understand a society's ideological project, which is crucial since it is ideology that shapes us: 'it is hard to be gay until you have some kind of slot, however ambiguously defined, in the current framework of ideas' (Sinfield 1994a, 17). Wilde's exposure gave homosexuality a definition, a narrative: the leisured, effeminate, aesthetic dandy having sex for money with lower class boys. Such an image showed the homosexual as disruptive of all forms of Victorian social order. It also created a stereotype, a recognizable picture of the homosexual which men who were so inclined could model themselves after or rebel against. Central to this picture is effeminacy, which ties the homosexual to a rigid, fictional masculine-feminine binary, but at the same time gave many twentieth-century homosexuals a mode of affirmation: 'Effeminacy has over manliness the advantage of being a central gay cultural tradition which we may proudly assert' (Sinfield 1994a, 196).

The Wilde Century joins Dollimore's *Sexual Dissidence* and other volumes devoted to Wilde's centrality in the creation of a gay persona that was both limiting and liberating. Neil Bartlett's 'personal meditation' *Who Was That Man* analyses the historical and symbolic Wildes: the writer who became a scandalous sexual criminal and the supposed father of the modern gay community. Bartlett accumulates historical and literary details to demonstrate that the historical Wilde was not an anomaly: 'the gay culture of London was there. It was organized in a variety of forms, spoke both private and public languages, inhabited both private and public spaces, was both terrified and courageous' (1988, 127–8). Wilde, then, was not intolerable to his society because he was homosexual: 'he was intolerable because he was a public man who was homosexual' (Bartlett 1988, 148). Bartlett scans historical writing and Wilde's *oeuvre* to discover what homosexuality meant to Wilde and what Wilde meant to a gay man in the 1980s:

> There was no real Oscar Wilde, if by real we mean homosexual. He did not, like us, have the alibi of 'being like that'. London in 1895 had no conception of a man being 'naturally homosexual'. A man who loved other men could only be described as an invert, an inversion of something else, a pervert, an exotic, a disease, a victim, a variation. Wilde was an artist as well. He was entirely uninterested in authenticity. (1988, 163–4)

Joseph Bristow's *Effeminate England* (1995) begins with the same idea asserted in Sinfield's *The Wilde Century* – that effeminacy only became a stereotype of homosexuality after the Wilde scandal. Given this taint of effeminacy and the Uranian notion that a homosexual was some sort of hermaphrodite caught in the middle of the gender binary, Bristow asserts that 'homoerotic writing after 1885 constantly defines itself against the predominant assumption that to be a man-loving man necessarily meant that one was weakened, morally and physically, by the taint of effeminacy' (Bristow 1995, 10), which informed the writer's presentation of male-male desire and their often contemptuous treatment of women. Sinfield's *The Wilde Century* asserts that 'the villain of the piece is the masculine/feminine binary structure as it circulates in our cultures' (Sinfield 1994a, vii). Bristow's work is also built on this assumption.

Most of Alan Sinfield's recent work focuses on gay culture and discourse. *Cultural Politics – Queer Reading*, published the same year as *The Wilde Century*, contains lectures Sinfield gave at the University of Pennsylvania critiquing the relationship of what he calls 'Englit' the profession of literary criticism as it is practised in English departments, and homosexuality and queer studies. In essence, he is writing a clear, articulate argument for his cultural materialist approach. Sinfield is particularly interested in the dynamics of subcultures, particularly the gay subculture: 'the advantage of subculture as an interpretive tool is that it designates a distinctive framework of understanding that is neither determined by the dominant nor immune to it' (Sinfield 1994b, 68). For him, gayness is a mode of categorizing, not a property of individuals.

Sinfield is always concerned with the ways in which his ideas affect the political reality of present-day queers and how we can effect social change, how we realize the possibility of 'subcultural strategies'. *Gay and After* (1998), Sinfield's contribution to what is called 'post-gay' writing, begins from the notion that ' "gay" as we have produced it and lived it, and perhaps "lesbian" also, are historical phenomena and now may be hindering us more than they help us' (Sinfield 1998, 5). Post-gay, for Sinfield, is a time 'when it will not seem so necessary to define, and hence to limit, our sexualities' (1998, 14). There is not one monolithic homosexuality, but a variety of homosexualities shaped by different circum-stances of class, education, race and ethnicity. Gay readers neither live nor read the same way. The only condition those defined as gay share is that of being not heterosexual. Therefore the term 'gay' neither reflects this variety nor allows for changes in the sex-gender system.

A sense of the ways in which queer studies were influencing literary studies can be found in a collection of essays edited by Joseph Bristow (1992). A central concern of the volume is the elimination of the notion of gay and lesbian identity and readership. In his introduction, Bristow begins challenging the monolithic notion of homosexuality which 'denies the gendered difference between men and women who desire their own sex. It produces sameness where there is not necessarily any at all' (1992, 3). In her essay 'What Is Not Said', Diana Colecott elaborates Bristow's argument: 'The male body dominates current discussion in gay studies, while the female body is doubly deleted: is deleted as maternal body, and as both subject and object of lesbian desire' (Colecott, in Bristow 1992, 93). Even more than in the writings of gay men, the key words in lesbian criticism are 'silence' and 'erasure': silence about the desire and experience of lesbians and erasure of their difference. 'This situation leaves the lesbian conscious of herself as an absence from discourse, and the lesbian writer, teacher, or theorist is in an historical position that does not synchronize with the relative recognition and the relative freedom of gay men to write, teach, and theorize' (Colecott, in Bristow 1992, 93).

The first British collection of essays by lesbians on literature was not published until 1991. *What Lesbians Do in Books*, edited by Elaine Hobby and Chris White, reinforces what might be called the lesbian canon (Sappho, Radcliffe Hall, Virginia Woolf, Audre Lorde, Adrienne Rich), but expands into areas like the lesbian detective story. What is most provocative about the essays are their rethinking of accepted ideas of queer theory. Chris White offers a rebuttal to both Michel Foucault and Jeffrey Weeks's account of the history of sexology. For White, Foucault's 'one way' power dynamic between society and the individual does not take into account the fact that much of the change in discourse about homosexuals that took place in the nineteenth century was instigated by homosexuals trying to find neutral, if not positive, definitions. Katherine Phillips asserts that the accounts she has found of female–female desire before the nineteenth century raise doubts about Foucault's primary thesis that there could not be a homosexual without the language to define her. More important to the writers of this volume are feminist theorists like Luce Irigaray and the psychoanalytic theories of Jacques Lacan. As the essays in the volume make clear, lesbian writers, critics and theorists draw their ideas and empowerment more from the body of feminist criticism than the work of gay male writers.

John M. Clum

Further reading and works cited

Bartlett, N. *Who Was That Man*. London, 1988.
Bray, A. *Homosexuality in Renaissance England*. London, 1982.
Bristow, J. *Sexual Sameness*. London, 1992.
—. *Effeminate England*. New York, 1995.

Dollimore, J. *Sexual Dissidence*. Oxford, 1991.

Dyer, R. *Gays and Film*. New York, 1984.

—. *Now You See It*. London, 1990.

Hobby, E. and White, C. (eds) *What Lesbians Do in Books*. London, 1991.

Meyers, J. *Homosexuality and Literature*. London, 1977.

Plummer, K. (ed.) *The Making of the Modern Homosexual*. Totowa, 1981.

— (ed.) *Modern Homosexualities*. London, 1992.

Shepherd, S. *Because We're Queers*. London, 1989.

Simpson, M. (ed.) *Anti-gay*. London, 1996.

Sinfield, A. *The Wilde Century*. New York, 1994a.

—. *Cultural Politics – Queer Reading*. Philadelphia, 1994b.

—. *Gay and After*. London, 1998.

Smith, A. M. *New Right Discourse on Race and Sexuality*. Cambridge, 1994.

Smyth, C. *Lesbians Talk Queer Notions*. London, 1992.

Still, J. and Worten, M. (eds) *Textuality and Sexuality*. Manchester, 1993.

Weeks, J. *Coming Out*. London, 1977.

—. *Sex, Politics and Society*. London, 1981.

—. *Sexuality and Its Discontents*. London, 1985.

—. *Against Nature*. London, 1991.

22. Ernesto Laclau (1935–), Chantal Mouffe (1948–) and Post-Marxism

The suggestion that there could be an intimate link between literary theory and political philosophy might come as something of a surprise in certain circles, not least perhaps in those of literary theory and political philosophy themselves. Yet it was precisely by applying literary theoretical, psychoanalytic and semiotic concepts and techniques to the analysis of the political that Ernesto Laclau and Chantal Mouffe developed a radical version of marxist political theory. This new theory, which they termed 'post-marxism', found its first thoroughgoing articulation in their co-authored work, *Hegemony and Socialist Strategy: Towards a Radical Democratic Politics* (1985). This work carries out a methodical historical critique and conceptual deconstruction of 'classical Marxism' (1985, 3), which enables them to identify why classical marxist theory could not predict, account for, or adequately explain the behaviour of political struggles and socio-political or economic 'classes'. This 'failure' became increasingly apparent throughout the nineteenth and twentieth centuries, and represented a severe challenge to the validity of marxism, threatening its credibility, while also initiating a 'crisis' *within* marxism itself. For this 'failure' ran entirely contrary to the claims that marxism could be the *objective science* of historical processes (1985, 2). As such, Laclau and Mouffe begin their analysis by identifying an antagonism, between marxism's claims about the socio-political world on the one hand, and the 'reality' or observable development of actual societies on the other (1985, 122).

As 'objective science', marxism aimed to predict the course history must *necessarily* take, culminating in the revolution of a 'universal class' of workers. But, in the face of the failure of this prediction, marxism could most readily survive by switching the emphasis of its claims, away from being the *declarations* of an *objective science* (of the order: 'This *will* happen'), and changing to those of *injunctions* made in the name of an *ethical programme* (of the order: 'This *should* (be made to) happen') (Derrida 1994; Laclau 1996, 66). However, for Laclau and Mouffe, any move which entails abandoning the idea of marxism's objective and scientific aspirations, and the subsequent – and supplementary (Laclau and Mouffe 1985, 51; Derrida 1974, 141) – adoption of a position in which marxism would be considered merely *ethical*, was simply unsatisfactory – academically and politically.

Although they would not disagree that marxism entails an *ethical dimension*, especially regarding the primary question of *justice*, which is always in some measure at the heart of democratic struggles (1985, 174), their analysis does not remove itself from the matter of the *mechanisms* governing social and political 'reality'. However, where classical marxism concerned itself with *objective* 'reality', Laclau and Mouffe see objectivity itself as only one part of 'reality'. So, as 'objectivity' is only one part of a social totality, it is not, therefore, coterminous or coextensive with 'reality' as such, and any analysis of the *totality* should not therefore concern itself with only that one *part* (1985, 111). Accordingly, their emphasis moves from the objectivity of that which exists, 'is', or has being or presence (Spivak, in Derrida 1974, xiv ff.), and focuses instead upon the 'logic' of the social and political – the *logic* of socio-political mechanisms. They do not ignore the status of the 'objective' and objectivity, but in their analysis the focus is more upon the logical mechanisms through which 'objective reality' actually gains that status of being – or what they term 'the *conditions of possibility* of any objectivity' (Žižek 1989, xiii). But this logic is far from being a logic organized by 'identity' and the law of 'non-contradiction' (Laclau and Mouffe 1985, 124). It is rather a deconstructive logic, which is intelligible most readily in terms of the Saussurean semiotic notion in which the identity of any sign (or, in Laclau and Mouffe, any *entity* at all) is constituted on the basis of defining and asserting itself in terms of *that which it is not* – that is, on the basis of difference (de Man 1978, 22).

Their revaluation and overhaul of marxist theory in *Hegemony and Socialist Strategy* constituted a concerted attempt to 'save' the project of marxism from obsolescence, while not abandoning the aspirations, aims and objectives (*telos*) of marxism: namely, the hope of egalitarian emancipation for all from the exploitation and subjection attendant to capitalist production. Hence the term 'post-marxism': the reference to the *telos* of marxism remains in place, as a guiding idea, but the 'post' signifies 'after', 'more than', 'other than' marxism. In addition, of course, the term 'post-marxism' carries more than a passing allusion to 'post-modernism': in a sense, post-marxism is marxism reformulated in light of profound changes in the topography of what has become a postmodern world (Laclau 1993, 329). The 'post-' of post-marxism thereby signifies the abandonment of those axioms that Laclau and Mouffe call 'essentialist' (1985, 47). Their deconstruction of these essentialisms has caused much controversy among other marxist theoreticians (Geras 1985), and in a sense this controversy exists actually *because* their analysis of the social, political, ideological and economic takes the form of a *deconstruction*.

For, deconstruction itself is controversial. Often, it is not generally recognized as being 'political' at all, or of any use to political analysis – especially not before Laclau and Mouffe's intervention (Bennington 1994, 6). As a tool for literary analysis, and occasionally for drawing out philosophical themes within texts, deconstruction is often construed as being something worthwhile only in so far as it constitutes a radical form of *reading* (Weber 1987). But Laclau and Mouffe use deconstruction to read the texts of classical marxism, and to reassess and reformulate them according to this peculiar reading practice.

Already it is possible to see that 'post-marxism' is far from being *proper* marxism: the way that it denies some of the central tenets of marxism and applies a form of analysis, often deemed anarchic and even irrational, to political texts, has led 'post-marxism' to be received as a *transgression* of marxism, or even as *not marxist at all*. But, Laclau and Mouffe argue, their critical analysis of marxist categories and their subsequent construction of a deconstructed and deconstructive post-marxist paradigm (1985, 14; Mowitt 1992, 17), constitutes a necessary reinvigoration and radicalization of the tradition, which is the only way to keep open the possibility of the marxist project, as a valid and viable political force. Let us trace the outline of their argument, as presented in *Hegemony and Socialist Strategy*, and indicate its subsequent development, and the ways it has contributed to contemporary understanding of the nature of 'the political' (Beardsworth 1996, xi), before suggesting its limitations.

In the opening movement of the book, Laclau and Mouffe focus on the social conditions characterizing 'revolutionary situations'. Reading Rosa Luxemburg's analysis of these situations, they argue that

> in a revolutionary situation, it is impossible *to fix the literal sense* of each isolated struggle, because each struggle overflows its own literality and comes to represent, in the consciousness of the masses, a simple moment of a more global struggle against the system. And so it is that while in a period of stability the class consciousness of the worker ... is 'latent' and 'theoretical', in a revolutionary situation the *meaning* of every mobilization appears, so to speak, as split: aside from its specific literal demands, each mobilization represents the revolutionary process as a whole; and these totalizing effects are visible in the overdetermination of some struggles by others. This is, however, nothing other than the defining characteristic of the symbol: the overflowing of the signifier by the signified. *The unity of the class is therefore a symbolic unity.* (1985, 10–11)

Here, the 'literal meaning' of an event is shown to depend on the context in which it occurs, or in which it is interpreted and given meaning. The literal meaning of anything – what semiotics calls 'denotation' – cannot be divorced from its 'connotation' (Hall 1980, 133), and both the connotation and denotation of a signifier (whether a word, image or historical event) will always be established within the confines of a certain context: the same signifier will connote and denote very different things (signifieds or referents) in different contexts, depending on the context in which it occurs (as well as the infinite range of possible contexts in which it could thereafter be interpreted) (Derrida 1977, 1–25). In the case of a revolutionary political situation, as Laclau and Mouffe argue, any particular event in that struggle will attain a meaning in which it is 'equivalent' to all other events in that struggle, no matter how 'different' it might *literally* be. The *meaning* of any event (what it 'stands for', what it 'symbolizes') will arise as a result of the 'overdetermination' (Laplanche and Pontalis 1988, 292) of the context in which it occurs, or the context in which it is interpreted.

In the revolutionary situation described by Laclau and Mouffe, the 'event' and its 'interpretation' take place in the same 'context' – that of the 'revolutionary situation' itself. But it is important to note that the meaning of an event is open to the possibility of being renarrated in different contexts, so that it will *mean* – and even '*be*' – something entirely different. In this example, though, Laclau and Mouffe are concerned with the meaning of an event within the interpretive context of a 'revolutionary situation', and not with its meaning 'outside' or 'after' that situation. Later on, they consider the importance of the reiteration of an event's meaning *into* different discursive contexts, as a key moment of articulating (connecting, constructing, saying, representing) a certain desired *meaning* to *any* event, so that its meaning becomes *relatively fixed* within the socio-political imaginary, thus enabling it to work (or, to *tend* to work) for the purposes of a certain political project.

That is to say, in a revolutionary situation, the meaning of all events will be over-determined by the revolutionary factors bearing on their significance or status as events. So, in a non-revolutionary situation, were a group of workers to strike for better pay or better working conditions, then that strike would not *necessarily* symbolize any general cause or struggle. In a revolutionary situation, in which an entire society has become polarized into two opposing camps (say, the 'people' versus the 'aristocracy' or '*ancien régime*', in the manner of the French Revolution), then when a particular group strikes, it will symbolize the entire struggle, the entire plight of 'the people'. In Laclau and Mouffe's terms, in such a situation, or context, whatever 'the people' do – however *different* each act is – it will be *equivalent* in status and meaning when considered in terms of the general struggle: it will be a symbol of and for it. For as long as the struggle persists, it will be immensely important to each side of the struggle to *reiterate* a certain meaning for these events, in order that, over time, and through the 'regularity in dispersion' of these reiterations, the meaning which best serves the cause will become consolidated and sedimented as 'true' in the minds, or imaginary, of as many people as possible. The meanings which *tend* to become dominant in the social-political imaginary, and which work to strengthen a particular cause, political position or power structure, will, in Laclau and Mouffe's terms, have become hegemonic, working to constitute, represent and perpetuate the dominant hegemony or dominant hegemonic political position.

Another way to put this would be to say that, in such a situation, certain acts or events would have a *synonymous meaning*. In a revolutionary situation, then events as ostensibly *different* as strikes, graffiti, petitions, pamphlets, the formation of unions and other social bonds, even terrorism, violence, conflict, law-breaking and refusals to conform to certain tasks (taxpaying, voting, etc.), would all be synonymous with and symbols *of and for* 'the cause'. On the other hand, in a non-revolutionary situation, then such events would not necessarily be interpreted as *equivalent* symbols of a unified struggle against the dominant hegemony in the popular imaginary (the 'hearts and minds' and practices of the populace). They would perhaps *tend* to be interpreted as unique 'differences' *within* the hegemony, or differences (classified, say, as differences of personal opinion) that could be resolved without changing the established institutional dynamics of society (the *status quo* of a social hegemony).

The example of the synonym is helpful. For, whereas in conventional usage, any given word will have a certain set of general synonyms – for example 'truth' is conventionally synonymous with 'fact', 'reality', 'certainty', 'accuracy', 'genuineness', 'precision', and so on – in a precise discursive context, for example that of a novel, poem (or literary genre, generally), a political manifesto or philosophical treatise, it might become synonymous with very different words (note that none of the synonyms of 'truth' listed above actually name a concrete or tangible *referent* themselves). Staying with our hypothetical revolutionary situation, 'truth' might become synonymous with 'the cause', 'the plight of the people', 'emancipation from exploitation and oppression'. That is because, in that situation, the context is highly overdetermined. But, it is important to note, the same process of *the overdetermination of meaning takes place in all contexts*. In fact, the *tendency* to establish (articulate) certain meanings in certain ways can be viewed as one of the ways of defining or delimiting the notion of 'context' itself. So, where, in existentialist philosophy, 'truth' will be constructed in such a way as to be read as 'absurdity', perhaps, elsewhere, as in romantic poetry, it will be constructed so as to be synonymous with 'nature', or, in religious contexts, it will mean 'God' or 'the Divine', and so on.

In this way it can be seen that 'truth' itself is a 'floating signifier' (Laclau and Mouffe 1985, 171; Laclau 1996, 36). That is, as semiotics has shown, it is not *necessarily* attached to any final signified, or precise referent. It all depends, in Laclau and Mouffe's terms, on 'precise discursive conditions of emergence'. In the discourse of classical marxism, the 'truth' of social 'reality' lies with the economic base of any given society. This means that, for such marxists, the *real, fundamental* situation of human societies is that there are, first and foremost, *material economic factors* which determine everything about that society. For instance, the location of a source of raw materials, along with the viability, presence or possible presence of the other factors of production (land, labour, capital) will govern the decision (Mouffe 1996, 54) to locate (or not to locate) a factory thereabouts. As such, it is by way of the dictates of the economic base that the presence and form of *any* social activity is determined. So, for classical marxism, it is true to say that *the economy is determinant in the first and last instance of social relations*. In marxist terms, the effects of the determination of all aspects of society by the economy are felt nowhere more profoundly than in a society operating under a capitalist economy, where the population is displaced and located according to the dictates of profitability, and where the fate of nations is determined according to decisions made by capitalists. In terms of this 'truth', then, classical marxism sees a distinction between the constitutive factor of the 'economic base', and the subordinate element of the 'ideological superstructure'. This second term, the 'super-structure', names the lived relations of a society: its beliefs, practices and relationships – the family structure, the educational apparatus, religious institutions, the whole infrastructure and its attendant systems of values, truths or 'ideology'. (But, immediately, post-marxism points out, it is really quite impossible to maintain the distinction between base and superstructure, as they are symbiotic, overlapping and non-separable, which is why they offer the more Foucauldian term of 'discourse', to indicate the entire structure, rather than maintain the impossible *essentialist* distinction (1985, 174).)

For marxism, this base/superstructure relationship is held in place and operates success-fully (for capitalists, who hold power and extract excess profit) only on the basis of 'false consciousness' or 'ideology'. 'False consciousness' is anything which prevents 'the masses' from perceiving the 'truth' of their situation: namely, anything which blocks their 'knowledge' of the 'fact' that they are exploited, in so far as the fruits of their labour ('profit': 'surplus value') are being illegitimately extracted from their work (alienation) and are going to those who do not, *by rights* or *justifiably*, deserve it, i.e. the capitalists who own the factors of production, including, actually, *the workers themselves*.

In the terms of classical marxism, then, it is the blinkers of 'false consciousness' instituted by 'capitalist ideology' that need to be overcome, overthrown: the classical argument therefore emphasizes that the workers of the world need consciously to realize their own economic exploitation (Marx and Engels 1967). But before this can happen, they must realize that their beliefs as to what is 'natural' and 'true' about society and social relations are all part and parcel of capitalist ideology. This is the realm of the ideological super-structure: the lived beliefs and practices of everyone's everyday lives. Louis Althusser's statements about the 'ideological state apparatuses' in 'Ideology and Ideological State Apparatuses' exemplify this position (Althusser 1971).

However, as Laclau and Mouffe argue, the base/superstructure argument of marxism is flawed by a certain essentialism. This essentialism, they argue, takes the form of a belief in the simple fixed identity of notions like 'individual', 'class' and 'society'. Instead of preserving the kind of thinking which takes an 'individual' to be a member of a 'class' a class which is itself a coherent part of a coherent 'society', Laclau and Mouffe focus on these terms themselves. What is an 'individual'? What is a 'class'? And what is 'society'? They subject such notions to a rigorous deconstruction, by way of inquiring into the relationship between the *concept* (for example, the concept of 'working class') and the *referent* which is thought to be signified by that term (in this example, the concept or signifier of 'working-class subject' would be tied necessarily to some specific living person, exemplifying and representing *the* 'working class').

The first essentialism that Laclau and Mouffe point to is this kind of referential thinking: namely, *that* someone who occupies at certain times a 'working-class subject position' *is therefore* 'a member of the working class', purely, simply and entirely. They argue that while it is true that at certain times in certain people's lives, they will quite literally occupy what are deemed to be working-class subject positions, it is equally likely that such a person who at times qualifies as being 'working class', will at other times occupy a contradictory 'subject position', one not consistent with being a 'working-class subject'. They argue that this referential essentialism has led to theoretical 'confusion' in marxist theory (1985, 119), as it has led thinkers to either the 'logically illegitimate conclusion . . . that the other positions occupied by these agents are also "working-class positions" ' or, alternatively, to argue that these contradictions in the variety and inconsistency of 'subject positions' occupied by 'working-class' subjects has come about as the result of some 'separating' power of capitalism, working in the 'superstructure'. That is to say, Laclau and Mouffe disagree with much marxist theory in the sense that they deny it is ever simply the case that there is an essential unity to the 'working class', a unity extending to all the possible subject positions occupied by all the 'individuals' who make up the 'class'. Whereas earlier marxist theory would consider ideological contradictions to be the result of the divisive power of capitalism, used in order to perpetuate the mystification and delusion of subjects who would otherwise be able to see the truth of their situation as the exploited working class, Laclau and Mouffe disagree. They argue that many of the problems of theoretical marxism have been brought on by their own manner of theorizing: marxism they argue, theorizes the 'individual' as being a referent, 'individuals' as the being 'origin and basis of social relations' (1985, 115), and 'society' itself as actually *being a 'thing'*, a referent.

However, as the passage cited above reveals, Laclau and Mouffe argue that any 'class unity' that might occur – a unity in which individuals see themselves as part of a class, and act as a class, in unity – will only by a *symbolic identification*. It is the work of symbolic signification which has the power to make or break the notion of 'class' as a valid political force. But what this means is that, in stark distinction to traditional marxist theories of political action and transformation, it is quite possible that members of many different classes could identify with the symbol of a political struggle, and become identifiable as a *consciously unified* group, struggling for a particular political transformation.

The key point here is that political groups need not essentially consist of members of the same class: the traditional conception of 'class' is 'essentialist' and 'confused'. Nor are 'political groups' total and complete – they are rather *partial and provisional identifications* with a cause. Unity will not be complete, total or permanent. As soon as the cause is lost, won or dissipates, the group will effectively cease to exist. The *identity* of the group has no *essence* outside of the *antagonism,* around, against and in terms of which it constructed itself. Thus, they argue, one should not *identify* political agents with named or real *referents.* A political identity will be formed in relation to a political issue (an antagonism); that identity is not the whole or entire identity of the person or persons who hold it, even though some political antagonisms persist to such an extent that the identities of certain people and groups will be dominated and overdetermined to a massive extent by these political antagonisms. One need only mention those political antagonisms that can be expressed under the headings of racism, sexism, homophobia, xenophobia, ethnocentrism, anti-Semitism, imperialism, exploitation, oppression and discrimination on many other grounds in order to appreciate this possibility – and also to see the implication of very many contextual factors in the determination and establishment of all 'individual' subjectivity.

Thus a theory of the political cannot theorize in terms of 'individuals'. For the 'identity' if an individual will depend on contextual factors in precisely the same way that, in Saussurean linguistics and semiotics, the identity of a signifier will depend on the position it occupies within a signifying structure – it will be overdetermined by a context. This application of semiotic insights to the theory of the identity of 'individuals' or 'subjects' constitutes a radical contribution to political theory. But, Laclau and Mouffe also bring psychoanalytic considerations to bear on political analysis (especially since Slavoj Žižek's involvement with their project), exploring the roles played by the imaginary and fantasy within the political domain (Žižek 1989). All of these perspectives expand the field of the political and transform the nature of any consideration of the political from the simplicity of thinking about 'individuals' *in* 'society'.

For, just as looking at 'individuals' will miss profound *discursive* or *structural* elements relevant to the study of political issues – especially the political issues related to the construction of an 'individual' subjectivity itself (for the notion of the 'individual' implicitly takes the identity of that 'individual' to be set and already established, while Laclau and Mouffe show how any 'individual identity' will be constituted by factors such as the very fact of their involvement in a struggle) – they also point out that the object of political analysis termed 'society', 'the social' or 'socius', is not only *not* pre-given, already-existing, established, unified and 'objectively real' (which it is often assumed to be), but that, in actual fact, *society does not exist* (Žižek, in Laclau 1990, 249).

This point deserves further clarification. The point is that 'society' or 'the social' is not a *thing* (or *referent*). It is a 'construct', or a 'figure', without a final signified. You cannot put your finger on any object and declare that *it is society*. There is no object which objectively *is* society. Laclau and Mouffe proceed broadly in accordance with semiotics, in arguing that 'society' functions as a signifier, but it has no final signified. Everyone 'knows' what it 'means' (although this meaning will differ in its representation, from context to context), but no one could put their finger on some*thing* that '*is*' the '*essence*' of the social. Semiotically speaking, 'society' or 'the social' has no denotative signified of itself, 'essentially', there being no *thing* which *is* the social. There are *figures* of and for the social/society (metonymies, metaphors, symbols, etc.), but 'society' is itself already a 'figuration' or a 'construct' for something which, Laclau and Mouffe argue, is *constitutively absent* (Laclau and Mouffe 1985, 125). It is in this sense that they can argue that 'society' does not exist.

But, of course, 'society' or 'the social' *does exist.* It is just that our thinking of what it means to say that something exists has to be reassessed (Spivak, in Derrida 1974, xiv).

'Society' does not exist as an *essence* residing somewhere, fully present and intelligible in any way. It is rather a construct, or as Slavoj Žižek says, it exists as 'ideological fantasy'. It is a signifier that has no adequate signified, but only partial, provisional and insufficient signifiers of 'itself'. Indeed, whenever a signifier of 'society' or 'the social' is presented as being *the* signifier *of* 'society' – examples might range from the figure of the monarch (or a rebel) to the results of a census or a table of statistics about a society – it is immediately obvious that this representation is not that society *itself*, that it in no way captures the 'essence' of the society, that there would seem to be so much more to it than that. This is because, as Laclau and Mouffe point out, 'the totality is not a datum but a construction' (1985, 144), and always both less and more than any given signifier of it. They refer to this effect as that of the 'surplus of meaning', an effect which is the result of the semiotic fact that because 'identities are purely relational ... there is no identity which can be fully constituted' (1985, 111).

This formulation of the relational character of identities here means not only the identity of linguistic or discursive terms, but also even what we tend to think of as the 'identity' of 'individuals', the identity of institutions and even those of historical events. None of these identities are 'fixed', but rather all identities are the effect or result of their relationships with other identities, and the relationships between identities (it being the *relationship* in which an identity is placed or articulated that determines the meaning and being of that identity) are established in what Laclau and Mouffe term 'discourse'.

To stay with the concept of 'the social' or 'society', we can say that, because it is intelligible, or because we all know what it is, even though 'it' is a construct with no ultimate referent, this intelligibility has been constructed by *discourse*: discourses of value, which assert what society *is like* or *should be like*, using the term rhetorically (through analogy), and empirical discourses, using statistical constructs which take parts as indicators of the whole (metonymically). The features of rhetorical or value-based discourses and those of empirical discourses mark the coordinates of all discourses of the social. Historical, literary, anthropological, governmental and bureaucratic discourses and so on, all incorporate the *evaluatory* and the ostensibly *referential* in order to suture the meaning of 'society'.

Sutured means stitched together, weaved or fabricated. It is a textile and textual metaphor, as is the notion or concept of 'text' itself. The suturing of the notion of 'society', so that it means something whole, complete, knowable, etc., implies what Laclau and Mouffe call (using a Foucauldian expression) the 'regularity in dispersion' of its reiteration in many and varied discursive contexts (1985, 142): the signification of 'society' (or any term) becomes partially fixed (yet always open to the polysemy of many possible meanings) only on the basis of its regular deployment as a signifier, in familiar ways, in everyday discourses (educational, governmental, familial, media and so on), throughout time and space. Laclau and Mouffe invoke the Lacanian concept of the *point de capiton*, or 'quilting point', to explain the way that meaning becomes relatively fixed within different discursive contexts. These quilting points are overdetermined by their status within discourses (examples might include the idea of 'Man', the 'individual' or 'God'), and they prevent the slippages of meaning that would occur in interpretation were there no relatively stable terms to refer to in communicating or interpreting. Their stability is a result of the work of their 'regularity in dispersion' throughout dominant discourses. But a deconstructive analysis of the situations in which they are used to structure meaning reveals that, despite their 'obvious' intelligibility or their transparency of meaning, it remains impossible to identify a concrete signified or referent for them other than through connotation, metaphor, metonymy, symbol and other such literary or poetic techniques. This leads to the peculiarity in which even the ostensible literality of speaking about the 'individual' reveals itself to be figurative language! Thus it can be shown that even the objectivity of objective language is itself a construction which relies on rhetorical, textual, poetic, and otherwise literary techniques, or, as Laclau and Mouffe say, 'all discourse of fixation becomes metaphorical: literality is, in actual fact, the first of all metaphors' (1985, 111).

In a sense, all of this runs contrary to all discourses that claim to be objective. It goes against them, and it implicitly rejects all claims made in the name of *neutral* objectivity. Even objectivity, in post-marxism, is *not neutral*, but is rather *contestable* and, hence, *political*. This reading of objectivity as a non-neutral (hence, political) construct subverts the notion of objectivity and the authority of discourses claiming to be objective. As such, for 'objective discourses', what we have just asserted will always be inadmissible – for, were it to be accepted, then it would enable the contestation of the authority of authoritative discourses and authoritative structures of power and knowledge. In Laclau and Mouffe's terms, we have just located a site of antagonism (1985, 122). Antagonism cannot be objective, as it will arise by virtue of an experience of objective relations that are experienced as being *unjust* or *wrong* (1985, 125). They explore the example of the development of feminism (1985, 154), in which the claims for the equal rights of women were *articulated* with reference to the *ethos* and *telos* of equality and democracy. But, they point out, 'in order to be mobilized in this way, the democratic principle of liberty and equality had first to impose itself as the new matrix of the social imaginary; or, in our terminology, to constitute a fundamental nodal point in the construction of the political' (1985, 154–5).

Thus it was the institution of 'democracy' as a *point de capiton* which paved the way for the possibility of the birth of feminism. In their terms, it was the democratic revolution which constituted the conditions of possibility for the emergence of feminist/sexist antagonisms *as* antagonisms and for the construction of a democratic feminist struggle. In fact, Laclau and Mouffe locate, in the democratic revolution, or in the concept of democracy itself, a profound transformation of the range of possibilities for 'politics', in a radical extension of the entire political terrain, moving *the political* into every relation and institution which has a place (or does not yet have a place) in every aspect of every sense that can be signified by the notion of 'society'. As they argue:

> The 'democratic revolution', as a new terrain which supposes a profound mutation at the symbolic level, implies a new form of institution of the social. In earlier societies, organized in accordance with a theological-political logic, power was incorporated in the person of the prince ... the radical difference which democratic society introduces is that the site of power becomes an empty space ... The possibility is thus opened up of an unending process of questioning ... (1985, 186)

When society is no longer considered to be organized according to some theological hierarchy based on 'divine right', then the members of that society must bear the responsibility for *its* (*their own*) organization. If society's hierarchies and institutions are deemed to be unjust, then democratic principles enable the contestation of that situation on the basis of appeals to justice and equality. In post-marxism, then, democracy promises to be the best means of assuring that any injustice, exploitation and oppression can be countered, and that *all* power be accountable, precisely because democratic principles contain within themselves the basis of their own critique and contestation. The advent of this new kind of politics, Laclau and Mouffe argue, initiated a political logic that they term 'hegemony'.

Their theory of hegemony and hegemonic politics takes its inspiration from the work of Antonio Gramsci, who theorized hegemony as the name of a mechanism of socio-political organization in which:

> previously germinated ideologies become 'party', come into confrontation and conflict, until one of them or at least a combination of them tends to prevail, to gain the upper hand, to propagate itself throughout society – bringing about not only a unison of economic and political aims, but also intellectual and moral unity, posing all the questions around which the struggle rages, not on a corporate but on a 'universal' plane, and thus creating the hegemony of a fundamental group over a series of subordinate groups. (Gramsci 1971, 181–2)

The key difference between Gramsci's model and that of Laclau and Mouffe lies in the latter's emphasis on the discursive construction of every political identity, in that identities do not exist *before* their construction around antagonisms. This is the reason why the post-marxists talk of 'subject positions' as opposed to 'subjects', as political identities are partial, provisional and constantly in a state of flux. Accordingly, Laclau and Mouffe emphasize the prime importance of the '*tendency*': the *tendency* to represent certain issues or figures in a certain way, the *tendencies* by which certain issues are articulated as equivalent or different, related or separate, and so on. For it is the 'regularity in dispersion' of manners of representation and modes of articulation that governs the character of a political hegemony, and so any changes at the point of representation or articulation will affect changes throughout an entire hegemonic structure – a structure that encompasses all areas of the social, political and institutional make-up of a society.

Strong criticisms of post-marxism have come from within marxist political theory itself, and these have been widely detailed elsewhere (Lechte 1994, 191). But perhaps the most interesting, challenging and *widely unacknowledged* critique of post-marxism actually comes from within the very field of literary and cultural studies from which post-marxism took its formative analyses of the symbol and other 'literary' tools. As you will recall, post-marxist political theory developed by way of recourse to literary theoretical and deconstructive techniques of textual analysis. Yet, in reading Laclau and Mouffe, the *debt* (Derrida 1994) they owe to the theory of the text, as developed by Barthes, Derrida, Kristeva and so on, is given little attention. John Mowitt has argued that both this oversight, as well as their use of the Foucauldian notion of 'discourse' in preference to that of 'text' (even though they actually use 'text' to define 'discourse' (Mowitt 1992, 15)), constitutes *a limitation of the radical implications of the theory of the text – a theory that was already, from the outset, profoundly political and subversive*. Mowitt urges 'political' academia not to forget the 'textual paradigm' by accepting the 'discourse paradigm' of the post-marxists, because, in his sense, the concept of 'discourse' is a lot less radical and political than that of 'text' in the work of Barthes, Derrida and Kristeva (Mowitt 1992). Indeed, there would be a certain compelling logic at play – a deconstructive logic, at least – were we to *return* to the 'literary' theory that *supplemented* the genesis of post-marxism, in order to look once again at that ostensibly purely '*literary* theory', and to examine how profoundly political it already is, *or could be – were it read accordingly*. The relationship between the 'literary' and the 'political' is intimate, and perhaps it would be a political error to subordinate the one to the other, as is the *tendency* of many modes and manners of *articulation* and *representation* within the *hegemony* of political or literary study.

Paul Bowman

Further reading and works cited

Althusser, L. *Lenin and Philosophy*. New York, 1971.

Arditi, B. and Valentine, J. *Polemicization*. Edinburgh, 1999.

Beardsworth, R. *Derrida and the Political*. London and New York, 1996.

Bennington, G. *Legislations*. London, 1994.

de Man, P. 'The Epistemology of Metaphor', in *On Metaphor*, ed. S. Sacks. Chicago, 1978.

Derrida, J. *Of Grammatology*, intro. G. Chakravorty Spivak. Baltimore, MD, 1974.

—. *Limited Inc*. Evanston, IL, 1977.

—. *Specters of Marx*. London, 1994.

Geras, N. 'Post-Marxism?', *New Left Review*, 163, 1985.

Gramsci, A. *Selections from the Prison Notebooks of Antonio Gramsci*, eds Q. Hoare and G. Nowell Smith. New York, 1971.

Hall, S. *Culture, Media, Language*. London, 1980.

Laclau, E. *New Reflections on the Revolution of Our Time*. London, 1990.

—. 'Politics and the Limits of Modernity', in *Postmodernism*. London, 1993.

—. *The Making of Political Identities*. London, 1994.

—. *Emancipation(s)*. London, 1996.

— et al. *Contingency, Hegemony, Universality*. London, 2000.

—. 'Politics, Polemics and Academics: An Interview by Paul Bowman', *parallax*, 11, 1999.

— and Mouffe, C. *Hegemony and Socialist Strategy*. London, 1985.

Laplanche, J. and Pontalis, J.-B. *The Language of Psychoanalysis*. London, 1988.

Lechte, J. *Fifty Key Contemporary Theorists*. London, 1994.

Marx, K. and Engels, F. *The Communist Manifesto*. St Ives, 1967.

Mouffe, C. *The Return of The Political*. London, 1993.

— (ed.) *Deconstruction and Pragmatism*. London, 1996.

—. *The Challenge of Carl Schmitt*. London, 1999.

Mowitt, J. *Text: The Genealogy of an Antidisciplinary Object*. Durham, NC, 1992.

Smith, A. M. *Laclau and Mouffe*. London, 1998.

Torfing, J. *New Theories of Discourse*. London, 1999.

Weber, S. *Institution and interpretation*. Minneapolis, MN, 1987.

Žižek, S. *The Sublime Object of Ideology*. London, 1989.

23. Psychoanalysis in Literary and Cultural Studies

In 'In Memory of Sigmund Freud', W. H. Auden expresses the challenge represented by Freud to entrenched powers, to systems and structures that satisfied some by oppressing others, evidenced by the burning of Freud's books by the Nazi regime and by his death in exile. While it is by no means unique, this explicitly political reading of the significance of psychoanalysis is useful as the starting point for an exploration of the relationship between psychoanalysis and literary and cultural studies over the last sixty years. The poem reveals that which constitutes the core of the relationship. Auden celebrates Freud's lifework in part because he sees its effects – 'the fall of princes' – as analogous to those of poetry. Psychoanalysis, like poetry, has effects beyond its own boundaries as theory and practice. Indeed, for Auden, both poetry and psychoanalysis challenge the very boundaries that keep in place the political status quo. It is this analogy, its interactions, enmeshments and various consequences, that has come to dominate the current cultural use of psycho-analysis. In the contemporary life of the humanities in Britain, the relationship between psychoanalysis and cultural criticism is not that of a couple, but rather of a *ménage à trois*. To put this another way, if ideally the relationship between literary and cultural studies and psychoanalysis is that of a dialogue (Donald 1991, 3), what they speak to each other about is politics.

The difficulty with this *ménage*, however, is that none of the participants holds one position for very long. If literature and psychoanalysis occupy analogous positions in their relationships to politics, it can also be said that literary studies came to need psychoanalysis because of the revelation of its own political implications. As postwar Britain experienced a shift in terms of established loyalties, an expanding educational sector and the beginnings of a consumer culture, so an English studies dominated by Leavisite definitions of cultural value seemed less and less viable. Leavis had eschewed all approaches to literature, psychoanalytic criticism included, which privileged a pre-existing agenda over the literary work itself. In contrast, the work, among others, of Raymond Williams and Richard Hoggart in the 1950s concerned itself with making 'the experiences of ordinary people and the texture of everyday life. . . a legitimate and necessary focus of concern' (Donald 1991, 4) for explicitly political purposes. Rather than something to be defended against or 'cured' by Leavis's 'minority culture', working-class *culture* became itself an object of critical interest and a site of potential political change. As part of this challenge, traditional definitions of literary value were revealed as complicit with the operation of self-interest on the part of the powerful. 'Great' literature was that which upheld the status quo, which reconfirmed the validity of bourgeois privilege, which mystified economic determinacy. It is in these marxist critiques that British cultural studies originates and consequently so too does the problem of talking about a specifically 'literary' studies. Just as the position of English studies became established within the British academy, Williams and others began its undoing. It is less the texts themselves that come under scrutiny, rather the methods and values of the literary critical establishment.

The desire of critics such as Williams and Hoggart to focus on the 'everyday' and 'lived' experiences of 'ordinary people', both as individuals and collectively, would seem to overlap with psychoanalysis's concentration on the quotidian. The marxist critics of the 1950s too began to question orthodox explanations for the relationship between the individual and the social, between consciousness and history, between inside and outside. Their focus on working-class culture and identity forced a rereading and reinterpretation of literary and cultural production and of historical events. What they also did, however, was to assume that 'working-class identity', however sophisticated its critical construction, fitted neatly with individual consciousness; that indeed 'identity' as such was what was being observed. Here, rather than mirroring it, psychoanalysis, with its central concept of the unconscious, 'explodes the very idea of complete or achieved identity to which [the marxist critics] ascribe such critical and political importance' (Donald 1991, 5). The unconscious as theorized by psychoanalysis is that which does not fit, which exceeds our control, our reason, our ability to know. It is that which intrudes when it is least wanted, which undoes our mastery, which challenges the whole notion of identity. In his analysis of the Rat Man, Freud uses the concept of ambivalence to explain his patient's symptoms, in particular his habit of constructing long prayers to cover his unconscious wishes.

> This became clearly evident in our patient on one occasion, for the disturbing element did not remain unconscious but made its appearance openly. The words he wanted to use in his prayers were, '*May God protect her*', but a hostile '*not*' suddenly darted out of his unconscious and inserted itself into the sentence. (*SE*, 10, 242)

It is the presence of that 'not' wherein lies the 'not enough' of Williams's matching of politics with literary and cultural criticism; it is the explanation of that 'not' that constitutes the significance of psychoanalysis as a theory. While for later political positions it is precisely for this reason that use is made of psychoanalysis, what the application of psychoanalysis to such marxist analyses demonstrates is something that is repeated over and over in its conjunction with politics and cultural criticism. First, it is the place and definition of the unconscious that is of the essence (Rustin 1995, 241); second, any position that is predicated on the notion of the unconscious contains the seeds of its own undoing, of the revelation of its own 'not enough'. In the historical survey which follows, the relations between the participants in our *ménage à trois* are effects of the unconscious as much as of any theoretical choice, and as such undo, reform, regroup and shout 'not' at awkward moments. What is significant, though, is that each case, each position, each relation resists stasis, and, in its contradictions and paradoxes, points beyond. It is the theoretical possibilities and problematics of going 'beyond' in which the significance of psychoanalysis for literary and cultural studies in the British academy originated and by which it is still constituted – beyond common-sense ways of reading, beyond conventional categories, beyond the either/or of traditional debate. Further, it is this question of a going 'beyond' which forms psychoanalytic criticism's debates with other theoretical and critical positions, most significantly those with deconstruction.

The origins of the current importance of psychoanalysis in British literary and cultural studies can be found in the wider political and intellectual change of the 1960s. In part because of the expansion of higher education, the academy began to be seen as complicit with the establishment, and this cosy consensus was challenged from a number of positions. The belief that intellectual life produced 'objective knowledge' was revealed as a powerful fantasy by those who were not white or male or from a privileged class. Identity and its political implications began to move to the centre of debates in the humanities. Interest began to focus on its construction, its meaning, its place in continuing traditional divisions of privilege and power. Two things marked this as different from both earlier left-wing political analyses and from early marxist cultural criticism. First, analysis moved from a focus on economics, the 'base' in traditional marxist terms, to a consideration of culture, the 'superstructure', as also a determinant in the construction of the social world. Second, identity was no longer defined just as a matter of class, but of ethnicity, gender and sexuality, and an awareness grew that class-based methods could not simply be transferred unchanged to these. The question became: what part does culture play in constructing or challenging identities which perpetuate the status quo? As suggested above, however, previous attempts to unite cultural criticism and an explicit left-wing position had come unstuck around the very concept of identity. In the 1960s, the work of two structuralist analyses provided frameworks within which the question could begin to be answered; this work, taken together, suggested possibilities for the coming together of political and cultural analyses via a renewed psychoanalysis.

Jacques Lacan had begun his 'return to Freud', first within and then outside the French psychoanalytic institution, during the 1930s. His work only began to be more widely disseminated outside psychoanalytic training circles, however, in the 1960s, with the publication of *Écrits* in Paris (1966). Lacan reread Freud as a radical challenge to conventional assumptions about the stability of identity, the primacy of the conscious and the autonomy of the individual that had come to dominate the psychoanalytic institution, particularly in the United States. In the notions of, most particularly, the imaginary, the symbolic and the 'mirror stage', Lacanian psychoanalysis provided cogent readings of the self-deceiving properties of language and culture. Identity is acquired and constantly renewed, not only through the oppressive operations of an external force, but because it affirms the human subject. 'Identity', however seemingly negative or oppressive, is a product of fantasy. Moreover, identity is acquired through the subject's insertion into and subjection to the determining systems of the symbolic, pre-eminently that of language.

At around the same time the work of Louis Althusser, who had long been a significant presence in French intellectual life, became more widely known with the publication of *For Marx* (1965), an attempt to retrieve marxism from the, for Althusser, distorting grasp of Christianity, humanism and economic determinacy. From Freud's *The Interpretation of Dreams*, and via Lacan's rereading of Freud, Althusser took the concept of 'overdetermination' to explain the relation between the economic level and ideology, that is the cultural, the social, the linguistic. For Freud, the relation between the latent content and the manifest content of a dream is one of overdetermination, carried out through, principally, condensation and displacement. Further, this relation exists between unconscious wishes and each place where, in a disguised form, they force their way into the conscious – slips of the tongue, jokes, day dreams, hysterical symptoms. For Althusser, although the modes of production are determining in 'the last instance', their effects are not self-evident at the level of ideology, but rather have to be read symptomatically, that is to say, they must be *analysed*. Ideology functions, then, as a disguise; it

> represents in its necessarily imaginary distortion not the existing relations of production (and the other relations that derive from them), but above all the (imaginary) relationship of individuals to the relations of production and the relations that derive from them. (Althusser 1971, 155)

Crucially, what both Lacan and Althusser focus on in their structuralist rereadings of Freud and Marx is the determining function of language in the creation of the subject. Whereas previous cultural criticism from the left struggled with the notion of subjectivity, a renewed psychoanalysis and a renewed marxism seemed to offer a coherent theory of the relation between the individual and the social.

While some literary and cultural critics have made use of psychoanalytic traditions other than the Lacanian, such as Klein, Winnicott and Hanna Segal, which can be broadly described as humanist, this has occurred mainly in the American academy (see Holland 1990). It is Lacanian psychoanalysis that dominates intellectual life in Britain. More particularly, the pattern of engagement between literary and cultural studies and psychoanalysis in the last three decades of the twentieth century is incomprehensible without an understanding of the intellectual history of feminism. It is largely feminist politics that has driven forward psychoanalytic engagement with cultural criticism. Indeed, this situation can be seen in part as a result of the problems inherent in the left's appropriation of psychoanalysis. Althusser had taken from Freud an account of subjectivity that he saw as useful for his explication of ideology. However, of course, psychoanalysis is an account of the construction of a *gendered* identity, not a class-based one. Increasingly, the use of psychoanalysis in cultural criticism became dominated by feminism. In his introduction to a series of talks given at the ICA in 1987 on psychoanalysis and cultural theory, James Donald admits that 'psychoanalysis' in British intellectual debate means 'psychoanalysis after the feminist rereading of Lacan's rereading of Freud' (Donald 1991, 2).

The significance of this in a British intellectual life increasingly concerned with a political reading of identity and its relation to the social and cultural can be seen in *Feminism and Psychoanalysis* (1974) by Juliet Mitchell. During the late 1960s she was closely associated with the British journal *New Left Review* and with its importation of Althusser. As Mitchell makes clear in her introduction, the feminists of the early second wave, particularly in the United States, were almost unanimous in seeing Freud and psychoanalysis as the enemy. For Germaine Greer, for example, psychoanalysis may accurately describe femininity as constructed within patriarchy, but it does nothing to undermine, critique or dismantle it. Rather, the theories of Freud and his followers are 'a farrago of moralism and fantasy unillumined by any shaft of commonsense' (Greer 1981, 95). For Mitchell, however, to continue this rejection would be 'fatal' for feminism precisely because psychoanalysis provides a theoretical model at odds with commonsense. An analysis that asserts things as self-evident will inevitably find itself re-enmeshed with the operations of oppression. While Freud's practice may or may not have been conservative, his 'discovery' of the unconscious provides a radical *theory* which is vital as the basis of a truly radical politics. Without it, any political theory or activism will inevitably collapse back into oppressive notions of identity and self, ultimately oppressive because reliant on an essence rather than seeing identity as constructed. Significantly, Mitchell makes clear both the influence of Lacan's theories and the absolute necessity of using it in tandem with Althusserian marxism.

> So where Marxist theory explains the historical and economic situation, psychoanalysis, in conjunction with the notions of ideology already gained by dialectical materialism, is the way into understanding ideology and sexuality. (Mitchell 1974, xxii)

What is particularly significant about Mitchell's reading of the situation is her assertion of a positive correlation between an openness to psychoanalytic theory and feminism as a radical political agenda (1974, 297–9). Psychoanalysis is paired, then, not with bourgeois orthodoxy, but with radical critiques concerned to reveal at the deepest level the workings of capitalism and patriarchy.

Although Mitchell does not foreground language, a general outcome of this position for cultural criticism can be seen by comparing two feminist readings of the same novel. In *Sexual Politics*, Kate Millett sees psychoanalysis as merely 'cloth[ing] the old doctrine of the separate spheres in the fashionable language of science' (1985, 178). In her reading of Charlotte Brontë's *Villette* (1853) she is concerned to read the novel as subversive, as radical in its critique of patriarchy. However, without a notion of the unconscious, Millett is forced to do this, not only by a problematic reading of the main character, Lucy Snowe, as if she were a real woman, but more problematically still, by assuming that both Brontë and Lucy Snowe are in control, that they know what they are doing, that their actions and behaviour are the results of conscious choice. Anything that contradicts this reading is dismissed by Millett as Brontë's necessary compromise with orthodox Victorian sensibility, what she describes as 'mawkish nonsense' (1985, 147). In comparison, Mary Jacobus' reading of the novel, which sees both it and literature in general as the reserve of both the repressed and its uncanny return, finds that it is at these very moments of 'nonsense' that the subversive, destabilizing effects of the novel are located (Jacobus 1987, 41–2). Significantly, what is being analysed is neither character nor writer, but *language*; *Villette* is 'a text formally fissured by its own repressions' (41). Psychoanalysis shows how, because of the effects of repression, things both say and do not say at the same time. Without this, criticism will merely repeat the obfuscations of ideology – in this case that reasoned choice is the foundation of political subversion. What this comparison makes clear then is the centrality of the unconscious for political readings of cultural products.

> The force of the psychoanalytic metaphor in this discourse derived from the idea that ideology was most effective when its distortions, its one-sidedness, its silences, and omissions became implicit and taken-for-granted routines, not depending on overt prohibition. (Rustin 1995, 229–30)

Interestingly, despite Mitchell's very early use of Lacan, it was American feminist writers that produced the first full-length attempts to work together Lacanian psychoanalysis, feminism and literary and cultural criticism. Shoshana Felman and Jane Gallop, in particular, developed sophisticated critical positions aware of the relationships *between* the three discourses, rather than taking for granted the usefulness of one as a meta-discourse. However, the feminism of Felman and Gallop lacks the materialist base of the dominant strands of British feminism, and as a result their use of psychoanalysis can seem a matter of hermeneutics rather than politics. So, for example, in her *Feminism and Psychoanalysis* (1982), Gallop criticizes Mitchell for her implicit assumption that together feminism and psychoanalysis point the way unproblematically to a political *practice*. In Mitchell's final claims for psychoanalysis, then, it would seem that she has forgotten the very thing which began her assertion of its necessity – the unconscious. In Gallop's own work, then, rather than making claims for psychoanalytic models of social change, she instead suggests 'attending to the odd truths revealed in the accidental material of language' (Gallop 1982, 29). For Gallop and Felman, Lacan's importance is as a theorist of language, and it is as a hermeneutics that it is potentially radical.

In Britain in the 1970s and early 1980s, feminist analyses using Lacanian psychoanalysis were most visible in politically radical interventions into and critiques of culture which went beyond the traditional focus of British literary criticism. The feminist journal *m/f*, co-founded by Parveen Adams and Elizabeth Cowie and published between 1978 and 1986, was the forum for many of the central debates, in particular the continued friction between the role of subjectivity and the place of materialist, class-based critiques. What the work published in *m/f* makes clear, though, is that this relation, however fraught, had come to occupy a pre-eminent place in intellectual critical debate. A 'pure' psychoanalytic criticism had become impossible in the British context.

The tensions and debates generated by this can be seen very clearly in another journal, *Screen* (which included Elizabeth Cowie on its editorial board, and published the work of, among others, Juliet Mitchell, Jacqueline Rose, Stephen Heath and Colin MacCabe), in particular the way in which a feminist political position sharpens the focus of a more general relation between psychoanalysis and cultural criticism. So, for example, in Laura Mulvey's seminal 'Visual Pleasure and Narrative Cinema', which first appeared in *Screen* in 1975, Lacanian psychoanalysis is explicitly used as a 'political weapon' to challenge the reproduction of the status quo through the 'magic' of the cinema (6). At the same time, however, Mulvey challenges *Screen* itself for ignoring 'the importance of the representation of the female form' and at the end suggests the implications of her analysis for feminist and other sorts of radical film-making (see essay on *Screen* for more detailed discussion of this). What Mulvey's intervention suggests, though, is that 'total', stable critical position is likely somewhere to be covering up its partial, self-interested position. Of course, it is this insight into and theorization of the non-rational in rational thought for which psychoanalysis is primarily responsible. What can be seen in the history of its use in the humanities in Britain is an acting out of this very insight.

A further inflection of this jostling for position can be seen in Lola Young's *Fear of the Dark: 'Race', Gender and Sexuality in the Cinema* (1996). Citing Mulvey's article, Young suggests how 'race' has been left out of feminist debates *because* of the latter's relation with psychoanalysis and its privileging of gender. Mulvey, she argues, in attempting to work out this relation ignores historical perspectives, does not differentiate between women and is oblivious to the extent to which her essay is about *white* people (16–17). Despite this, Young herself makes use of psychoanalysis in her theoretical framework because, she argues, materialist explanations of racial oppression privilege class over race and are unable to explain 'how the power relations embedded in textual systems and forms of representation may be unconsciously sustained' (17). On the other hand, she argues, critics who use psychoanalysis to unpick the construction of 'race' in cultural representation have ignored the difference that gender makes. Young criticizes the work of Homi K. Bhabha for this, and for precisely the absence of a materialist analysis.

> Bhabha does not express reservations about the use of psychoanalysis as a cultural theory: neither does he refer to any difficulty or tension which might exist because of what might be characterized as the cultural and temporal specificity of psychoanalytic theory or its lack of an historical and materialist base. (Young 1996, 29)

What is significant is that Young argues that the absence of a gender-based analysis *allows* Bhabha's other theoretical and methodological failings. To put it another way, it is the repression of one aspect that makes possible a supposedly water-tight theoretical position. Again, we see the insights of psychoanalysis being acted out in the very discourses that use psychoanalytic methods.

In the British context, the attempt to create a politically engaged critical position which uses psychoanalysis to investigate cultural representation without covering over these problematics finds its exemplar in the work of Jacqueline Rose. Situated at the intersection of psychoanalysis, feminist theory and literary studies, it attempts to use the insights of each to interrogate each from an explicitly political position and resists the use of any one discourse as a 'meta-discourse' (Rose 1993, 242–3). In 1982 Rose co-edited and, with Juliet Mitchell, translated and provided one of the introductions for a collection of articles by Lacan and other members of the *école freudienne*, most of which had not appeared in English before (Mitchell and Rose 1982). As well as contributing practically to the debate around Lacan's work in British intellectual life, what both introductions insist upon is that, rather than being just one aspect, debates about feminine sexuality have constructed psychoanalytic theory and psychoanalytic traditions as we know them. Its significance for feminist theory and practice is, then, incontrovertible. In her subsequent work, though, what is clear is that, while the concept of the unconscious is absolutely central, and is used, as in Lacan, to resist any normalizing focus on the ego, she resists any idealization of it as an 'outside' of oppressive political structures, as some feminist engagements with psychoanalysis have done, 'whether as writing or pre-oedipally or both' (Rose 1993, 42). In this way, Rose's work can be seen as different from and critiquing aspects of French feminism, for example *écriture féminine*. Rose's use of Melanie Klein in the 1990s has been a way of countering this idealization through an investigation of aggression and violence that does not just place it at the door of an 'external' patriarchy (1993, 41–71). While critiquing the position that sees 'woman's writing' as inherently subversive, though, Rose allows the language of the literary text its own interpretative status, its own strangeness and difficulty. Rose's *The Haunting of Sylvia Plath* (1991) is a celebrated example of this type of reading, and its exemplary position is shown by selections from it being included in a number of anthologies on psychoanalysis and literary criticism.

> In Rose's work, poetry and theory, feminism and psychoanalysis, politics and fantasy meet without either identifying with the other or affirming identity against the other. The assurance of stable identity that forgets the aberrant ways of sexuality, the fantasies of culture, or the autocracy of patriarchy has in her work been subjected to a sustained and eloquent critique. (Rose 1993, 12)

She is keen, though, not to privilege the literary sphere, for which she again criticizes a number of French theoretical positions (1993, 238), in particular that of Kristeva, and her work includes analysis of the visual, popular culture and contemporary political culture. It shows a nuanced and delicate balance between the critical discourses with which she engages.

However, the problem for feminism and indeed all politically engaged critical positions is that the psychoanalytic questioning of the constructions of identity lessens the possibility of the assertion of autonomous identity, and points to an impossibility in organizing politically around such claims. For example, Rose's claim that '[t]he question of identity is . . . the central issue through which psychoanalysis enters the political field' (1986, 5) partly informs her critique of Derrida's critique of psychoanalysis and of deconstruction generally (1986, 19–23). For example, deconstruction cannot answer the question of 'how we can begin to think the question of violence and fantasy as something that implicates us as women' (Rose 1993, 106). However, on the other hand, her answer to the charge from cultural materialist feminists (Rose 1986, 11–12) that psychoanalysis does not provide adequate models of social change insists that it is vital for feminism because of its very questioning of the limits of subjectivity. A rejection of this would mean that oppression is sent out 'wholesale into the real from which it can only return as an inevitable and hallucinatory event' (1993, 106).

If politically radical critical positions have been responsible for the primacy of Lacanian psychoanalysis in literary and cultural studies over the last three decades, then in this relation can also be seen their discomfort. The question of whether anti-humanist positions can really inform radical political praxis remains. In Terry Eagleton's chapter on Freud in *The Ideology of the Aesthetic*, after a cogent analysis of the political implications of the superego and of the Freudian notion of desire, and of Freud's challenge to a separate realm of the aesthetic, the argument strangely retreats to an assertion of the transformative possibilities of morality or love. Freud is criticized for concentrating too much on Eros and not enough on Agape (Eagleton 1990, 284). In the end, as a resolution, Eagleton implies a distinction between Freud's theories and psychoanalysis as a practice. Freud provides no political solution to the problems of authority and aggression, but '[t]o acquire a more reciprocal, egalitarian style of loving is thus one of the goals of psychoanalysis as it is of revolutionary politics' (1990, 285). The problem here is that psychoanalysis is being forced to answer something, to solve something.

> Both Marxism and feminism, then, in incorporating psychoanalysis, have tried to use it as a way of articulating the individual with the social, or subjectivity with society. But they then tend to get caught up in acting out the conflict between the psychic and the social, rather than, as psychoanalysis itself does, producing a theory of that incompatibility. The lesson of psycho-analysis is that they have to be lived simultaneously as two irreconcilable positions – which is why we have an unconscious. (Donald 1991, 142)

It may be, however, that some kind of re-engagement with psychoanalysis as a practice will be the next set of repositionings in our ménage, indeed that it has already begun (Rose 1993, 255; Shamdasani 1994). British psychoanalysis has remained mostly impervious to the debates within the humanities. Any therapy cannot but retain some connection to the idea of cure, and since the structuralist and marxist challenges of the 1960s, the questioning of literary value, of the 'healing' possibilities of aesthetics and of a stabilizing identity has made crossover between the two unlikely. It may be that the feminist questioning and reformulation of psychoanalytic orthodoxies is located in the academy because of the inflexibility of psychoanalytic institutions themselves. However, what this survey has shown is that the profound importance of psychoanalytic theory is due to its ability to contain and explain contradictions, impossibilities, the presence and not-presence of that 'not' discussed above, and to describe a 'place' between two seemingly bounded positions, thereby unsettling them both. The poles of the ultimate failure of interpretation and of interpretation as cure are present indeed in Freud's work; it is perhaps time for a renegotiation of their mutual impossibility.

Leigh Wilson

Further reading and works cited

Adams, P. and Cowie, E. (eds) *The Woman in Question*. Cambridge, MA, 1990.
Althusser, L. *Lenin and Philosophy and Other Essays*. London, 1971.
Auden, W. H. *Collected Poems*. London, 1976.
Brennan, T. (ed.) *Between Feminism and Psychoanalysis*. London, 1989.
Donald, J. (ed.) *Psychoanalysis and Cultural Theory: Thresholds*. London, 1991.
Eagleton, T. *The Ideology of the Aesthetic*. Oxford, 1990.
Easthope, A. *Literary into Cultural Studies*. London, 1991.
—. *The Unconscious*. London, 1999.
Elliott, A. and Frosh, S. (eds) *Psychoanalysis in Contexts*. London, 1995.
Ellman, M. (ed.) *Psychoanalytic Literary Criticism*. London, 1994.
Freud, S. *The Standard Edition of the Complete Psychological Works of Sigmund Freud*, eds J. Strachey and A. Freud, 24 vols. London.
—. 'Notes upon a case of obsessional neurosis', *Standard Edition*, vol. 10, 1909.
Gallop, J. *Feminism and Psychoanalysis*. Basingstoke, 1982.
Greer, G. *The Female Eunuch*. London, 1981.
Holland, N. N. *Holland's Guide to Psychoanalytic Psychology and Literature-and-Psychology*. New York, 1990.
Jacobus, M. *Reading Women*. London, 1987.
Lacan, J. *Ecrits: A Selection*. London, 1977a.
—. *The Four Fundamental Concepts of Psycho-analysis*. London, 1977b.

—. 'Desire and the Interpretation of Desire in Hamlet', in *Literature and Psychoanalysis*, ed. S. Felman. Baltimore, MD, 1982.

—. 'Seminar on "The Purloined Letter" ', in *The Purloined Poe*, eds J. P. Muller and W. J. Richardson. Baltimore, MD, 1988.

Lechte, J. (ed.) *Writing and Psychoanalysis*. London, 1996.

Millett, K. *Sexual Politics*. London, 1985.

Mitchell, J. *Psychoanalysis and Feminism*. London, 1974.

— and Rose, J. (eds) *Feminine Sexuality*. London, 1982.

Mulvey, L. *Visual Pleasure and Narrative Cinema*. London, 1989.

Rose, J. *Sexuality in the Field of Vision*. London, 1986.

—. *The Haunting of Sylvia Plath*. London, 1991.

—. *Why War?* Oxford, 1993.

Rustin, M. 'Lacan, Klein and Politics: The Positve and Negative in Psychoanalytic Thought', in *Psychoanalysis in Contexts*, eds A. Elliott and S. Frosh. London, 1995.

Shamdasani, S. 'Introduction', in *Speculations After Freud*, eds S. Shamdasani and M. Münchow. London, 1994.

Wright, E. *Psychoanalytic Criticism*. Cambridge, 1998.

Young, L. *Fear of the Dark*. London, 1996.

Young, R. 'Psychoanalysis and Political Literary Theories', in *Psychoanalysis and Cultural Theory: Thresholds*. London, 1991.

24. Feminism, Materialism and the Debate on Postmodernism in British Universities

While there are obvious dangers in classifying a number of theoretical endeavours in terms of national boundaries, we can probably safely agree with the American feminist Alice Jardine that there is a delicate '*pas-de-deux*' of current American and French feminist, or post-feminist, theory and also agree with Toril Moi that this dance excludes certain strands of materialist feminist theory, more often associated with British feminism. Yet both 'transatlantic' and British feminism are informed by radical feminism and radical feminism has itself been described as Anglo-American. Interestingly, each theory has, for a variety of reasons, claimed to be materialist. There are three main meanings of the term 'materialism' that concern us in this essay: realism, physicalism and historical or dialectical materialism. Toril Moi once said that 'a feminist intellectual is one who seeks to stress her own politics, not one who seeks to replace it with geography'. This essay will aim to keep these materialisms conceptually distinct while showing that the exclusion from the dance of the type of materialism, linked not only with British feminist theory but also socialist feminism, leads to a form of postmodernism which aims to be one of resistance but which must end up being merely concerned with the mechanics of signification.

The first form of materialism (M1) can be identified as a realism about the existence of a mind-independent world. A materialist, in this sense, need not believe that there is direct access to that world nor need they dismiss the existence of consciousness. We should not confuse materialism with empiricism. The term empirical usually denotes the belief that a proposition can be confirmed or denied by immediate sense experience. Empiricism attempts to tie knowledge to experience in such a way that anything that cannot be immediately before the senses, or inferred from the class of things observed to be true, is not considered to be a legitimate road of inquiry. This means that we must distinguish between empiricism and scientific analysis.

The second form of materialism that concerns us is often linked with physicalism (M2) and is prevalent in the philosophy of mind and cognitive sciences. It is the theory that because cognition is a matter of computational data processing, the best way to approach the human mind is as though it were a computer. Behaviour is understood as being caused by internal mental states and these mental states are thought to be reducible to physical processes or brain states. Within the philosophy of mind there is a tendency towards reductionism, the belief that one science can be better explained by a more general, lower level, science but this is not unproblematic.

Dialectical or historical materialism (M3) is the final form of materialism that is of interest to us and its most famous exponents were Marx and Engels. It was first fashioned as a response to Hegel's idealism. This is basically the doctrine that the world is essentially a mental construct or image and is contrasted with the common-sense realist view that there is something 'out there', mind-independent and distinct from the perceiver. Marx, though, does concede that the human world is fashioned from human activity but makes a sharp distinction between this sort of production and the 'production' of concepts or thinking. Consciousness, ideas and concepts, according to Marx, result from the social experience of production. Production itself takes various forms and changes over time and therefore our social experience must also alter.

The second aspect of Marx's materialism relates to his methodology and can be referred to as a 'context principle'. Taking from Hegel the idea that each thing needs to be understood in its relationships with other things, Marx 'turned Hegel on his head' and argued that the relations between things are not conceptual but are historical and social. To grasp what a thing is we must first place it in its context which is at once social, political and historical. Any attempt to analyse a thing abstracted from its context will lead to erroneous, and often ideological, judgement. Historical materialism is thus a theory of relations such that individual identity can be seen to be a consequence of antecedent social processes.

Lastly, the term 'materialism' in historical materialism conveys a commitment to a scientific method of inquiry. This brings the two previous points together. It is the belief that there is a 'mind-independent' world, that events in that world can only be understood in context and that the situation of the knower might well effect knowledge claims. The scientific hypothesis includes within its explanatory framework abstract entities such as 'the family', 'state' and 'culture' and these entities are taken to designate something actual. Economic, social and psychological processes are presumed to be open to scientific assessment, but because they are processes only a method which can accommodate change, non-conformity and difference has sufficient explanatory potential. The appropriate scientific method is dialectical and the underlying epistemic position fallibilist; we can make truth claims with the understanding that what counts as true now might well alter over time.

Materialist feminism has been defined as a synthesis of postmodern, Anglo-French, feminism and socialist, British, feminism. For any synthesis to be even possible we must allow that postmodernism and marxism are not incommensurable theories. 'Postmodernism' has been defined as a historical era corresponding to a new mode of production, post-fordism, and as an 'attitude', a new way of thinking about, and experiencing, modernity. The point of contention is whether or not it is possible to adopt a new attitude, to break from specific patterns of thought, while our social and political context remains the same, if, indeed, it does. Benhabib encourages us to separate postmodernisms into 'strong' and 'weak'. The former postmodernists, with the exception of Derrida, tend to believe that it is possible to adopt a 'postmodern' attitude even if our socio-economic climate is still modernist. Strong postmodernism is a response to specific philosophies of language and tends to extreme relativism. According to Benhabib, feminist theory can ally itself with it only at the risk of incoherence and self-contradictoriness. Weak postmodernism is an attempt to combine realism with a number of postmodern insights, specifically the relevance of the context principle to questions of epistemology (1992, 213–30). I shall be arguing that unless we take the softest form of postmodernism then the theories are indeed incommensurable, due to disagreements over what counts as 'materialism' and thus to divergent accounts of 'the real context'. The *pas-de-deux* is necessarily an exclusive dance.

Kristeva, in her now seminal essay 'Women's Time', argues that the feminist movement can be divided into three distinct phases (1982, 31–53). The first phase is associated with liberal and existentialist feminism, the second with radical and socialist feminism and the third with postmodernism. Liberal and existentialist theorists have shared a surprising number of political assumptions and political aspirations. They believed that the political demands for rights and inclusion in the decision-making processes ought to be central to a feminist politics. Because they shared a philosophical lineage, liberal and existentialist feminists, such as Wollstonecraft, Taylor, de Beauvoir and, more recently, Radcliffe Richards, agreed that there is no relevant difference between the two sexes and that the human subject is essentially rational. Any marked differences between men and women can thus be explained as the consequence of education or the general cultural milieu. Because they considered the property of rationality to be the only quality relevant for participation in political decision-making processes, they also believed that there could be no plausible argument for the exclusion of women. For this reason, the first phase of feminism has been described as one which promoted the moral equality of autonomous rational agents.

British materialist feminism is associated with the second wave of feminism. The symbolic beginning of the second wave has often been assumed to be 1968. In Britain it is coupled with the first national conference of the Women's Liberation Movement at Ruskin College in 1970. The four simple demands, adopted at Ruskin, were equal pay, equal education and opportunity, twenty-four-hour nurseries, free contraception and abortion on demand. Later conferences added demands for financial and legal independence, an end to discrimination against lesbians, a woman's right to choose her own sexuality and freedom from intimidation and violence (1974, 1978). From the 1970s we can detect a change in emphasis from the liberal or existentialist political agenda to a much broader set of political goals and strategies. This can, in part, be explained by the influence of left politics from the 1960s onwards. Liberal, socialist and radical politics coexisted, within the women's movement of the 1970s, with ecofeminism, peace campaigns and anarchism. Underlying the change was a general acceptance that women had never been simply excluded from the social contract. Modern social structures, it was agreed, managed to include women in the political order in such a way that formal demands could be met without the substantial changes that it had been thought would necessarily follow.

The second wave of feminism began with an analysis of these structures. Influenced by

American feminist theorists such as Friedan, Millett and Firestone, radical feminists began to analyse the family, sexuality and forms of cultural representations. They concluded that the political gains of the first wave had been quite empty because traditional structures and values had been left in place and it was these very structures which defined the roles of men and women and gave femininity and masculinity different values. Radical feminists can be divided into two broad camps: essentialists and anti-essentialists. Men and women, it was agreed, are allocated different categories of activities, considered useful or socially necessary for social production or reproduction. A generally held rationale for this was that certain types of work can be identified with certain behavioural characteristics or dispositions (gender). The argument was whether or not these traits can be thought to be caused by primary or secondary sexual characteristics (sex) or whether sex and gender were brought together through various social processes, including educational and religious practices, family, labour and the learning of conceptual schemes. This was, therefore, a disagreement as to the role and type of causal processes involved in the oppression of women.

Radical feminism is characteristically concerned with the differences between men and women, differences in power and authority as well as different dispositions and character-istics. Essentialists and anti-essentialists agreed that the liberal political slogan 'equal but different' obviously mystifies the base fact that masculinity is valued over femininity and men are guaranteed sanctioned domination over women. The structures themselves would need to be revised and revised according to different values. Some argued that the appropriate values were those associated with femininity. Others argued that characteristics associated with femininity were a product of the very system to be replaced, hence a 'revaluation of all values' was required. But connecting these arguments was a real belief in the moral equality and value of men and women. This belief in the 'metaphysical' equality of all human beings existed side by side with the belief that the two sexes are biologically different and the belief that because social systems change over time, the type of human subject who is a result of such social processes, their abilities and characteristics, also changes. This theory of the changing human subject inaugurated a break from the 'abstract individualism' of the liberal and existentialist project and this would, in the end, remove from the feminist project its ability to sustain a defensible moral position.

We can see that a number of questions concerning the nature of patriarchy and the causal origins of oppression perplexed second wave feminists during the 1970s. Socialist and marxist feminists were not inured from such arguments raging within the women's movement. Fundamentally they wished to analyse the material structures of patriarchy and capitalism but had to first decide whether or not patriarchy should be analysed as a set of social institutions distinct from capitalism, with its own history and its own causal origins. Dual systems theorists argued that patriarchy and capitalism are two distinct systems that may, or may not, intersect. Unified systems theorists argued that capitalism and patriarchy can be seen as a set of social relations and that therefore one conceptual scheme ought to be adequate. In a nutshell, the problem was how to explain the relation of production to reproduction: whether women's subordination to men is an effect of economic depen-dency, a dependency that is the result of women's role in sexual reproduction, a role that is required by capitalism or whether economic dependency is another facet of a more general system of male power and that this might or might not coincide with a specific organization of labour defined as capitalism. This discussion came to a head in the domestic labour debate of the 1970s. The argument concerned the function of domestic labour and its role in the reproduction of capitalism.

The initial argument was between those who drew on Engel's speculative comments about the pre-capitalist sexual division of labour and those who argued that sex-based labour roles were brought about by capitalism. Within the marxist frame of reference, this argument was significant for only those involved in productive labour; those producing commodities and surplus labour were considered to be part of the revolutionary class. The Wages for Housework Campaigners argued that domestic labour indeed produces a commodity which is central to capitalism – labour power. For this reason, Selma James, Dalla Costa and others proposed a domestic wage. Apart from signalling the productive nature of domestic labour, the proposal was also designed to cut at the heart of the assumption that the principal, or male, wage earner was paid a family wage. This point intersected with arguments being made by various dual systems theorists such as Juliet Mitchell and Mary McIntosh. Not only had no man ever been paid a 'family wage', it was argued, but also the very idea of the family wage hid the fact that many women were either primary or important, if supplementary, earners and that women were paid less than men for work 'of the same value'. Inevitably these views threw the socialist and marxist feminist movement into conflict with the trade union and labour movement. As Bea Cambell and Val Charlton wrote in 1979: 'the labour movement has managed to combine a commitment to equal pay with a commitment to the family wage, you can't have both'.

Marxist feminists recognized that the categories of economic analysis tended to reduce questions of power to the simple matter of who owned and controlled the means of production and who had surplus labour extracted. Setting themselves the task of redressing this, marxist feminists tried to identify the operation of gender relations as and where they may be distinct from, or connected with, the process of production and reproduction, understood by historical materialism. The marxist concepts of exploitation, alienation and the labour theory of value, with the implied exchange principle, were worked through theoretical explanations to clarify just how the intricate relationship between 'the private' and 'the public' was entwined through, and dependent upon, material conditions. The term 'material conditions' refers to a mind-independent set of practices which can be analysed scientifically but which, in turn, affect our ideas and beliefs. The analysis provoked heated debate due to the obvious inclination to separate the base, economic structures, from the superstructural beliefs, the family, forms of cultural representations, but, at the same time, to think of the two in a continual process of (dialectical) interaction.

As pointed out by Sheila Rowbotham and Veronica Beechey, dual systems theorists, often referred to as socialist feminists, had a tendency to be softer on marxism. This was because they could accommodate gender analysis within an exposition of patriarchy, rather than forcing the economic analysis of marxism to answer the questions outlined above. Mitchell contended that the two systems are theoretically irreducible and argued that there had been a tendency in marxism towards reductionism, such that the function and role of reproduction, sexuality and socialization were taken to be determined by the economic base (Mitchell 1971). The merits of this particular interpretation of marxism aside, it is instructive to see a number of questions being posed concerning the acquisition of mature subject identity. If we accept that an adult subject will actually desire things that will, in effect, maintain the current social organization and if we believe that the congruence of sex, gender and sexual orientation is the result of various processes that secure desires and that our sense of who we are depends on these beliefs, desires and behaviours then it makes sense to look for a theory which describes ways in which the individual is assigned a place in the social order. By extending and developing Marx's account of ideology it seemed possible to make some sense of women's 'false consciousness' (Barrett 1988). For this reason various dual systems theorists looked to Althusserian marxism and hoped to find in his theory of 'interpellation' an account of ideology which would be able to explain the exigencies but force of patriarchal ideology. Mitchell herself tried to combine insights of structural linguistics with psychoanalysis, to flesh out an analysis of the development of subject identity. Her argument is that women's relation to production, low pay, part-time work and economic dependency is a cause of oppression but that this operates in tandem with biosocial considerations and more general ideas circulating in society concerning masculinity and femininity (Mitchell 1974). Her psychoanalytic analysis of patriarchy, the supposed transition from monocausal to polyvalent analyses, has been called non-materialist because it is concerned with ideas, feelings and the unconscious. But this is to mistake, rather than to criticize, the Freudian insistence on psychoanalysis as a science and is a simplistic understanding of the meaning of the term 'materialism'.

Radical feminist ideas about the complex nature of subject identity, and the ways in which heterosexuality functions to maintain social stability, influenced the arguments between dual and unified systems theorists (Keohane, in Kristeva 1982, 1–30). Issues relating to sexuality were brought to the fore of the political agenda by work in women's refuges and rape crisis centres and around pornography, and culminated in the separatist and political lesbianism debates of the middle 1970s to early 1980s (Evans 1995, 54–74). These arguments, centring on subject identity and sexuality, occurred as the British left, most notably the *New Left Review*, moved onto a philosophical terrain that could accommodate psychoanalysis and theories concerning the cultural significance of various forms of representation. This move, especially that of Juliet Mitchell and Jacqueline Rose into Lacanian psychoanalysis, was not uncontested, for example by Parveen Adams in *m/f*, but from it rose a curious hybrid of literary and cultural studies. Although two schools of literary criticism are often distinguished, the French and the Anglo-American, it has been suggested that this is to overplay the part of British feminist theory. Instead, and unsurprisingly given the history of feminist theory, what we find is that British feminist theory contributes to the international debate mainly through its sociologists and cultural theorists. The development of cultural theory in Britain was largely guided by Hoggart and Hall, who founded and ran the Centre for Contemporary Cultural Studies (CCCS) at Birmingham University. Lovell suggests that the convergence of textual with sociohistorical analysis made cultural studies a natural habitat for feminist theory.

Cultural studies has a tendency towards eclecticism and humanist and economist readings of Marx were replaced by an interest in 'marxian' theorists such as Gramsci, Althusser, Lacan, Barthes and Foucault. Perhaps the most important question at the time was whether or not a socialist history could incorporate a historicized notion of human subjectivity. Those such as Cora Kaplan warned that unless semioticians and psychoanalytic theorists retained their materialist and class analyses they would end up producing no more than 'an anti-humanist avant-garde version of romance'. Thus, the critique of the subject, the idea that apparent unified subject identity is actually a consequence of antecedent linguistic and psychosexual processes, led to a series of arguments about the nature of psychoanalysis. Marxism and psychoanalysis share three basic characteristics. They present themselves as scientific and materialist, they question the viability of the idea of value-free scientific method and they are interested in the socialized human subject. However, although marxism and psychoanalysis are concerned with processes of change, conflict and resolution, there is fundamental disagreement as to the nature of the processes in question. Those influenced by psychoanalytic theory argued that marxists socialized structures which caused conflict and aggression and that their explanations of commodity fetishism and ideology were profoundly one dimensional. Marxists argued that psycho-analysis naturalized human motivation and posited invariant and universal psychic structures. In effect, marxists argued that psychoanalysis was an individualized response to the misery of alienation and that the abstraction of the experience of alienation from its context resulted in a theory of individual reconciliation to the status quo.

The philosophical argument over the 'principle of identity' was a fairly natural consequence of, or at least a fellow traveller with, 'identity politics' and signalled a move from psychoanalytically influenced cultural theory into postmodernism: Kristeva's third wave. The philosophical argument was that the belief in subject identity, the autonomous rational agent of liberalism, the proletariat of marxism or the individual of radical feminism was premised on a prior commitment to an ontology of natural kinds underlying certain forms of materialism or to principles of rational, logical identity, underlying forms of rationalism. Individuals, postmoderns argued, are subsumed under general concepts according to features which they supposedly share. These concepts become organizational categories, according to which bodies are subjected to various regimes of power. Influenced by Derrida, Kristeva, Cixous and Irigaray poststructuralist feminists argued that radical and marxist feminists used this principle of identity and this explained how they suppressed varieties of experiences and silenced the women who did not conform to their cognitive framework: black women, lesbian women and working-class women. The critique of the subject hence led to an investigation of the differences between men and women, differences within the group 'women' and differences embodied in 'one' woman. Feminist theory became aligned with a method of reading, a way to uncover the hidden or suppressed Other in texts. This, in turn, became a matter of looking at the ways in which meaning is constructed and values percolated through language and texts. Thus we have a radical break from realism (M1) and a separation of the term 'materialism' from 'scientific analysis'. Questions concerning representation became questions about 'reality' itself.

Identity theory made its appearance in the 1980s, theoretically prefigured by the pivotal role of experience, almost an extreme form of empiricism, in radical feminism, the left turn to psychoanalytic marxism in the 1970s and French literary criticism. At the same time 'identity politics' was making its appearance felt on the national political stage. The 1980s saw a tremendous change in the political culture of Britain. There was an intricate and complicated relationship between the rise of Thatcherism, 'free market' fiscal policy, left disunity and the demise of feminism as a political force. It has been suggested that what distinguishes and shapes British feminism is its roots in the high levels of working-class action in the 1960s and 1970s (Rowbotham 1990). And during the 1980s, with a number of extremely important exceptions, including the Miner's Strike and anti-Section 28 demonstrations, there was a general decline in trade union and labour activity. However, a contributory factor in the demise of feminism as a political force were the tensions within the Women's Liberation Movement that had been brewing for over a decade. Conflicts between radical and socialist feminists, between middle-class and working-class feminists, between black feminists and white feminists, heterosexual and lesbian feminists were played out in local organizations, at conferences and through the editorial boards of *Spare Rib*, *Trouble and Strife* and the *Feminist Review*. These conflicts forced feminists into recognizing their own location and acknowledging the universalizing tendencies within feminist thought itself. Suddenly, it was no longer feasible to argue that just because an individual had a certain sexed body s/he ought to align with a particular political movement, and the goals of feminism as a political movement became hard to justify. This recognition occurred as divisions concerning the appropriate place for feminist activity became entrenched. Some, such as Sheila Rowbotham and Hilary Wainwright, attempted to transform labour politics from within, while others argued that a more open and democratic political movement was incompatible with old-style labour or workers' political groups.

Corresponding to this demise of feminism as a political force was a consolidation of academic feminism (Oakley and Mitchell 1986). Academic feminism has, in turn, been described as a deradicalization of feminist theory and this has been linked to the rise of 'municipal feminism', the filtering through of women and feminist theory into public institutions, including, but not exclusively, those of Higher Education (Lovenduski and Randall 1993). There are two main reasons why an increase in the mass of women in Higher Educational Institutions could be causally related to a deradicalization of feminist theory. The first refers us to the ways in which the institutional body manages to exert a determining influence on the type of work done. The second refers us to the type of academic theory which became prevalent. To take the first. An institution can be defined as a form of physical organization which includes sedimented relations of power and lines of funding management. A certain 'norm' of academic practice and an image of an 'ideal' academic practitioner filter through. The rules of academic practice constrain and inform the content of the subject matter itself (Garry and Pearsall 1989, 1–46). In addition to these problems which are endemic to all forms of academic inquiry, as women's studies courses were gaining ground, the vicious spending cuts and actualization programmes of the 1980s and 1990s took place. There is a prima facie case for arguing that the type of academic work which was done was the type which could be safely funded and published.

The second explanation for the deradicalization of theory concerns the nature of the theory itself. Identity politics and theory have provided strategic and theoretical problems. It has been argued that feminist discourses of difference pulled the rug from under feminism as politics (Soper 1990). This is for two main reasons. Firstly, once the diversity of women is recognized and privileged over community, any sort of collective and goal-directed action becomes problematic. Secondly, the substance of feminist theory became itself and the purpose of theory became the reflection upon and the interrogation of internal divisions and conflicting subject positions (Whelehen 1995). The type of feminist theory inhabiting cultural and media and English departments was directly influenced by psycho-analytic literary theory, which, in effect, amounted to a rejection of realism (M1). Various arguments blossomed. If feminist theory could be reduced to a way of reading then women could no longer claim a privileged standpoint and men could justifiably call themselves 'feminist' (Jardine and Smith 1987). If feminism was still a political practice what were its goals? Due to its rejection of the values of modernity and to its anti-realism in ethics, feminist strategy had to be limited to the demonstration of the vagueness or fluidity of conceptual discrimination. The only aim left was to experience, perhaps desire, outside the parameters of western logic. This return to the 'body' or 'embodiedness' had every claim to materialism but without any sort of realist purchase.

If we abandon our realist commitments in epistemology, it becomes extremely difficult to argue, with any conviction, about the causal origins, effects and even nature of material practices. Against the grain, some, such as Liz Stanley, Michèle Barrett and Alison Assiter, have attempted to revise traditional epistemology, in light of feminist criticisms, and to take subjectivity into account while retaining a form of realism. Along with Benhabib, we can call this a form of 'soft' postmodernism. Others have responded by using 'discourse analysis' as proposed by Foucault, in the belief that he successfully keeps an idea of material social conditions but manages to marry this with the recognition of the located and social nature of knowledge claims and an anti-essentialism (Shildrick 1997). This appears to be materialist (M3) but due to its rejection of realism (M1) is actually unable to justify its own descriptions.

In conclusion, it is clear that feminism is fundamentally a modern project and this can be seen in the fact that the political goal of feminism has been, in various guises, to end the oppression of morally valuable human subjects. Where 'hard' postmoderns insist on being post-humanist, they are in fact arguing for an anti-realism in epistemology and in ethics (Weedon 1987). This makes it virtually impossible not only to talk meaningfully about material conditions, but also to argue against the current form of social organization and to consider alternatives. There have been three main solutions proposed to this. The first, following Donna Haraway, replaces the concept of the moral agent with the concept of the (unnatural) body and attempts to give content to the term 'oppression' by referring to 'negative and positive' physical effects. The second is a revision of identity politics as 'queer theory', where images and representations are deployed in a way which is supposed to force a renegotiation of basic political categories and a reappraisal of purposes of political action. But, again, this tends to mean that the arena of political struggle is that of cultural representation, cloistered conferences and textual exchange. The last, more honestly, eliminates all talk of the human subject, moral agency and consciousness by reducing the mind to the brain and the brain to a computational data processing organ (Kemp and Squires 1997, 468–529). But the idea of 'cyberfeminism' must be recognized to be an oxymoron. Physicalists eliminate the very gender categories on which feminism bases its politics and then they reduce subjectivity to causally determined physical laws (M2). Indeed, I would argue that we are left with a perfect coincidence of a certain form of global capitalism, a 1990s backlash against feminism and a deradicalization of theory masked as radical postmodern chic. This would be to return to my original point. There are certain versions of postmodernist feminism which a marxist feminist would describe as the cultural logic of developed capitalism and the graceful *pas-de-deux* as a dance to the death.

Gillian Howie

Further reading and works cited

Assiter, A. *Enlightened Women*. London, 1996.
Barrett, M. *Women's Oppression Today*. London, 1988.
—. *The Politics of Truth*. Cambridge, 1991.
Benhabib S. *Situating the Self*. Cambridge, 1992.
Bock, G. and James, S. (eds) *Beyond Equality and Difference*. London, 1992.
Brennan, T. (ed.) *Between Feminism and Psychoanalysis*. London, 1989.
Bryson, V. *Feminist Political Theory*. London, 1992.
Evans, J. (ed.) *Feminist Theory Today*. London, 1995.
Garry, A. and Pearsall, M. (eds) *Women, Knowledge and Reality*. London, 1989.
Hennessy, R. *Materialist Feminism and the Politics of Discourse*. New York, 1993.
Jardine, A. and Smith, P. (eds) *Men in Feminism*. New York, 1987.
Jeffreys S. 'Creating the Sexual Future', in *Feminist Theory Today*, ed. J. Evans. London, 1995.

Kemp, S. and Squires, J. (eds) *Feminisms*. Oxford, 1997.

Kristeva, J. 'Women's Time', in *Feminist Theory*, ed. N. O. Keohane, M. Z. Rosaldo and B. C. Gelpi. Brighton, 1982.

Lovell, T. (ed.) *British Feminist Thought*. Oxford, 1990.

Lovenduski, J. and Randall, V. *Contemporary Feminist Politics*. Oxford, 1993.

MacKinnon, C. 'Feminism, Marxism, Method and the State: An Agenda for Theory', *Feminist Theory*, eds N. O. Keohane, M. Z. Rosaldo and B. C. Gelpi. Brighton, 1982.

McNay, L. *Foucault and Feminism*. Cambridge, 1992.

Mitchell, J. *Woman's Estate*. Harmondsworth, 1971.

—. *Psychoanalysis and Feminism*. London, 1974.

Mitchell, J. and Oakley, A. (eds) *What is Feminism?* Oxford, 1986.

Moi, T. *Sexual/Textual Politics*. London, 1985

Nicholson, L. *Feminism/Postmodernism*. New York, 1990.

Oakley, A. and Mitchell, J. (eds) *Who's Afraid of Feminism?* New York, 1997.

Rowbotham, S. *The Past is Before Us*. Harmondsworth, 1990.

Shildrick, M. *Leaky Bodies and Boundaries*. London, 1997.

Soper, K. *Humanism and Anti-Humanism*. London, 1986.

—. *Troubled Pleasures*. London, 1990.

Stanley, L. *Feminist Praxis*. London, 1990.

Tong, R. *Feminist Thought*. Sydney, 1989.

Weedon, C. *Feminist Practice and Poststructuralist Theory*. Oxford, 1987.

Whelehen, I. *Modern Feminist Thought*. Edinburgh, 1995.

25. British Poststructuralism since 1968

There are several ironies involved in the title 'British poststructuralism since 1968'. At first glance the phrase 'British poststructuralism' may seem something of a contradiction in terms. 'Poststructuralism' is characteristically French, the common noun designating a heterogeneous collection of texts by Jacques Derrida, Hélène Cixous, Julia Kristeva, Michel Foucault, Jacques Lacan, Roland Barthes, Louis Althusser *et al.* However, 'poststructuralism' is not a French word, nor is it a translation of a French word. The later neologism in French, 'poststructuralisme', is a translation of the English to describe an experience of appropriation and translation. Poststructuralism is what happens to a certain strand of French thought in the Anglo-American academy. For example, in France the work of Jacques Derrida and those associated with him, colleagues or students, has been met with resolute resistance by the academic institution. In 1980 when it appeared likely that Derrida would succeed Paul Ricoeur's chair of philosophy the then education minister Alain Saulnier-Seite abolished the post. When another professorship was set up as a replacement, with certain preconditions, the university colleagues who had invited Derrida to apply voted against him. Meanwhile in America, Derrida has occupied chairs in the most prestigious institutions, including Yale and Irvine. As director of studies at the Centre Études Féminines in Paris, Hélène Cixous faces annual threats of closure for the only inter-disciplinary and only 'women's studies' programme in France. In 1980 the conservative Barre government abolished the doctorate in Études Féminines; it was re-established in

1982 by the new socialist government. Meanwhile in America, Cixous has occupied chairs in the most prestigious institutions, including Northwestern and Virginia. Such stories seem anathema to the easy understanding of 'poststructuralism' often invoked in the English-speaking world, the '1968 and all that' version of critical theory.

Indeed it could be argued that far from being a contradiction, 'British poststructuralism' is a tautology. 'Poststructuralism' designates a history of reception of certain French philosophers and literary critics, originally in the Anglo-American academy and later in all its colonial satellites, including France. In this respect 'poststructuralism' is made in Britain. Claims can be made for the American origins of 'poststructuralism'. In many respects the 'Structuralist Debate' conference at Johns Hopkins University, Baltimore, at which Derrida met Lacan and de Man for the first time in 1966, was already 'post-structuralist' in character. However, to attempt any such historicization of this term would be to adopt an idea of history which has been thoroughly 'deconstructed' by poststructuralism itself. It would be a mistake to think it possible that one might identify an origin of poststructuralism, a moment when this intellectual interest in the Anglo-American academy began. Indeed, if we take deconstruction as a metonym for poststructuralism, as it so often was in the 1980s (see, for example, Eagleton on 'Poststructuralism' (1983) or the 1987 collection of essays on deconstruction *Poststructuralism and the Question of History*) then how can we speak of something like 'British deconstruction'? Such a phenomenon would certainly resist the temporal limits implied by the qualifying phrase 'since 1968'. Deconstruction will have been a situation in Britain and British writing for as long as the idea of Britain has existed. Perhaps one might say that Britain has been in/under deconstruction for a long time. It might also be possible to identify a tradition of deconstruction in Britain prior to, and in ignorance of, Jacques Derrida. Here one could identify the texts of Oscar Wilde, James Joyce, Lewis Carroll, Mary Shelley, Tom Paine, Jonathan Swift and so on. In this respect, the question of Britishness also comes into question.

'British poststructuralism' is in fact a contradiction because the first word in this coupling presupposes an idea of continuity, stability and exclusion which the second word works to undo. In order to ask what is 'British poststructuralism' one must ask the prior question of what is 'Britain'? Britain is a concept. It involves the ideological union of heterogeneous identities (English, Scottish, Welsh, Irish, protectorates) around an idea of sovereignty derived from a colonial history. As such the question of 'British poststructuralism' is a complicated arrangement of competing interests. For example, one might think of English scholars such as Christopher Norris and Catherine Belsey working in the Centre for Critical and Cultural Theory at Cardiff, a Scottish scholar like Thomas Docherty working at the University of Kent, English scholars such as Nicholas Royle and David Punter working at the University of Stirling. The only identity that such people share might be the nomadic internationalism of the professional academic. While Scotland and Wales have always had a strained relationship with England, recent constitutional reform has redefined that relation and so rewritten the concept of Britain. Furthermore, an understanding of 'British poststructuralism' will have to negotiate the double problematic of Ireland and black Britain. This would be a matter of examining the displacement of 'Britain', as both a concept and a political entity, by postcolonial theory. In the case of Ireland, poststructuralist analysis by Seamus Deane, David Lloyd and Luc Gibbons (among others) has questioned the geographical certainty of the term 'British' in relation to Britain's historical occupation of Ireland and continued governance of Ulster. In the case of black Britain, the poststructuralism of Paul Gilroy, Homi Bhabha and Angela MacRobbie (among others) has disrupted the stability of 'Britishness' by proposing that this term is constructed in opposition to and exclusive of 'blackness'. If there is a form of 'poststructuralism' which is characteristically 'British' then it is one that has persistently questioned the term 'British'.

The formulation 'since 1968' will also have to be interrogated. The adverb 'since' both presupposes a historical point of origin for 'British poststructuralism', namely 1968, and implies the non-originary nature of such a starting point, 'British poststructuralism before 1968' would be another entry in this encyclopaedia. Perhaps, in the sense outlined above, it suggests that poststructuralism became British after 1968. The date 1968 refers to the events in May of that year in which student protest for academic reforms combined with nationwide trade union action to precipitate a general strike in France. Momentarily it seemed that revolution was possible but disputes between the various factions on the left resulted in the dissipation of the protests. It would seem odd then that 'British post-structuralism' should be defined by events in another country. For the British 1968 is perhaps more significantly marked by the rise of the civil rights movement in Northern Ireland and the beginnings of what has been euphemistically called 'the Troubles'. In this sense, 'British poststructuralism' might be more accurately situated within a sustained encounter with the dissolution of Britishness than with the appropriation of the exoticism of Paris in 1968.

May 1968 retains a talismanic quality for the Left (another term that would require to be unpacked with care) as a metonym for both the possibility of revolution in an advanced liberal democracy and the failures of revolutionary practice. It is most often described as a 'lost historic opportunity'. Accordingly, if poststructuralism can be characterized as a rethinking of the aporias of the marxist project after the experience of the inadequacy of its programme then 1968 seemingly stands as a significant moment in this task of revaluation. However, even though the principle players of poststructuralism participated in *les événements* they certainly did not direct them – Derrida, for example, retained a certain distance from them – and they have never been the explicit topic of any prolonged analysis by these theorists. If the emergence of 'poststructuralism' can be tied to a specific historical conjunction there are more convincing candidates than 1968. Derrida cites the importance of 1958:

> What we had known or what some of us for quite some time no longer hid from concerning totalitarian terror in all the Eastern countries, all the socio-economic disasters of Soviet bureaucracy, the Stalinism of the past and the neo-Stalinism in process (roughly speaking from the Moscow trials to the repression in Hungary, to take only these minimal indices). Such was no doubt the element in which what is called deconstruction developed – and one can understand nothing of this period of deconstruction, notably in France, unless one takes this historical entanglement into account. (1994, 15)

For Derrida the influences of French thought lie elsewhere. Similarly, Robert Young, a British poststructuralist, cites a moment in which the idea of 'Frenchness' is called into question:

> If so-called 'so-called poststructuralism' is the product of a single historical moment, then that moment is probably not May 1968 but rather the Algerian War of Independence – no doubt itself both a symptom and a product. In this respect it is significant that Sartre, Althusser, Derrida and Lyotard, among others [add here Cixous and Deleuze], were all either born in Algeria or personally involved with the events of the war. (1990, 1)

As such the tropes and interests of poststructuralism (history, marginality, origins, authority, etc.) may be the result of a colonial rather than a revolutionary experience.

In this sense the 'post' in 'poststructuralism' may be the same 'post' in 'postcolonialism'. However, such an assertion would merely beg the question of the nature of the 'post' itself. Certainly, the 'post' here does not imply a simple idea of 'after', 'poststructuralism' coming after structuralism. 'Post' as a temporal marker is implied at least twice in the phrase 'British poststructuralism since 1968', with 'since' suggesting 'after' 1968. However, while 'post' in a temporal sense means 'coming after' in its spatial sense it means 'behind'. We might think here of the ambiguities implied by the word 'posterior'. Robert Young writes:

> 'Poststructuralism' suggests that structuralism itself can only exist as always already inhabited by poststructuralism, which comes both behind and after. It is always already unfolding as a repetition not of the same but as a kind of *Nachtraglichkeit*, or deferred action. In this sense, poststructuralism becomes structuralism's primal scene. (1982, 4)

If we take this logic of *Nachtraglichkeit* [deferral] seriously then something like 1968 as a 'symptom and product' of poststructuralism, or poststructuralism as a symptom and product of 1968, looks more like an experience of repetition than a point of origin – a primal scene that is never primal enough. Thus, the question of 'poststructuralism' becomes a question of the meaning of structuralism and vice versa. If the difference between the two signifiers cannot be resolved in terms of a historical break this is because the conceptual difference between the two remains elusive. At what point does structuralist narratology become poststructuralist narrative theory? When does Lacan's 'structuralist' rereading of Freud in the 1950s become 'poststructuralist' psychoanalytic theory? How can we characterize Derrida's essay 'Structure, Sign and Play in the Discourse of the Human Sciences', given at the 'Structuralist Debate' conference in Baltimore in 1966, as anything other than 'poststructuralist'? The very term 'poststructuralism' seems to contain within itself the impossibility of a clean break from structuralism. Rather than 'poststructuralism since 1968' one may as well speak of the continued operation of structuralism since 1968, but again this would be to imagine that structuralism was somehow less resistant to the holistic demands of historicism than 'poststructuralism'.

The phrase 'British poststructuralism since 1968' is taken from Antony Easthope's seminal study of the same name. Professor Easthope died a few months before this entry was written and the encyclopaedia is dedicated to his memory. In his preface to that book he rehearses similar reservations as those outlined above to his own title, noting that the 'book should be called 'English poststructuralism' (Easthope 1988, xiv), and starts its historical analysis in 1965 as an important year for British (English) marxism. However, despite his preliminary worries Easthope goes on to offer a historical overview of so-called 'British poststructuralism' between 1965 and 1988. His aim in the book, as he told me on a separate occasion, was to commit to print important facts before they were lost to distant memory for all time. In this respect, his study provides a wealth of information on the origins of critical theory in England during the 1970s and 1980s, from the politics of the founder members of the film journal *Screen* to the development of the Open University module on popular culture. The value of Easthope's book is that it views 'British poststructuralism' as a consequence of inter-disciplinary research rather than a product of, say, literary studies. He provides us with accounts of the emergence of theoretical inquiry in film studies, the social sciences, art history and philosophy, among others. In short, the argument runs that an indigenous British marxism had come to a moment of conceptual impasse in the 1960s and found a revitalizing force in the spaces opened up by certain French philosophers at that time. 'British poststructuralism' began with the translation of Althusser and Lacan in *Screen* and blossomed out into a full-blown paradigm-shift in the humanities. This may explain the autobiographical path of the author of *British Poststructuralism since 1968* but I am not sure that it will do as an account of the complexity and heterogeneity hinted at by Robert Young when he talks of 'so-called "so-called poststructuralism"', in which the 'so-called' is indicative of histories of misunderstanding and institutional contest. 'British marxism' – there is not enough time to unpack this phrase – has always been suspicious of 'poststructuralism' and remains today the primary reactionary force against it in the British academy. Even now after more than thirty years of theoretical inquiry in British universities, it is still more acceptable to the majority of British academics to be a 'marxist' than a reader of Derrida.

However, Easthope's book lacks insight as an account of 'poststructuralism' because, as a matter of choice, it adheres to a historicist account of origins, causes and effects which 'poststructuralism' itself rejects. It cannot historicize theory because it does not sufficiently theorize history. Undoubtedly, 'poststructuralism', if such a thing exists and it is one, has a history and this history remains to be written. However, such a history will first have to think through the question of history itself as a precondition of telling the story of 'poststructuralism'. When it is finally told this story will be inseparable from the history of something like 'deconstruction in America' (see Derrida 1989, 18, 122–3) and the history of France *per se*. Since it has been a minimum requirement of this entry to provide a number of basic facts and events which would make up the story of 'British Poststructuralism since 1968', on reflection, this essay may prove as arbitrary as the date from which it is obliged to commence.

Martin McQuillan

Further reading and works cited

Attridge, D. et al. (eds) *Poststructuralism and the Question of History*. Cambridge, 1987.

Barker, F. et al. (eds) *Literature, Politics and Theory: Papers from the Essex Conference 1976–1984*. London, 1986.

Barthes, R. *Image-Music-Text*. London, 1977.

Belsey, C. *Critical Practice*. London, 1980.

Bennett, T. *Formalism and Marxism*. London, 1979.

Bennington, G. *Legislations*. London, 1994.

Bhabha, H. K. (ed.) *Nation and Narration*. London, 1990.

Brennan, T. (ed.) *Between Feminism and Psychoanalysis*. London, 1989.

Culler, J. *Structuralist Poetics*. London, 1975.

—. *On Deconstruction: Theory and Criticism after Structuralism*. London, 1983.

Derrida, J. *Of Grammatology*, trans. G. Chakravorty Spivak. Baltimore, MD, 1976.

—. *Memoirs for Paul de Man*. New York, 1989.

—. *Specters of Marx*. London, 1994.

—. 'Honoris Causa: "This is *also* extremely funny"', *Points: Interviews, 1974–1994*, ed. Elisabeth Weber. Stanford, CA, 1995.

Dews, P. *Logics of Disintegration*. London, 1987.

Dollimore, J. *Sexual Dissidence: Augustine to Wilde, Freud to Foucault*. Oxford, 1991.

Drakakis, J. (ed.) *Alternative Shakespeares*. London, 1985.

Eagleton, T. *Literary Theory: an Introduction*. Oxford, 1983.

Easthope, A. *British Poststructuralism since 1968*. London, 1988.

Foucault, M. *The Order of Things*. New York, 1970.

Gilroy, P. *There Ain't no Black in the Union Jack*. London, 1987.

Hawkes, T. *Structuralism and Semiotics*. London, 1977.

Lacan, J. *Ecrits: A Selection*. London, 1977.

Laclau, E. and Mouffe, C. *Hegemony and Socialist Strategy*. London, 1985.

Lyotard, J.-F. *The Postmodern Condition*. Manchester, 1984.

McQuillan, M. et al. (eds) *Post-Theory*. Edinburgh, 1999.

Mitchell, J. *Psychoanalysis and Feminism*. London, 1974.

Mulvey, L. 'Visual Pleasure and Narrative Cinema'. *Screen*, Autumn 1975.

Norris, C. *What's Wrong with Postmodernism*. Baltimore, MD, 1994.

Readings, B. *The University in Ruins*. Cambridge, MA, 1993.

Royle, N. *After Derrida*. Manchester, 1995.

Salusinsky, I. *Criticism in Society: Interviews*. London, 1987.

Sinfield, A. *Cultural Politics – Queer Readings*. London, 1994.

Young, R. (ed.) *Untying the Text*. London, 1981.

—. 'Poststructuralism: The End of Theory', *Oxford Literary Review*, 5, 1982.

—. *White Mythologies*. London, 1990.

— (ed.) '(Neocolonialism)', *Oxford Literary Review*, 13, 1991.

—. *Torn Halves*. Manchester, 1996.

26. Developments in Literary Theory since 1995

Literary theory moves, not from pillar to post, but from post to post – post-structuralism, post-modernism, post-colonialism and the rest – but the post to end all posts is the widespread belief that we have been in the era of 'post theory' for more than a decade now. 'Is there life after theory?' a major UK conference wanted to know in 2003 (Derrida et al. 2004), and Eagleton's *After Theory* in the same year shows that what comes after theory might be his own version of despairing moral theology (see later). Eagleton's book is 'post' Valentine Cunningham's *Reading After Theory* (2001), which it doesn't mention, but 'post-theory' books were around as early as 1990, when Thomas Docherty's *After Theory* was published. Yet the notion of 'after theory' is a self-contradiction, just like 'life after death', for on the one hand, if there's life after it, it can't be death, and on the other, if *we're* after it, it can't have been theory. Of course, theory has changed, but that doesn't mean it's dead – on the contrary.

As this suggests, we haven't always understood the extent of changes taking place in theory. In the recent past, the anti-theory books argued that major theorists had misread the authors they claimed as their predecessors, especially the foundational work of Ferdinand de Saussure (see Tallis 1988; Washington 1989; Jackson 1991). More recently still, pro-theory books claim that we have misread (or not read) major theorists like Derrida (see Rapaport 2001; Davis 2004). But both the pro and the anti books risk missing the point, since the influence of theory never depended on the accuracy of its readings of its predecessors, nor on that of its supporters' readings of theory itself – what intellectual movement could flourish if the thought police made arrests on such grounds? Rather, it depended (and – residually – depends) on the power of its rhetoric, and on the institutional circumstances of its interventions, matters which are beyond refutation.

The signs of a major seismic shift in theory were there, indeed, as far back as 1986 when J. Hillis Miller's MLA Presidential Address noted (in effect) that the 'Triumph of Theory' was being interrupted by regrettable outbreaks of historicism:

> Literary study in the past few years has undergone a sudden, almost universal turn away from theory in the sense of an orientation toward language as such and has made a corresponding turn toward history, culture, society, politics, institutions, class and gender conditions, the social context, the material base. (1991, 313)

Historicism (as distinct from history) is what the theory-weary (in the main) moved on to, and to ever more elaborate forms of it, entailing extensive archival work, the setting up of interdisciplinary research centres, and the pursuit of cross-institutional collaborations.

But in what precise ways *did* theory change between, say, 1995 and 2005? One general shift has been that theory became less willing than hitherto to suspend disbelief in the face of vast, but uncorroborated, intellectual claims, and more committed to engaging with its material at an empirical level, so that findings are now more likely to be demonstrated, rather than just magisterially asserted. Indeed, the old Gallic disdain for 'mere' empiricism seems as dated as the assumption that French *cuisine* and French fashions are superior to all others. Clarity is now expected, even of literary theorists, and the poetic licences liberally issued to Francophone theorists in the 1970s and 1980s are no longer valid (or, at least, are not valid abroad). The current 'afterlives' of theory, then, are characterized by a strategic 'downsizing' of the old intellectual 'mega-zones': thus, structuralism has been eclipsed by narratology, originally one of its own specialist sub-sets, and the recent upsurge of interest in the work of Paul Ricoeur has been symptomatic of that shift, particularly the popularity of his major work' *Time and Narrative* (1990). His recent death (in 2005) allows comparisons to be made between his career, philosophy and influence and those of Derrida, who died in 2004, and in the long run the former may come to be regarded as the more significant figure. Likewise, the abstractions of 'Ideology' and 'Politics', which were the subject of Marxist-materialist theory, have been replaced by minute attention to the cultural logistics of specific periods – especially Early Modernism, Romanticism and Victorianism. In addition, such areas as the body (see Atkinson 2005), the uncanny (Royle 2003), and the environment (Bate 2001) have become the more precise theoretical foci for energies which a decade or two ago would probably have been devoted to deconstruction and poststructuralism – intellectual attitudes or processes which claimed a universal applicability, and had no designated sphere of operations other than the totalities of 'Western Metaphysics' or 'Language'.

Secondly, there is evidence of a turning away from the dominant materialism epitomized by British Cultural Materialism and American New Historicism, and a drift towards aspects of 'the spiritual', whether conceived of as metaphorical renderings of various aspects of reading, writing and textuality (see Wolfreys 2001), or as metonymic representations of a world more real (in the sense of deeper, more fundamental) than material reality. Thus, Fernie (2004) argues that Cultural Materialism has so pervaded our thinking that 'history is now the far horizon and sole explanatory hypothesis in contemporary criticism' (2004, 10).

The 'turning' from materialism was seen in the intense 'religiosity' (if that is the right word) of Greenblatt's *Hamlet* book (2002) and as Fernie points out, Derrida had already anticipated this 'spiritualist' turn (or turn-about) in his examination of the implications of the ghost in *Hamlet* in *Specters of Marx* (1994). Indeed, the religious turn seems much in evidence in literary studies in the present millennial era, far more so than for several decades, and perhaps the recent widespread preoccupation with Shakespeare's religion (dating from Honigmann 1998, but see also Wilson 2004) is indicative, as is the founding of the ISRLC (the International Society for Religion, Literature and Culture) in September 2000, linked to the journal *Literature and Theology*.

Thirdly, the recent trend of critical 'Presentism' is another reaction against the historicist materialism which has dominated the study of literature since the early 1980s. That emphasis on history was consolidated later in the 1980s, and into the 1990s with the rise of postcolonialism, and was built upon antecedents in the work of Michel Foucault, who had stipulated, in *The Archaeology of Knowledge* (1972), that in the analysis of the discursive field 'we must grasp the statement in the exact specificity of its occurrence'. It built too upon Raymond Williams's emphasis (1977) on understanding 'the whole lived social process, as practically organized by specific and dominant meanings'. The somewhat intimidatory use of the word 'specific' in such proclamations drove us towards exhaustive historicist study, so that literary scholars became pre-occupied by historical method, turning themselves into, if not historians exactly, then at least 'historianists'. By the late 1990s, historicism had (arguably) become the most prevalent form of what Paul de Man called 'resistance to theory', and it seemed to be taken for granted that only an amateur reader of literature would deny that literature can best be understood through history.

Yet paradoxically, the emergent trend of Presentism embodies the paradox of accepting the radical 'alterity' and unique 'unrecoverability' of the past. Talk of 'exact specificity', and the like, fosters the delusion that if only we are relentless enough in the archival grind, we will one day recover the past and again walk the streets of Shakespeare's London, making for the playhouse to see a performance of *Hamlet* (Stephen's intellectual fantasy in the 'Scylla and Charybdis' section of Joyce's *Ulysses*). Further, it's not the mere streets which are to be rescued by historicist archaeology, but the mind-set. Hollywood and the Bankside Globe, after all, can give us the *mise-en-scène*, but it's the *mentalité* which is the Grail of historicists. Presentism paradoxically rejects that historicist aim, 'in favour of embracing [Shakespeare's] true historicity as something irreversibly changing in time' (Fernie 2004, 186). Hence – as the catalogue description of Terence Hawkes's *Shakespeare in the Present* (2002) puts it – 'Presentism is a critical manoeuvre which uses relevant aspects of the contemporary as a crucial trigger for its investigations. It deliberately begins with the material present and lets that set the interrogative agenda.'

Of course, Presentism is not universally accepted. In an article in *Textual Practice*, Andrew Hadfield points to the exhaustion of the *theoretical* impetus of New Historicism and cultural materialism, seeing it as an intellectual formation which is 'in danger of losing a vital aspect of its political significance, and, while properly foregrounding the problem of subjectivity, it is at the expense of an analysis of politics' (2003, 462). Thus, there comes 'a time when theory ceases to be radical and even properly theoretical, because it has become hegemonic and inscribed within the academic culture at large' (454). Everyone, these days, is keen to examine Early Modern 'identities' and 'subjectivities', but to consider 'citizens' rather than 'subjects', and the 'state' and the extent of its powers over those citizens, is to change the emphasis from cultural theory, or cultural materialism, to politics. Thus,

Hadfield is distrustful of Hugh Grady's Presentist leanings, rightly pointing out the circularity of Grady's pronouncement that 'in studying the configuration and reconfiguration of the themes of power and subjectivity in central Shakespearean plays, I have come to the conclusion that these plays, in effect, constitute interventions within our own theoretical discourses on these topics within late modernity' (464). The notion that Shakespeare's value lies in his anticipating our 'discourses' on such topics is somewhat bizarre, and there is a danger of Presentism becoming yet another crudely 'de-oxygenating' form of literary theory – the kind which, when theory was in its pomp, smothered the text in 'discourse', making *Hamlet* an enactment of Lacanian notions of desire and lack, or Harold Pinter's enigmatic play *The Homecoming* a practical demonstration of object relations theory.

Presentism, then, is one currently active (if limited) form of resistance to a too-long dominant historicism. New Aestheticism, a fourth aspect of recent developments in theory, is another. The 'new' aestheticism, in effect, seeks to move on from theory without just going back on theory. The two recommended starting points in this area would be Armstrong (2000), and Joughin and Malpas (2003). The publisher's description of the Joughin and Malpas collection signals its approval of 'specificity' (which has become the new apple pie of theory):

> The rise of literary theory spawned the rise of anti-aestheticism, so that even for cultural theorists, discussions concerning aesthetics were often carried out in a critical shorthand that failed to engage with the particularity of the work of art, much less the specificities of aesthetic experience.

This has become a familiar constellation of words – 'specificity', 'singularity', 'particularity'. But an element of readerly suspicion is appropriate whenever such words are used without being, well, *specific*. To announce a programme of responding to the 'specifics' of literary works is actually a commitment to a generalization – we should always ask what *specific* 'specificities' the critic is concerned about, how they are to be prioritized and how analysed. Notoriously, New Historicism's totalizing readings of culture seemed to rule out the possibility of contradiction and subversion within literary works, and this is what the 'new specificisms' are supposed to counter. Early Modern cultural authoritarianism (so Early Modernist scholars believed) made resistance unthinkable, and the 'singularity' of literature was constantly tidied up and tidied away by New Historicists as they explored the enmeshing of literature in the Tudorbethan political order.

The resurgent aestheticism announced in Armstrong is consonant with the call by Edward Pechter, in another *Textual Practice* article, for a reversal of 'the repudiation of literary interest as a fundamental motivation for our work' – exemplified, as he sees it, in the voguish tendency to downgrade Folio texts of Shakespeare plays which are typically 'rich in metaphor and verbal energy' (2003, 508) for starker Q text versions characterized by 'narrative efficiency and technical simplicity' (513). He sees this as a 'dumbed-down', 'phallic' sense of theatrical value – 'get it on, move it along, get it over with; and God forbid the performance should sag' (513) – a 'Shakespeare without Act IV'. Such classic 'Act IV' episodes as the account of Ophelia's death, Cordelia's reunion with Lear, Mariana at the grange, and so on, tend to leave the action hovering on pause, so to speak, providing reflective, meditative sections which are not about mere forward movement. After all, the 'verbal energy' of literature resides not in the dash for the blood-boltered climax, but in such 'reverberating' scenes, the devaluation of which Pechter protests against, scenes which contribute powerfully to the 'singularity' and 'reciprocality' of literary effects which the New Aestheticism seeks to rehabilitate.

'Singularity', 'particularity', and 'specificity', then, are the professed goals of all forms of theory-literate criticism today. Nobody is interested any more in the general, a reversal of the 1970s and early 1980s when structuralism enjoyed its brief heyday and 'specificity' was seen as the passé focus of old-style literary-critical effort. Thus, the specificity and singularity of *Middlemarch* or 'The Turn of the Screw' were the denigrated and rather patronized concerns of the liberal humanists, while the theorists investigated the generalities, the glamorous abstractions – not how *Middlemarch* worked, but how *narrative* worked is what fired the cutting-edge theoretical imagination in that era.

The stance which New Aestheticism seeks to correct might also be described as the superiority complex which criticism and theory had indulged in, unchecked, for something like a quarter of a century. Disdaining the (usually un-exemplified) enthusiastic 'gushing' of the critics of the past about 'great' authors, theory went to the opposite extreme: authors were always presumed guilty and the job of the critic was to read them against the grain, catching them out on what they didn't say but obviously meant, or what they did say but obviously didn't mean. Laying bare their racist, sexist and classist assumptions, opening up their fault-lines and exposing their fissures made theorized criticism sound like a sadistic ritual of textual harassment. It was a great time for inquisitorial theorists, who were allowed to be 'over-arching' when this was forbidden to everybody else, and whose motives were never questioned. This instinctive distrust of writers is what Ricoeur calls the 'hermeneutics of suspicion' (in *Freud and Philosophy*), 'a method of interpretation which assumes that the literal or surface-level meaning of a text is an effort to conceal the political interests which are served by the text. The purpose of interpretation is to strip off the concealment, unmasking those interests' (27). Of course, all forms of criticism tend to read and interpret the text counter-intuitively, so the only thing distinguishing the 'hermeneutics of suspicion' from the rest is the word 'political', but aestheticism in particular was usually condemned without trial as a disguise for various forms of political self-interest.

That 1980s era already seems distant, and if aestheticism is reinstated, then the whole theoretical construct of the past twenty years will have to be re-constructed from the ground up. If we are going to allow aestheticism back, then we will have to allow the existence of literature and the literary too, and this has long been (to say the least) a 'site of struggle'. Indeed, the very existence of literature has been hotly contested in some of the most widely used undergraduate primers. Thus, Eagleton's *Literary Theory: an Introduction* (1987) opens with sixteen pages on the question 'What is literature?', concluding (surprisingly) that 'literature does not exist in the sense that insects do' and (unsurprisingly) that the value judgements by which it is constituted 'have a close relation to social ideologies' (16). Bennett and Royle, too, after lengthy wresting in the same vein, reach the inevitable conclusion that 'literature in a sense does not exist. It has no essence', (2004, 86), while for Peter Widdowson (in *Literature*), 'perhaps the only way to represent it [literature], as a *passé* presence or determinate absence, is under erasure'. He views 'what has gone on, in its sullied name, and under its tattered banner' (1999, 2) with great distaste, and Chris Hopkins, clearly of similar mind, carefully avoids even the sullied name of literature in his title (his book, published in 2001, is called *Thinking about Texts*), but still spends the regulation fifteen or sixteen pages evading the question, 'How do we define literature?' But Pechter's question, 'What's wrong with literature?' must somehow be faced, even if we still can't bring ourselves quite to look it in the eye. Isobel Armstrong, thankfully, *does* face such questions as 'What is wrong with the aesthetic?' (and with Kant) in the early sections of her book, and thereby signals a decisive shift in the literary-theoretical climate.

So the difficult revisionist questions being raised in criticism and theory today refuse to be confined to some safe and remote corner of the field of literary studies. There cannot be a controlled explosion (or a series thereof) carefully calculated to remove a specific bit of the thirty-year-old intellectual formation of theory, while leaving all the rest intact. We cannot afford to be seen as a discipline which refuses to ask the most fundamental questions of its own subject matter, and the inevitable result of trying to do so would be our deserved cultural marginalization. Admitting that we got some things wrong in theory during the past quarter-century won't be easy, but it is the only way forward.

Of course, it isn't possible to be comprehensive about new directions in theory in such a brief adumbration as this, and there is much else going on. The 'Cultural Criticism' (a development from Cultural Studies) associated with Catherine Belsey and the distinguished Centre for Critical and Cultural Theory at Cardiff University is ambitious, but seems to want to retain intact too much of the high theory project of the 1980s, in particular an un-nuanced belief in the deconstruction of the concept of human nature, a continuing adherence to the notion of language as independent of external reality, and an acceptance of the whole intellectual corpus of Lacan and Lyotard (a pair who seem oddly exempt from the critique to which everything else is to be subjected). The approach seems too much restricted to considering the effects of 'sexual alignments, family values, racial politics, the implications of economic differences' – the familiar determining agenda of cultural materialist critique. Belsey's 2005 New Accents book 'follows on', she says, from her *Critical Practice* of 1980, and there is too little engagement with shifts in the cultural and intellectual climate since then. Neil Badmington's *Posthumanism* (2000), in Belsey's 'Readers in Cultural Criticism' series, rounds up a collection of eminent contributors whose very contiguity seems to epitomize the superseded paradigm of 1980s theory.

Belsey's Cardiff colleague Christopher Norris, on the other hand, has long been a major force in dismantling the prestige of the 'textual sublime' (that 'constructivist' notion of language as a world-making force), and suspicious of the view that language speaks to us rather than vice versa, a notion which, he says, (presumably with Heidegger and de Man in mind), too easily allows us to deny responsibility for our pronouncements. He has vehemently attacked the 'anti-realists' in philosophy (those who deny the existence of 'mind-independent' reality and tend to see everything as 'mind-determined'). Even the much discussed 'third way' between the 'realist' and 'anti-realist' poles he has tended to see as really just another form of the latter. Likewise, he has taken issue with the 'endless, playful, polysemic interpretation' offered 'at the expense of systematic argument' in such theorists as Baudrillard, Fish, Rorty and Lyotard, seeing that kind of thing as typical of postmodernist relativism (see Norris 1998; 2000; 2005).

Norris's 'pro-realist' stance is cognate with calls, from critics such as Jonathan Bate, for English to become more of a 'fact-based' discipline than it has been. Bate has been outspoken against the 'anti-Stratfordians' (those who think that Shakespeare did not write Shakespeare's plays), putting the view that 'partly it's to do with honouring truth, honouring fact. And, you know, without being melodramatic about it, if you deny the reality of Shakespeare one moment, you can deny the reality of the Holocaust the next.' Bate's strong 'pro-realism' (his evident belief in a mind-independent and language-independent reality) is partly a consequence of his eco-critical sympathies, calling to mind Kate Soper's frequently quoted remark (in her seminal book, *What is Nature?*) that 'it isn't language which has a hole in its ozone layer' (250). A similar sense of a situation which is increasingly desperate lies behind the recent work of Terry Eagleton (2003; 2004; 2005), which provides a cultural critique increasingly pre-occupied with violence, terror, and evil, a form of writing which might be called 'Crisis Critique' (of which eco-criticism could plausibly be seen as a sub-branch). It is much burdened by a sense of catastrophe as both pervasive and impending, and the more usual concerns of literary and cultural criticism are made to seem darkly complicit with the forces poised to destroy us. Of course, Crisis Critique is also a way of seizing the moral high ground, and it might at least provide that consolation if the worst happens. In the 1980s, theory enjoyed decentring human nature, toying endlessly with that notion as a kind of thrillingly apocalyptic intellectual game. It is inevitable that we should lose our taste for the game once that metaphor threatens to become all too real.

Peter Barry

Further reading and works cited

Armstrong, I. *The Radical Aesthetic*. Oxford, 2000.

Atkinson, T. (ed.) *The Body*. London, 2005.

Bate, J. *The Song of the Earth*. London, 2001.

Bate, Jonathan. 'Much Ado about Something'. http://www.pbs.org/wgbh/pages/frontline/shows/muchado/forum/bate.html

Bennett, A. and Royle, N. *An Introduction to Literature, Criticism and Theory*, 3rd edn. Harlow, 2004.

Cunningham, V. *Reading After Theory*. Oxford, 2001.

Davis, C. *After Poststructuralism*. London, 2004.

Derrida, J. *Specters of Marx*. New York, 1994.

— et al. *Life After Theory*. London, 2004.

Docherty, T. *After Theory*. London, 1990.

Eagleton, T. *Literary Theory: An Introduction*. Oxford, 1987.

—. *Sweet Violence*. Oxford, 2003.

—. *After Theory*. London, 2004.

—. *Holy Terror*. Oxford, 2005.

Fernie, E. *Spiritual Shakespeares*. London, 2004.

Foucault, M. *The Archaeology of Knowledge*. London, 1972.

Greenblatt, S. *Hamlet in Purgatory*. Princeton, NJ, 2002.

Hadfield, A. 'Shakespeare and Republicanism: History and Cultural Materialism', *Textual Practice*, 17(3), 2003.

Honigmann, E. A. J. *Shakespeare: The Lost Years*. Manchester, 1998.

Hopkins, C. *Thinking about Texts*. London, 2001.

Jackson, L. *The Poverty of Structuralism*. London, 1991.

Joughin, J. J. and Malpas, S. *The New Aestheticism*. Manchester, 2003.

Miller, J. H. 'Presidential Address: The Triumph of Theory, the Resistance to Reading, and the Question of the Material Base', *PMLA*, May 1987. Rpt. in *Theory Now and Then*. Durham, NC, 1991.

Norris, C. *What's Wrong with Postmodernism?* London, 1998.

—. *Quantum Theory and the Flight from Realism*. London, 2000.

—. *Truth Matters: Realism, Anti-Realism and Response-Dependence*. Edinburgh, 2005.

Pechter, E. 'What's Wrong with Literature?', *Textual Practice*, 17(3), 2003.

Rapaport, H. *The Theory Mess*. New York, 2001.
Ricoeur, P. *Freud and Philosophy*. Yale, CT, 1977.
—. *Time and Narrative*, (5 vols). Chicago, IL, 1990.
Royle, N. *The Uncanny*. London, 2003.
Soper, Kate. *What is Nature? Culture, Politics, and the Non-Human*. Oxford, 1995.
Tallis, R. *Not Saussure*. London, 1988.
Washington, K. *Fraud: Literary Theory and the End of English*. London, 1989.
Widdowson, P. *Literature*. London, 1999
Williams, R. *Marxism and Literature*. Oxford, 1977.
Wilson, R. *Secret Shakespeare*. Manchester, 2004.
Wolfreys, J. *Victorian Hauntings: Spectrality, Gothic, the Uncanny and Literature*. London, 2001.

Contributors

Ortwin de Graef, Katholieke universiteit, Leuven
Jonathan Loesberg, American University
Megan Becker-Leckrone, University of Nevada, Las Vegas
Jeremy Tambling, Hong Kong University
Jean-Michel Rabaté, University of Pennsylvania
Jane Goldman, University of Dundee
K. M. Newton, University of Dundee
William Flesch, Brandeis University
David Alderson, Manchester University
Andrew Milner, Monash University
John Brannigan, Queen's University, Belfast
Moyra Haslett, Queen's University, Belfast
Antony Easthope, Manchester Metropolitan University
Niall Lucy, Murdoch University
Peter Barry, University of Wales, Aberystwyth
Ashley Tauchert, Exeter University
Ian Baucom, Duke University
Gail Ching-Liang Low, University of Dundee
John M. Clum, Duke University
Paul Bowman, Leeds University
Leigh Wilson, University of Westminster
Gillian Howie, University of Liverpool
Martin McQuillan, Leeds University

Index